T0192009

Communications in Computer and Information Science 1545

More information about this series at https://link.springer.com/bookseries/7899

Steven Furnell · Paolo Mori · Edgar Weippl ·
Olivier Camp (Eds.)

Information Systems Security and Privacy

6th International Conference, ICISSP 2020
Valletta, Malta, February 25–27, 2020
Revised Selected Papers

 Springer

Editors
Steven Furnell
Plymouth University
Plymouth, UK

Edgar Weippl
University of Vienna
Vienna, Austria

Paolo Mori 🅱
Istituto di Informatica e Telematica
Pisa, Italy

Olivier Camp
MODESTE/ESEO
Angers Cedex 2, France

ISSN 1865-0929   ISSN 1865-0937 (electronic)
Communications in Computer and Information Science
ISBN 978-3-030-94899-3   ISBN 978-3-030-94900-6 (eBook)
https://doi.org/10.1007/978-3-030-94900-6

This Springer imprint is published by the registered company Springer Nature Switzerland AG
The registered company address is: Gewerbestrasse 11, 6330 Cham, Switzerland

Preface

This book includes extended and revised versions of a set of selected papers from the 6th International Conference on Information Systems Security and Privacy (ICISSP 2020), which was held in Valletta, Malta, during February 25–27, 2020.

The International Conference on Information Systems Security and Privacy aims at creating a meeting point for researchers and practitioners who address security and privacy challenges that concern information systems, especially in organizations, including not only technological issues but also social issues. The conference welcomes papers of either practical or theoretical nature, presenting research or applications addressing all aspects of security and privacy that concern organizations and individuals, thus creating new research opportunities.

ICISSP 2020 received 114 paper submissions from authors in 36 countries, of which 10% were included in this book.

The papers were selected by the event chairs and their selection is based on a series of criteria including the classifications and comments provided by the Program Committee members, the session chairs' assessment, and the program chairs' global view of all papers included in the technical program. The authors of selected papers were then invited to submit a revised and extended version of their papers having at least 30% innovative material.

The papers selected for inclusion in this book contribute to the understanding of relevant trends of current research on information systems security and privacy in a number of areas, including network attacks and security, protection of IoT devices security, secure protocols, and human aspects of cyber security. In all cases, the papers make research contributions that advance the topics beyond the current state of the art.

We would like to thank all the authors for their contributions and the reviewers who have helped to ensure the quality of this publication.

February 2020

Steven Furnell
Paolo Mori
Edgar Weippl
Olivier Camp

Organization

Conference Co-chairs

Edgar Weippl   University of Vienna/SBA Research, Austria
Olivier Camp   Graduate School of Electronics of the West, France

Program Co-chairs

Steven Furnell   University of Nottingham, UK
Paolo Mori   Consiglio Nazionale delle Ricerche, Italy

Program Committee

Carlisle Adams   University of Ottawa, Canada
Ja'far Alqatawna   Higher Colleges of Technology, UAE
Saed Alrabaee   United Arab Emirates University, UAE
Mario Alvim   Federal University of Minas Gerais, Brazil
Morteza Amini   Sharif University of Technology, Iran
Thibaud Antignac   CEA/DRT/LIST, France
Hugo Barbosa   Lusofona University of Porto, Portugal
Montserrat Batet   Universitat Rovira i Virgili, Spain
Matt Bishop   University of California, Davis, USA
Chiara Bodei   Università di Pisa, Italy
Reinhardt Botha   Nelson Mandela Metropolitan University, South Africa
Christos Bouras   University of Patras, Greece
Francesco Buccafurri   University of Reggio Calabria, Italy
Ismail Butun   Chalmers University of Technology, Sweden
Luigi Catuogno   Università di Salerno, Italy
Hervé Chabanne   Idemia/Télécom ParisTech, France
Rui Chen   Samsung Research America, USA
Thomas Chen   City, University of London, UK
Feng Cheng   Hasso-Plattner-Institute at the University of Potsdam, Germany
Yannick Chevalier   Université Paul Sabatier Toulouse III, France
Hung-Yu Chien   National Chi Nan University, Taiwan, Republic of China
Stelvio Cimato   Università degli Studi di Milano, Italy
Miguel Correia   Universidade do Porto, Portugal
Gianpiero Costantino   Consiglio Nazionale delle Ricerche, Italy
Lorenzo De Carli   Worcester Polytechnic Institute, USA
Andrea De Salve   Consiglio Nazionale delle Ricerche, Italy
Rafael de Sousa Junior   University of Brasilia, Brazil

Yong Wang	Dakota State University, USA
Bing Wu	Fayetteville State University, USA
Alec Yasinsac	University of South Alabama, USA
Nicola Zannone	Eindhoven University of Technology, The Netherlands

Additional Reviewers

Shashank Arora	State University of New York at Albany, USA
Joakim Brorsson	Lund University, Sweden
Linda Guiga	Idemia, France
Lara Mauri	Università degli Studi di Milano, Italy
Bruno Praciano	University of Brasilia, Brazil
Veena Ravishankar	University of Mary Washington, USA
Rhea Rinaldo	DFKI, Germany
Arianna Rossi	University of Luxembourg/SnT, Luxembourg
Antonia Russo	University of Reggio Calabria, Italy
Borce Stojkovski	University of Luxembourg/SnT, Luxembourg
Nima Tavangaran	Princeton University, USA
Florian Wilkens	Universität Hamburg, Germany

Invited Speakers

Sokratis K. Katsikas	Norwegian University of Science and Technology, Norway
Stefan Schmid	University of Vienna, Austria

Contents

Inferring Sensitive Information in Cryptocurrency Off-Chain Networks Using Probing and Timing Attacks

Utz Nisslmueller[1], Klaus-Tycho Foerster[1(✉)], Stefan Schmid[1], and Christian Decker[2]

[1] Faculty of Computer Science, University of Vienna, Vienna, Austria
klaus-tycho.foerster@unive.ac.at
[2] Blockstream, Zurich, Switzerland

Abstract. Off-chain networks have recently emerged as a scalable solution for blockchains, allowing to increase the overall transaction throughput by reducing the number of transactions on the blockchain. However, off-chain networks typically require additional bootstrapping and route discovery functionality to determine viable routes. For example, the Lightning Network (LN) uses two mechanisms in conjunction: gossiping and probing. This paper shows that these mechanisms introduce novel vulnerabilities. In particular, we present two attacks. The first one, which we shall call a probing attack, enables an adversary to determine the (hidden) balance of a channel or route through active probing and differentiating the response messages from the route participants. The second one, which we shall call a timing attack, enables the adversary to determine the logical distance to the target in hops, given that geographical data of LN nodes is often publicly listed, or can be inferred from allocated IP addresses. We explore the setup and implementation of these attacks and address both the theoretical and practical limitations these attacks are subject to. Finally, we propose possible remediations and offer directions for further research on this topic.

Keywords: Lightning · Confidentiality · Probing attack · Timing attack

1 Introduction

Decentralized cryptocurrencies such as Bitcoin and Ethereum revolutionized the way monetary transactions can be performed, without requiring a trusted third party, central bank or intermediaries. The underlying technology, the blockchain, allows to record transactions reliably in a public distributed ledger. A key challenge faced by today's cryptocurrencies concerns their scalability. Supporting only tens of transactions per second, compared to the thousands of transactions per second supported by systems such as Visa. The bottleneck is the required global consensus algorithm.

A promising solution to mitigate the blockchain scalability problem are off-chain networks [9], a.k.a. payment channel networks (PCNs) or second-layer blockchain networks. These networks allow participants to make payments directly through a network of *peer-to-peer* payment channels, and hence to avoid the overhead of global consensus protocols and committing transactions on-chain. Bitcoin Lightning [18], Ethereum

© Springer Nature Switzerland AG 2022
S. Furnell et al. (Eds.): ICISSP 2020, CCIS 1545, pp. 1–21, 2022.
https://doi.org/10.1007/978-3-030-94900-6_1

Raiden [22], XRP Ripple [8], and other off-chain networks promise to reduce load on the underlying blockchain and hence to increase transaction throughput. PCNs may also reduce transaction fees, since only one counterparty is responsible for validating a payment initially, rather than the whole network.

PCNs can be represented as graphs, where each node represents a user and each weighted edge represents funds escrowed on a blockchain; these funds can be transacted only between the endpoints of the edge. Many payment channel networks employ source routing: the source of a payment specifies the complete route for the payment. If the global view of all nodes is accurate, source routing is highly effective because it finds all paths between pairs of nodes. Naturally, nodes are likely to prefer paths with lower per-hop fees, and are only interested in paths which support their transaction, i.e. which have sufficient channel capacity.

The fact that nodes need to be able to find routes however also requires mechanisms for nodes to learn about the payment channel network's state. The two typical mechanisms which enable nodes to find and create such paths are *gossip* and *probing*. The gossip protocol defines messages which are to be broadcast in order for participants to be able to discover new nodes and channels and keep track of currently known nodes and channels [15]. *Probing* is the mechanism which is used to construct an actual payment route based on a local network view delivered by gossip, and ultimately perform the payment. In the context of Sect. 4, we are going to exploit probing to discover whether a payment has occurred over a target channel. The gossip store is queried for viable routes to the destination, based on the desired route properties [24]. Because the gossip store contains global channel information, it is possible to query payment routes originating from any node on the network. Due to privacy concerns, gossip messages only include the *total* balance for any given channel rather than the balance each node is holding.

We explore whether the inherent need for nodes to discover routes in general, and the gossip and probing mechanisms in particular, can be exploited to infer sensitive information about the off-chain network and its transactions.

This paper improves upon the preliminary research in [20] in several aspects. Generally, there is a clearer distinction between design and implementation of the analyzed attacks. The implementation for both attacks now covers a lab implementation (Sects. 4.2, 5.2) and actual BTC Testnet runs (Sects. 4.3, 5.3). For the probing attack in Sect. 4, we have formalized the procedure into three algorithms (Algorithms 1, 2 and 3). For the timing attack, our research has shown that the timing attack might be more promising than initially stated in [20], which is discussed in Sect. 5.4.

1.1 Our Contributions

We uncover and analyze two novel threats for the confidentiality of off-chain networks. As a case study, we consider the Lightning Network. We present two attacks, an active one and a passive one. The active one is a *probing attack* in which the adversary wants to determine the maximum amount which can be transferred over a target channel it is directly or indirectly connected to, by active probing. The passive one is a *timing attack* in which the adversary discovers how close the destination of a routed payment actually is, by acting as a man-in-the middle and listening for/analyzing certain well-defined messages. We then analyze these attacks, identify limitations and also propose remediations for scenarios in which they are able to produce accurate results.

1.2 Organization

The remainder of this paper is organized as follows. We introduce some preliminaries in Sect. 2 and discuss related work in Sect. 3. We describe the probing attack in Sect. 4 and the timing attack in Sect. 5. We conclude in Sect. 6.

2 Preliminaries

While our contribution is applicable to the concept of off-chain networks in general, to be concrete, we will consider the Bitcoin Lightning Network (LN) as a case study in this paper. In the following, we will provide some specific preliminaries which are necessary to understand the remainder of this paper.

The messages which are passed from one Lightning node to another are specified in the Basics of Lightning Technology (BOLTs) [17]. Each message is divided into a subcategory, called a layer. This provides superior separation of concerns, as each layer has a specific task and, similarly to the layers found in the Internet Protocol Suite, is agnostic to the other layers.

For example in Lightning, the `channel_announce` and `channel_update` messages are especially crucial for correct payment routing by other nodes on the network. `channel_announce` signals the creation of a new channel between two LN nodes and is broadcast exactly once.

`channel_update` is propagated at least once by each endpoint, since even initially each of them may have a different fee schedule and thus, routing capacity may differ depending on the direction the payment is taking (i.e., when c is the newly created channel between A and B, whether c is used in direction AB or BA). Once a viable route has been determined, the sending node needs to construct a message (a transaction "request") which needs to be sent to the first hop along the route. Each payment request is accompanied by an onion routing packet containing route information. Upon receiving a payment request each node strips one layer of encryption, extracting its routing information, and ultimately preparing the onion routing packet for the next node in the route. For the sake of simplicity, cryptographic aspects are going to be omitted for the rest of this chapter. We refer to [14] and [16] for specifics.

Two BOLT Layer 2 messages are essential in order to to establish a payment chain:

– `update_add_htlc`: This message signals to the receiver, that the sender would like to establish a new HTLC (Hash Time Locked Contract), containing a certain amount of millisatoshis, over a given channel. The message also contains an `onion_routing_packet` field, which contains information to be forwarded to the next hop along the route. In Fig. 1, the sender initially sets up an HTLC with Hop 1. The `onion_routing_field` contains another `update_add_htlc` (set up between Hop 1 and Hop 2), which in turn contains the ultimate `update_add_htlc` (set up between Hop 2 and Destination) in the `onion_routing_field`.

– `update_fulfill_htlc`: Once the payment message has reached the destination node, it needs to release the payment hash preimage in order to claim the funds which have been locked in the HTLCs along the route by the forwarded `update_add_htlc` messages. For further information on why this is necessary and how HTLCs ensure trustless payment chains, see [4]. To achieve this, the preimage is passed along the route backwards, thereby resolving the HTLCs and committing the transfer of funds (see Steps 4, 5, 6 in Fig. 1).

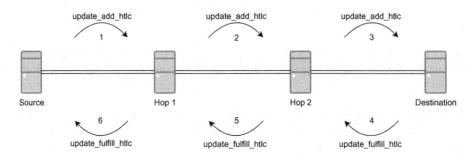

Fig. 1. An exemplary transaction from source to destination, involving two intermediate nodes [20].

The gossip messages mentioned earlier are sent to every adjacent node and eventually propagate through the entire network.

`update_add_htlc` and `update_fulfill_htlc` however, are only sent/ forwarded to the node on the other end of the HTLC.

In order to test the attacks proposed in Sect. 4 and Sect. 5, we have set up a testing network consisting of four c-lightning [2] nodes, with two local network computers running two local nodes each (Fig. 2). Nodes 1 and 2 are connected via a local network link and can form hops for payment routes between Nodes 3 and 4. In order to interact with the nodes, we have made use of c-lightning's RPC interface and built our software tool set in Python [19]. The tests and their corresponding results in Sect. 5 have also been verified with LND [3], another BOLT-conform Lightning Network implementation, written in Go.

3   Related Work

Off-chain networks in general and the Lightning network in particular have recently received much attention, and we refer the reader to the excellent survey by Gudgeon et al. [9]. The Lightning Network as a second-layer network alternative to pure on-chain transactions was first proposed by [21], with the technical specifications laid out in [18]. Despite being theoretically currency-agnostic, current implementations such as c-lightning [2] and LND [3] support BTC exclusively. A popular alternative for ERC-20 based tokens is the Raiden Network [22].

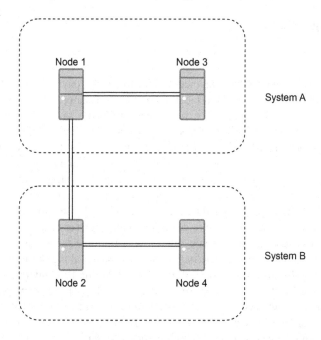

Fig. 2. Local testing setup [20].

Several papers have already analyzed security and privacy concerns in off-chain networks. Rohrer et al. [23] focus on channel-based attacks and propose methods to exhaust a victim's channels via malicious routing (up to potentially total isolation from the victim's neighbors) and to deny service to a victim via malicious HTLC construction. Tochner et al. [26] propose a denial of service attack by creating low-fee channels to other nodes, which are then naturally used to route payments for fee-minimizing network participants and then dropping the payment packets, therefore forcing the sender to await the expiration of the already set-up HTLCs.

[10] provides a closer look into the privacy-performance trade-off inherent in LN routing. The authors also propose an attack to discover channel balances within the network. Wang et al. [27] examine the LN routing process in more detail and propose a split routing approach, dividing payments into large size and small size transactions. The authors show that by routing large payments dynamically to avoid superfluous fees and by routing small payments via a lookup mechanism to reduce excessive probing, the overall success rate can be maintained while significantly reducing performance overhead. Beres et al. [6] make a case for most LN transactions not being truly private, since their analysis has found that most payments occur via single-hop paths. As a remediation, the authors propose partial route obfuscation/extension by adding multiple low-fee hops. Currently still work in progress, [5] is very close to [4] in its approach and already provides some insights into second-layer payments, invoices and payment channels in general. The Lightning Network uses the Sphinx protocol to implement onion routing, as specified in [14]. The version used in current Lightning versions is based on [7] and [11], the latter of which also provides performance comparisons between competing protocols.

4 Probing Attack

4.1 Design

The Lightning Network uses an invoice system to handle payments. An LN invoice consists of a destination node ID, a label, a creation timestamp, an expiry timestamp, a CLTV (Check Lock Time Verify) expiry timestamp and a payment hash. Paying an invoice with a randomized payment hash is possible (since the routing nodes are yet oblivious to the actual hash) and will route the payment successfully to its' destination, which forms the basis of this attack. Optionally it can contain an amount (leaving this field empty would be equal in principle to a blank cheque), a verbal description, a BTC fallback address in case the payment is unsuccessful, and a payment route suggestion. This invoice is then encoded, signed by the payee, and finally sent to the payer.

Having received a valid invoice (e.g. through their browser or directly via e-mail), the payer can now either use the route suggestion within the invoice or query the network themselves, and then send the payment to the payee along the route which has been determined. In this section, we will use the c-lightning RPC interface via Python exclusively - the functions involved are `getroute()` [24] and `sendpay()` [25], which takes two arguments: the return object from a `getroute()` call for a given route, a given amount and a given riskfactor, as well as the payment hash. Using `sendpay()` on its own (meaning, with a random payment hash instead of data from a corresponding invoice) will naturally result in one of two following error codes:

- **204 (Failure Along Route):** This error indicates that one of the hops was unable to forward the payment to the next hop. This can be either due to insufficient funds or a non-existent connection between two adjacent hops along the specified route. If we have ensured that all nodes are connected as depicted in Fig. 2, we can safely assume the former. One sequence of events leading up to this error can be seen in Fig. 3.
- **16399 (Permanent Failure at Destination):** Given the absence of a 204 error, the attempted payment has reached the last hop. As we are using a random payment hash, realistically the destination node will throw an error, signalling that no matching preimage has been found to produce the payment hash. The procedure to provoke a 16399 error code can be seen in Fig. 4.

The goal of this attack is to trace payment flow over a channel, which the attacker node is directly or indirectly connected to. The attacker node will therefore initially attempt to determine whether a payment has occurred over the observed channel between the penultimate and final node along the route. To this end, the attacker will send out periodic probes to the final node (the "victim"), containing the amount which has been determined by the initial probe. If channel weights remain unaltered, each of these probes should return a 16399 error code. If a payment does occur however, the penultimate node will find itself unable to forward the payment on the outgoing channel to our target, yielding a 204 error response. Upon receiving this message, we can then restart the process of our initial probe and ultimately arrive at the exact amount of millisatoshis (msat), which have been transferred.

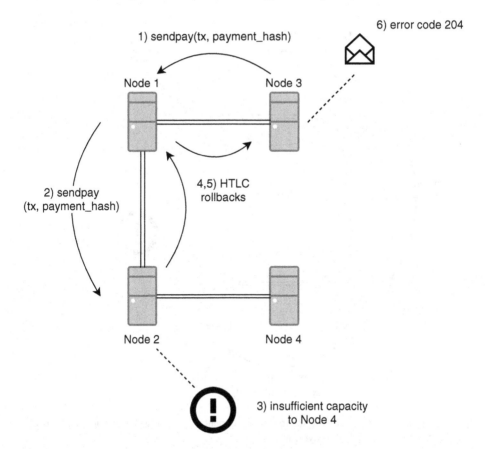

Fig. 3. Causing a 204 error by trying to send a payment to Node 4, which Node 3 is unable to perform [20].

4.2 Lab Implementation

Recalling Fig. 2, we have chosen Node 3 as our attacker node and Node 4 as our target node - hence, the initial goal of Node 3 is to determine the maximum payment flow between Nodes 2 and 4. To conduct our tests, each of the channels has been set up with a balance of 200,000,000 msat, with each node holding a stake of 100,000,000 msat in each of its channels. Node 3 will hold a slightly higher balance in order to accommodate probing fees. We can use the total channel balance, as received via gossip, as an upper ceiling for this value (200,000,000 msat in this case). We can then send payments from Node 3 to Node 4 with random payment hashes - resulting in either error code 16399 or error code 204 (Sect. 4.1). To this end, we perform a binary search on the available funds which we can transfer, searching for the highest value yielding a 16399 error instead of a 204 error. The algorithms used for both initial probing and deriving the actual channel balance from Node 2 to Node 4 are depicted in Algorithms 1 and 2.

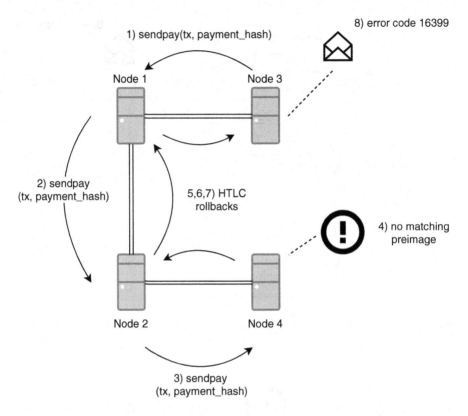

Fig. 4. Causing a 16399 error by trying to send a payment to Node 4, who can't produce a matching preimage and thus fails the payment [20].

We thus arrive at the approximate maximum amount, which Node 2 can transfer to Node 4. The next step is to continuously probe for this amount of msat in regular intervals. The expected response is a 16399 error code, with a 204 error code implying that the amount we are trying to send is higher than the available amount which Node 2 can transfer to Node 4 (or that it has disconnected from Node 4). Upon receiving a 204 response, we start looking for the maximum payable amount to Node 4 once more. Subtracting the new amount from the old amount, we arrive at the size of the transaction which has occurred between Nodes 3 and 4. After 17 probes by Node 3, Algorithm 2 has yielded an initial balance of 99,999,237 msat, which is in line with the channel balance we have allocated between Nodes 2 and 4. The next step is to monitor the channel for potential weight changes (Algorithm 3).

To verify this, we have transferred 50,000,000 msat from Node 2 to Node 4, with our program detecting this soon after (we have set t to 5 s in order to avoid excessive probing) and returning an updated balance of 49,998,237 msat. We then transferred another 30,000,000 msat from Node 1 to Node 4, with our program again picking up the change and reporting the new channel balance at 19,997,389 msat.

Algorithm 1. Probing a channel for a given amount of msat

Result: Either error code 204 or 16399
payment_hash = random.hex();
node_id = node ID of final node on victim channel;
msat = *value to probe for*;
route = getroute(node_id, msat);
sendpay(route, payment_hash);

Algorithm 2. Finding the initial maximum channel balance.

Result: amount_msat - initial channel balance
min_msat = 0;
max_msat = channel.balance;
amount_msat = channel.balance / 2;
while *True* **do**
    if *probe(amount_msat) == 16399* **then**
        | min_msat = amount_msat;
    else
        if *amount_msat) == 204* **then**
        | max_msat = amount_msat;
        else
        | return "No suitable route found.";
        end
    end
    if *max_msat - min_msat < 1000* **then**
        | return amount_msat;
    else
        | *// continue to minimise maximum error*
    end
    amount_msat = (min_msat + max_msat) / 2
end

Figure 5 shows the trade-off between probing run time and the error in the channel balance estimate we observed for test runs on our lab setup. As we wanted to avoid overly excessive probing while conducting our tests, we were generally satisfied with any answer which is less than 1000 msat (the actual minimum BTC denomination) lower than the actual channel balance. Another possible approach could be keeping the number of probes sent out to the target constant, hence providing a more uniform level of balance error and probing duration.

4.3 BTC Testnet Evaluation

For analysis on the feasibility of our attack over the BTC Testnet, we connected Nodes 1, 2 and 3 from Fig. 2 to the "ion.radar.tech" Testnet Lightning node. We chose this host in particular, since their website allowed us to alter the channel weights by generating payable invoices with parameters of our choosing. The exact connections along with the corresponding channel weights can be seen in Fig. 6. Our goal was to verify the results we obtained in Sect. 4.2 and see whether probing duration (see Fig. 5) was affected by

---

Algorithm 3. Finding the initial maximum channel balance.

Result: New maximum flow from penultimate to final node
init_max = *initial channel balance*;
new_max = init_max;
t = *time to wait between checks*;
while *True* **do**
    sleep(t);
    if *probe(init_max)* == *204* **then**
        // *channel balance has decreased*
        return find_init_max();
        // *potentially calculate delta*
    else
        if *(init_max + 1000)* == *16399* **then**
            // *channel balance has increased*
            return find_init_max();
            // *potentially calculate delta*
        else
            return error;
        end
    end
end

---

the public Testnet hop in place of the local hop(s) used in Sect. 4.2. Running an initial series of probes from Node 3 to Node 1, we arrived at a channel balance of 149,926,757 msat between the radar.ion.tech node and Node 1 (99.95% accuracy). We attribute this comparatively high error in regard to our tests in Sect. 4.2 due to the Testnet nodes' differing fee structure, which is necessarily taken into account when constructing the payment route. Then, we sent a payment containing 50,000,000 msat from Node 2 to Node 1 - predictably, Node 3 returned the updated maximum payment flow on the observed channel correctly with 99,902,343 msat (99.9 % accuracy).

After verifying the correct operation of our program for 16399 error codes, we were keen on discovering whether 204 error code scenarios would be dealt with correctly as well. In order to test this, we transferred back any amounts which have been redistributed as part of our initial test, increased the channel balance between Node 1 and radar.ion.tech by a factor of 10 and modified the setup from Fig. 6 slightly by placing an intermediary hop between radar.ion.tech and Nodes 2 and 3. The updated infrastructure can be seen in Fig. 7.

It became apparent however, that we would need to rethink the weights we allotted to the respective nodes, as we were initially unaware of the true channel weights between the radar.ion.tech and "lnd.vanilla.co.za" nodes. Naturally, we were inclined to simply run the find_init_max() function (Algorithm 2) from Node 3 on the ion.radar.tech node. However, we found that the two nodes were connected by 6 channels rather than one. To circumvent this route ambiguity, we queried a route for 1,000, 1,000,000 an 1,000,000,000 msat using default parameters, hoping all of them would return the same route, thus allowing us to treat the resulting channel as the only one connecting these two nodes. Unfortunately though, we received varying responses for all of these amounts, introducing a large uncertainty in any subsequent measurements.

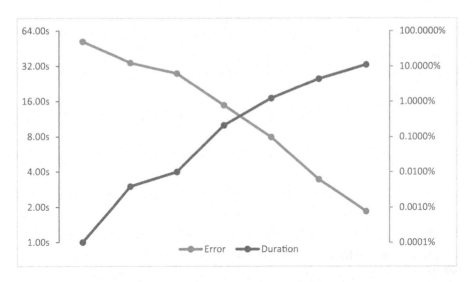

Fig. 5. Visualizing the trade-off between probing accuracy and duration [20].

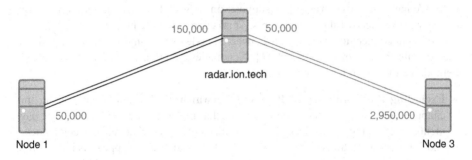

Fig. 6. Setup and balance allocations of our first Testnet evaluation (balances given in satoshis).

We then tried to run our tests on these channels, with all of them reporting failure in establishing a route to the target. We are not sure why even the initial probes failed and only further analysis and testing of our program will unveil the error in our approach. We decided to conclude our Testnet evaluation at this point, since despite extensive refactoring, we were not able to produce meaningful results for this constellation of nodes and channels, leaving route ambiguity and handling of multiple channels to be explored by further research in this area.

4.4   Results, Implications, and Further Considerations

In Sect. 4.2 we have demonstrated that it is in fact possible to trace channel payments if the network is structured in a certain way. In theory, this method should hold true for any node which is reachable from the attacking node and has only one channel whose balance is lower or equal to the second lowest balance on the route from the attacking

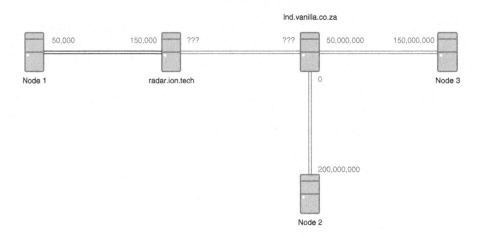

Fig. 7. Initial setup and balance allocations of our second Testnet evaluation (balances given in satoshis).

node. We have partially verified this supposition in Sect. 4.3 while maintaining a high accuracy in our successful measurements. This is particularly a threat to end users, since most of them connect to a single well-connected node over a single channel, in order to interact with the rest of the network [1]. Nonetheless, there are several caveats to this method, the most significant of which are:

– **Excluding the Possibility of Payment Forwarding:** The attack laid out in this chapter does not take into account the fact that nodes can be used to forward payments. Hearkening back to Fig. 2, if we were to select the channel between Nodes 1 and 2 as our target, transactions between Nodes 1 and 4 would appear as if they were transactions to Node 3. One opportunity of accounting for this would be to monitor *every* channel to and from Node 3 for changes in directed channel balance, which would create problems on its own (see below).
– **Surge of Unresolved HTLCs While Probing:** Recalling steps 5–7 in Fig. 4, each probe sets up a chain of irredeemable HTLCs (since a matching preimage would have to be brute-forced). Eventually, running multiple probes over the same channels will escrow its funds in these HTLCs, effectively DOSing the probe route and forcing the nodes to wait until the HTLCs time out before being able to forward other payments. This is an issue we encountered over and over during Sect. 4.2 and Sect. 4.3, often giving us one shot at probing before having to wait multiple hours for the HTLCs to expire. This is also why we chose the channels leading up to our final target to have a much higher balance, so that we would have enough balance left after initial probing to monitor the channel for a reasonable period of time.
– **Insufficient Sensitivity for High-frequency Transactions:** Looking back at Algorithm 3, we have defined the parameter t as the time, for which to wait during probes for monitoring the channel balance, one the initial maximum value has been discovered. If more than one transaction would occur during this timeframe, it would still only show up as a singular payment with our tool. In the worst-case scenario, two

transactions covering the same amount could take place in opposite directions, not changing the weighted balance at all and thus eluding our detection mechanisms.

- **Omission of Private Channels:** Upon creating a channel, the node can declare the channel as private, and thus prevent it from being broadcast via gossip. The channel is fully functional for both nodes which are connected by it, but no foreign payments can be routed through it. Looking ahead to increasing adoption of the Lightning Network, this provides an intriguing opportunity for nodes, which do not wish to participate in routing (e.g. mobile wallets) or nodes with limited uptime (personal computers). Routing would only occur between aggregating nodes (such as payment providers), with most of the channels (and therefore nodes) on the network remaining invisible to malicious participants as the gossip protocol would only propagate public channels. This further exacerbates our ability to detect forwarded payments (see above) as opposed to actual payments, since private channels can't be monitored by design.

- **Disregard of Potential Bottlenecks:** The proposed method of monitoring channel transactions does not hold, if a single channel along the route has a lower balance than the target channel in the desired direction. The node which has an insufficient amount of msat on its' outgoing channel would return a 204 error (Fig. 3) This can often happen if an end user node is used as a hop prior to a high-capacity node. It is easy to detect which channel acts as a bottleneck, however a bit trickier to circumvent this obstacle - we would like to point the interested reader to [26] for suggestions on route hijacking and thus effectively bypassing the bottleneck along the route.

During the tests we conducted in Sect. 4.3, we also encountered the hops between Node 1 and Node 3 being connected via multiple channels. As confirmed by our observations, it is entirely possible to receive varying routes for differing amount_msat, risk-factor, cltv and fuzzpercent [24] combinations. Our tool failed to produce accurate results in this scenario, as it was designed assuming singular channels between pairs of nodes. It is however perfectly reasonable to have multiple channels between two nodes, as channel balances are final and can't be increased after creation. We expect this to be the predominant form of retrospectively increasing potential payment flow between nodes and further research on how to deal with this complication would be highly appreciated.

All in all, the probing attack we laid out in this chapter can be seen more as a proof of concept rather than a realistic attack vector, due to the limitations discussed in Sect. 4.4. We are confident that certain aspects such as the exact algorithm and route construction could be refined to provide more reliable results. However other aspects such as the binding of channel funds in irredeemable HTLCs and the incomplete network view due to private channels provide a much more consistent barrier to uncovering payment flows in real-world scenarios.

5 Timing Attack

5.1 Design

The Lightning Network is often referred to as a payment channel network (PCN). Performing payments over multiple hops is possible due to the use of HTLC's [21], a special bitcoin transaction whose unlocking conditions effectively rid the Lightning Network and its users of all trust requirements. An exemplary chain of HTLCs along with their shortened unlocking conditions is shown in Fig. 8. Note that any node can only retrieve the funds locked in the HTLCs if they share R, and that each HTLC starting from Node 4 is valid for 2 h longer than the previous HTLC to provide some room for error/downtime.

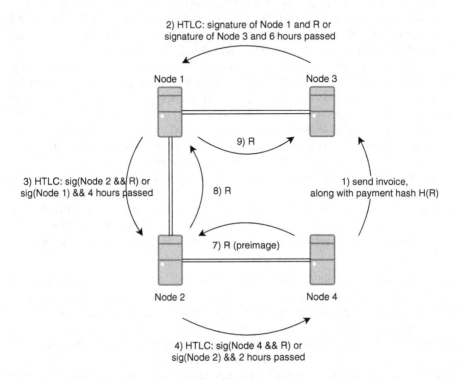

2) HTLC: signature of Node 1 and R or signature of Node 3 and 6 hours passed

Node 1   Node 3

9) R

3) HTLC: sig(Node 2 && R) or sig(Node 1) && 4 hours passed

8) R

1) send invoice, along with payment hash H(R)

7) R (preimage)

Node 2   Node 4

4) HTLC: sig(Node 4 && R) or sig(Node 2) && 2 hours passed

Fig. 8. Paying a LN invoice over multiple hops. Messages 2–4 are `update_add_htlc` messages, messages 7–9 are `update_fulfill_htlc` messages [20].

Due to the Onion Routing properties of the Lightning Network, it is cryptographically infeasible to try and determine where along the route a forwarding node is located, since each node can only decrypt the layer which was intended for it to decrypt. Attempts to analyze the remaining length of the routing packet have been thwarted at the protocol level by implementing a fixed packet size with zero padding at the final layer [14].

The only opportunity left to analyze the encrypted traffic between the nodes is to extract time-related information from the messages. One possibility would be to analyze the `cltv_expiry_delta` field (analogous to "hours passed" in Fig. 8, measured in mined blocks since the establishment of the HTLC): By looking at the delay of both the incoming and the outgoing HTLC, a node could infer how many hops are left until the payment destination. However, this possibility has been accounted for by the adding "shadow routes" to the actual payment path, with each node fuzzing path information by adding a random offset to the `cltv_expiry_delta` value, hence effectively preventing nodes from guessing their position along the payment route [15].

The method we propose, is to time messages at the network level, rather than at the protocol level (e.g. through `cltv_expiry_delta`). Recalling Fig. 8, Node 2 can listen for response messages from Node 4, since there is currently no mechanism in place to add delay to `update_fulfill_htlc` responses (in fact, [13] states that "*a node SHOULD remove an HTLC as soon as it can*"). Based on response latency, Node 2 could infer its position along the payment route to a certain extent, as examined in Sect. 5.2.

5.2 Lab Implementation

Initial analysis has shown that analyzing packets directly (e.g. via Wireshark) is of little avail, since LN messages are end-to-end encrypted - meaning that even if we know the target nodes' IP address and port number, we can not detect the exact nature of the messages exchanged. We hence chose to redirect the output of the listening c-lightning node to a log file, which we then analyze with a Python script. As in Sect. 4, the source code can be found at [19].

Looking at the log file, we are particularly interested in the two messages discussed in Sect. 2: `update_add_htlc` and `update_fulfill_htlc`. The node output includes these events, complete with timestamps and the corresponding node ID with which the HTLC is negotiated. By repeatedly sending money back and forth between Nodes 1 and 3 in our test setup (Fig. 2), we arrive at a local (and therefore minimum) latency of 182 ms on average. The latency distribution for small (1,000 msat) payments can be seen in Fig. 9. We have found that latencies remain largely unaffected by transaction size - increasing payment size by a factor of 100,000 actually slightly reduced average settlement time and standard deviation (Fig. 10).

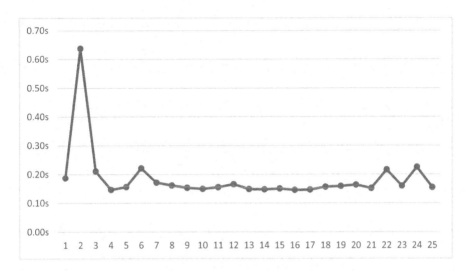

Fig. 9. Latency times for local payments containing 1,000 msat ($\mu = 0.1892$, $\sigma = 0.1168$, $n = 25$) [20].

Next, we examined whether an increase in hop distance would yield predictable results. To this end, we first timed payments over 1 network hop from Node 2 to Node 1 (Fig. 11). Then, we timed payments over the same amount over 1 network and 1 local hop from Node 2 to Node 3 (Fig. 12). Based on these results, we derive that timing messages on a local network with little to no interfering traffic scales predictably over several hops, with 1 network hop roughly corresponding to 1.284 local hops in terms of latency.

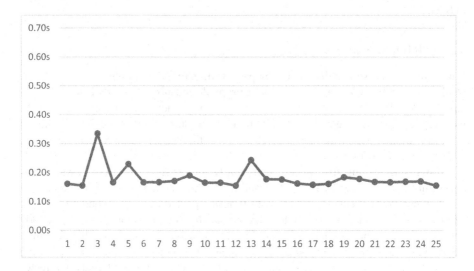

Fig. 10. Latency times for local payments containing 100,000,000 msat ($\mu = 0.1798$, $\sigma = 0.0385$, $n = 25$).

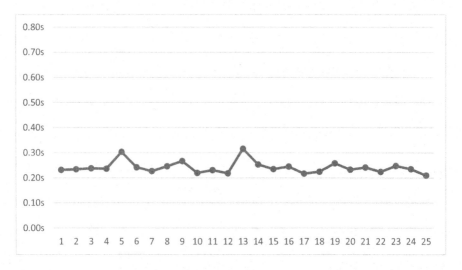

Fig. 11. Latency times for payments containing 100,000,000 msat over 1 network hop ($\mu = 0.234$, $\sigma = 0.025$, $n = 25$).

5.3 BTC Testnet Evaluation

Building on the results obtained in Sect. 5.2, we were keen to discover whether the they would carry over into real-world evaluations. To this end, we connected Node 1 and Node 3 from Fig. 2 to the "endurance" Lightning Testnet node. Located in Dublin, Ireland and being connected to over 500 other Lightning Testnet nodes [1], we concluded that this node would provide a good entry point to test network latency from our location in Vienna, Austria, with the possibility to construct longer and more complicated routes over it as we saw fit. In order to constitute an initial RTT value, we established an HTTP connection to Lightning's default port 9735 [12], since the target host appeared to drop our ICMP ping requests. Alternating our requests between Systems A and B (Fig. 2) in an attempt to prevent cached responses, we have found that HTTP response times were fairly constant from this node, with an average response time of 0.067 s ($\sigma = 0.0206$).

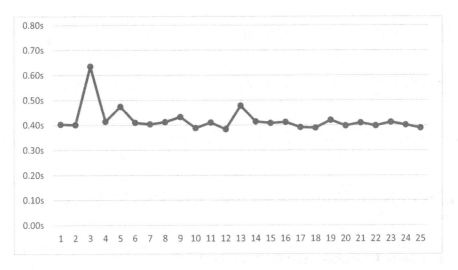

Fig. 12. Latency times for payments containing 100,000,000 msat over 1 network hop and 1 local hop ($\mu = 0.414$, $\sigma = 0.05$, $n = 25$).

Next, we were interested whether payments over the public hop were subject to an equally uniform latency as in Sect. 5.2. Thus, we created 25 invoices over 1,000,000 msat each (having found in Sect. 5.2 that response latency is independent of payment size) at Node 3 and sent the payment from Node 1. As seen in Fig. 13, the fulfill message response times were remarkably consistent, however latency did not scale to our expectations. Based on Fig. 12, we expected to be overall latency to be in the ballpark of 0.5–0.7 s (2x local network RTT + HTTP request RTT), however actual latency was twice that value. Results from the aranguren.org Testnet node, located in Melbourne, Australia, proved equally consistent with an average ping time of 0.314 s ($\sigma = 0.035$) and an average HTLC fulfillment latency of 1.68 s ($\sigma = 0.0972$)

Finally, we were curious about HTLC fulfillment delays over 2 public hops. To this end, we closed the channel between Node 3 and endurance and opened a new channel to the "aranguren.org" Testnet node, which in turn has a channel with endurance and thus re-establishes the chain of channels from Node 1 to Node 3. Timing results for this route can be seen in Fig. 14. This marked the end of our timing tests, since we were not able to establish an acyclic payment route over 3 or more publicly available LN nodes. This coincides with the observation that neither the attempted nor the actual payments we performed during the course of Sect. 4 and Sect. 5 were routed over more than two public hops.

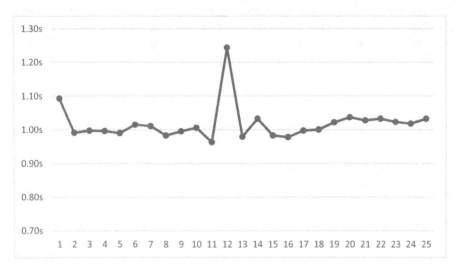

Fig. 13. Latency times for payments between Node 1 and Node 3 over the endurance Lightning node ($\mu = 1.0179$, $\sigma = 0.0542$, $n = 25$).

5.4   Results, Implications and Further Considerations

Considering the findings in Sect. 5.2, we can see that timing produces fairly reliable and uniformly distributed results over a local network with little outside interference. Yet, due to the nature of LN routing, it is not possible to determine the distance or path to the initial payment source. To our surprise however, RTT remained equally consistent over 1–2 internet hops. Data acquired during monitoring of the local (mostly idle) network suggests that the timing node won't be able to distinguish traffic originating from a local node from the traffic in Sect. 5.2 without further information due to low latency deltas ranging from 2 ms to 5 ms.

While performing timing measurements for payments across the BTC Testnet network, we have found that HTLC settlement takes long enough over even 1 hop to make traffic RTT volatility negligible. Over 1 hop, we conclude that HTLC settlement for our Vienna-based node should be in the ballpark of 0.86 − 1.97 s with 2-hop latency amounting to roughly 1.99 − 2.68 s, depending on the geographical location and assuming a normal distribution for the measured latency deltas. Further research could include

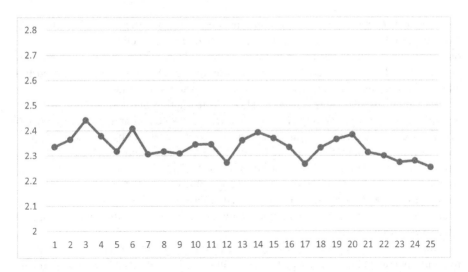

Fig. 14. Latency times for payments between Node 1 and Node 3 over the endurance and aranguren.org Lightning nodes ($\mu = 2.3349$, $\sigma = 0.0475$, $n = 25$).

a further statistical examination of the ability to differentiate distances for HTLC deltas at the sub-2-second threshold. We suggest that overall network bandwidth does not affect the acquired results significantly, since after performing all payments in Sect. 4, Node 1 has sent 64 KB and Node 3 has received 55 KB - only a fraction of which were outgoing/incoming HTLCs (alongside gossip, pings, etc.).

Our results open many new avenues for further timing-based research on the Lightning Network. The next step for us would be to develop a tool to predict the distance to the final destination of an HTLC which is passing through the listening node, based on the measurements laid out in Sect. 5.3. It would be interesting to see whether there is a possibility to force payment-unrelated response messages, e.g. by forging ping messages [12] in order to estimate (possibly network-wide) RTTs, correlate HTLC settlement latencies against them and finally arrive at a set of nodes which must have been the ultimate recipient of the forwarded payment. Furthermore, experiments could be conducted on the feasibility of adding a random time offset to HTLC fulfillments, and the trade-offs involved therein.

6   Conclusion

This paper has shown that off-chain routing and payment settlement mechanisms may be exploited to infer confidential information about the network state. In particular, considering the Lightning Network with Bitcoin as the underlying blockchain as a case study, we set up a local infrastructure and proposed two ways in which two current state-of-the-art implementations, c-lightning and LND, can be exploited to gain knowledge about distant channel balances and transactions to unconnected nodes: By deliberately failing payment attempts, we were able to deduce the exact amount of (milli-)satoshis on a channel located two hops away on our local lab infrastructure. Using this technique repeatedly, we were able to determine whether a transaction occurred between one node and another over the monitored channel. To a certain extent, we were able to reproduce these results in the public Bitcoin Testnet chain. We also identified this attacks' limitations and proposed some workarounds to these obstacles.

By timing the messages related to HTLC construction and termination, we were able to infer the remaining distance of a forwarded packet accurately in our test lab. These results transferred well into our Testnet evaluation, while being free of the partially restrictive limitations which we discovered during our examination of the probing attack. We concluded that RTT volatility of the HTLC message cycle was low enough for public Testnet hops which were within geographical vicinity to our node in Vienna, Austria, as well as for hops which were located in East Asia, to establish latency approximate latency boundaries for the number of remaining hops along the payment route of a forwarded transaction.

Our work raises several interesting research questions. In particular, it remains to fine-tune our attacks, to improve the flexibility of our software tools and to finally conduct more systematic experiments including more natural/interconnected network topologies, particularly on other off-chain networks. More generally, it will be interesting to explore further attacks on the confidentiality of off-chain networks exploiting the routing mechanism and investigate countermeasures. Furthermore, our work raises the question whether such vulnerabilities are an inherent price of efficient off-chain routing or if there exist rigorous solutions.

Bibliographical Note

A preliminary version of this article appeared at ICISSP 2020 [20].

References

1. 1ML - Bitcoin Lightning Analysis Engine (2019). https://1ml.com/. Accessed 10 Nov 2019
2. c-lightning GitHub Repository (2019). https://github.com/ElementsProject/lightning. Accessed 26 Dec 2019
3. LND GitHub Repository (2020). https://github.com/lightningnetwork/lnd. Accessed 18 Jan 2020
4. Antonopoulos, A.M.: Mastering Bitcoin: Unlocking Digital Crypto-Currencies. O'Reilly Media Inc, 1st edn. Newton (2014)
5. Antonopoulos, A.M., Osuntokun, O., Pickhardt, R.: Mastering the Lightning Network (2019). https://github.com/lnbook/lnbook. Accessed 22 Nov 2019
6. Béres, F., Seres, I.A., Benczúr, A.A.: A cryptoeconomic traffic analysis of bitcoins lightning network. arXiv abs/1911.09432 (2019)
7. Danezis, G., Goldberg, I.: Sphinx: A compact and provably secure mix format. In: IEEE Symposium on Security and Privacy, pp. 269–282. IEEE Computer Society (2009)
8. Fugger, R.: Money as IOUs in social trust networks & a proposal for a decentralized currency network protocol. Hypertext document. Available electronically at http://ripple.sourceforge.net 106 (2004)
9. Gudgeon, L., Moreno-Sanchez, P., Roos, S., McCorry, P., Gervais, A.: Sok: off the chain transactions. IACR Crypt. ePrint Arch. **2019**, 360 (2019)

10. Herrera-Joancomartí, J., et al.: On the difficulty of hiding the balance of lightning network channels. In: AsiaCCS, pp. 602–612. ACM (2019)
11. Kate, A., Goldberg, I.: Using sphinx to improve onion routing circuit construction. In: Sion, R. (ed.) FC 2010. LNCS, vol. 6052, pp. 359–366. Springer, Heidelberg (2010). https://doi.org/10.1007/978-3-642-14577-3_30
12. Lightning Network: BOLT 1: Base Protocol (2019). https://github.com/lightningnetwork/lightning-rfc/blob/master/01-messaging.md. Accessed 23 Jan 2020
13. Lightning Network: BOLT 2: Peer Protocol for Channel Management (2019). https://github.com/lightningnetwork/lightning-rfc/blob/master/02-peer-protocol.md. Accessed 6 Jan 2020
14. Lightning Network: BOLT 4: Onion Routing Protocol (2019). https://github.com/lightningnetwork/lightning-rfc/blob/master/04-onion-routing.md Accessed 3 Jan 2020
15. Lightning Network: BOLT 7: P2P Node and Channel Discovery (2019). https://github.com/lightningnetwork/lightning-rfc/blob/master/07-routing-gossip.md Accessed 4 Dec 2019
16. Lightning Network: BOLT 8: Encrypted and authenticated transport (2019). https://github.com/lightningnetwork/lightning-rfc/blob/master/08-transport.md. Accessed 4 Jan 2020
17. Lightning Network: Lightning Network Specifications (2019). https://github.com/lightningnetwork/lightning-rfc/. Accessed 29 Nov 2019
18. Lightning Network: Lightning RFC: Lightning Network Specifications (2019). https://github.com/lightningnetwork/lightning-rfc. Accessed 18 Nov 2019
19. Nisslmueller, U.: Python code repository (2020). https://github.com/utzn42/icissp_2020_lightning. Accessed 02 Jan 2020
20. Nisslmueller, U., Foerster, K.T., Schmid, S., Decker, C.: Toward active and passive confidentiality attacks on cryptocurrency off-chain networks. In: Proceedings of 6th International Conference on Information Systems Security and Privacy (ICISSP) (2020)
21. Poon, J., Dryja, T.: The bitcoin lightning network: Scalable off-chain instant payments (2016). https://lightning.network/lightning-network-paper.pdf. Accessed 3 Jan 2020
22. Raiden Network: Raiden Network (2020). https://raiden.network/. Accessed 02 Jan 2020
23. Rohrer, E., Malliaris, J., Tschorsch, F.: Discharged payment channels: quantifying the lightning network's resilience to topology-based attacks. In: EuroS and P Workshops, pp. 347–356. IEEE (2019)
24. Russell, R.: lightning-getroute - Command for routing a payment (low-level) (2019). https://lightning.readthedocs.io/lightning-getroute.7.html. Accessed 6 Dec 2019
25. Russell, R.: lightning-sendpay - Low-level command for sending a payment via a route (2019). https://lightning.readthedocs.io/lightning-sendpay.7.html. Accessed 4 Jan 2020
26. Tochner, S., Schmid, S., Zohar, A.: Hijacking routes in payment channel networks: a predictability tradeoff. arXiv abs/1909.06890 (2019)
27. Wang, P., Xu, H., Jin, X., Wang, T.: Flash: efficient dynamic routing for offchain networks. In: CoNEXT, pp. 370–381. ACM (2019)

Secure Ownership Transfer for Resource Constrained IoT Infrastructures

Martin Gunnarsson[1]([✉])[ID] and Christian Gehrmann[2][ID]

[1] RISE, Ole Römers väg 5A, Lund, Sweden
martin.gunnarsson@ri.se
[2] Department of Electrical and Information Technology, Lund University, Lund, Sweden
christian.gehrmann@eit.lth.se

Abstract. Internet of Things or IoT deployments are becoming more and more common. The list of use-cases for IoT is getting longer and longer, but some examples are smart home appliances and wireless sensor networks. When IoT devices are deployed and used over an extended time, it is not guaranteed that one owner will control the IoT devices over their entire lifetime. If the ownership of an IoT system shall be transferred between two entities, secure ownership transfer arises.

In this paper we propose a protocol that enables secure ownership transfer of constrained IoT devices. The protocol is resource-efficient and only rely on symmetric cryptography for the IoT devices. The protocol has been rigorously analyzed to prove the state security requirements. The security analysis has been done partially using formal protocol verification tools, particularly Tamarin Prover. To show our proposed protocol's resource efficiency, we have done a proof of concept implementation. This implementation, for constrained IoT devices, has been used to verify the efficiency of the protocol. The results presented in this paper, an extend version of previously published work on secure ownership transfer protocols for constrained IoT devices by the same authors.

Keywords: IoT · Ownership transfer · Constrained devices

1 Introduction

Internet of Things or IoT is a relatively well-established term in computer science research and the IT industry. IoT is a concept or vision where *things* are connected to some network, usually the internet. Network connectivity enables connected devices to send and receive data and interact with other computing resources connected to the same network. The types of devices that have gained networking capability are, to name a few: industrial sensors and actuators, connected medical devices, and smart consumer devices. One application of IoT is vast deployments with many devices [40]; these deployments can be used to monitor large areas such as cities for thins such as pollution

Supported by SSF project SEC4Factory under grant RIT17-0032 and EU H2020 project Cloudi-Facturing under grant 768892.

S. Furnell et al. (Eds.): ICISSP 2020, CCIS 1545, pp. 22–47, 2022.
https://doi.org/10.1007/978-3-030-94900-6_2

and noise levels. Large deployments of connected devices can be a challenge to manage for the owner of the devices and research on how to manage large IoT deployments [10,22].

Like any computing device network, a large IoT deployment must be managed and supervised to be secure. An IoT deployment is expected to facilitate secure communication between devices, confidentiality and integrity protection, etc. for the transmitted data. To enable this, each IoT device in the deployment needs keys. These keys need to be issued and updated [29] to each IoT device. The problem of key management has been explored and investigated before, and protocols and standards exist that describe how key management can be done securely. Examples of such key management standards are: IKE [14] and HIP [30]. These standards are tried and proven for a scenario when one organization is managing devices over their entire life cycle.

However, if the IoT deployment's owner wishes to sell or otherwise transfer the entire deployment to a new owner, existing key management solutions are no longer sufficient. For IoT systems deployed into an environment such as a factory or a city, it might not be feasible to physically access each IoT device to reprogram the devices to change ownership. The process of transferring the ownership must be done remotely, without physical access to the individual IoT devices. It is also essential that the old owner have all access revoked after the new owners assume ownership of the devices. It should not be possible for the new owner to access any data, or decrypt any messages sent by the old owner before the ownership transfer. When deploying IoT devices, especially in large numbers, it is important that the cost of devices must be kept low. Cost constraints typically result in IoT devices with limited performance, or *constrained* IoT devices. The limited capability of these types of IoT devices make certain types of cryptography to resource intensive.

Secure ownership transfer has been studied in the research for IoT devices and also for RFID tags. Deployments of RFID tags can be used for inventory tracking and supply chain management. For these use-cases, with many RFID tags that switch owners, the problem of secure ownership transfer has been studied [36]. For IoT, the question of secure ownership transfer has been studied for several applications, such as medical IoT and smart home appliances. The proposed solutions for these applications do not work for our intended use case with a system of constrained IoT devices.

In this paper we provide our extended work on the problem of secure ownership transfer for constrained IoT deployments. This work is the extended version of our previous work [16]. In this paper we have extended the security evaluation, provide more results from an experimental evaluation and have included a more comprehensive overview of related work.

We started by analyzing the intended deployment scenario for our protocol, including trust assumptions for the different entities in the system. We have stated formal security requirements for a secure ownership transfer protocol in the domain of constrained IoT devices from these preliminaries and prior research. Next, we present a protocol, with a trusted third party, referred to as a "Reset Server" (RS) in this work. We have performed a rigorous security analysis of the protocol we proposed. We have used formal protocol verification with Tamarin Prover to aid in proving the previously stated security requirements. In addition to proving that the protocol fulfills the security requirements, we have done a proof of concept implementation of our protocol to experimentally verify that the protocol performs as desired when deployed in a constrained IoT environment.

The contribution of this paper is as follows:

- We analyze the IoT infrastructure ownership transfer problem and conclude that it has similar but not equal security requirements than those identified in previous analyses of group ownership transfer for tags.
- We suggest a novel IoT infrastructure ownership transfer model and protocol. The protocol uses a Trusted third party (TTP) and only symmetric cryptography to facilitate secure ownership transfer of constrained IoT devices.
- We present a proof of concept implementation and performance evaluation of the proposed ownership transfer scheme.
- We make a security analysis of the proposed ownership transfer protocol using both Tamarin Prover and logical reasoning.

We proceed as follows: first, we introduce our system model in Sect. 2, identify security requirements, and give a problem definition in Sect. 3. In Sect. 4, we present our ownership transfer model and protocol design; we perform a security analysis of the proposed transfer protocol in Sect. 5. We then describe our proof-of-concept implementation, including performance benchmarks in Sect. 6. Finally, we present and discuss related work in Sect. 7 and conclude with a discussion of our contribution and future work in Sect. 8.

2   System Model and Assumptions

In this paper, we consider IoT deployments, as seen in Fig. 1. The IoT deployment consists of many IoT devices, deployed and managed by a Device Management Server (DMS) that is owned and operated by some entity. The entity will typically be a company but can also be an individual or an institution. The IoT deployment can serve a variety of purposes; it can, for example, be a part of an industrial control system, a building automation system, or a smart sensor network deployed to monitor the environment for pollution. The DMS is typically not located physically adjacent to the IoT devices, and communicate with the IoT devices through intermediary networks, typically the Internet. The last hop in communication.

The IoT devices considered in this paper are typically constrained devices described in this document [7], which means that their computational capabilities, such as processing power and memory, are limited. In this paper, we assume that the IoT devices are capable of symmetric cryptography. Asymmetric cryptography is not feasible for these devices due to the complex computation needed. These computations consume energy and memory that is scarce on these types of constrained devices. The wireless communication technology available to constrained devices is usually Low-Power and Lossy Networks (LLNs) [39]. As the name implies, LLNs have limited bandwidth, range and suffer from packet loss. These constraints restrict the amount of data that can be transmitted to and from the IoT devices. The DMS is assumed to be a computationally powerful server, either located on-premise in the entity owning and operating the IoT deployment or running in a cloud environment.

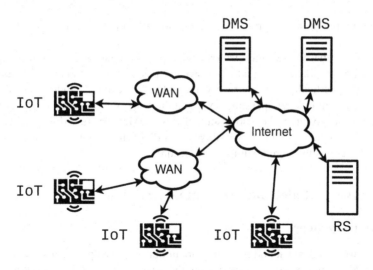

Fig. 1. An overview of the considered system.

We show a schematic overview of a considered IoT deployment in Fig. 1; the IoT units use LLNs or WAN to communicate locally, connectivity to the DMS is provided over the Internet. Since the IoT devices are connected to the Internet, they are vulnerable to remote attacks. Because of this threat of a remote attack, the IoT units must be properly secured against these threats. The IoT devices must authenticate all incoming messages, and the DMS must authenticate all messages believed to originate from an IoT device. Since messages traverse networks that cannot be trusted not to eavesdrop on the communication, messages between the DMS and IoT devices must be encrypted. Thus, independent of the particular communications technology used, secure communication requires keys in place on the IoT units to mutually authenticate with the back-end DMS.

The protocol we propose uses several keys to perform secure ownership transfer. These symmetric keys are shared between individual IoT devices and the owner's DMS. In this paper we refer to these key(s) collectively as *credentials*.

Ownership transfer implies that the ownership is transferred from one organization to another. In this paper, we have assumed that another entity, be it another company, individual, or other organization that wishes to acquire ownership of the IoT deployment. We assume that the parties, in this paper called *old owner* and *new owner*, can agree on eventual payment and other compensation outside the scope of this protocol. Of more relevance for our protocol, we assume that the new owner has its own DMS and that the old owner and new owner can establish mutual authentication, possibly with a Public Key Infrastructure (PKI).

To facilitate secure ownership transfer using symmetric keys, we assume a trusted third party called the RS. The RS will aid in the deployment and ownership transfer of the IoT deployment. Since RS is a trusted third party, it is naturally trusted to a high degree by both new owner and old owner. In this paper, RS refers only to the server directly participating in the protocol. The organization operating the RS is left out of scope.

We suppose that the RS and DMS are servers of standard computational capabilities. There are no practical limitations in what types of cryptographic operations they can perform, specifically asymmetric cryptography. But, even if resources are abundant on the RS we want to keep operating costs and the computation and storage needed for the RS as low as possible. We also assume that the DMS servers and RS can exchange keys and authenticate each other, possibly with a PKI. Throughout this paper, the cryptographic functions used are assumed to be secure.

3   Adversary Model and Problem Description

3.1   Adversary Model

To enable structured and sound reasoning about our proposed protocol's security properties, we have chosen to use a model for the adversary and its capabilities. In this paper, we assume an adversary according to the Dolev-Yao model [11]. The attacker can intercept, delete, re-order, or modify all messages sent over any entity's communication channel. The adversary can also destroy messages but can not break cryptographic functions that are assumed secure.

We also assume that the IoT devices are placed in an environment where physical attacks from an insider are possible. One such attacker could be the current owner. The DMS and the RS are assumed to be in a secure location or in protected, isolated environments protected from external and insider software attacks.

Concerning direct physical attacks on the IoT units, we assume that an adversary and the old and new DMS can compromise, with a given effort, some or a limited number of IoT units through direct physical attacks on the devices. Here a compromised device refers to a device where the attacker has full control of the execution environment and volatile and persistent storage units of the device. Such a model is motivated by the fact that the needed effort for direct physical attacks is proportional to the number of compromised devices. Attacks from the current or new owner on a large scale can be difficult to perform in practice due to the location of the IoT devices or hardware protection mechanisms on the IoT units.

3.2   Trust Model

The RS is assumed to be "honest but curious" [26]: The RS will be a legitimate and honest participant in the protocol execution, it will not deviate from the defined protocol, but will attempt to learn all possible information from legitimately received messages.

Realistically, there needs to be a certain level of trust between New owner and Old owner to transfer the IoT deployment ownership. It is, for example, difficult to imagine two companies with mutual distrust to do business. However, a company might have malicious insiders or might change its operating values and actions after a leadership change. Therefore, it is essential to design a protocol that assures both the New owner and the Old owner's security and privacy, even if the other party is malicious. For the security analysis of our proposed protocol, the Old owner and the New owner are assumed not to trust each other; the Old owner is interested in learning the New owner's secrets. Similarly, the New owner would like to learn the secrets held by the Old owner.

3.3 Requirements

We have started from the previously introduced adversary model for security protocols and have added general ownership transfer security requirements identified in previous work on RFID tags [36]. These security requirements for ownership transfer schemes for RFID tags have been adapted them to our system of IoT devices and our considered adversary model:

R1. **IoT Unit Impersonation Security:** The protocol shall not allow an adversary to impersonate legitimate IoT units during or after the ownership transfer process.

R2. **Old DMS Impersonation Security:** The protocol shall not allow an adversary or the new DMS to impersonate the old DMS.

R3. **New DMS Impersonation Security:** The protocol shall not allow an adversary or the old DMS to impersonate the new DMS.

R4. **RS Impersonation Security:** The protocol shall not allow an adversary, any IoT unit or any DMS in the system to impersonate the RS.

R5. **Reply Attack Resistance:** The protocol shall be resistant against attacks where an adversary tries to complete sessions with any entities in the system by replaying old, observed messages.

R6. **Resistance to Man-in-the-Middle Attacks (MitM):** The protocol shall not allow insertion or modification of any messages sent between trusted entities in the system.

R7. **Resistance to De-synchronization Attack:** The protocol should not allow the IoT units and the new or old DMS to enter a state where necessary secure communications is prevented by a credential mismatch.

R8. **Backward Security:** During and after an IoT ownership transfer, the new owner shall not be given access to any secrets allowing the new owner to get access to any identities or confidential information used in past sessions between the old DMS and the IoT units.

R9. **Forward Security:** During and after an IoT ownership transfer, the old owner shall not be given access to any secrets allowing the old owner to get access to any identities or confidential information used in sessions between the new DMS and the IoT units.

R10. **No Double Ownership:** There shall not be any time period during the ownership transfer process when both the old and the new owner has control over an IoT unit in the system.

In addition to these requirements, our adversary model does not imply full trust in the RS, and we also take into account the risk that IoT units might be compromised through attacks with direct physical access. These two assumptions result in the following additional two security requirements:

R11. **Protection of New Credentials:** After completing the ownership transfer, the RS shall not know the new IoT credentials and shall not be able to set impersonate the new DMS or have access to secure sessions between the new DMS and the IoT units in the system.

R12. **IoT Compromise Resilience:** A successful compromise of an IoT unit by an external or internal adversary shall only give the adversary the power to impersonate this single IoT unit in the system and not impersonate or break any secure sessions between other, non-compromised IoT units in the system and the new DMS.

To make our proposed protocol usable for different types of IoT infrastructures, we must add more requirements. In some IoT deployments, the IoT units are connected to local networks, not publicly accessible, and only accessible by the owner system. For our purposes, this means that the current only DMS can access the IoT devices but not the RS. If a protocol was designed in such a way that RS needed to connect directly to the IoT devices, each IoT device would require a public IP-address. It would limit the suitability of our protocol for certain IoT deployments. Instead, by imposing this requirement on the protocol, our proposed protocol can be more general and fit for more IoT deployments. We add the following additional requirement to the system solution:

R13. **IoT Unit Isolation:** An ownership transfer shall not require any direct interactions between the IoT unit and the RS but only between the IoT unit and the DMS (old or new) in the system.

3.4 Problem Statement

We define ownership as holding the credentials needed to authenticate to and securely communicate with the individual IoT devices. Each individual IoT device has credentials that it shares with a remote entity, i.e., its owner. The purpose of the protocol we propose is to transfer the ownership of a set of deployed IoT devices from the current owner to a new owner. The problem of ownership transfer then thus the process of updating credentials shared with the old owner to credentials shared with the new owner. We want to find an ownership transfer protocol that is secure under the specified adversary model and prove that the protocol fulfills the security properties stated in Sect. 3.3.

4   IoT Infrastructure Ownership Transfer Model and Protocol Design

In our solution, we divide the process of ownership transfer into three phases:

- Deployment
- Ownership transfer preparation
- Ownership transfer

In the deployment phase, the RS and the first owner of the IoT units provisions keys to the individual devices. The devices are then deployed and placed into the environment where they will be active.

In the ownership transfer preparation phase, the owner, from now on called *old owner*, and the entity that will assume ownership, from now on *new owner*, signs a list of all devices that shall be transferred and forwards this list to the RS. The RS verifies both signatures on the list of IoT devices. The RS distributes the keys needed for the ownership transfer and generates an ownership transfer token and the individual intermittent keys to the new owner.

In the final ownership transfer stage, the old owner receives the ownership transfer token from RS and forwards it to the IoT units. After receiving the token, each IoT devices verify the authenticity of the token. If the token is authentic, the IoT device decrypts it. In the token is information, such as IP-addresses and URLs: specifying how the IoT devices shall contact the new owner. The new owner and the IoT units can then mutually authenticate, and new credentials can be provisioned by the new owner to the IoT devices.

We describe the protocol in detail below, using terminology defined in Table 1. A schematic overview of messages transmitted between the entities in the protocol, the contents of the messages, and the computations done by each entity is illustrated in Fig. 2. The steps from Fig. 2 are references by bold numbers e.g. (**1.1**) in the subsections below.

4.1 Deployment

RS generates the keys KR_E, KR_M and K_{RS}. RS provides each IoT device with a unique identifier ID_i. K_{RS} is then used to generate a device unique key, $K_i = PRF(K_{RS}||ID_i)$, for each IoT_i. Each device IoT_i is provided with the corresponding KR_E, KR_M, ID_i and K_i. After transferring the keys RS can discard all keys K_i. RS sets its counter $Ctr_{RS} = 0$ and all IoT devices counters Ctr_i are also set to zero. These counters are used to verify the freshness of the ownership tokens later on. The first owner, DMS_{old}, takes control of the system and provides the owner-key $KO_i = \{KO_{i1}, KO_{i2}\}$ to each device IoT_i. The system is then ready for deployment and regular use, with KO_i used for securing the communication with DMS_{old}.

4.2 Ownership Transfer Preparation

The ownership transfer process starts with a preparation phase with interactions between the RS, DMS_{old} and DMS_{new}. DMS_{old} creates a list of all IoT device identities ID_i called **ID** and a list of identities and partial keys $\{ID_i, KO_{i2}\}$ called **ID-K** that shall switch owner (**1.1**). The list of identities is signed $Sign(DMS_{old}, \textbf{ID})$. Both lists are sent to DMS_{new} (**1.2**), DMS_{new} first verifies the signature of the list, the list of identifiers are then signed by DMS_{new}. The result is $Sign(DMS_{new}, Sign(DMS_{old}, \textbf{ID}))$, the list **ID-K** is kept by DMS_{new} (**1.3**). The list **ID** is sent to RS, to prove that ownership transfer shall take place and that both DMS_{old} and DMS_{new} are agreeing to the transfer (**1.4**). DMS_{new} also sends its

Table 1. Notations used in protocol description. Originally published in [16].

DMS_{old}	Old Device Management Server
DMS_{new}	New Device Management Server
RS	Reset server
$Sign(P, d)$	Digital signature of data d by party P
$E(k, m)$	Symmetric encryption of message m with key k
$D(k, c)$	Symmetric decryption of ciphertext c with key k
$MAC(k, m)$	Message Authentication Code of message m with key k
$PRF(s)$	Pseudo-random function with seed s, generating a pseudo random key
IoT_i	IoT device number i
ID_i	Identifier of IoT device i
ID_{new}	Identifier of DMS_{new}
URL_{new}	Uniform resource locator to DMS_{new}
K_i	Key for IoT device number i, shared with RS
KR_E	Reset-key used for encryption
KR_M	Reset-key used for message authentication
KO_i	Owner-key for IoT device number i, divided into two parts $KO_i = \{KO_{i1}, KO_{i2}\}$
K_{RS}	Master-key for RS used for deriving K_i
N	Ownership-transfer nonce
Ctr_i	Counter for device i is used for verifying freshness of nonces
Ctr_{RS}	Counter for RS, incremented at every ownership transfer. Used for verifying freshness of nonces
KS_i	Ownership transfer key for device i composed by: $KS_i = PRF(K_i\|N\|Ctr_{RS})$
T	Ownership-transfer token, calculated by: $T = E(KR_E, ID_{new}\|URL_{new}\|N\|Ctr_{RS}\| MAC(KR_M, ID_{new}\|URL_{new}\|N\|Ctr_{RS}))$
PSK_i	DLTS-PSK for IoT device i, generated by $PSK_i = PRF(KS_i\|KO_{i2})$
ID	List of IoT device identities $\mathbf{ID} = \{ID_1, ID_2, ..., ID_i\}$
ID-K	List of pairs of IoT device identities and KO_{i2}: $\mathbf{ID\text{-}K} = \{(ID_1, KO_{12}), ..., (ID_i, KO_{i2})\}$
K	List of keys K_i $\mathbf{K} = \{K_1, K_2, ..., K_i\}$
KO	List of owner-keys KO_i, $\mathbf{KO} = \{KO_1, KO_2, ..., KO_i\}$
KS	List of keys KS_i, $\mathbf{KS} = \{KS_1, KS_2, ..., KS_i\}$
ID-KS	List of IoT device identities and keys: $\mathbf{ID\text{-}KS} = \{(ID_1, KS_1), ..., (ID_i, KS_i)\}$

identifier and URL to RS. After verifying that the list **ID** is correctly signed by both DMS_{old} and DMS_{new} (**1.5**), RS can start the ownership transfer protocol.

4.3 Ownership Transfer

RS start the ownership transfer process by re-generating the keys K_i. A nonce N is generated, that together with Ctr_{RS} is used to generate the individual owner-ship transfer keys $KS_i = PRF(K_i||N||Ctr_{RS})$ (**2.1**). The list of ownership trans-fer keys **ID-KS** is sent to DMS_{new} (**2.2**). The RS creates the ownership transfer token T, with information needed by the IoT devices, authorizing an ownership trans-fer and information for how to do it. $T = E(KR_E, ID_{new}||URL_{new}||N||Ctr_{RS}|| MAC(KR_M, ID_{new}||URL_{new}||N||Ctr_{RS}))$ RS sends the token T to DMS_{old} (**2.3**). DMS_{old} forwards the Ownership Transfer Token T to all IoT devices (**2.4**). The devices decrypts T with KR_E and verifies the MAC with KR_M. If the MAC veri-fication succeed, the freshness of the nonce is checked by verifying $Ctr_{RS} > Ctr_i$ (**2.5**). After these checks each IoT device IoT_i can compute the ownership transfer key $KS_i = PRF(K_i||N||Ctr_{RS})$ (**2.6**). With KS_i and KO_{i2} the IoT devices can connect to DMS_{New} using DTLS-PSK [38]. The parameters used are PSK-ID = ID_i and PSK = $PRF(KS_i||KO_{i2})$ (**2.7**). After a successful contact has been made with DMS_{new} IoT_i destroys KO_{i1} (**2.8**). DMS_{new} then generates a new key KO_i' (**2.9**). The new key KO_i' is sent to IoT_i, that also sets Ctr_i to the received value Ctr_{RS} (**2.10**). After DMS_{new} has provisioned new keys to all IoT devices the ownership transfer process is concluded. DMS_{new} can securely communicate with all IoT devices using the new keys KO_i'.

4.4 Handling of Ownership Transfer Failures

In the previous sections we have described the ownership transfer process in detail. However, there is a risk that the ownership transfer succeeds for one set of IoT units but not for another set due to communication errors or similar. Such situation will be detected by the DMS_{New} as it will notice that it has not been able get in contact and authenticate some units part of the IoT transfer list given in step 1.2. DMS_{New} can first retransmit the ownership transfer token T to the devices that has not changed ownership. Some protocols provide a mechanism of notifying a sender that a message has been received. Such a mechanism can be used to verify the proper delivery of T. If T has been delivered but an IoT device still does not connect to DMS_{New} the issue lies with the device IoT_i, that situation will have to be resolved by DMS_{Old} before a new attempt can be made. In such situation, it is possible is for DMS_{New} to issue a "recovery" procedure by sending a signed list of missing units back to DMS_{Old}, which then will be requested to contact each of the missing IoT units (still under ownership of DMS_{Old}) over a mutual authenticated DTLS channel re-sending the transfer token, T. Such procedure can be repeated, until the whole set of IoT units are successfully transferred to DMS_{New}.

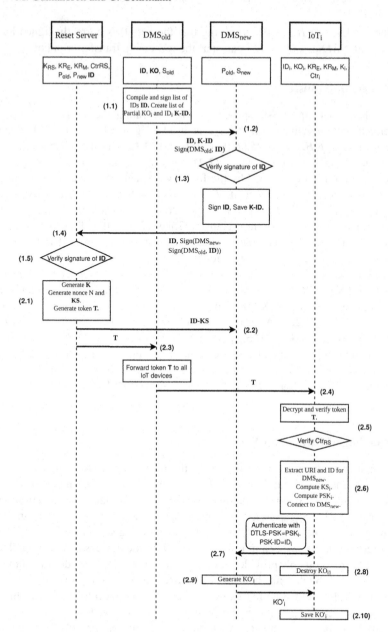

Fig. 2. Messages and computations done during the ownership transfer. The figure is an updated version of a figure originally from [16].

5   Security Analysis

We will now analyze our proposed ownership transfer protocol in the scope of the system model presented in Sect. 2 and the threat model from Sect. 3. We will address each requirement from Sect. 3.3 except R13 that is a functional requirement. We give special attention to the requirements R8, R9 and the requirement for PSK_i to be secure. We formally prove these requirements with Tamarin Prover [5]. The requirement to protect PSK_i from an outside adversary is important for requirements R1, R3 and R6 while backward (R8) and forward (R9) secrecy are a core features of the suggested protocol.

R1. **IoT Unit Impersonation Security:** Each IoT unit i holds a unique key K_i. The nonce and counter in the token together with this key are used to calculate KS_i. In turn, KS_i and the second part of KO_i are used to calculate the PSK, used to authenticate the connection between the IoT unit and DMS_{New}. Both key parts needed to calculate the PSK are only known to DMS_{New} apart from the IoT unit as long as the RS and old owner do not collude, which contradicts the trust assumption regarding the reset server. Hence, given that the IoT unit itself can securely store and keep K_i, IoT impersonation is not possible for an external attacker or DMS_{Old}.

R2. **Old DMS Impersonation Security:** The ownership transfer is triggered by letting DMS_{Old} send a signed list of IoT identities (step 1.2). This signature is verified by the RS at step 1.5. As long as the signature scheme is secure and the private key of the DMS_{Old} not is compromised, an attacker cannot impersonate the DMS_{Old} at the ownership transfer "triggering moment". As we do not require protected transfer of the token (step 2.4), DMS_{Old} impersonation at this step is possible. However, it is not crucial for the protocol that it is indeed DMS_{Old} that sends the token but it can be transferred in arbitrary way, as the IoT unit does not finally accept the token unless the authentication in step 2.7 is performed successfully. The latter requires the genuine key KO_{i2} from old owner, and this key is sent protected to the DMS_{New} at step 1.2.

R3. **New DMS Impersonation Security:** Similar to the DMS_{Old}, DMS_{New} signs the list of IoT IDs subject to ownership transfer (step 1.3). This signature is verified by the RS at step 1.5. As long as the signature scheme is secure and the private key of the DMS_{New} not is compromised, an attacker cannot impersonate the DMS_{New} at the ownership transfer "trigering moment". Mutual authentication applies at step 2.7 when the IoT unit connects to the DMS_{New}. Impersonation at this step requires knowledge of the PSK, which (similar to the reasoning regarding R1 above), requires knowledge of both KS_i and KO_i, and if not the RS and old owner collude, these two values are only known to DMS_{New} and the IoT unit itself. Hence, DMS_{New} impersonation is not possible unless DMS_{New} is compromised such that the secure keys leaks or the secure key transfers at step 1.2 or step 2.2 are broken. The latter is only possible if the mutually authenticated secure channel is weak.

R4. **RS Impersonation Security:** Only DMS_{New} and DMS_{Old} communicate directly with RS. They do so over a secure channel that protects against impersonation of RS.

R5. **Reply Attack Resistance:** All messages between RS, DMS_{Old} and DMS_{New} are sent over secure channels that provides protection against replay attacks (steps 1.2, 1.4, 2.2 and 2.3). The Token T transferred from DMS_{Old} to IoT_i (step 2.4) contains Ctr_{RS} that is verified against Ctr_i by IoT_i. This provides replay attack resistance since a replayed T will be rejected due to the counter check. When IoT_i connects to DMS_{New} (step 2.7) it is done with DTLS protected by PSK_i, which is only known to DMS_{New} and IoT_i. This DTLS channel is also used to protect the transfer of the new credentials KO_i' (step 2.10).

R6. **Resistance to Man-in-the-Middle Attacks (MitM):** All messages between RS, DMS_{Old} and DMS_{New} are sent over secure channels that provides mutual authentication (steps 1.2, 1.4, 2.2 and 2.3) and thus prevents against MitM attacks. Communication with the IoT devices and DMS_{New} (steps 2.7 and 2.10) is done over DLTS-PSK that provides mutual authentication and with MitM protection. An attacker with knowledge of the keys KR_E and KR_M[1], can perform a successful man-in-the-middle substitution attack at step 2.4. Potential values to substitute are ID_{new}, URL_{new}, N or Ctr_{RS}. The IoT unit will not accept a wrong Ctr_{RS} as it is checked against the internal counter. Furthermore, substituted ID_{new} or N will not match the PSK values used in the mutual authentication in step 2.7 and the MitM substitution attack will fail. A substitution of URL_{new} will have no affect as long as the IoT unit still reach the legitimate DM_{new} with the given URL. If this not is the case, the ownership transfer for the affected unit will simple be aborted (see also the recovery discussion in Sect. 4.4).

R7. **Resistance to De-synchronization Attack:** If DMS_{Old} should send a modified token, T' (through access to the keys KR_E and KR_M), with modified nonce N', in step 2.4, the key KS_i' will not match the key KS_i held by DMS_{New}. Hence, in this case, the IoT device will not remove the KO_i key, and will remain in the ownership of DMS_{Old}.

R8. **Backward Security:** All traffic sent between the DMS_{Old} and the IoT devices is sent over a channel protected by the key KO_i, the IoT devices destroy KS_i when contact is made with DMS_{New}. DMS_{New} can not recover KO_i and is unable to learn any previous secrets (see also the Tamarin proof of Sect. 5.1).

R9. **Forward Security:** After DMS_{New} has made contact with the IoT devices and the old key KO_i has been destroyed, DMS_{New} provisions a new key KO_i' and sends it to the IoT devices over a secure channel protected by the key KS_i that DMS_{Old} does not hold. DMS_{Old} is thus unable to decrypt any future message sent to the IoT devices (see also the Tamarin proof of Sect. 5.1).

R10. **No Double Ownership:** The ownership hand-over is made when the IoT device connects to DMS_{New} with PSK_i and removes ownership from DMS_{Old} by removing KO_i. DMS_{New} takes ownership when it provisions KS_i' to IoT_i. Failure in any protocol step might results in that some IoT units are still owned by the DM_{old}. However, as we discuss in Sect. 4.4 below, such situation can be detected by DMS_{New} and a recovery process can be initiated.

R11. **Protection of New Credentials:** After the ownership transfer process IoT_i is provided with new credentials KO_i'. The only way RS can gain access to the system is by launching a MitM attack on the DLTS connection between IoT_i and DMS_{New}. Thus this property hinges on PSK_i, RS does not know KO_{i2} needed to derive PSK_i. As long as RS does not gain access to KO_{i2} by collusion

---

[1] These keys are included not to give protection against IoT compromise but to make denial-of-service type of attacks less likely.

with DMS_{Old}, the new credentials are protected (see also the Tamarin proof of Sect. 5.1).

R12. **IoT Compromise Resilience:** If an adversary compromises an IoT device IoT_i it will gain the following keys: KO_i, KR_E, KR_M and K_i. KO_i is only shared with the current owner and used for securing communication between the owner and IoT device, the adversary can not impersonate or compromise any other IoT device. KR_E and KR_M are shared with all IoT devices, an adversary could try to spoof an ownership transfer token T. Since the adversary only have KO_i it is impossible for the adversary to complete a malicious ownership transfer with an other IoT device IoT_j since the adversary does not know KO_j, thus providing resilience against compromises.

5.1 Tamarin Prover

Tamarin Prover [24] is a tool for formal analysis of security protocols. By creating a symbolic model of a protocol, stating security lemmas and then using the automatic reasoning to analyse the model the prover can show that the security lemmas hold or show a counter-example of when they do not hold. Tamarin represents protocols as a multi-set rewrite rules using first order logic. The automatic prover represent the state of the execution as a bag of multi-set of Facts. The adversary model used in Tamarin is the Dolev-Yao model [12]. In the Dolev-Yao model the adversary is able to read, modify, replay and send any message to any participant in the system. One way of phrasing this, is to say that the adversary *is* the network itself.

5.2 Modeling the Ownership Transfer Protocol

We have modeled a simplified version of our proposed Ownership Transfer Protocol in Tamarin. We have excluded the steps 1.1–1.5 and 2.7–2.10 to prove the correctness of the core ownership transfer steps. During our process to verify the security of our proposed protocol we have introduced five lemmas. We have created one lemma, Protocol Correctness, to verify that our protocol can execute with a successful conclusion of the ownership transfer process. We have created another lemma, Outsider secrecy, to prove that PSK_i is secret from an outside adversary. The next two lemmas Old Owner Secrecy and New Owner Secrecy are lemmas about attacks done by a party in the protocol that misbehaves. These types of attacks are not included in a standard Dolev-Yao model. To solve this problem, we have chosen to give the Dolev-Yao adversary all keys and secrets from the malicious party. The Dolev-Yao adversary then has all the capabilities to intercept, replay and send any message together with the capability to decrypt, encrypt and sign messages with the keys from the malicious party. We argue that this is a stronger attacker than a real-world malicious Old owner or New owner would be. We have assumed that to provide New Owner secrecy PSK_i has to be kept secret from DMS_{Old}. To Provide Old Owner Secrecy the two keys KO_{i1} and KO_{i2} have to remain secret from DMS_{New}. For the Outsider Secrecy Property we state that no outside party can learn PSK_i. The last lemma is used to prove that the RS indeed will not learn the long term secret of the IoTs after the ownership transfer is completed. Our Tamarin model of our proposed protocol can be found here[2].

Below we list the five lemmas:

L1 **Protocol Correctness.** The modeled protocol shall execute as specified.

$$lemma\ protocol\_correctness:$$
$$exists\_trace$$
$$\text{"}\exists\ PSK1\ PSK2\ \#i\ \#j.$$
$$((New\_owner\_PSK(PSK1)\ @\ \#i)\ \wedge$$
$$(IoT\_PSK(PSK2)\ @\ \#j))\ \wedge$$
$$(PSK1\ =\ PSK2)\text{"}$$

L2 **Outsider secrecy.** The Ownership Transfer protocol shall be secure against outside attackers. No outside party shall be able to learn PSK_i.

$$lemma\ outsider\_secrecy:$$
$$all\ -\ traces$$
$$\text{"}\forall\ PSK\ \#i\ \#j.$$
$$((((IoT\_PSK(PSK)\ @\ \#i)\ \wedge$$
$$(New\_owner\_PSK(PSK)\ @\ \#j))\ \wedge$$
$$(\neg(\exists\ Old\_owner\ \#k.\ Reveal(Old\_owner)\ @\ \#k)))\ \wedge$$
$$(\neg(\exists\ New\_owner\ \#l.Reveal(New\_owner)\ @\ \#l)))\ \rightarrow\ (\neg(\exists\ \#k.\ K(PSK)\ @\ \#k))\text{"}$$

L3 **Old Owner secrecy.** The New Owner shall not be able to learn anything that has been sent before the ownership transfer, thus KO_{i1} and KO_{i2} has to be secure against an adversary that knows everything DMS_{New} knows.

$$lemma\ backwards\_secrecy:$$
$$all\ -\ traces$$
$$\text{"}\forall\ New\_owner\ PSK\ \#i\ \#j\ \#k.$$
$$((((IoT\_PSK(PSK)\ @\ \#i)\ \wedge$$
$$(New\_owner\_PSK(PSK)\ @\ \#j))\ \wedge$$
$$(Reveal(New\_owner)\ @\ \#k))\ \wedge$$
$$(\neg(\exists\ Old\_owner\ \#l.\ Reveal(Old\_owner)\ @\ \#l)))\ \rightarrow$$
$$(\neg(\exists\ OwnerKey1\ OwnerKey2\ \#m\ \#n.$$
$$(K(OwnerKey1)@\ \#m)\ \wedge\ (K(OwnerKey2)@\ \#n)))\text{"}$$

L4 **New Owner secrecy.** The Old owner shall not be able to learn anything that occurs after the ownership transfer is complete. No adversary that knows everything DMS_{Old} knows shall be able to learn PSK_i.

---

[2] https://github.com/Gunzter/iot-ownership-transfer-protocol-tamarin-model.

$lemma\ forward\_secrecy :$
$all-traces$
"$\forall\ Old\_owner\ PSK\ \#i\ \#j\ \#k.$
$((((IoT\_PSK(PSK)@ \#i)\wedge$
$(New\_owner\_PSK(PSK)@ \#j))\wedge$
$(Reveal(Old\_owner)@ \#k))\wedge$
$(\neg(\exists New\_owner\ \#l.\ Reveal(New\_owner)$
$@ \#l))) \rightarrow (\neg(\exists\ \#m.K(PSK)@ \#m))$"

L5 **RS secrecy from.** The RS shall not be able to learn anything that occurs after the ownership transfer is complete. No adversary that knows everything RS knows shall be able to learn PSK_i.

$lemma\ secrecy\_from\_rs :$
"$\forall\ RS\ PSK\ \#i\ \#j\ \#k.$
$(IoT\_PSK(PSK)@ \#i\wedge$
$New\_owner\_ownership\_transfer\_key(PSK)@ \#j\wedge$
$Reveal(RS)@ \#k\wedge$
$\neg(\exists Old\_owner\ \#l.\ Reveal(Old\_owner)@\#l)\wedge$
$\neg(\exists New\_owner\ \#l.\ Reveal(New\_owner)@\#l))$
$\rightarrow \neg(\exists OwnerKey1\ OwnerKey2\ \#m\ \#n.$
$K(OwnerKey1)@ \#m\ \wedge\ K(OwnerKey2)@ \#n)$"

Using our modeled protocol we let Tamarin prove the five stated lemmas. All of them were found to hold. We conclude that our protocol fulfills the previously stated security properties.

6 Implementation and Experimental Evaluations

We have implemented our proposed protocol for an IoT environment running Contiki-NG[3]. Contiki-NG is a light-weight operating system designed for constrained devices. We have used some other protocols to structure our data. Most significantly we use COSE [32] to encode and encrypt the ownership transfer tokens. We assume secure communication between the RS, DMS_{old} and DMS_{new}. The connections to the IoT devices are secured with DTLS [28]. Since SHA256 is assumed to be included on the IoT device from DTLS, we have selected HKDF-SHA256 as our key derivation function.

We have designed the system to use the REST-model [15]. Sending the ownership transfer token to the IoT device is done with a POST operation to/transfer-ownership. The IoT device then sends a GET message to/key to receive the new keys K_i' and KO_i'.

---

[3] https://github.com/contiki-ng/contiki-ng.

6.1   Test Setup

The evaluated scenario is executed on the following setup. One Desktop PC running the RS, DMS_{Old} and DMS_{New}. The PC is connected to a Border-Router that acts as an IEEE 802.15.4 network interface. We have used four Zolertia Firefly-A development boards[4] that are going to transfer from owner Old to New. The experimental setup is illustrated below in Fig. 3. The IoT devices are based on the cc2538 system on chip made by Texas Instruments [37]. They have an ARM Cortex-M3 CPU clocked at 32 MHz together with 32 KB of RAM and 512 KB of flash. Connectivity is provided by an IEEE 802.15.4 radio providing about 100 Kb/s of bandwidth.

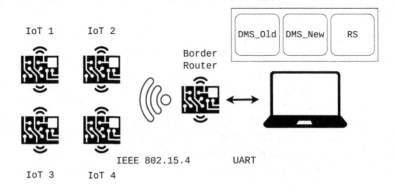

Fig. 3. Experimental setup used in the evaluation.

6.2   Test Scenario

The test scenario consists of an initial setup phase where keys are distributed to the individual IoT devices and an ownership transfer phase. The initial setup phase is not in scope for the performance evaluation, only the ownership transfer process is included. We ran the ownership transfer scenario, of the four IoT devices, ten times.

6.3   Ownership Transfer Time

In order to evaluate the efficiency of our proposed scheme from a system perspective we timed the entire ownership transfer process. We measured the time elapsed from that the RS sends out the token T to when all IoT devices has been provisioned with new owner keys KO'_i. The time taken for the ownership transfer process is measured to a mean of 4.7 s with a 95% confidence interval between 4.4 s and 5 s.

It should be noted that these times are for a single link-layer hop. Doing the ownership transfer process over another network, with higher latency, such as the internet would take longer time.

---

[4] https://github.com/Zolertia/Resources/wiki/Firefly.

6.4   Energy Consumption

Since the devices considered for this protocol usually are powered by a battery it is important that the energy consumed by the IoT device when executing the ownership transfer protocol is reasonable.

We have measured the energy usage on the constrained devices for both the radio modem and the CPU. The total energy consumption was measured to a mean of 0.18 mJ. With a 95% confidence interval of the mean between 0.14 mJ and 0.22 mJ. For comparisons sake, the mean energy consumption of 0.18 mJ is equal to the energy consumed by the CPU executing at full power for four seconds.

6.5   Memory Overhead

Constrained devices usually have a limited amount of memory available to store both code in ROM and variables and data in RAM. It is important for all protocols aimed at these types of devices are efficient in terms of memory usage. This is especially true for an ownership-transfer protocol, that is not used often.

To evaluate the memory utilization of our proposed protocol we have used the GNU-tools **size**[5] and **nm**[6] to evaluate and break down the the memory utilization of our implementation. The detailed breakdown of memory utilization can be seen in Table 2 below.

Table 2. Memory utilization.

Functions	Storage location	Utilization
HKDF-SHA256	ROM	256 Bytes
CBOR	ROM	165 Bytes
COSE	ROM	292 Bytes
Ownership transfer	ROM	340 Bytes
Keys	RAM/ROM	100 Bytes

In summary; 100 Bytes of keys needs to be stored, together with around ∼500 Bytes of ROM for extra functions. Another ∼500 bytes is needed for the COSE functionality. Since DTLS is assumed to be existing on the device, AES-128 and SHA256, or equivalent are assumed to exist on the device. Either implemented in software or accelerated in hardware.

7   Related Work

Protocols for ownership transfer have been studied in several fields. Both recently for IoT devices and earlier for RFID-tags. IoT infrastructures and RFID systems are not

---

[5] https://ftp.gnu.org/old-gnu/Manuals/binutils-2.12/html_node/binutils_8.html.

[6] https://sourceware.org/binutils/docs/binutils/nm.html.

equal but have some common characteristics. RFID-tags and IoT systems are deployed in large numbers and efficient management of a large number of devices is necessary. IoT devices might have constrained resources and RFID-tags typically even less resources for computation and storage. IoT units are connected, usually wireless, and the ability to initiate communication with external entities. RFID-tags however are only capable of responding to requests. RFID-tags can only be read and written to locally, a reader must be in physical proximity to the RFID-tag to be able to communicate with the device. An IoT device can however receive communication originating practically anywhere, this creates a bigger attack surface on IoT devices since an attack on the system can, in theory, originate from anywhere on the planet.

7.1   IoT Ownership Transfer

Internet of Things (IoT) are a very wide category of devices for a wide variety of purposes, with the common property that they are connected to a network in some way. When ownership transfer is studied in the realm of IoT devices authors often have different views of what types of devices constitute an IoT device. Devices considered can be connected medical equipment, wearables, smart consumer electronics such as fridges and CCTV-cameras. Other devices that are often grouped into IoT are sensor networks, building automation and connected sensors and actuators for industrial applications.

Tam and Newmarch state the problem of transferring ownership in [35] for Ubiquitous Computing Networks, a term that predates IoT. They define the term ownership and provide requirements for an ownership system. They also provide an example of an ownership transfer protocol. The protocol is based on public-key cryptography and defines how two parties transfer the ownership of a device.

Khan et al. discuss ownership transfer for connected consumer products [21]. The focus of the ownership transfer process is less about re-keying the device and more about preserving privacy for information stored on the device. They also propose a novel idea of how to automatically start the ownership transfer process by detecting changes in the environment to determine if the device has been sold or given away.

Pradeep and Singh propose a protocol in [27] utilizing a trusted third party that they call a Central Key Server. The protocol requires physical proximity when the ownership transfer process is about to take place. The protocol does not specify exactly what type of IoT device that is considered, but only one device is transferred during each execution of the protocol.

In [23] the authors, Leng et al., propose an ownership transfer protocol for IoT devices with a TTP in the system. The authors intended use-case is traceability and monitoring of supply chains rather then re-keying an IoT deployment. The TTP needs, like in our system to establish secret keys, from the beginning, with IoT devices that will be transferred. Since the use-case of the protocol is traceability of IoT devices and the security analysis provided in the paper is brief, it is uncertain if this protocol can fulfill the use-case we present in this work. No implementation and experimental results are provided, but owing to the large amount of direct communication between the IoT device and TTP the network overhead of an ownership transfer will be big. In this work we have done a rigorous security analysis using formal verification methods and implemented our protocol on a physical constrained IoT device to verify its efficiency.

In [25] Müller et al. propose HomeCA. A life-cycle management system for consumer IoT. HomeCA uses certificates and by extension asymmetric cryptography, making it unsuitable for our use-case of constrained IoT devices. The authors present a comprehensive work, based on open standards, that is intended for more powerful devices compared to the very constrained devices that we consider in this work.

In [1] medical IoT unit authentication as well as ownership transfer is considered. The authors propose a new scheme called LACO, which is an improvement to an earlier medical three factor authentication protocol proposed by Zhang et al. in [42]. The authors have done a formal verification of their proposed protocol. Different from our work, the authors behind the LACO, do not considered the ownership transfer with respect to the IoT units themselves but only ownership transfer between users connected to a medical server, which in turn controls the medical IoT units.

7.2 IoT Ownership Transfer with Blockchain Technology and Smart Contracts

Many proposed protocols for Ownership Transfer utilize a TTP. In later years work has been done investigating if the TTP can be replaced with either entries on a Blockchain or Smart contracts. Some works aim to just keep track of the changing owners of an IoT device, this can be used to keep track of the current ownership status. For such an application a distributed ledger, on a Blockchain is a suitable solution instead of a TTP. For protocols where the TTP is used to facilitate the transfer of ownership, more functionality is needed, compared to a traditional Blockchain. Smart contracts is one such solution. The most common platform for smart contracts is Ethereum [41].

In [6] Borah et al. present a Blockchain based, used for Supply chain management. In this work the considered IoT devices are Mobile phones. In this work the ownership transfer is logged to a Blockchain as to later being auditable without needing a TTP in the system. The work of Borath et al. and other similar works such as [33] is one example of how Blockchains and Smart contracts can be used in the field of ownership management. The difference between these works and our, is that they present how to monitor who owns an asset after the ownership has changed whereas we are interested in *how* the ownership transfer is facilitated with regards to IoT security. However the present work can show the utility of Blockchains and Smart contracts as TTPs.

In [3] Altun et al. present an IoT ownership and management scheme for home appliances with Digital Twins in a fog-computing environment. Digital Twins is a concept where a physical device has a digital replica, the Digital Twin. This Digital Twin can be used to synchronize data.

The authors Islam et al. propose a smart contract-based ownership transfer scheme in [18]. It is intended for use in the sharing economy or rentals, such as AirBnB etc. The specified use use case is an IP camera in a rented property. An IP camera is a more powerful devices compared to the one we consider. The system use a PUF to authenticate the IoT device to outside parties. The authors use a smart contract on a Blockchain to eliminate TTP. The re-keying of the IoT device is done with a TPM in the IP-camera. The scheme uses public-key cryptography on the IoT device to securely transport keys to the IoT device and is thus to resource intensive compared for our intended use-case.

In a paper by Alblooshi et al. [2], the authors propose an ownership transfer protocol for Medical IoT devices, the scheme uses Smart contracts (Ethereum) to eliminate a TTP in the system. The intended use-case of this protocol is to track ownership with the purpose of establishing authenticity of medical IoT devices.

As can be seen from the previous work with replacing the TTP with a Blockchain together with smart contracts there seem to be promise in the field. However, some drawbacks with smart contracts and Blockchains exist. Blockchains uses asymmetric cryptography, that might be to resource intensive for very constrained devices. The idea of replacing the TTP with a smart contract looks attractive, but there are still issues. A smart contract is difficult or impossible to update or patch, either with bug-fixes or additional functionality. In addition, an incorrect smart contract can be a major security vulnerability, for example as in the case with the DAO vulnerability in 2016, where an implementation error caused large monetary losses.

7.3   Ownership Transfer Protocols for RFID-Tags

The subject of secure ownership transfer has been studied in the field of RFID technology since 2005 [31]. In the paper "Tag Ownership in RFID systems: Survey of Existing Protocols and Open Challenges" [36] the authors list the research done in the field from 2005 to 2018. The authors also group protocols by features; Group transfer protocols and individual tag transfer protocols, trusted Third Party (TTP) protocols, and protocols where only the new and current owner take part. Lastly EPC-C1G2 [13] compliant protocols and protocols that require more resources from the tags. The first papers for RFID-tag ownership transfer generally suffered from not satisfying some important security requirements. The early Satio paper [31], does for instance not provide forward and backwards secrecy for the owners.

We are considering a model with IoT ownership transfer with the assistance of a trusted third party, the so-called "Reset Server" (RS) (see Sect. 2 and Sect. 4). This entity has a very similar role as a TTP in RFID ownership transfer solutions. However, *different* from prior art work, we think that for IoT infrastructures, one would like to avoid the TTP to actual *choose* the credentials for the devices in the system but merely "supervise" the transferring process. This has the main advantage that the RS, unlike the TTP in prior-art solutions, will not have complete knowledge of the final device credential after completing the ownership transfer process. TTP based protocols in prior-art are the ones that most closely resemble the model we consider and we will in the related work summary below, focus on TTP based protocols.

7.4   RFID Single Ownership Transfer

Much work has been done for owner transfer of single RFID-tags. Since we consider group transfer of IoT devices these protocols are mainly mentioned for completeness sake. Protocols that are intended for EPC-compliance are often forced to use non-standard solutions due to the extremely constrained nature of EPC-compliant RFID-tags. One such scheme can be found in [9]. The protocols that are not restricted by EPC-compliance often make use of standard cryptological functions such as symmetric ciphers and hash functions. One example of an ownership transfer protocol using a TTP can be found in [43].

7.5 RFID Group Ownership Transfer

Several group transfer protocols with a TTP have been proposed in the literature [4, 17, 20, 34, 44]. The design goals of the different protocols are not uniform. They do not work with the very same security requirements. They also differ with respect to that one solution wants to achieve EPC-C1G2 compliance [34] and another want to have a group of RFID-tags to switch ownership simultaneously for instance [44].

A core characteristic we expect from an ownership transfer protocol, is backward and forward secrecy. This is not offered by the protocol suggested by Sundaresan et al. [34]. The group transfer protocol by Kapoor [20] is an extension of an earlier variant for singe tag transfer [19]. Even if this is a simple and rather straightforward protocol, these protocols were later shown by Bagheri et al. [4] to be vulnerable to de-synchronization attacks (due to the simple fact that the message exchange between the TTP and the tag was not authenticated). The authors in [4] also showed how to fix these shortcomings, but unlike our suggested protocol, their solution is dependent on a direct session between the tag (the IoT unit in our case) and the TTP. They also give the full power to the TTP that must have access to all key information (both the old and the new).

Inspired by an earlier work on grouping proofs for RFID tags [8], Zuo proposed a new TTP based protocol for RFID ownership transfer [44]. Similar to the earlier grouping proof protocols, the design goal is to provide a proof of the ownership transfer of all tags in a group *simultaneously*, i.e., without the need of having connection to the back-end system representing the tag owner during the ownership switch. This means that the ownership transfer interactions only take place locally between the tag reader and the tags in the group connected to this reader. Later, the back-end system just can verify that the transfer has occurred. In and RFID system scenario this has some communication overhead reduction advantages but not in a system scenario with distributed IoT units. Hence, the off line requirement makes the ownership transfer unnecessarily complex for the IoT scenario we are considering. Furthermore, similar to other ownership protocols, the TTP is given full power by selecting all the new credentials using the solution in [44].

In [17] another group ownership transfer protocol was proposed. This protocol shares our design goals with respect to forward and backward secrecy. Furthermore, it allows arbitrary location and grouping of tags based on group keys. This is a property most suitable also for IoT infrastructures. However, similar to other prior art, the solution in [17] gives the TTP full knowledge of the key information. It also must has active sessions with all tags taking part in the ownership transfer process. Our protocol does not have these two limitations.

8 Conclusion

In this paper, we have presented the extended version of our previous work, where we presented an ownership transfer protocol for constrained IoT devices [16]. In our previous work, we identified the need for an ownership transfer protocol for constrained IoT devices. The constrained nature of the considered IoT devices necessitates that the protocol is resource-efficient, both in computational overhead and communication overhead. These requirements require a solution based on symmetric cryptography. We have investigated previous models and protocols for ownership transfer in the fields of IoT and RFID tags. Since IoT is such a different field, there are many different IoT devices with different capabilities. We have found that protocols for RFID-tags most closely related to the requirements we have identified.

We stated formal requirements from the related work, having investigated the state-of-the-art protocols for ownership transfer for both IoT devices and RFID-tags. We have formulated security requirements and functional requirements for a protocol for ownership transfer of constrained IoT devices. After stating the requirements, we have proposed and presented our protocol. After describing our proposed protocol, we have performed a rigorous security analysis of our proposed protocol. We have used two security analysis methods: formal protocol verification with Tamarin Prover and traditional reasoning, based on the security requirements. In the security analysis, we show that the previously stated security requirements hold. Next, the protocol was implemented as a proof-of-concept to be evaluated in terms of performance. The protocol proved to be as resource-efficient as hoped. The time required to transfer ownership is small for resource-constrained IoT units, and ownership transfer will not be frequent in the use-case we envision. We have also investigated the energy consumption of the protocol and found it to be reasonable. The memory footprint needed for the implemented protocol is small and is not prohibitively large for code that will be executed relatively infrequent.

The research field of ownership transfer protocols for IoT deployments has previously been explored for more powerful IoT devices, especially medical and consumer IoT devices. The area of constrained IoT devices is still relatively unexplored. However, there are many open possibilities for further work. For example, evaluating the performance of protocols in large infrastructures, i.e., hundreds to thousands of IoT units, is an interesting question to investigate. Implementing and deploying our protocol for real systems, such as industrial control systems or building automation, is another interesting question. Furthermore, investigating other trust models where no trusted third party is required is also an exciting research question. Last but not least is the question about the ownership models of the future. Data and computational devices are shared in a larger and larger extent, and it will be necessary to investigate how IoT devices will be handled in the future. Will devices always belong to one owner? Will they be transferred between owners, or will they be rented out to clients from one owner? These questions need to be considered when designing protocols that can accommodate more complex ownership structures for future infrastructure.

References

1. Aghili, S.F., Mala, H., Shojafar, M., Peris-Lopez, P.: LACO: lightweight three-factor authentication, access control and ownership transfer scheme for e-health systems in IoT. Future Gener. Comput. Syst. **96**, 410–424 (2019). https://doi.org/10.1016/j.future.2019.02.020, http://www.sciencedirect.com/science/article/pii/S0167739X18331297

2. Alblooshi, M., Salah, K., Alhammadi, Y.: Blockchain-based ownership management for medical IoT (MIoT) devices. In: 2018 International Conference on Innovations in Information Technology (IIT), pp. 151–156. IEEE (2018)
3. Altun, C., Tavli, B., Yanikomeroglu, H.: Liberalization of digital twins of IoT-enabled home appliances via blockchains and absolute ownership rights. IEEE Commun. Mag. **57**(12), 65–71 (2019)
4. Bagheri, N., Aghili, S.F., Safkhani, M.: On the security of two ownership transfer protocols and their improvements. Int. Arab J. Inf. Technol. **15**(1), 87–93 (2018). https://iajit.org/PDF/January%202018,%20No.%201/8266.pdf. Accessed 07 Jan 2022
5. Basin, D., Cremers, C., Dreier, J., Sasse, R.: Symbolically analyzing security protocols using tamarin. ACM SIGLOG News **4**(4), 19–30 (2017). https://doi.org/10.1145/3157831.3157835, https://hal.archives-ouvertes.fr/hal-01622110
6. Borah, M.D., Naik, V.B., Patgiri, R., Bhargav, A., Phukan, B., Basani, S.G.M.: Supply chain management in agriculture using blockchain and IoT. In: Kim, S., Deka, G.C. (eds.) Advanced Applications of Blockchain Technology. SBD, vol. 60, pp. 227–242. Springer, Singapore (2020). https://doi.org/10.1007/978-981-13-8775-3_11
7. Bormann, C., Ersue, M., Keranen, A.: Terminology for constrained-node networks. Internet Engineering Task Force (IETF): Fremont, CA, USA, pp. 1721–2070 (2014)
8. Burmester, M., de Medeiros, B., Motta, R.: Provably secure grouping-proofs for RFID tags. In: Grimaud, G., Standaert, F.-X. (eds.) CARDIS 2008. LNCS, vol. 5189, pp. 176–190. Springer, Heidelberg (2008). https://doi.org/10.1007/978-3-540-85893-5_13
9. Cao, T., Chen, X., Doss, R., Zhai, J., Wise, L.J., Zhao, Q.: RFID ownership transfer protocol based on cloud. Comput. Networks **105**, 47–59 (2016). https://doi.org/10.1016/j.comnet.2016.05.017, http://www.sciencedirect.com/science/article/pii/S1389128616301621
10. Díaz, M., Martín, C., Rubio, B.: State-of-the-art, challenges, and open issues in the integration of internet of things and cloud computing. J. Network Comput. Appl. **67**, 99–117 (2016)
11. Dolev, D., Yao, A.C.: On the security of public key protocols. In: Proceedings of the 22nd Annual Symposium on Foundations of Computer Science, pp. 350–357. SFCS 1981. IEEE Computer Society, Washington, DC (1981). https://doi.org/10.1109/SFCS.1981.32
12. Dolev, D., Yao, A.: On the security of public key protocols. IEEE Trans. Inf. Theor. **29**(2), 198–208 (1983)
13. EPCglobal Inc.: EPC Radio-Frequency Identity Protocols Generation-2 UHF RFID. Report 1.2.0, EPCglobal Inc. (2008)
14. Eronen, P., Nir, Y., Hoffman, P.E., Kaufman, C.: Internet Key Exchange Protocol Version 2 (IKEv2). RFC 5996 (2010). https://doi.org/10.17487/RFC5996, https://rfc-editor.org/rfc/rfc5996.txt
15. Fielding, R.: Representational state transfer. In: Architectural Styles and the Design of Network-Based Software Architecture, pp. 76–85 (2000)
16. Gunnarsson, M., Gehrmann, C.: Secure ownership transfer for the internet of things. In: 6th International Conference on Information Systems Security and Privacy, ICISSP 2020, 25 February 2020 through 27 February 2020, pp. 33–44. SciTePress (2020)
17. He, L., Gan, Y., Yin, Y.: Secure group ownership transfer protocol with independence of old owner for RFID tags. Comput. Model. New Technol. **18**(12B), 209–214 (2014). http://www.cmnt.lv/upload-files/ns_63brt035
18. Islam, M.N., Kundu, S.: IoT security, privacy and trust in home-sharing economy via blockchain. In: Choo, K.-K.R., Dehghantanha, A., Parizi, R.M. (eds.) Blockchain Cybersecurity, Trust and Privacy. AIS, vol. 79, pp. 33–50. Springer, Cham (2020). https://doi.org/10.1007/978-3-030-38181-3_3

19. Kapoor, G., Piramuthu, S.: Protocols for objects with multiple RFID tags. In: 2008 16th International Conference on Advanced Computing and Communications, pp. 208–213, December 2008. https://doi.org/10.1109/ADCOM.2008.4760450
20. Kapoor, G., Zhou, W., Piramuthu, S.: Multi-tag and multi-owner RFID ownership transfer in supply chains. Decis. Support Syst. **52**(1), 258–270 (2011)
21. Khan, M.S.N., Marchal, S., Buchegger, S., Asokan, N.: chownIoT: enhancing IoT privacy by automated handling of ownership change. In: Kosta, E., Pierson, J., Slamanig, D., Fischer-Hübner, S., Krenn, S. (eds.) Privacy and Identity 2018. IAICT, vol. 547, pp. 205–221. Springer, Cham (2019). https://doi.org/10.1007/978-3-030-16744-8_14
22. Lanza, J., et al.: Managing large amounts of data generated by a smart city internet of things deployment. Int. J. Semant. Web Inf. Syst. 12(4), 22–42 (2016). https://doi.org/10.4018/IJSWIS.2016100102
23. Leng, X., Mayes, K., Lien, Y.: Ownership management in the context of the internet of things. In: 2014 International Conference on Cyber-Enabled Distributed Computing and Knowledge Discovery, pp. 150–153. IEEE (2014)
24. Meier, S., Schmidt, B., Cremers, C., Basin, D.: The TAMARIN prover for the symbolic analysis of security protocols. In: Sharygina, N., Veith, H. (eds.) CAV 2013. LNCS, vol. 8044, pp. 696–701. Springer, Heidelberg (2013). https://doi.org/10.1007/978-3-642-39799-8_48
25. Müller, R., Schmitt, C., Kaiser, D., Waldvogel, M.: HomeCA: Scalable Secure IoT Network Integration. Gesellschaft für Informatik eV (2019)
26. Oded, G.: Foundations of Cryptography: Basic Applications, vol. 2, 1st edn. Cambridge University Press, New York (2009)
27. Pradeep, B.H., Singh, S.: Ownership authentication transfer protocol for ubiquitous computing devices. In: 2013 International Conference on Computer Communication and Informatics, pp. 1–6, January 2013. https://doi.org/10.1109/ICCCI.2013.6466133
28. Rescorla, E., Modadugu, N.: Datagram Transport Layer Security Version 1.2. RFC 6347, January 2012. https://doi.org/10.17487/RFC6347, https://rfc-editor.org/rfc/rfc6347.txt
29. Roman, R., Najera, P., Lopez, J.: Securing the Internet of Things. Computer **44**(9), 51–58 (2011). https://doi.org/10.1109/MC.2011.291
30. Saied, Y.B., Olivereau, A.: D-hip: a distributed key exchange scheme for hip-based internet of things. In: 2012 IEEE International Symposium on a World of Wireless, Mobile and Multimedia Networks (WoWMoM), pp. 1–7, June 2012. https://doi.org/10.1109/WoWMoM.2012.6263785
31. Saito, J., Imamoto, K., Sakurai, K.: Reassignment scheme of an RFID tag's key for owner transfer. In: Enokido, T., Yan, L., Xiao, B., Kim, D., Dai, Y., Yang, L.T. (eds.) EUC 2005. LNCS, vol. 3823, pp. 1303–1312. Springer, Heidelberg (2005). https://doi.org/10.1007/11596042_132
32. Schaad, J.: CBOR object signing and encryption (COSE). RFC 8152, RFC Editor, July 2017
33. Sedlak, K., Zih, J., Pirc, M., Osvald, U.: 0xcert protocol (2019)
34. Sundaresan, S., Doss, R., Zhou, W., Piramuthu, S.: Secure ownership transfer for multi-tag multi-owner passive RFID environment with individual-owner-privacy. Comput. Commun. **55**, 112–124 (2015). https://doi.org/10.1016/j.comcom.2014.08.015, http://www.sciencedirect.com/science/article/pii/S0140366414003053
35. Tam, P., Newmarch, J.: Protocol for ownership of physical objects in ubiquitous computing environments. In: IADIS International Conference E-Society, vol. 2004, pp. 614–621 (2004)
36. Taqieddin, E., Al-Dahoud, H., Niu, H., Sarangapani, J.: Tag ownership transfer in radio frequency identification systems: a survey of existing protocols and open challenges. IEEE Access **6**, 32117–32155 (2018)
37. Texas Instruments, I.: CC2538 powerful wireless microcontroller system-on-chip for 2.4-GHz IEEE 802.15. 4, 6lowpan, and ZigBee applications. CC2538 datasheet, April 2015

38. Tschofenig, H., Fossati, T.: Transport layer security (TLS)/datagram transport layer security (DTLS) profiles for the internet of things. In: RFC 7925. Internet Engineering Task Force (2016)
39. Vasseur, J.: Terms used in routing for low-power and lossy networks. Technical Report, RFC 7102, January 2014
40. Vögler, M., Schleicher, J.M., Inzinger, C., Dustdar, S.: A scalable framework for provisioning large-scale IoT deployments. ACM Trans. Internet Technol. **16**(2), 11:1–11:20 (2016). https://doi.org/10.1145/2850416
41. Wood, G., et al.: Ethereum: a secure decentralised generalised transaction ledger. Ethereum Project Yellow Pap. **151**(2014), 1–32 (2014)
42. Zhang, L., Zhang, Y., Tang, S., Luo, H.: Privacy protection for e-health systems by means of dynamic authentication and three-factor key agreement. IEEE Trans. Ind. Electron. **65**(3), 2795–2805 (2017)
43. Zhou, W., Yoon, E.J., Piramuthu, S.: Simultaneous multi-level RFID tag ownership and transfer in health care environments. Decis. Support Syst. **54**(1), 98–108 (2012)
44. Zuo, Y.: Changing hands together: a secure group ownership transfer protocol for RFID tags. In: 2010 43rd Hawaii International Conference on System Sciences (HICSS), pp. 1–10. IEEE (2010)

Untangling the XRP Ledger: Insights and Analysis

Lara Mauri[1], Stelvio Cimato[1(✉)], and Ernesto Damiani[1,2]

[1] Computer Science Department, Università Degli Studi di Milano, Milan, Italy
{lara.mauri,stelvio.cimato,ernesto.damiani}@unimi.it
[2] Center for Cyber-Physical Systems, Khalifa University, Abu Dhabi, UAE

Abstract. Over the last few years, the interest in blockchain platforms has fostered the implementation of a number of distributed ledger-based solutions for the exchange of information, assets and digitized goods in both the private and the public sectors. While proposing promising alternatives to the original Bitcoin protocol is an important goal that the bulk of the effort in blockchain community has been focused on, it may not be enough. A major challenge faced by blockchain systems goes beyond the ability to superficially explore their attack surface, and firstly must consider the importance of studying the functioning of their underlying consensus protocols also in the form of non-functional properties such as security and safety. It is to this extent that recent research has started to rigorously analyze the Bitcoin protocol and its close variants, whilst BFT-like systems have not received equal attention so far. In this paper, we focus on the XRP Ledger with the aim to lay down the first steps towards the complete formalization of its unique consensus mechanism. We provide a thorough description of its different phases and present an analysis of some of its properties, which will be suitable as a basis for future research in the same vein.

Keywords: XRP ledger · Ripple · Consensus · Distributed trust · Blockchains

1 Introduction

Blockchain (or more generally, distributed ledger technology) platforms hold great promise to shapeshift the nature of centuries-old business models and pave the way for new, unprecedented levels of transparency for users, who, as a direct consequence, can gain more proactive control over their data. The key success of blockchains essentially stems from the idea that led to the birth of the Bitcoin protocol [28], i.e. allowing mutually mistrusting parties to perform financial payments and autonomously reach agreement on an ever-growing linearly-ordered log of transactions. The ability of blockchains to maintain the integrity of the system without relying on a trusted third party enables to move the control from the center to the edge and makes this technology an attractive option to truly concretize the promises of edge-centric computing. This and other fundamental properties such as transparency and resilience have progressively increased the interest in distributed ledger protocols, causing the flourishing of countless proposals for

S. Furnell et al. (Eds.): ICISSP 2020, CCIS 1545, pp. 48–72, 2022.
https://doi.org/10.1007/978-3-030-94900-6_3

new features and completely new blockchain-based applications beyond the financial sector [6,7,33]. Over the last years, a concurrent research trend has focused towards the development of entire categories of newly designed consensus protocols [5,9,41] that aim at overcoming the disadvantages due to the use of the so-called *Nakamoto consensus*, which is the mechanism adopted by Bitcoin and similar approaches to consistently update the state of the network. The Nakamoto consensus is purposefully designed to be energy-intensive and relies on the notion of *Proof-of-Work* (PoW), which involves competition between participants to incentivize the creation of new blocks of transactions. The most popular alternative to the Bitcoin's cryptographic puzzle-solving scheme is represented by *Proof-of-Stake* (PoS). This technique gives involved parties the chance to affect the behavior of the system on the basis of the stake they possess, instead of requiring them to invest computing power.

Despite the existence of numerous exciting lines of work investigating distributed ledger protocols, current research is predominantly addressing aspects that only target improving the performance and usability of this technology. An even more important priority for the wide adoption and acceptance of blockchain-based solutions is the rigorous analysis of their underlying consensus algorithms, which are the defining element of any distributed ledger system [21]. The reason why it is important to formalize their behavior is twofold. On one hand, it helps in gaining confidence that the protocol works exactly as expected and meets its specification. On the other hand, it serves to prove that the protocol achieves its goals in terms of a set of desirable properties. The conjunction of formal argumentation and detailed security analysis can provide the backbone for a more conscious understanding of both the potentialities and vulnerabilities of the blockchain paradigm in general [37]. Furthermore, capturing the actual functioning of consensus protocols not only makes it easier to identify their limitations, but can also be useful to study them under new perspectives that go beyond those conventionally considered.

1.1 Why the XRP Ledger Calls for a Deeper Investigation

As said, Bitcoin-like approaches employ resource-based techniques to achieve consensus. So, they represent a natural fit for settings where anyone can arbitrarily join and leave the computation. At the opposite end of the spectrum lie protocols that rely on communication-based schemes, where participating entities are known and typically achieve consensus by means of a voting mechanism that runs through several rounds of communication. Essentially, these types of consensus protocols are provided with a security layer for access control that allows only a restricted set of participants to affect the behavior of the system. An intriguing distributed ledger protocol that incorporates the above characteristics is represented by the *XRP Ledger*[1] payment system [34]. This protocol uses a unique consensus mechanism, known as the *XRP Ledger Consensus Protocol* (XRP LCP), that sets it apart from previous approaches in several ways. The fact that the XRP LCP is not based on a mining process and does not need

---

[1] The XRP Ledger is better known as "Ripple" because originally this was the name used to refer to the protocol. Recently, in order to differentiate it from the company, the term "XRP Ledger" has been adopted to refer to the technology.

several confirmations before transactions can be accepted as settled clearly brings many advantages, compared to Bitcoin and other cryptocurrencies [26,40]. Indeed, while for Bitcoin-like protocols transactions are confirmed after an hour on average, in the XRP Ledger network the settlement process takes around 5 s, with a throughput of up to 1500 transactions per second. Although it exhibits several fascinating and innovative features, current research on the XRP Ledger protocol either addresses issues that do not concern the consensus protocol itself or compares it generically with other systems [12,20,32,43]. By now the original white paper [38] is deprecated, and available documentation about how the XRP LCP works is restricted to the developer portal [35] and a recent analysis provided by its creators [11]. Even if the latter presents a detailed explanation of the XRP Ledger algorithm and derives conditions for its safety and liveness, there remains a degree of uncertainty around many aspects of the protocol and, in any case, not all steps have actually been described. Furthermore, to date the only existing peer-reviewed analysis of the protocol was conducted on the original white paper and showed that some specifications were flawed [2].

Therefore, what is really missing today is an in-depth study and analysis of the XRP Ledger Consensus Protocol in all its parts. The objective of this work is to narrow this gap by digging deep into the underlying technical components that contribute to the construction and proper functioning of the XRP Ledger consensus mechanism. This paper has its roots in a previous work of ours [27], and can be considered as its natural extension towards the overall goal of providing a thorough, clear and exact description of the behaviour of the XRP LCP.

Contribution. The contributions of this paper are the following:

- In order to frame the context where some of the essential concepts incorporated by the XRP Ledger arose and developed, we first offer an overall historical perspective of the trust assumptions commonly used in the distributed systems panorama, tracing the evolution of the choices of trust in the different distributed ledger protocols.
- Drawing from a scattered corpus of information, we identify three core technical components of the XRP Ledger protocol design - *Peer-to-peer communication network*, *Consensus*, and *Transactions*. This concept decomposition enables a more insightful characterization of the protocol's behavior and can be used as a reference point for future investigation.
- The aforementioned three main technical components are further decomposed so as to clarify the role each element/participant plays during the different phases of the protocol. Especially for the Consensus and Transactions components we present thorough technicalities which, to the best of our knowledge, have never been covered in such detail by other research papers. For example, we provide a careful characterization of the three different ledger versions that each participant has to maintain during the execution of a single round of consensus. Also, we describe in detail the conditions under which the result of a transaction is considered final in relation to the ledger version in which it has been included, as well as the way initially discarded transactions are handled.

– Lastly, the step-by-step protocol description is preceded by a new enriched workflow showing a linear representation of the three phases of the protocol and their intermediate and final outputs for a single consensus round.

A direct benefit of our contributions is that they make the formalization and security analysis of XRP LCP provided in the subsequent sections clearer and can drive the reader towards a deeper understanding of the interactions that occur during each stage of the consensus process. This work, in conjunction with our prior effort [27], has shed light on many aspects of the XRP LCP that had remained unclear so far.

Overall, our research resulted in a comprehensive identification and characterization of the different phases governing the XRP Ledger Consensus Protocol. The careful analysis of all the available documentation and source code of the XRP LCP has allowed us to create an in-depth description of the protocol for every step and then, to conduct an accurate analysis of its security guarantees in terms of safety and liveness. Furthermore, we have proved that the correlation between some protocol parameters can be leveraged to achieve specific security goals.

The remainder of this paper is structured as follows. In Sect. 2 we provide an overview of the different trust assumptions underlying distributed ledger approaches. Then, we describe the flexible notion of trust introduced by the XRP Ledger. Section 3 presents the three core components at the basis of the XRP Ledger system and provides a detailed description of their utility during the protocol execution. Section 4 presents a set-theoretic formalization of the different phases of the XRP LCP. Section 5 shows the security guarantees of the protocol in terms of safety and liveness and how to increase the desired liveness/fault tolerance by changing the value of specific protocol parameters. Section 6 reviews recent work on the formalization of blockchain protocols. Finally, Sect. 7 concludes the paper and proposes directions for future research.

2   The Faces of Trust in Distributed Ledger Systems

Distributed ledger (DL) systems appear to bring forth a new form of trust where individuals who want to exchange valuable assets amongst each other are not required to trust either the interacting party or a central entity. Rather, trust seems to be placed only in a collection of components (firstly, hard code and cryptographic algorithms). The simple fact that all actors follow the same identical rules with the ultimate goal of reaching agreement on how to consistently update the state of the network causes the whole system to be perceived as trustworthy. Although blockchain approaches presuppose shifting trust to the veracity of the system and, consequently, to the overall control mechanism, it is essential to carefully consider the trust assumptions that underlie their consensus mechanisms. Indeed, trust assumptions, whether implicit or explicit, strongly influence the extent to which any distributed system maintains its stability and correctness and have a fundamental impact on how security analyses are conducted on models.

Successful blockchain platforms such as Bitcoin and Ethereum guarantee that consistency holds as long as more than half of the voting power (expressed in terms of energy consumption or wealth distribution) is controlled by participants that honestly follow the protocol. The model used in these systems is *permissionless*, in the sense that participants can join or leave the network at any time, without coordinating with any other party. On the contrary, the *permissioned* model, which is the one used traditionally in research, imposes restrictions on its nodes, in the sense that only an authorized set of known and identifiable participants is explicitly responsible for the advancement of the consensus protocol [1]. The trust assumptions underlying protocols in this setting – usually referred to as *Byzantine fault tolerant* (BFT) *consensus* – are generally stated with respect to a number of nodes behaving correctly. Typically, consensus is achievable if the maximum number of malicious nodes is less than one third of all participants in the system. *Byzantine quorum* (BQ) *systems* [25, 39] are a classic abstraction for ensuring system-wide consensus in distributed fault-tolerant computing. In a Byzantine context, a quorum can be defined as a collection of subsets of all the nodes, such that each pair of quorums intersect in a set containing sufficiently many correct nodes to guarantee consistency. Traditional BFT and BQ systems make use of a *symmetric* notion of trust, meaning that all the nodes involved in the system trust other network members in the same way, thereby adhering on a uniform trust view. However, this does not truly reflect the individual choices of trust taken in reality, where users may trust some participants more than others. Abandoning the idea of a global fail-prone structure, the work in [14] has laid the foundations of *asymmetric* trust, aiming at capturing a more subjective notion of trust for secure computation protocols. Recently, new approaches for designing BFT and BQ protocols have been proposed [8, 10, 19, 24]. This search for evolved models with more sophisticated trust assumptions is currently receiving a lot of attention because of their potential application to consensus algorithms for permissioned blockchains.

2.1   The XRP Ledger Through the Lens of Trust

The XRP Ledger was arguably the DL protocol that first introduced the idea of flexible trust structures. Influenced by the BQ approach, the XRP Ledger operates as a quorum-based system where the process for reaching agreement is driven by decisions taken by specific nodes, known as *validators*. The most important task of a validator is that of issuing special messages to communicate its opinion on which transactions to insert in the ledger. However, the mere act of sending messages does not automatically give the validator a say in the consensus process. In effect, the key idea is that a validator does not need to be listened to or to communicate with everyone. In the XRP Ledger, this concept is embodied in the so-called *Unique Node List* (UNL), which essentially resembles the classical notion of quorums, but is tailored so as to reflect the subjectiveness of trust choices. Each validator maintains its own UNL and uses it for designating which nodes it trusts. During the protocol execution, validators ignore other validators' messages unless those validators are included into their UNL. This means that if a validator is part of a UNL, it is *trusted* and its messages are considered in the consensus process by the validators that trust it. A viable way to assess the trustworthiness of validators is by inspecting the Validator Registry[2], which provides identity information and performance statistics for all network validators. Conceptually, the XRP Ledger can

---

[2] https://xrpcharts.ripple.com/#/validators.

be sited at some intermediate level between a BFT-based protocol and a permissionless blockchain. On one hand, the protocol goes beyond the traditional form of consensus by not prescribing only one global trust assumption for all validators. On the other hand, nodes determine individually if they want to act as validators. So, in principle, anyone can participate in the consensus process. Nevertheless, this freedom in participating is in fact limited by the discretion in selecting which nodes to trust. Practically, by expressing their own trust assumptions, validators determine with which other participants they wish to stay in consensus with, thereby entailing a certain degree of permissioning.

3   Core Technical Components

3.1   Peer-to-Peer Communication Network

As in any other DL system, the XRP Ledger enables a peer-to-peer network designed around the notion of equal participation by nodes, where any node is free to join the network in order to interact with other peers.

Network Topology, Discovery and Communication. The peer-to-peer network is supported by an overlay logic that creates a virtualized network layer on top of the physical network topology. This overlay network can be thought of as a directed graph whose vertices are the nodes and whose edges define the connections allowing nodes to directly communicate with each other. In general, a node maintains multiple outgoing connections and optional incoming connections to other peers. Whenever a node joins the network, it needs a way to find out about other nodes. By default, the XRP Ledger achieves this via a gossip protocol such that once a node has connected to a peer, it asks that peer for the connection information of other peers that may also be attempting to establish peer connections. The node can then connect to such peers, and ask them for the information of some other peers to connect to, thereby triggering a cascade mechanism of contact data exchange. Inter-party interaction, which for example involves sharing information on the network connection status and consensus progress, takes the form of signed messages. Each node possesses a key pair that is generated using any of the XRP Ledger's supported digital signature schemes, which, at present, are the ECDSA with secp256k1 (by default) and the EdDSA with Ed25519. The fact that all communications are signed guarantees the integrity of the message to the receiver as well as provides a reliable means to authenticate the identity of the sender.

3.2   Consensus

An essential part of the XRP Ledger is the consensus mechanism used to reach agreement on changes in the ledger, which is the shared state of the system. The overall consensus process, which will be thoroughly described in Sect. 4, consists of several phases that are continually repeated. The result is a chain of fully validated ledgers growing over time.

Open, (Last) Closed and Fully Validated Ledgers. In the XRP Ledger, the actual ledger destined to become part of the immutable history of transactions is nothing more than what results from successive refinements of individual versions of the ledger itself. In fact, during the consensus process, the content of the initial (parent) ledger taken as a basis is subject to continuous updates until a final ledger is validated by the whole network. We can roughly distinguish three different ledger versions, namely *open*, *last closed* and *fully validated*. In a sense, this series of individual ledgers is part of an evolutionary line expressed in terms of content validity and finality that leads from an initial provisional ledger version reflecting only the view of the single validator to a permanent and authoritative one that is globally accepted. Table 1 outlines the main differences between the ledger versions. Getting into details, each validator maintains a single open ledger that represents its own current working version of the next ledger and is used as a temporary workspace to group all incoming transactions in the order they arrive. At a certain point in time, the ledger is *closed*[3], and no new transaction can be considered as candidate for inclusion in the next ledger (but it may be considered for inclusion in a later ledger version). The set of transactions it contains forms the reference point for the start of the actual consensus phase. The closed ledger does not constitute another version of the ledger, rather a particular state associated with the open ledger, which simply serves to indicate that, for the current consensus round, all possible transactions to be considered as candidates are known (as such, we have not included it in the summarising table). The last closed ledger is the most recent ledger that the validator believes the network reached agreement on. The process for calculating a new last closed ledger involves taking the previous last closed ledger and applying the transaction set resulting from consensus[4]. In the last closed ledger, transactions are applied according to deterministic protocol rules (canonical order), instead of the order in which they are received, as is the case with the open ledger. This make sure that validators process the same sequence of transactions in the same way. However, the last closed ledger only reflects the personal belief by each validator on which transactions should be permanently included in the ledger. Thus, the content of a last closed ledger cannot yet be considered as neither final nor reliable. Only the transactions appearing in a fully validated ledger are final and hence truly irrevocable. This can be easily clarified by considering two basic parameters specified in the ledger header: the *ledger index* (or *sequence number*) and the *ledger hash*. The ledger index is a progressive number used to identify the ledger so as to keep all the ledgers in order. The ledger hash serves as a unique identifier of the exact contents of the ledger. As said, the contents of the open ledger change over time, reflecting the arrival of new submitted transactions (that is obviously affected by network delays). Since it is very likely that validators have very different ledgers at the early phase of the process, the ledger hash is calculated

---

[3] In the XRP Ledger documentation [35], the term "closed" is used to denote what here we refer to as "last closed". Our choice is dictated by the desire to make the exposition clearer and more consistent with what is in the current implementation [36].

[4] Even if it appears counterintuitive, in practice the open ledger is never really closed. When certain conditions are met, the validator throws away its open ledger, builds a new last closed ledger by starting with the prior last closed ledger, and then creates a new open ledger using the newly created last closed ledger as a basis.

only for last closed ledgers. Nevertheless, due to Byzantine failures, different validators can come to a different conclusion about the last closed ledger. This means that there may be multiple last closed ledgers with the same ledger index but different ledger hash competing to be fully validated. As a result, unless the last closed ledger is fully validated, it might be replaced by a completely different last closed ledger having a differing set of transactions.

Table 1. Differences between ledger versions.

	Open	Last closed	Fully validated
Purpose	Temporary workspace	Propose the next ledger state	Confirm the previous ledger state
Total number in the network	One per validator (periodically recreated)	One per validator per ledger index (for each consensus round)	One per ledger index (advancing the chain of ledger history)
Are both the hash value and the ledger index calculated?	No, only the ledger index	Yes, and two validators might have ledgers with the same ledger index but different hash value	Yes
Can contents change?	Always	No, but the whole ledger could be replaced	Never
In which order are transactions applied?	The order they arrive	Canonical order	Canonical order

Proposal, Dispute and Validation. Most of the consensus process is devoted to the exchange of so-called *proposals* between validators. A proposal is a signed message containing the position taken by the validator with regard to which set of transactions it believes should be included in the next ledger. Throughout the process, each validator broadcasts several proposals in an attempt to achieve consensus, but it is up to the receiving validators to decide whether or not to consider those proposals as part of their local decision-making process. As mentioned in Sect. 2.1, the UNLs give structure to the XRP Ledger network and can be thought of as the convincing set that each validator listens to. Thus, proposals are evaluated only if submitted by trusted validators. This exchange of proposals logically implies the occurrence of divergences between the various positions taken by the validators. This concept is expressed by the term *dispute*, which denotes an individual transaction that is either not included in a validator's proposal or not included in a trusted validator's proposal. The purpose of *validations* is to let trusted validators know which particular ledger has been built by the other validators and to come to a common conclusion about which ledger version should be declared as fully validated. In essence, a validation is a signed message containing the hash of the last closed ledger.

3.3 Transactions

Transactions represent the means by which making changes to the state of the world in the XRP Ledger. Every transaction has an identifying hash that serves as a globally distinguishing ID and has to be authorized through digital signatures before submission.

Transaction Finality. Every validator processes transactions independently and then verifies that its outcome corresponds to that of the rest of the network. When a validator receives a transaction, it provisionally applies it to its current open ledger and returns the corresponding tentative result. As mentioned earlier, the set (and the order) of transactions is not final until a ledger is approved by the consensus process. Depending on circumstances, this can cause a transaction that succeeded initially to eventually fail or a transaction that failed initially to eventually succeed. Furthermore, as long as a transaction is not incorporated in a fully validated ledger, it is also possible to cancel it. In addition to the hash, each transaction has a sequence number that starts at 1 and increments for each transaction that an XRP Ledger account submits. The purpose of this sequence number is analogous to that of the ledger index, that is keeping transactions in order. By signing a transaction, the owner of an account effectively authorizes it to take place. However, if the same account sends another transaction with the same sequence number, that transaction can be theoretically deleted. Whether or not the cancellation process is successful depends on a number of factors, including the network topology and workloads, but generally it is more likely to succeed when the transaction has not yet been proposed as a candidate transaction in a validator's proposal.

Queuing. In order to protect the network from excessive load (for instance due to denial-of-service attacks), each transaction must destroy a small amount of XRP, the native cryptocurrency of the XRP Ledger. Each validator maintains a cost threshold based on its local load, so if the transaction fee specified by a transaction is lower than the validator's load-based transaction cost, the validator simply discards the transaction without relaying it to the other peers. Also, a transaction can be included in an open ledger only if it meets the open ledger cost requirement, which serves to set a target number of transactions in any given ledger. When that is not the case, the validator may add the unsuitable transactions to its local *queue* after having estimated whether they are likely to be included in a later ledger version. This queuing structure is useful for selecting candidate transactions for the creation of the next ledger. If the queue is full, transactions drop out from it, starting with those with the lowest transaction cost. At each consensus round, transactions with the highest transaction cost are given priority.

4 Digging into the XRP Ledger Consensus Protocol

4.1 Protocol Overview

The ultimate goal of the XRP LCP is to advance the chain of ledgers by agreeing on a new set of transactions to apply to the prior fully validated ledger. At a high level, a ledger can be represented as a quintuple of the form $L = \langle sn, h, h_{-1}, ts, T \rangle$ where sn is the sequence number (or ledger index) of the ledger, h is the unique identifying hash of the ledger's contents, h_{-1} is the h value of the previous ledger version this ledger was derived from, ts is a timestamp, and T is a set of transactions. Of the many last closed ledgers independently built by validators, only one can become fully validated. Hence, there exists always only one fully validated ledger hash for each ledger index in history; all the other candidate ledger versions are destined to be discarded. A tuple $L = \langle sn, h, h_{-1}, ts, T \rangle$ is valid with respect to a predecessor (fully validated) ledger $L' = \langle sn', h', h'_{-1}, ts', T' \rangle$ if and only if the following holds:

1. $h_{-1} = h'$;
2. $sn = sn' + 1$;
3. $|\Sigma_L| \geq q_v$, where $|\Sigma_L|$ is the support of the ledger L and q_v is the minimum percentage of participation required to reach network agreement.

Note that the above third condition essentially says that a ledger is only validated by the consensus process as soon as a quorum q_v of trusted validators votes for the same exact ledger version L. Specifically, the threshold q_v, which we refer to as *validation quorum*, is a parameter that roughly specifies the minimum number of agreeing trusted validators each validator needs to hear from to commit to a decision. The distinguishing characteristic of the XRP LCP is that it makes use of two different thresholds serving two different purposes. In addition to the validation quorum, which is utilized at the very end of the entire consensus process, the XRP Ledger specifies another quorum, which we refer to as *consensus quorum*. This additional threshold is utilized at the intermediate phase of the consensus protocol to determine when a validator can build its own last closed ledger. Even though both quorums are subject to changes and do not necessarily need to be equal, in the current implementation they are exactly the same, as we will see later. By default, the two quorums are automatically set to a safe number of trusted validators based on how many there are. However, in principle it is possible to manually set their value.

The overall consensus process, which can be viewed as a progression through three phases – *collection*, *deliberation* and *validation* – involves multiple rounds of vetting where validators continually propose and revise their candidate sets of transactions in order to determine the final, authoritative version of the ledger. Figure 1 shows the flow of the primary operations that each of the three phases involves for a single ledger round, while a brief description of each phase is provided below:

⋄ *Collection*: Validators collect all received new transactions and apply the well-formed ones to their open ledger before relaying them to the other members of the network. When certain conditions are met, validators close their ledger and propose their initial candidate transaction set to their trusted validators.

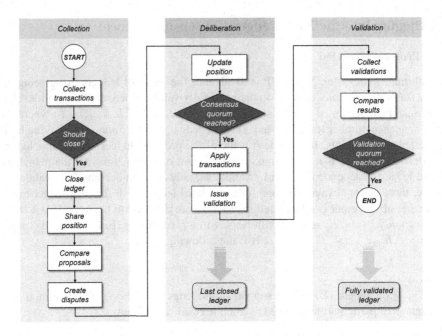

Fig. 1. Workflow of the protocol phases for a single round of consensus.

◇ *Deliberation*: Validators begin an iterative process during which they try to establish consensus by exchanging proposals with their trusted validators. Starting from their own position, they continuously change their view of the candidate transaction set by adding or removing disputed transactions from their proposal. After each update, validators check the percentage of trusted validators agreeing with them and declare that consensus has been reached only when there is a supermajority agreement. Then, they create a new last closed ledger by applying the consensus transaction set to the last fully validated ledger and issue a validation.

◇ *Validation*: Validators determine whether to consider the contents of their last closed ledger as final by comparing the results received from their trusted validators. The decision is taken on the basis of the percentage of agreement on the newly-created ledger. Only when a quorum of validations for the same ledger is reached, that ledger is deemed fully validated.

4.2 Preliminaries

Synchrony and Timing Assumptions. An important aspect that must be considered when designing any consensus protocol is the ability of parties to reach a certain degree of synchronization during the protocol execution. In the XRP Ledger network, the protocol execution is driven by a heartbeat timer which allows nodes to advance the consensus process. In practice, at regular intervals each validator checks whether the necessary conditions to move to the next phase of the consensus protocol are met. Although each validator can begin a new round of consensus at arbitrary times based on when the initial round started and the time taken to apply the transactions, the transition to both deliberation and validation phases can only occur at the end of the heartbeat timer. Furthermore, each node maintains an internal clock that it uses when calculating its own *close time*, i.e. the time at which the ledger has been closed. In practice, at the closure of the ledger (which reflects the end of collection phase) each validator uses its own current time as the initial close time estimate and includes this value in its initial position. Later, this approximate time is rounded based on a dynamic resolution. As a result, each validator uses the consensus process not only to reach agreement with its trusted nodes about the set of transactions, but also to attempt to agree on a common time for the closure of the ledger. Validators update their close time positions in response to the effective close time included in their trusted nodes' positions, and in this way, they can derive a common close time for the ledger without the need to synchronize their clocks. When there is no clear majority of trusted validators agreeing on a close time, nodes agree to disagree on an actual close time. Even though in this case the network has no official close time, the effective close time of the ledger is set to 1 s past the close time of the previous ledger.

The XRP LCP as a whole reaches agreement on both the effective close time and the final ledger version. Nevertheless, here the focus is on the ledger content aspect, thus our formalization includes only the fundamental protocol timing parameters.

Notation. We denote by N the universe of nodes of the peer-to-peer XRP Ledger network. Nodes play different roles: client applications submit transactions to server nodes, which are differentiated in tracking nodes and validators. The consensus process is exclusively driven by the latter. Since only validators actively participate, check and validate all transactions taking place in the system, we believe that for the purposes of formalization it is meaningful to consider only the subset $N_v \subset N$ of participants, where N_v denotes exactly the nodes acting as validators. As already mentioned, during the consensus process, validators only evaluate proposals and validations issued by their trusted nodes, discarding those received from validators not belonging to their UNL. For any node $i \in N_v$, $UNL_i = \{u : u \in N_v, F(u)\}$ denotes the set of all nodes u for which $F(u)$ is true, where $F(u)$ means that validator i trusts u. Also, we use $n_i = |UNL_i|$ to denote the size of node i's UNL. Giving as a fact that the individual choice to include (or omit) a given transaction in the next ledger is influenced only by the trusted nodes' messages, we decide not to directly specify UNL membership every time (in our formalization, we will specify this dependency only in the context of the last phase). Deliberation and validation phases are parameterized by q_c and q_v, respectively. In particular, q_c specifies the consensus quorum (i.e. the minimum number of validators having issued the same proposal needed to declare consensus), whereas q_v represents the validation quorum (i.e. the minimum number of validations needed to fully validate a ledger) – see Sect. 4.1. Both these parameters are a function of a constant k and n_i, where n_i is the previously defined size of UNL_i. We let $\tilde{L}_i$, $\tilde{L}_i^c$ and L_i' denote the open ledger, the closed ledger and the last closed ledger of node i, respectively. Moreover, we use $\hat{L}$ to denote the last fully validated ledger. tx is used to represent a single transaction under consideration by consensus. Any transactions excluded from a node's proposal are added to its local queue we denote by T_Q. For notational simplicity, we suppose the existence of another set T_I which contains all received new transactions. Also, we use P_i to denote the node i's proposal of candidate transactions and the symbol θ to indicate the threshold for including a given transaction in the proposal P_i. Lastly, D_i denotes the node i's set of disputed transactions, whereas σ_i denotes a validation issued by i. Table 2 provides a summary of the notation (over the course of the presentation, some elements will be slightly modified to better suit the context).

Table 2. Summary of notation [27].

Symbol	Description
N_v	The set of validators
i	A validator in the network
UNL_i	i's Unique Node List
n_i	The size of UNL_i
tx	A single transaction
T	A set of transactions
T_Q	The set of queued transactions
T_I	The set of new transactions
q_c	The consensus quorum
q_v	The validation quorum
$\tilde{L}_i$	i's open ledger
$\tilde{L}_i^c$	i's closed ledger
L_i'	i's last closed ledger
$\hat{L}$	The last fully validated ledger
P_i	i's proposal of transactions
D_i	i's set of disputed transactions
σ_i	i's validation

4.3   The XRP LCP Step-by-Step

We are now ready to proceed with the formalization of the three main phases of the XRP LCP. In order to formalize the behaviour of the protocol, we referred to the current implementation of the server software at the heart of the XRP Ledger (known as `rippled`), whose source code is available at [36]. Each `rippled` server running in a validator mode actively participates in the consensus process and contributes to the advancement of the ledger chain structure and to the overall health of the system.

The XRP Ledger chain of ledgers starts with the *genesis ledger*[5] (the first ledger ever created) and ends with the last fully validated ledger. Generally, given the prior fully validated ledger $\hat{L}$ and a set T of new candidate transactions, the execution of the XRP Ledger Consensus Protocol determines an output ledger $\hat{L}'$ which, together with the previous validated ledgers, forms the ledger history. Note that in our formalization we have considered the perspective of a single validator $i \in N_v$, which makes decisions only by listening to its unique node list UNL_i. Bearing the above in mind, the outcomes produced by each validator i for each of the three phases are as follows:

⋄ The output expected from collection is i's initial proposal P_i^0, which contains the starting position taken by the validator i before considering any trusted validator's position;
⋄ At the end of deliberation, i builds a new last closed ledger L_i';
⋄ Validation establishes which last closed ledger, amongst those proposed by all participants, must be considered the authoritative one ($\hat{L}'$).

Collection. The first stage of the process is a quiescent period allowing the validator i to create an individual perception of the state of the network. This perception is created thanks to the use of the open ledger that the validator fills with the candidate transactions that failed to be included in the last round (i.e. those queued in T_Q), as well as with newly submitted ones. i's open ledger $\tilde{L}_i$ contains the set of transactions T:

$$T = T_Q \cup T_I, \ T \in \tilde{L}_i \tag{1}$$

Under normal circumstances, the closure of the ledger occurs after a predetermined minimum time $t_{minclose}$ has elapsed and only if the open ledger contains at least one transaction. Thus, i closes its open ledger if the following holds:

$$T \neq \emptyset \wedge (t_{open} \geq t_{minclose}), \ T \in \tilde{L}_i \tag{2}$$

where t_{open} is used to denote how long the ledger has been open. We let $\tilde{L}_i^c$ indicate that i's open ledger has been closed (superscript letter c). In other cases, the protocol either *(1)* closes the ledger if more than half of the proposers have closed the ledger or validated the last closed ledger, or *(2)* postpones the closure to the end of a certain idle interval so that it is more likely to include some transactions in the next ledger. Regardless of the condition which led to the closure of the ledger, once the pre-close phase is completed, i establishes its initial position on the basis of the transactions included in the newly closed ledger. Then, i proposes it to its trusted validators in the form of a proposal, i.e. a signed message containing the transactions it believes should be included in the next ledger:

$$P_i^0 = \{tx : \ tx \in T, \ T \in \tilde{L}_i^c\} \tag{3}$$

Here the notation used for the proposal slightly differs from that given in Sect. 4.2; we introduced the superscript 0 to denote that P_i is the initial proposal shared by i.

---

[5] In the XRP Ledger network, the very first ledger started with ledger index 1. However, since in practice this is no longer available, the ledger #32570 is considered the actual genesis ledger.

Like ledgers, also proposals have a sequence number that is incremented each time a validator updates the transaction set contained therein. As easy to guess, different nodes may receive different unconfirmed transactions due to network delays. As this variation in arrival time allows for each potential new ledger version to be different for each node, immediately after sharing its initial position, i considers all the proposals received from its trusted validators and creates a dispute for each transaction discovered not to be in common with the peer's position under consideration. We define the validator i's dispute set D_i as:

$$D_i = \{tx : (tx \in P_i^r \land tx \notin P_{j \neq i}^r) \lor (tx \notin P_i^r \land tx \in P_{j \neq i}^r)\} \qquad (4)$$

where r refers to one of the subsequent proposals issued by i during deliberation (at this time, $r = 0$). Also, the validator keeps track of each peer's vote on each disputed transaction (voting in favour of a disputed transaction simply means believing that such transaction should be included in the next ledger). For each $tx \in D_i$, we use $v(tx)$ to denote the support given to tx by i's trusted validators:

$$v(tx) = |j \neq i : tx \in P_j^r| \qquad (5)$$

where, as before, r at this time is 0 (in a more advanced stage of the process, i.e. during deliberation, P_j^r will refer to the most recent proposal issued by j). Unless they are part of a peer's proposal, transactions received after the closure of the ledger are not considered until the next round.

Deliberation. In order to achieve consensus on the specific set of transactions to be processed next, i begins an iterative process during which it issues updated proposals (i.e. updates of its initial position), which are modified based on the support each individual transaction receives. The heartbeat timer is the key ingredient that drives the consensus process forward (see Sect. 4.2). In fact, it is only on timer calls that i adjusts and issues new proposals. Going into detail, the mechanism allowing differences between peers' proposals to converge is based on a majority voting scheme. The evaluation of the achieved convergence degree is performed taking the value of a certain threshold θ as a reference. In turn, the value θ depends on a parameter d which expresses the percentage of time that consensus is expected to take to converge. Specifically, d is a function of the previous round duration, which corresponds to the duration of the last deliberation phase (measured from closing the open ledger to accepting the consensus result) and the duration of the deliberation phase for the current consensus round:

$$d = f(t_{(deliberation-1)}, t_{deliberation}) = \frac{t_{deliberation} \cdot 100}{max(t_{(deliberation-1)}, t_{minconsensus})} \qquad (6)$$

where $t_{minconsensus}$ (currently, 5 s) expresses the minimum amount of time to consider that consensus was reached in the previous round. As deliberation proceeds, i changes its candidate transaction set in response to what its trusted validators propose. As a result, i may either add a disputed transaction to its current set if the percentage of trusted validators that have proposed the same transaction in their most recent proposal exceeds the aforementioned threshold θ or, otherwise, remove it. New proposals are formalized as follows:

$$P_i' = \{tx : (tx \in P_i^r \wedge tx \notin D_i) \vee (tx \in D_i \wedge (v(tx) \geq \theta))\}. \tag{7}$$

The current implementation uses an initial threshold for inclusion of 0.5. This means that if a particular disputed transaction is supported by half of the validators or more, i agrees to include it in its set. On the contrary, a transaction that, at this early stage, does not have the support of at least 50% of the trusted nodes, is removed from i's position. Omitted transactions are added to the transaction queue T_Q and considered again for inclusion in the next ledger version. Therefore, the queue is updated whenever a transaction is removed from a proposal:

$$T_Q' = T_Q \cup \{tx : tx \in D_i \wedge (v(tx) < \theta)\}. \tag{8}$$

The specific values of θ are subject to change, in accordance to the XRP Ledger implementation. Depending on the value of the function d (defined in Eq. 6), θ can currently assume one of the following values:

$$\begin{cases} 0.5 & d < 50 \\ 0.65 & 50 \leq d < 85 \\ 0.7 & 85 \leq d < 200 \\ 0.95 & otherwise \end{cases} \tag{9}$$

After changing its transaction view, i broadcasts its new proposal (increasing the related sequence number) and determines whether consensus has been reached – in case i has not changed its set of transactions, no new proposal needs to be issued. Consensus can be declared only if there is a supermajority support for each of the transactions the candidate set contains. Formally, the support of a proposal P_i^r is expressed as follows:

$$v(P_i^r) = |\{j \neq i : P_j^r = P_i^r\}|. \tag{10}$$

Actually, consensus is reached when the following three conditions are met: *(a)* a certain minimum amount of time has elapsed since deliberation began, *(b)* at least $3/4$ of the previous round proposers are participating or the current deliberation phase is longer (of a given minimum amount of time) than the deliberation phase of the previous round, *(c)* i, together with its trusted peers, has reached the percentage threshold q_c above which consensus can be declared. However, for the purpose of formalization, the really meaningful condition is the third. Hence, we assume i declares consensus reached when the following holds:

$$v(P_i^r) \geq q_c, \quad q_c = k \cdot n_i \tag{11}$$

where n_i is the number of trusted nodes belonging to UNL_i (see Sect. 4.2) and $k = 0.8$ in the current implementation. Once consensus is reached, i builds a new last closed ledger L_i' by adding the agreed-upon set of transactions to the prior fully validated ledger $\hat{L}$:

$$L_i' = \hat{L} \cup \{tx \in P_i^r : v(P_i^r) \geq q_c\} \tag{12}$$

and then, it broadcasts its resulting ledger in the form of a signed message σ_i containing the identifying hash of this ledger. At this point, the round is completed and i now builds a new open ledger on top of the last closed ledger. As previously said, the open ledger represents the basis of any validator's initial proposal and hence, the first transactions to be added to the new open ledger are those pending from the previous consensus round. Next, all valid transactions that in the previous round were received after the ledger was closed are applied. In practice, the protocol starts a new round of consensus before the third phase, i.e. validation, ends. Each participant begins a new collection phase concurrently, preparing its proposal for the next ledger version meanwhile the consensus process related to the prior ledger version progresses. Accordingly, at any given time, the process is characterized by a series of in-progress open ledgers, individual participants' last closed ledgers that have not been fully validated and historical ledgers that have been fully validated (see Sect. 3.2).

Validation. At the end of deliberation, as seen above, validators independently build what they believe the next state of the ledger should be. Due to latency in propagating transactions throughout the network, different validators may compute different last closed ledgers. These ledger versions have the same sequence number, but different hash values that uniquely identify their contents (see Sect. 3.2). It is important to note that the sequence number and the hash correlate 1:1 only for fully validated ledgers. Thus, for a given sequence number, only one ledger version can ever be fully validated. In order to converge on a universal status of the ledger and, consequently, resolve the above differences, i checks how many trusted validators have built a last closed ledger identical to its own by comparing its validation, i.e. the hash of the ledger it computed, with the hashes received from its peers; amongst all the most recent validations, i considers only those with the greatest sequence number. We denote by $\Sigma_{L_i'}$ the set of trusted validators that published the same validation hash as the validator i:

$$\Sigma_{L_i'} = \{j \in UNL_i : \sigma_j = \sigma_i\}. \tag{13}$$

Based on these validations, i recognizes whether the previous consensus round succeeded or not. In particular, the node declares its last closed ledger L_i' fully validated in the event that a supermajority agreement on the calculated hash is reached. Therefore, if i detects that it is in the majority, having built a ledger that received enough matching validations to meet the validation quorum q_v, it considers the ledger fully validated. Formally, L_i' is declared fully validated iff:

$$|\Sigma_{L_i'}| \geq q_v, \quad q_v = k \cdot n_i \tag{14}$$

where, as for the consensus quorum q_c (cf. Eq. 11), the constant k is 0.8. Conversely, if i is in the minority, it cannot consider its ledger instance fully validated. Instead, it has to find the supermajority ledger, i.e. the one with the sufficient number of validations (and highest sequence number), and accept it as the new fully validated ledger:

$$\hat{L}' = L_x' : (x = i \vee x \in UNL_i) \wedge (|\Sigma_{L_x'}| \geq q_v). \tag{15}$$

Lastly, in case for a given sequence number no last closed ledger meets q_v, no ledger is declared fully validated and i switches to a strategy allowing it to determine the preferred last closed ledger for the next consensus round (we refer the reader to [11] for an overview on this strategy).

5 Security Analysis

5.1 Desiderata and Adversary Model

Consensus protocols typically have some desired properties they wish to obtain. For example, one of the fundamental problems they have to face is to ensure that all the correct processes operating in a system with dynamic participation make decisions and eventually share a single common view of the state of the system even in the presence of corruptions and network failures. However, understanding under which conditions do these protocols achieve their desiderata is often not so trivial. Even though there exist several nuances of the Byzantine agreement protocol [31], all variants are subject to conditions similar to the following:

◇ *Validity*: If every process begins with the same initial value v, then the final decision of a non-faulty process must be v;
◇ *Agreement*: Final decisions by non-faulty processes must be identical;
◇ *Termination*: Every non-faulty process must eventually decide.

These conditions are intended to capture two crucial properties, namely *safety* and *liveness*. The former, which derives from the conjunction of validity and agreement, traditionally guarantees that something bad will never happen. The latter guarantees that something good will happen eventually, and derives from the termination condition. In the XRP Ledger context, the above definitions can be reformulated as follows:

◇ *Safety*: If an honest validator fully validates a ledger L, then all honest validators cannot fully validate a contradictory ledger $L' \neq L$;
◇ *Liveness*: If an honest validator broadcasts a valid proposal P, then P will eventually be accepted by all validators and included in a fully validated ledger.

As previously mentioned, the XRP Ledger features a layered notion of trust. The network is divided into subsets of nodes that are collectively trusted to not collude in an attempt to defraud the other peers, and each node has complete discretion in selecting its own UNL. Since validators only have influence over nodes configured to trust them, the presence of an honest validator in more UNLs directly implies a greater influence by that validator on the process of determining the next ledger state. Intuitively, the majority voting scheme on its own is not sufficient to guarantee network safety. Rather, it is essential to ensure that the majority of the validators act honestly and that the UNLs maintain a minimal degree of intersection between each other, in the sense that each validator chooses its own set of trusted validators so that it is reasonably similar to the set chosen by all the others. These two factors have a significant impact on the ability of systems to prevent the occurrence of a *fork* and to produce reliable results. Ledger forks constitute a major threat to the correct operations of every distributed system, and in the XRP Ledger ecosystem, this phenomenon corresponds to the situation in which *two honest validators fully validate conflicting ledgers, i.e. ledgers having the same sequence number, but different identifying hash value.* The original Ripple (XRP Ledger) whitepaper [38] provided an initial analysis of the overlap condition required to ensure consistency, coming to the conclusion that the needed minimum overlap was roughly 1/5 of the UNL size. Later, an independent analysis [2] proved that the above condition was insufficient and suggested that the correct bound was >2/5 of the UNL size. To be precise, they showed that in order to ensure the absence of any fork, the intersection set size between the UNL of any two validators needs to be >40% of the maximum UNL size. A recent work by Chase and MacBrough [11] provided a further analysis of the XRP LCP and derived new conditions for its safety and liveness, changing the expectation for the overlap requirement. Below, we report some of their major findings, which will be useful in the subsequent section. Prior to this, we introduce the adversary model used to analyze the safety and liveness of the protocol.

In the traditional distributed computing literature, the most common model employed to capture the role of attackers and their capabilities is the *Threshold Adversary Model*, where the threshold helps in easy characterization of an upper bound on the number of corrupted nodes. By adopting this approach, we can model the XRP Ledger network as if an adversary is in full control of at most t_i nodes in UNL_i for any validator i. The nodes controlled by the adversary are called Byzantine and can deviate from the protocol by performing at least one of the following actions: *(i)* not responding to messages; *(ii)* sending incorrect messages; *(iii)* sending differentiated messages to different nodes. In contrast, we consider as honest any node that follows exactly the prescribed XRP LCP. The honest proportion is equal to $n_i - t_i$. Due to the *FLP impossibility result* [15], safety and liveness cannot be simultaneously guaranteed by any consensus algorithm in the presence of arbitrary asynchrony and Byzantine nodes. In [11], the authors assumed a weak form of asynchrony in order to prove that the system is able to not fall in a state where some honest nodes can never fully validate a new ledger. This last assumption, however, does not seem to be sufficient to guarantee that the system cannot get stuck even in networks where two UNLs disagree only by few nodes. In this regard, the paper showed an example where even with 99% UNL overlap and no Byzantine faults, the system failed to successfully apply the preferred branch strategy, consequently maintaining a ledger chain with two distinct branches (in other words, the nodes were unable to determine a preferred chain of ledgers to converge on). It follows that the XRP LCP cannot get stuck only in the restricted case where the network consists of a single agreed-upon UNL with an arbitrary number of extra nodes.

The most relevant contribution by Chase and MacBrough was the re-analysis of the overlap condition required to ensure safety. According to them, the XRP LCP guarantees fork safety if for every pair of nodes i, j the following holds:

$$O_{i,j} > \frac{n_j}{2} + n_i - q_v + t_{i,j} \tag{16}$$

where $O_{i,j} = |UNL_i \cap UNL_j|$, $q_v = k \cdot n_i$ (cf. Eq. 14) and $t_{i,j} = min\{t_i, t_j, O_{i,j}\}$ is the maximum number of allowed Byzantine faults in $UNL_i \cap UNL_j$ – here we have slightly changed the original notation in order to adapt it to the one used in our formalization. Assuming 80% validation quorum (q_v) (as prescribed in the actual implementation) and 20% faults ($t_{i,j}$), the condition in essence requires roughly >90% UNL agreement.

5.2 Achieving Safety and Liveness in the XRP Ledger

In order to provide a more accurate view of the security provisions of the XRP LCP in terms of safety and liveness, here we make some observations about the three key parameters of the protocol, i.e. UNL overlap, validation quorum and tolerated Byzantine nodes, considering also the discussion recently appeared on the XRP Ledger GitHub repository [42]. We investigate the values $O_{i,j}$, q_v and $t_{i,j}$ displayed in Eq. 16 and in the following we show how safety and liveness tolerances are related to each other and vary according to the assumptions made on the above parameters. To this end, we find it convenient to introduce two additional parameters, namely μ_i and μ_j, which denote the size of the set of surplus nodes for UNL_i and UNL_j, respectively, that is the nodes in UNL_i that are not in common with UNL_j and viceversa: $\mu_i = n_i - O_{i,j}$, $\mu_j = n_j - O_{i,j}$ (Fig. 2). Moreover, we denote by t_s the safety fault tolerance and by t_l the liveness tolerance of the system, i.e. the maximum number of Byzantine nodes the XRP LCP tolerates in order to guarantee safety and liveness, respectively.

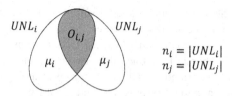

$$n_i = |UNL_i|$$
$$n_j = |UNL_j|$$

Fig. 2. μ_i and μ_j are the set sizes of surplus nodes in UNL_i and UNL_j [27].

Given a pair of nodes i, j with their respective UNLs, and assuming that $n_i < n_j$ and both UNLs have the same percentage of faulty nodes, $t_{i,j} = min\{t_i, t_j, O_{i,j}\} = t_i$. By substituting $O_{i,j}$ with $n_i - \mu_i$ in Eq. 16, we get the following inequality:

$$t_s < -\frac{n_i}{2} - \frac{\mu_i}{2} - \frac{\mu_j}{2} + q_v. \qquad (17)$$

On the other hand, the liveness tolerance t_l is given by:

$$t_l < n_i - q_v. \qquad (18)$$

In general, a consensus protocol providing results that can be relied upon is preferable, rather than one that is able to progress in the presence of faulty nodes but, at the same time, reports impaired results that could undermine consistency. As a result, in order to obtain a validation quorum q_v whose safety fault tolerance t_s meets or exceeds the liveness tolerance t_l, we can use $t_s \geq n_i - q_v$ and get the following:

$$n_i - q_v < -\frac{n_i}{2} - \frac{\mu_i}{2} - \frac{\mu_j}{2} + q_v$$

$$q_v > \frac{3n_i}{4} + \frac{\mu_i}{4} + \frac{\mu_j}{4}. \qquad (19)$$

Unique UNL. Let us now consider the simplest case where the XRP Ledger network consists of a single agreed-upon UNL. In this case, $n_i = n_j = n$, and, consequently, $\mu_i = \mu_j = 0$. By Eq. 19, we obtain $q_v > (3/4)n$, meaning that when there is 100% agreement on participants, reaching a 75% validation quorum is sufficient to fully validate a ledger. Therefore, in Eq. 16 we have $n > n/2 + n - (3/4)n + t_i$, from which we obtain $t_s(= t_i) < (1/4)n$, whereas from Eq. 18 we obtain $t_l < n - (3/4)n = (1/4)n$. As a result, in case $UNL_i = UNL_j$ and $q_v = 0.75n$, both the tolerances are $0.25n$. This means that when less than 25% of trusted nodes are Byzantine, the protocol functions properly.

Keeping valid the assumption $UNL_i = UNL_j$, now we show how t_s and t_l vary when q_v is equal to $0.8n$, as required by the current XRP LCP specification. In this case, the value of the two tolerances are no longer equal: $t_s < (3/10)n$, and $t_l < (1/5)n$. Compared to the previous case in which $q_v = 0.75n$, here the liveness tolerance is lower than the safety fault tolerance, and this implies that the system ability to not get stuck is slightly weakened.

Overlapping UNLs. So far the analysis has focused on the circumstance where the network is composed of a unique UNL. However, the validation quorum increase takes on greater significance in the context in which the UNLs of any two nodes i, j do not completely overlap, i.e. when at least one of the two parameters μ_i and μ_j is > 0. In this regard, we now turn our attention to the total non-overlapping component resulting from the sum of the two individual surpluses μ_i and μ_j of Eq. 17:

$$\mu_i + \mu_j < -n + 2q_v - 2t_s. \tag{20}$$

Let us now consider two cases in which we set the validation quorum first to 80% and then to 90% of the nodes. In the former case, $q_v = 0.8n$ and assuming $t_s = 0.2n$, we can safely allow up to a non-overlap of $0.2n$. In the latter case, $q_v = 0.9n$ and assuming $t_s = 0.1n$, the maximum non-overlap we can safely allow is $0.6n$. Thus, as the above bounds show, as q_v increases, the degree of freedom of any node in the choice of validators to trust, in turn, increases.

To conclude, if we want the system to have a little more liveness, we can increase the sizes of the surplus node sets μ_i and μ_j. Recalling that t_l depends on the quantity $n_i - q_v$, as the values μ_i and μ_j increase, we obtain a higher validation quorum (cf. Eq. 19), and hence the maximum number of allowed Byzantine nodes to guarantee liveness increases. Let us consider an overlap of 90%, i.e. a non-overlap of 10%. If the safety fault tolerance is $0.2n_i$, from Eq. 16 we obtain $q_v > 0.75n_i$, and $t_l < 0.25n_i$. In contrast, if the safety fault tolerance is $0.25n_i$, we obtain $q_v > 0.8n_i$, and hence, $t_l < 0.2n_i$. From this analysis, it emerges that safety and liveness tolerances, validation quorum, and UNLs overlapping set size are strictly correlated, and it is possible to tune these parameters according to the desired properties the system needs to satisfy.

Currently, if no configuration changes are made, each node adopts the default and recommended UNL provided by Ripple. This essentially implies that no disagreement on the participants in the network is allowed, since all the nodes listen to a single list of validators. Accordingly, the XRP LCP is really able to guarantee that the network cannot get stuck as long as the number of Byzantine nodes within the system is limited.

6   Related Work

Research on blockchain platforms has only recently focused on the problem of assessing their underlying consensus protocols on the basis of non-functional properties (with special emphasis on security and privacy). In literature, the work in [16] has been the first to formalize and analyze the fundamental principles behind the Nakamoto consensus, presenting an abstraction of the Bitcoin protocol in synchronous networks (referred to as the *Bitcoin backbone*) and proving that it satisfies certain security properties. This analysis was later extended in [29], where the authors proved that the protocol satisfies a strong form of consistency and liveness in an asynchronous network with a model allowing for dynamic participation and adaptive corruption (assuming a-priori bounded adversarial delays). Further refinements of the above original model of computation were subsequently presented in [17, 18]. Recently, the analysis conducted in [3] focused on the study of the economic forces governing the tension between honest participants and deviating ones, and showed that these forces affect participants' behavior in a way that rational participants end up behaving honestly because this strategy gives them the best utility. A number of other papers have studied the security of several Bitcoin-like consensus mechanisms in a rigorous manner [4, 13, 22, 30]. Although the majority of current research is dealing with blockchains in the permissionless setting, work begins to appear that explores the theoretical foundation and feasibility of reaching consensus in the permissioned setting. For example, the study in [23] formulated an abstraction of the Stellar network by introducing the notion of *Personal Byzantine Quorum Systems*, whereas the work in [19] established a correspondence between the federated voting protocol of Stellar and another protocol for reliable Byzantine broadcast with the aim at putting the basis for their rigorous formalization and proof of correctness.

7   Concluding Remarks

Blockchain technology is widely envisioned as a game-changer for facilitating the transfer of units of value and for securing data. The most important component that all existing DL approaches have in common is a consensus protocol allowing participants to agree on the exact series of events and their outcome at any point in time. The interest in consensus protocols has recently triggered a stimulating line of work aiming at in-depth analysis and rigorous formalization of the security properties holding for the blockchain-based protocols. As a result, in some cases, it has been possible to discover weaknesses or attacks against commonly used blockchain platforms resulting from unforeseen scenarios or weak assumptions that did not hold up during the execution of the protocol [29]. In other cases, the formalization effort has been directed to answer some fundamental questions about the required properties that a DL protocol and its implementation must satisfy [16].

In this paper, we presented a formalization of the XRP Ledger Consensus Protocol, analyzing in detail the process, the interactions amongst the participants, and the timing assumptions necessary for its correct functioning. We gave also a definition for two key security properties for the XRP LCP, that are safety and liveness, and the conditions under which they can be guaranteed, analyzing the correlation amongst some protocol parameters and showing how they can be leveraged to meet some desired liveness/fault tolerance.

Our work can serve as the basis for a further precise description of the XRP Ledger platform relying on some formal language that can be used as input to (semi-)automatic verification tools, in order to prove and verify the correct implementation of the consensus process. In this direction, we plan to provide a complete formalization of the XRP LCP, extending its coverage, and proving additional security properties, in relation also to other blockchain based protocols. The goal is to achieve a deep understanding of the underlying consensus mechanisms, and to foster a comparative analysis, considering both security and performance aspects.

Acknowledgment. This work has been partly supported by the EC within the Project CONCORDIA (H2020-830927).

References

1. Abraham, I., Malkhi, D.: The blockchain consensus layer and BFT. Bull. EATCS **3**(123) (2017). http://eatcs.org/beatcs/index.php/beatcs/article/view/506
2. Armknecht, F., Karame, G.O., Mandal, A., Youssef, F., Zenner, E.: Ripple: Overview and Outlook. In: Conti, M., Schunter, M., Askoxylakis, I. (eds.) Trust 2015. LNCS, vol. 9229, pp. 163–180. Springer, Cham (2015). https://doi.org/10.1007/978-3-319-22846-4_10
3. Badertscher, C., Garay, J., Maurer, U., Tschudi, D., Zikas, V.: But why does it work? a rational protocol design treatment of bitcoin. In: Nielsen, J.B., Rijmen, V. (eds.) EUROCRYPT 2018. LNCS, vol. 10821, pp. 34–65. Springer, Cham (2018). https://doi.org/10.1007/978-3-319-78375-8_2
4. Badertscher, C., Maurer, U., Tschudi, D., Zikas, V.: Bitcoin as a transaction ledger: a composable treatment. In: Katz, J., Shacham, H. (eds.) CRYPTO 2017. LNCS, vol. 10401, pp. 324–356. Springer, Cham (2017). https://doi.org/10.1007/978-3-319-63688-7_11
5. Bano, S., et al.: Consensus in the Age of Blockchains. CoRR abs/1711.03936 (2017). http://arxiv.org/abs/1711.03936
6. Braghin, C., Cimato, S., Cominesi, S.R., Damiani, E., Mauri, L.: Towards blockchain-based e-voting systems. In: Abramowicz, W., Corchuelo, R. (eds.) BIS 2019. LNBIP, vol. 373, pp. 274–286. Springer, Cham (2019). https://doi.org/10.1007/978-3-030-36691-9_24
7. Braghin, C., Cimato, S., Damiani, E., Baronchelli, M.: Designing smart-contract based auctions. In: Yang, C.-N., Peng, S.-L., Jain, L.C. (eds.) SICBS 2018. AISC, vol. 895, pp. 54–64. Springer, Cham (2020). https://doi.org/10.1007/978-3-030-16946-6_5
8. Cachin, C., Tackmann, B.: Asymmetric distributed trust. In: Felber, P., Friedman, R., Gilbert, S., Miller, A. (eds.) 23rd International Conference on Principles of Distributed Systems, OPODIS 2019, 17–19 December, 2019, Neuchâtel, Switzerland. LIPIcs, vol. 153, pp. 7:1–7:16. Schloss Dagstuhl - Leibniz-Zentrum für Informatik (2019). https://doi.org/10.4230/LIPIcs.OPODIS.2019.7
9. Cachin, C., Vukolic, M.: Blockchain Consensus Protocols in the Wild. CoRR abs/1707.01873 (2017). http://arxiv.org/abs/1707.01873
10. Cachin, C., Zanolini, L.: Asymmetric Byzantine Consensus. CoRR abs/2005.08795 (2020). https://arxiv.org/abs/2005.08795
11. Chase, B., MacBrough, E.: Analysis of the XRP Ledger Consensus Protocol. CoRR abs/1802.07242 (2018). http://arxiv.org/abs/1802.07242

12. Christodoulou, K., Iosif, E., Inglezakis, A., Themistocleous, M.: Consensus crash testing: exploring ripple's decentralization degree in adversarial environments. Future Internet **12**(3), 53 (2020)
13. Daian, P., Pass, R., Shi, E.: Snow White: Provably Secure Proofs of Stake. Cryptology ePrint Archive, Report 2016/919 (2016)
14. Damgård, I., Desmedt, Y., Fitzi, M., Nielsen, J.B.: Secure protocols with asymmetric trust. In: Kurosawa, K. (ed.) ASIACRYPT 2007. LNCS, vol. 4833, pp. 357–375. Springer, Heidelberg (2007). https://doi.org/10.1007/978-3-540-76900-2_22
15. Fischer, M.J., Lynch, N.A., Paterson, M.S.: Impossibility of distributed consensus with one faulty process. J. ACM **32**(2), 374–382 (1985). https://doi.org/10.1145/3149.214121
16. Garay, J., Kiayias, A., Leonardos, N.: The bitcoin backbone protocol: analysis and applications. In: Oswald, E., Fischlin, M. (eds.) EUROCRYPT 2015. LNCS, vol. 9057, pp. 281–310. Springer, Heidelberg (2015). https://doi.org/10.1007/978-3-662-46803-6_10
17. Garay, J., Kiayias, A., Leonardos, N.: The bitcoin backbone protocol with chains of variable difficulty. In: Katz, J., Shacham, H. (eds.) CRYPTO 2017. LNCS, vol. 10401, pp. 291–323. Springer, Cham (2017). https://doi.org/10.1007/978-3-319-63688-7_10
18. Garay, J.A., Kiayias, A., Leonardos, N., Panagiotakos, G.: Bootstrapping the blockchain, with applications to consensus and fast PKI setup. In: Abdalla, M., Dahab, R. (eds.) PKC 2018. LNCS, vol. 10770, pp. 465–495. Springer, Cham (2018). https://doi.org/10.1007/978-3-319-76581-5_16
19. García-Pérez, Á., Gotsman, A.: Federated byzantine quorum systems. In: Cao, J., Ellen, F., Rodrigues, L., Ferreira, B. (eds.) 22nd International Conference on Principles of Distributed Systems, OPODIS 2018, 17–19 December 2018, Hong Kong, China. LIPIcs, vol. 125, pp. 17:1–17:16. Schloss Dagstuhl - Leibniz-Zentrum für Informatik (2018). https://doi.org/10.4230/LIPIcs.OPODIS.2018.17
20. Gramoli, V.: From blockchain consensus back to byzantine consensus. Future Gener. Comput. Syst. **107**, 760–769 (2017)
21. Halpin, H., Piekarska, M.: Introduction to security and privacy on the blockchain. In: EuroS&P 2017 - 2nd IEEE European Symposium on Security and Privacy, Workshops, April 2017. https://doi.org/10.1109/EuroSPW.2017.43, https://hal.inria.fr/hal-01673293
22. Kiayias, A., Russell, A., David, B., Oliynykov, R.: Ouroboros: a provably secure proof-of-stake blockchain protocol. In: Katz, J., Shacham, H. (eds.) CRYPTO 2017. LNCS, vol. 10401, pp. 357–388. Springer, Cham (2017). https://doi.org/10.1007/978-3-319-63688-7_12
23. Losa, G., Gafni, E., Mazières, D.: Stellar consensus by instantiation. In: Suomela, J. (ed.) 33rd International Symposium on Distributed Computing (DISC 2019). Leibniz International Proceedings in Informatics (LIPIcs), vol. 146, pp. 27:1–27:15. Schloss Dagstuhl-Leibniz-Zentrum fuer Informatik, Dagstuhl, Germany (2019). https://doi.org/10.4230/LIPIcs.DISC.2019.27, http://drops.dagstuhl.de/opus/volltexte/2019/11334
24. Malkhi, D., Nayak, K., Ren, L.: Flexible Byzantine Fault Tolerance. In: Cavallaro, L., Kinder, J., Wang, X., Katz, J. (eds.) Proceedings of the 2019 ACM SIGSAC Conference on Computer and Communications Security, CCS 2019, London, UK, 11–15 November 2019, pp. 1041–1053. ACM (2019). https://doi.org/10.1145/3319535.3354225
25. Malkhi, D., Reiter, M.K.: Byzantine quorum systems. In: Leighton, F.T., Shor, P.W. (eds.) Proceedings of the 29th Annual ACM Symposium on the Theory of Computing, El Paso, Texas, USA, 4–6 May 1997, pp. 569–578. ACM (1997). https://doi.org/10.1145/258533.258650
26. Mauri, L., Cimato, S., Damiani, E.: A comparative analysis of current cryptocurrencies. In: Proceedings of the 4th International Conference on Information Systems Security and Privacy - Volume 1: ICISSP, pp. 127–138. INSTICC, SciTePress (2018). https://doi.org/10.5220/0006648801270138

27. Mauri, L., Cimato, S., Damiani, E.: A Formal Approach for the Analysis of the XRP Ledger Consensus Protocol. In: Furnell, S., Mori, P., Weippl, E.R., Camp, O. (eds.) Proceedings of the 6th International Conference on Information Systems Security and Privacy, ICISSP 2020, Valletta, Malta, 25–27 February 2020, pp. 52–63. SCITEPRESS (2020). https://doi.org/10.5220/0008954200520063

28. Nakamoto, S.: Bitcoin: A Peer-to-Peer Electronic Cash System (2008). https://bitcoin.org/bitcoin.pdf

29. Pass, R., Seeman, L., Shelat, A.: Analysis of the blockchain protocol in asynchronous networks. In: Coron, J.-S., Nielsen, J.B. (eds.) EUROCRYPT 2017. LNCS, vol. 10211, pp. 643–673. Springer, Cham (2017). https://doi.org/10.1007/978-3-319-56614-6_22

30. Pass, R., Shi, E.: The sleepy model of consensus. In: Takagi, T., Peyrin, T. (eds.) ASIACRYPT 2017. LNCS, vol. 10625, pp. 380–409. Springer, Cham (2017). https://doi.org/10.1007/978-3-319-70697-9_14

31. Pease, M., Shostak, R., Lamport, L.: Reaching agreement in the presence of faults. J. ACM **27**(2), 228–234 (1980)

32. Pérez, D., Xu, J., Livshits, B.: We Know What They've Been Put Through: Revisiting High-scalability Blockchain Transactions. CoRR abs/2003.02693 (2020). https://arxiv.org/abs/2003.02693

33. Rawat, D.B., Chaudhary, V., Doku, R.: Blockchain: Emerging Applications and Use Cases. CoRR abs/1904.12247 (2019). http://arxiv.org/abs/1904.12247

34. Ripple Labs Inc.: Ripple. https://ripple.com/ (a), https://ripple.com/. Accessed 01 June 2020

35. Ripple Labs Inc.: XRP Ledger Dev Portal. https://xrpl.org/index.html (b), https://xrpl.org/index.html. Accessed 01 June 2020

36. Ripple Labs Inc.: Ripple Source, GitHub repository. https://github.com/ripple/rippled/tree/develop/src/ripple (c), https://github.com/ripple/rippled/tree/develop/src/ripple. Accessed 01 June 2020

37. Saad, M., et al.: Exploring the Attack Surface of Blockchain: A Systematic Overview. CoRR abs/1904.03487 (2019). http://arxiv.org/abs/1904.03487

38. Schwartz, D., Youngs, N., Britto, A.: The Ripple Protocol Consensus Algorithm. Ripple Labs Inc., White Paper (2014). https://ripple.com/files/ripple_consensus_whitepaper.pdf

39. Vukolic, M.: The origin of quorum systems. Bull. EATCS **101**, 125–147 (2010). http://eatcs.org/beatcs/index.php/beatcs/article/view/183

40. Vukolić, M.: The quest for scalable blockchain fabric: proof-of-work vs. BFT replication. In: Camenisch, J., Kesdoğan, D. (eds.) iNetSec 2015. LNCS, vol. 9591, pp. 112–125. Springer, Cham (2016). https://doi.org/10.1007/978-3-319-39028-4_9

41. Wang, W., et al.: A Survey on Consensus Mechanisms and Mining Management in Blockchain networks. CoRR abs/1805.02707 (2018). http://arxiv.org/abs/1805.02707

42. Wilson, B.: Raise quorum/increase fault tolerance, June 2018. https://github.com/ripple/rippled/issues/2604. Accessed 01 Oct 2019

43. Xiao, Y., Zhang, N., Lou, W., Hou, Y.T.: A Survey of Distributed Consensus Protocols for Blockchain Networks. CoRR abs/1904.04098 (2019). http://arxiv.org/abs/1904.04098

End to End Autorship Email Verification Framework for a Secure Communication

Giacomo Giorgi[✉], Andrea Saracino, and Fabio Martinelli

Informatics and Telematics Institute (IIT) of National Research Council,
via G. Moruzzi 1, Pisa, Italy
{giacomo.giorgi,andrea.saracino,fabio.martinelli}@iit.cnr.it

Abstract. The paper proposes an alternative email account protection to prevent a very specific targeting email attacks where an attacker can impersonate a legitimate/trusted sender to steal personal information to the recipient. Authorship mechanism based on the analysis of the author's writing style and implemented through binary traditional and deep learning classifiers is applied to build the email verification mechanism. A flexible architecture, where the authorship component can be placed in different locations, is proposed. Due to its location and consequently to the email data available, can be exploited an individual writing style, or an end to end writing style learning related to the sender-receiver communication. The system is validated on two different dataset (i) the well-known public Enron dataset, with the experiments showing the author verification accuracy of 96.5% and 99% respectively for the individual and end to end writing style learning and (ii) our private dataset, with accuracy results of 98.3% and 97%. An alternative classification training, that exploits the partition of the dataset in subsets having approximately the same length, is presented. From the results obtained is proved how such training approach outperforms the traditional training where emails of different lengths are contained in the same training dataset. The overall results obtained proved that the authorship mechanism proposed is a promising alternative support technique exploitable as an email anti-scam or anti-theft tool to guarantee secure email communication.

Keywords: Machine learning · Deep learning · Privacy-preserving · Email authorship · Email spoofing · Scam emails · Spear-phishing

1 Introduction

Nowadays, email is one of the primary forms of communication used. Its large diffusion has allowed the physical distance reduction between the end-users, the speeding up of the communication, and the cost minimization. Despite the listed benefits, it has become one of the main instruments used by malicious users to compromise the end-user privacy information through identity theft, fraud, or scam techniques. The diffusion of spam emails have been used purely for advertising purposes, but have been used also

This work has been partially supported by H2020 EU-funded projects SPARTA, GA 830892, C3ISP, GA 700294 and EIT-Digital Project HII, PRIN Governing Adaptive.

by cybercriminals to perform damage to the victim in order to get money or deceiving recipients to share personal information (e.g. bank or financial data). The social engineering techniques used in the spam email are referred to as a category of security attacks in which someone manipulates others into revealing information that can be used to steal, data, access to systems, access to cellular phones, money, or even your own identity [11]. Such technique in conjunction with the spoofing email attack, that occurs when the imposter can forge an email header to bring up the message originated from someone or somewhere other than the legitimate source, can be one of the most dangerous email attacks to steal personal information to the victim. Other dangerous email attacks can come from forged email accounts. In such case, the attacker, performing an identity theft, can send emails to the victim impersonating the legitimate sender, and applying social engineering techniques, deceive the recipient to share personal information. One of the most important spam attacks that use social engineering techniques is the *spear phishing* where the scam email is personalized to the target victims. Such emails containing victim-specific instead of general content can appear more realistic, and thus, harder to detect. While the majority of spear phishing attacks are coming from an unknown or "pseudo-known" email address, in this paper we focus on identifying a specific class of spear-phishing emails where the attack is performed using a trusted email address with which the victim has already communicated in the past. In such a case, the attack can become more realistic and can achieve a high degree of success because people are more inclined to open an email when they think a legitimate or familiar source has sent it. In this paper, is introduced a new countermeasure mechanism based on email authorship verification able to verify the identity of the sender analyzing the writing style of his emails. Different architectures are presented where the authorship component is placed in a different location (client or server-side). It is shown as different locations can imply different learning writing style, and thus, as well as the traditional individual writing style learning, where the aim is to learn a specific unique writing style (like a biometric trait) associated to the sender, a novel learning related to the communication sender-receiver is presented (end to end writing style). The two learning approaches are applied to two different datasets (public and our private collected dataset). The results obtained proved the effectiveness of the end to end communication learning respect to individual learning since a person can assume different writing style depending on the recipient.

This paper extends the one presented in [9] by presenting as new contributions (i) the introduction of a new private dataset (ii) the extension of the attack scenario with a new attack based on the forged email account credentials (iii) the extension of the architecture based on different location of the authorship system component (iv) the experiments done on the new dataset in order to validate the effectiveness of the approach proposed. The rest of the paper is organized as follows: Sect. 2 describes the background concepts related to the spam emails and the authorship attribution system, in Sect. 3 is reported the related works related to the email spear-phishing detection and authorship attribution of textual information, in Sect. 4 is described the attack model considered and is detailed the architecture proposed with its different versions. In that section also a comparison between the different versions is given. Section 5 describes the implementation of the authorship component based on features based and word embedding classifiers. Section 6, provides details related to the dataset used (public and private), and an explanation of each training approach and experiments done is given.

Section 7 shows the results obtained from the experiments addressed. In Sect. 8 is discussed the effectiveness of the proposed approach. In Sect. 9 conclusions and future works are given.

2   Background

In this section, the background concepts related to the spam email attack, focusing on the spear-phishing and the spoofing attack techniques, are given. In addition, the introduction of the authorship problem defining the two possible writing style learning analyzed in the paper is presented.

2.1   Email Spoofing

The email spoofing is a form of spam attack where an attacker forges an email so that it appears sent by someone else. The attacker intends to force the victims to send back sensitive information or download infected file attachment (e.g., ransomware). Due to the structure of the Simple Mail Transfer Protocol (SMTP) used in the electronic mail transmission, email services by default are not capable of identifying and blocking deceptive emails with a forged sender name or email address. When the TCP connection between the sender and the receiver is established, the SMTP sender provides the following address information:

- RFC2821 Envelope: metadata that does not appear in the SMTP header contained: (i) MAIL FROM: specifies the email address of the sender and is presented to the SMTP receiver as the *Return-path* (the address where non-delivery receipts are to be sent) and (ii) RCPT TO: Specifies the email address of the recipient.
- RFC2822 Message: metadata contained in the SMTP header that begins when the DATA command is issued. It is composed of: (i) HEADER FROM: modifiable by the attacker and it specifies the email address of the sender. The protocol does not check if the sending system is authorized to send on behalf of that address and (ii) HEADER TO: The email address of the recipient.

Figure 1 shows the SMTP messages exchanged during a spoofing attack and a spoofing email where the Envelope message, hidden to the receiver, is different from the forged *From field* contained in the email header visible to the receiver. Such a technique can be used by the spear-phishing attack [15] that is a form of email scam intended to steal sensitive information from a specific victim. Unlike traditional spam attacks, spear phishing messages are tailored to the characteristics of the victim. Such characteristic requires much more effort on gathering victim information, but have a higher degree of success.

2.2   Authorship

The Authorship attribution process is defined as the problem of determining the likely authorship of a given document. It can be divided into two sub-problems: (i) authorship identification and (ii) authorship verification. The goal of the identification is to predict

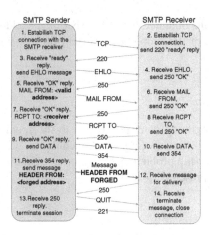

Fig. 1. Email spoofing attack.

the author of an unknown text within a closed set of candidate authors where, from the classification point of view, it is a multi-class text classification task. Conversely, the goal of the authorship verification is to predict whether a text is written by the declared author and it can be modeled as a binary classification problem in which we attempt to distinguish a single author (target class) from all other authors (not target class). In literature, the problem has been addressed through a study of the linguistic style of a person taking as assumption that each author has distinctive writing habits which can be represented by writing stylistic features. Through our analysis, the writing style of a person, can be considered under two different writing style abstraction level: (i) *individual writing style*, which is related to the generic writing style of a person discernible in every context (e.g. a biometric trait of the user) and (ii) *end to end writing style*, related to a user writing style used only with a specific receipts (e.g. a biometric train of the communication sender-receiver). The concept of *individual writing style* is related to the fact that it is possible to detect distinctive stylistic features that do not change respect to the context, situation, or recipient. Such independence led to consider the individual writing style as a measurable human trait such as a biometric characteristic. Therefore analyzing text/messages sent by an author to a subset of recipients, it is possible to understand the individual writing style of the sender and infers the author of the text/messages sent to new recipients. The new concept of *End to End writing style* is based on the fact that a person can assume different writing style depending on the recipient (e.g., colleague, friend, family member), therefore infer the author of a text/message it is possible only analyzing the interaction sender-receiver in order to learn a custom linguistic fingerprinting for each communication.

3   Related Work

In this section, the main spam email detection work is presented. In addition, an extensive panoramic related to the authorship work are given. In the field of spear-phishing email detection, different works are proposed on social media data. In [6], a deep study on the social and stylometric features used to distinguish spear-phishing from not spear-phishing emails is done. They applied machine learning algorithms to a labeled dataset, reaching an overall accuracy of 97.76% in identifying spear-phishing emails. In [13], is introduced four categories of email profiling features that capture various characteristics of spear-phishing emails. They applied a graph-based learning model for campaign attribute and detection. In [12], they propose a hybrid feature selection approach considering both content-based and behavior-based. They achieved 94% accuracy rate on a publicly test corpus. The aforementioned work concentrates on distinguishing phishing emails from legitimate ones, trying to learn the generic characteristics of the spear-phishing emails. To the best of our knowledge, there are no works that consider the phishing detection more oriented to understand the specific pattern of the legitimate sender or more specifically the communication sender-receiver.

Authorship is a topic widely treated in literature and in particular in the forensic linguistics field where the aim is to identify linguistic features that can give information about the identity of an anonymous text. We take into consideration the differentiation between feature-based and deep learning authorship classifiers, as well as the differentiation between authorship for identification and verification. A schematization of the different branches in the authorship field is shown in Fig. 2. The first works on authorship were related to the attribution of an author to a specific textbook or general text document well structured and having a long size. The new investigations are focused on authorship analysis of online documents that have reduced text size and in general, not well structured like social messages or emails [1, 23]. The main approach used to solve that problem is to use the stylometric features manually extracted to specify the writing style of a person through traditional machine learning algorithms. The effectiveness of deep learning neural networks in Natural Language Processing (NLP), have provided advantages in feature extraction, and some techniques have also been applied in the authorship field. Most of the authorship works are focused on the identification problem (attribution of identity to a given text), in [28] the authors present an online message authorship identification framework based on four types of writing style (lexical, syntactic, structural and content-specific).

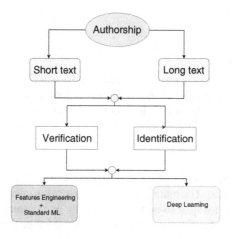

Fig. 2. Authorship domain.

They experimented with three features based on classification techniques on English online text with an average length of 169 words. They achieved 97% of accuracy in identifying 20 identities through 30, 40 messages per author. In [25] is presented another work on authorship identification of short messages based on a deep learning model. The authors presented a Convolutional Neural Network for the author attribution of tweets achieving 76% of accuracy for 50 authors with 1000 tweets each.

Another authorship subfield studied in short message analysis is the verification problem (verify whether the written text belongs to who declares to be). In such a context, in [3], the authors propose a machine learning model for authorship similarity detection of short text through the manual extraction of 150 stylistic features. Deep learning models have also been applied to the authorship verification problem for short messages, in [18] is presented a deep learning model for automatic feature extraction directly from the input text. They implemented a Convolutional Neural Network ables to analyze the raw input email text and extract the discriminate features to verify the genuineness of the author. A summary schema of the different research fields in the authorship domain is reported in Fig. 2. Table 1 summarizes the comparison between our authorship work and the studies in this field. To the best of our knowledge, there are no works that consider the authorship attribution as the process of determining the authorship of a given communication sender-receiver and the application of such a method in order to protect the email account from spear-phishing attacks.

Table 1. Authorship works comparison.

Ref.	Dataset	Text size	Identities	End 2 end verification	Sender verification
[2]	Enron	500 chars	87	-	EER 14.35%
[15]	Enron	<95 words	52	-	Accuracy 97%
[23]	Twitter	1000 chars	50	-	Accuracy 76%
Our	Enron	>20 words	67	Accuracy 99%	Accuracy 96.5%
Our	Our dataset	>20 words	5	Accuracy 98.3%	Accuracy 97%

4   Scenario

In this section are presented the possible attack scenarios and the architectures proposed to solve the problem analyzing each one under different viewpoints that taking into account the learning capabilities and the security offered.

4.1   Attack Model

In this section is detailed the threat model explaining how and which mail attacks are considered in our scenario. The main goal of the attacker is to steal sensitive information from a specific victim using a fooled mail account or the mail address of a trusted account for the victim. The two attack cases considered are presented in the following:

- **Targeting Scam Attack:** in such a case, we assume that the adversary knows only the recipient's email address (victim email address) and an email address of a trusted source for the victim. Despite the attacker does not have the control of the trusted mail account, it (forging the sender email address on the email header) can impersonate the trusted source and it can ask sensitive information to the victim.
- **Attack from a Forged Email Account:** in such cases, we assume that the sender mail account is under control of an attacker (identity theft) and it can send an email directly from that account to a specific victim known by the forged user. Unlike the scam attack, the adversary impersonates the trusted source without the need to forge the email header and can ask personal information to the victim.

Figure 3 and Fig. 4 show respectively the targeting scam attack and the email attack from a forged email account.

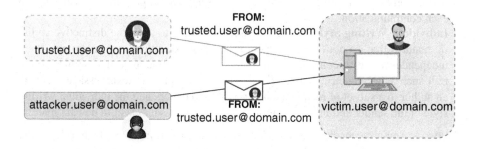

Fig. 3. Targeting scam attack [9].

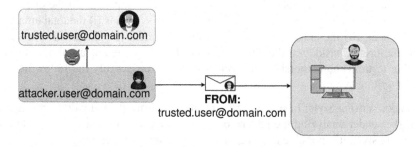

Fig. 4. Email attack with identity theft.

4.2 Architecture

In this section are proposed different system architectures based on the different locations of the authorship attribution component and the training data considered. In addition, are analyzed the advantages and disadvantages of each proposed architecture in terms of (i) learning capabilities and (ii) security offered. An email system is referred to as the exchange of information between one sender and one or more receivers. The email communication can be seen as a client-server communication where are involved the sender, the receivers, and the mail servers. The role of the mail server is to manage the user mailboxes storing the sent and received messages and implementing the delivery of email messages between users. Considering the nature of the email communication, the authorship attribution component can be located on (i) the client-side (sender or receiver) or on the (ii) mail server side. Depending on the location of the authorship attribution component, it can access different information, and consequently, it can offer different writing style learning degrees. Such degrees can be differentiated in the following learning writing styles:

- **End to End Communication Writing Style:** in such a case, the goal is to learn the specific style of sender-receiver communication. Considering that a person can assume different writing styles depending on the recipient (e.g., colleague, friend, family member), infer the author of a text/message it is possible only analyzing the interaction sender-receiver to learn a custom linguistic fingerprinting associated to each communication.
- **Individual Writing Style:** in such a case, the goal is to learn the distinctive stylistic features that do not change respect to the context, situation, or recipient. Such independence led to consider the individual writing style as a measurable human trait such as a biometric characteristic. Therefore analyzing text/messages sent by an author to a subset of recipients, it is possible to understand the individual writing style of the sender and infers the author of the text/messages sent to new recipients.

The two learning mechanisms need different data information from which to learn the specific writing style pattern. Data information can be different depending on the location of the authorship attribution component, and thus, it is possible to refer to different architectures as described in the following paragraphs.

Authorship on the Client Side. Placing the authorship component on the client-side, the exploitable data information with which trains the system is (i) the total email sent by the client, (ii) the email sent to each specific recipient (iii) the email received by a specific user. Considering the three different aforementioned data information, it is possible to train the authorship component to learn respectively the following three type of writing style:

- Sender Writing Style: In such a case, the aim is to learn the individual writing style of the sender analyzing the pattern of its sent emails. Once learned the individual writing style, it is possible to detect an email sent by a non-legitimate sender. Therefore an attacker although having access to the victim's email account cannot send an email without knowing his writing style. In that case, the sender authorship attribution system can be considered as an *anti-theft tool*.
- End To End Communication Writing Style: In such a case, the writing style is learned from each specific communication sender-receiver. As in the sender writing style case, an attacker although having access to the victim email account, not only cannot send an email without knowing his writing style but cannot send an email without known the exact sender writing style towards the specific receiver (victim) to be fooled. Also in that case the end to end authorship attribution system can work as an *anti-theft tool*.

– Receiver Writing Style: In such a case, the writing style is learned from the received emails. Knowing that information a scam email coming from an attacker through a forged account can be detected and marked as a non trusted email by the authorship system, working as a *scam tool*.

Figure 6 shows the architecture based on the authorship attribution component located on the client-side. The main disadvantage concerns the receiver's writing style learning. In such case the limited number of emails known by a client related to a specific receiver cannot sufficient to learn accurately the pattern of an individual receiver writing style, hence that case can be equal to the sender-receiver communication writing style due to the absence of additional information respect to that case.

Authorship on Server Side. Considering the server-side, the authorship component can be trained considering the sent or the received emails, in such case the data information available to train the system is the same as in the client-side with the additional information related to the receiver writing style. Considering the best case where the sender and the receiver belong to the same mail server, both the sender and the receiver emails are known. This allows us to learn the sender, the receiver and the sender-receiver communication writing style (Fig. 5 shows the best case). If the sender and the receiver accounts belong to different mail servers, the sender mail server can know only the received emails of its registered clients. The receiver writing style in that case is less characterized respect to the best case. The worst-case happens when the sender and the receiver belong to different mail servers and the sender mail server manages only the communication between the sender and the receiver. In such a case to learn accurately the pattern of the individual receiver writing style is possible only with a trusted sharing of the knowledge between the mail servers. Figure 5 shows the architecture where the authorship component is placed on the server-side.

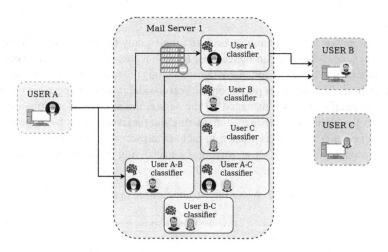

Fig. 5. Authorship on server side.

Comparison. In such paragraph is discussed the comparison between the authorship attribution architectures presented in the previous paragraph. As comparison parameters have been considered the different writing styles learnable by the authorship component, the degree of protection offered in terms of security, and the number of classifiers needed to build the architecture. Table 2 shows for each architecture (depending on the data information used to train the authorship and its location), the type of writing style learnable, and the type of security protection offered (anti-theft and/or anti-scam). Placing the authorship component on the client-side and considering as training data the email sent by a user, it is possible to learn both an end to end writing style for each sender-receiver communication and the individual writing style of the sender. Considering such implementation, the authorship attribution component acts as an anti-theft tool able to block a suspicious email send if the writing style does not match with the sender's writing style.

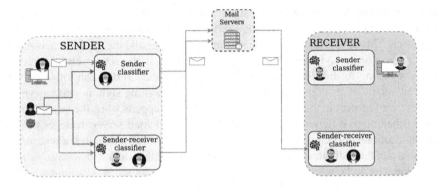

Fig. 6. Authorship on client side.

Considering as training data the received emails, only the writing style of the communication sender-receiver can be learned. In such a case, the system can work as an anti-scam tool able to detect and block the suspicious received emails. While considering the authorship component placed on the server-side, if the training set is composed by the sent emails of a user managed by the server, the amount of information is the same as in the client case, whereas considering the received emails by a specific user the number of data available is greater. In fact, a mail server despite that does not manage that account, can learn its user writing style accessing the mail sent by that user to

Table 2. Authorship architectures comparison.

Authorship location	Training data	E2E writing style	Individual writing style	Anti-theft	Anti-scam
Client	Sent emails	v	v	v	x
Client	Received emails	v	x	x	v
Server	Sent emails	v	v	v	x
Server	Received emails	v	v	v	v

multiple recipients managed by the mail server. Whereby the authorship system can be used as an anti-theft and anti-scam tool.

5 Authorship Implementation

The email authorship verification can be modeled as a text binary classification problem to distinguish the *target class* (email sent by the declared author) from the *not target class* (email sent by an author different from who declares to be). The two types of classifiers used in the experiments can be divided into two classes based on the feature extraction method used: (i) features engineering-based, which require domain knowledge of the data to extract features, and (ii) word embedding based, which perform an automatic feature extraction process to learn a words representation from the data. Such representation is learned during the training phase and it tries to assign to each word a vector in such a way that a similar word used in the target email has a similar vector in the word embedding representation, conversely, different words have distant vectors.

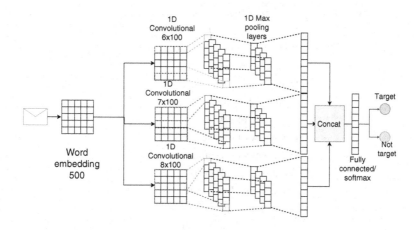

Fig. 7. CNN architecture [9].

5.1 Features Based Classifier

Features based classifiers used in the experiments, consider a set of linguistic features validated in many authorship verification works [2,28]. The three main elements that describe a language are lexis, syntax, and semantics. The language varies from one nation to another, to one context to another, or from one person to another one, and consequently, the lexical, syntactic, and semantic features undergo a variation. The features considered in our work are divided into lexical, syntactical, and structural features. The lexical features are text items that can be a word, part of a word, or a chain of words. Lexical items are the basic building blocks of a language's vocabulary and can be used to measuring the lexical richness of a writing style. By definition, the syntax is the set of rules, principles, and processes that govern the structure of sentences in a given language. Finally, the structural features measure the text organization in terms of the number of sentences or sentence length. The complete list of features used is reported in Table 3 [9]. As classifiers, seven different states of art machine learning algorithms are experimented: Nearest Neighbors [5], Radial Basis Function kernel SVM (RBF SVM) [26], Decision Tree [21], Random Forest [14], AdaBoost [8], SGD [16] and Logistic regression [20].

5.2 Word Embedding Classifier

Neural Networks (NN) require input data as sequences of encoded integers so that each word has to be represented by a unique integer. Therefore it is necessary an encoding schema that represents a sequence of text in an integer vector. Word embedding is a

Table 3. Linguistic features [9].

Category	Feature
Lexical	Number of characters (C)
	Number of lower characters/C
	Number of Upper characters/C
	Number of white space/C
	Number of special char/C
	Number of vowels/C
	Frequency of vowels
	Frequency of non Vowels
	Frequency of special char
	Number of words (W)
	Average length per word
	Number of unique words
	Word (W) - Char (C) ratio
	Most frequently words
	Word 2 and 3-grams
Structural	Number of short words/W
	Number of long words/W
	Number of Sentences (S)
	Average number of words in Sentences
	Number of sentences beginning with Uppercase/S
	Number of sentences beginning with Lowercase/S
Syntactical	Number of punctuation
	Punctuation frequency
	Number of symbols
	Symbols frequency

technique for representing words and documents using a dense vector representation [19], its aim, is a text description where for each word in the vocabulary corresponds a real value vector in a high-dimensional space. The vectors are learned in such a way the words that have similar meanings have similar representations in the vector space. Such text representation is more expressive than more classical methods like bag-of-words, where relationships between words or tokens are ignored, or forced in bigram and trigram approaches. In every network implemented, the embedding layer is initialized with random weights to learn, along with the model, an embedding space for all of the words in the training dataset (custom word embedding). In this way, the vocabulary created reflects the terms contained in the dataset, and it is independent of the language. Two different types of deep learning classifiers based on word embedding have been experimented: (i) Convolutional Neural Network and (ii) Recurrent Convolutional Neural Network.

Convolutional Neural Network. During recent years, Convolutional Neural Network (CNN) has achieved great performances in the Computer Vision field. The extension of the CNN in other fields has proved the effectiveness also in Natural Language Processing (NLP), outperforming state of the art [27]. The CNN architecture is composed of a combination of layers that, performing a non-linear operation (convolution and subsampling), can extract essential features from the input data (text sentences in our case). Convolutional layers apply a set of learnable filters to the input with small receptive fields. Such filters are a sort of mask that is applied to the word representation of the input text through a sliding window to detect different text patterns. The set of features extracted through the filters are called *feature map*. The convolutional operation is typically followed by a subsampling operation performed by a max-pooling layer. This layer aims to reduce the dimensionality of the feature map and extract the most significant features. The architecture implemented is composed of three essential part: (i) Custom Word embedding, (ii) Convolutional part, and (iii) Fully connected part. As convolutional neural network, we experimented a multi-channel Convolutional network [22], composed of a custom word embedding of dimension 2000 with 10000 maximal amount of words in the vocabulary, able to represent each text sequence with maximum length 500 through an integer vector of size 2000. The vector representations are routed to three different Convolutional channels having different learnable filter dimensions (3, 4, and 5) able to extract distinctive feature maps. On the bottom of the network, the feature maps extracted are concatenated, and a fully connected layer with 2 softmax units is applied in order to compute the probability of the input email to belong to the declared sender. The complete Convolutional architecture used, as reported in [9] is shown in Fig. 7.

Recurrent Convolutional Neural Network. Recurrent Neural Networks (RNNs) are successfully applied to sequential information such as speech recognition [10], video analysis [7], or time series [4]. Different from the traditional neural networks, it considers the dependency between each sequence input value. For this reason, it can successfully be applied to the text analysis context where the text sequences are related to each other. Bidirectional RNNs [24] is a variant of RNN based on the idea that the output at a specific time is dependent not only on the previous element but also on the future element of the sequence. The network designed and implemented to solve the authorship problem is a combination of a Recurrent (RNN) and a Convolutional (CNN) Neural network (RCNN). The RCNN is able to capture contextual information and text representation, applying respectively recurrent and convolutional layers. The network designed and implemented is composed of four part: (i) Custom word embedding, (ii) Recurrent, (iii) Convolutional and (iv) fully connected part. The text representation through word embedding as in the Convolutional network, is composed of 2000 dimension, a maximum vocabulary size of 10000 and maximum text sequence length set to 500. Figure 8, described in [9], shows the entire network implemented.

6   Experiments

In this section are described the two datasets used to test the classifiers and the approaches proposed for the training phase.

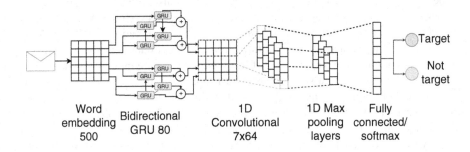

Word embedding 500   Bidirectional GRU 80   1D Convolutional 7x64   1D Max pooling layers   Fully connected/ softmax   Target   Not target

Fig. 8. RCNN architecture [9].

6.1   Dataset Analysis

To test the proposed classifiers in the context of email authorship, we considered (i) a public email dataset and (ii) our collected private email dataset.

Public Dataset. The public dataset used is the *Enron Email Dataset* [17]. It is a set of emails collected and mantained by the CALO Project (A Cognitive Assistant that Learns and Organizes)[1]. It contains data from about 150 users, mostly senior management of Enron company. This data was originally made public, and posted to the web, by the Federal Energy Regulatory Commission during its investigation. For each of the 150 identity the dataset contains the *inbox folder* and the *sent folder*. The total emails included in the dataset are 517401, sent by 20328 different email accounts to 58564 different receivers. The dataset is analyzed under the two following viewpoints: (i) end to end communication (sender-receiver) (ii) client email sent.

---

[1] https://enrondata.readthedocs.io/en/latest/data/calo-enron-email-dataset/.

Client Dataset. The dataset contains 20328 senders of which 136 of them have more than 500 emails sent, and only 67 have more than 1000 emails. Analyzing the email lengths of the dataset, we can identify three different email set: (i) Short emails: emails having less than 20 words, (ii) Medium emails: emails having more than 19 and less than 51 words and (iii) Long emails: emails having more than 50 words.

Table 4. Enron senders and communications [9].

Email length	Senders	Sender-receiver communications
No constraint	67	256
words >50	49	126
20 <words <50	13	256
words <20	5	256

That analysis shows as the majority of the identity sent long emails followed by the medium emails and only few identities sent short emails. The number of senders having more than 1000 emails considering different length is summarized in the second column of the Table 4 as reported in [9].

End to End Communication Dataset. In such scenario, we are interested in considering users that have a considerable number of emails received from the same identity to learn with more accuracy the end to end writing style of the sender toward the receiver. Considering 100 as the minimum number of emails that a single class has to contain to train a classifier, the number of receivers with more than 100 emails received from a single user and more than 100 emails received from other users is 26, while 256 are the total amount of sender-receiver interactions. Such information is reported in the third column of Table 4, published in [9].

Private Dataset. The private dataset is our collected dataset (not published for privacy reasons) used to test the flexibility of the framework in a real scenario. It has been built collecting emails from our institutional accounts. The accounts involved in the construction of the dataset are 5 formed by 2 receivers and 3 senders as showed in Fig. 9. It shows the number of emails exchanged between the user involved in the communication.

Through that dataset, it is possible to experiment the learning capabilities of the authorship component both in the client and the server scenario. In fact, considering the authorship on the sender scenario, it is possible to learn (i) the end to end communication between Sender A - Receiver A/B, Sender B - Receiver B and Sender C - Receiver A, (ii) the sender writing style of Sender A, Sender B, and Sender C.

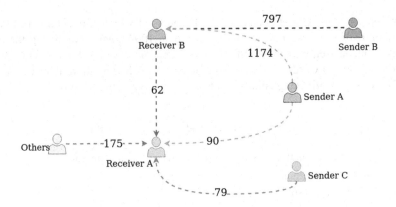

Fig. 9. Private dataset.

Table 5. Number of emails per communication.

	Sender A				Sender B				Sender C				Others			
	Total	< 20	20< w< 50	> 50	Total	< 20	20< w< 50	> 50	Total	< 20	20< w< 50	> 50	Total	< 20	20< w< 50	> 50
Receiver A	90	31%	50%	19%	-	-	-	-	79	21%	39%	40%	90	19%	32%	49%
Receiver B	1174	35%	55%	20%	797	44%	44%	12%	-	-	-	-	797	54%	35%	11%

While focusing the attention on the server-side and considering Receiver A and Receiver B belonging to the same mail server, it is possible experiments the individual learning writing style of the Sender A sharing the received emails by the Receiver A and Receiver B.

Table 5 shows the email distribution on each communication for each length subset.

6.2 Training and Evaluation

In this section, the training approaches used in both the scenario (individual writing style, end to end writing style) are detailed.

Individual Writing Style Training. For every sender identity contained in the dataset, a binary classifier has been trained, selecting its inbox emails as a positive class and a list of emails randomly selected from other senders as a negative class. In the client-side scenario, the negative class is taken from the received emails by the client, instead of in the case of authorship on the server-side that data are selected from the list of accounts managed by the mail server. During the training, we considered identities having more than 1000 emails sent and for each of one have been trained a binary classifier considering a balanced training set selecting randomly 1000 emails sent by the target class (sender) and 1000 emails randomly selected from the sent emails of other identities of the dataset. As a testing phase, a 10 cross-fold validation has been performed using 100 testing emails for the positive class and 100 emails for the negative class.

End to End Email Verification Training. In the end to end email verification context, for each recipient identity have been selected a set of sender identities, and in turn, choosing a single target sender (target communication) has been trained a binary classifier using the target emails as positive class and the remaining sender emails as negative class. During the training phase, 256 sender-receiver communications having more than 100 emails, have been considered. A random sub-sampling of the majority class to balance the training set has been performed. Such a training experiment includes both the client and the server scenario.

Training Approaches. Two different training approaches have been used to test the learning degree of the authorship attribution system. As shown in Sect. 6.1, the dataset can be split considering different email length. Therefore, as well as the standard training approach, where the training data are selected independently from the mail length, has been considered a training approach customized for the following subsets: (i) short emails (less than 20 words) (ii) medium emails (between 20 and 50 words) (iii) long emails (greater than 50 words). Each networks' training has been performed on balanced data (number of positive emails equal to the number of negative emails), performing a random subsampling of the majority class when required. A 10 cross fold-validation has been applied during the training phase to have a better evaluation of the machine learning models.

7   Results

In this section, the results obtained from the experiments described in Sect. 6 are shown. In particular, are reported the results obtained in the two scenarios already presented (individual writing style, End to End writing style) using the proposed training approaches.

7.1   Individual Writing Style Verification Results

For the individual writing style case, we reported the evaluation of the classifier in terms of accuracy both for the *training independent from the email length* and for the *training dependent from the email length*. Table 6, in part reported in the paper [9], shows the accuracy comparison between the classification mechanisms used in the public and in the private dataset. It shows the mean accuracy obtained in each testing set (short, medium, long) of each classifier used to train the individual writing style of the senders in the dataset without considering the length of the input emails.

The reported results are measured through the mean accuracy of 67 target senders having more than 1000 emails sent for the public dataset and 3 target senders for the private dataset. The results show the low accuracy of each classifier in recognizing the sender identities through short emails. Conversely, higher accuracy for the medium and long test set has been obtained. Such results can be because the email length influences accuracy until a certain threshold and short email means few data information to characterize the writing style patter of a sender. Splitting the training set basing on the email length and building a custom classifier for each subset as described in Sect. 6,

Table 6. Length independent individual writing style results.

Classifier	Public dataset			Private dataset		
	Accuracy short	Accuracy medium	Accuracy long	Accuracy short	Accuracy medium	Accuracy long
RCNN	89%	94%	94%	91%	96%	93%
CNN	90%	95%	95%	91%	97%	94%
Logistic Reg.	92%	95%	96%	89%	95%	93%
Nearest Neigh.	73%	65%	66%	82%	84%	83%
SVM	92%	95%	96%	90%	94%	94%
Decision Tree	77%	87%	93%	83%	91%	88%
Random For.	90%	94%	96%	90%	92%	94%
AdaBoost	83%	82%	95%	85%	86%	85%
SGD	88%	94%	94%	88%	92%	92%

we obtained the results reported in Table 7 where the results of the public dataset are detailed in the paper [9]. As in the previous experiment, the lower accuracy is given by the short email set, which does not take advantage of the custom training. Better results in the medium and long email testing set, have been reached, where the accuracy increases of 1–2% respect to the training independent from the email length. The results obtained shown as the email length is an important feature to recognize the author of an email and we can infer that a short email containing less than 20 words, does not include sufficient information for the author verification. Hence excluding the short email set from the results, it is possible to highlight the better accuracy obtained with the length-dependent respect to the length independent training.

Table 7. Length dependent individual writing style results.

Classifier	Public dataset			Private dataset		
	Accuracy short	Accuracy medium	Accuracy long	Accuracy short	Accuracy medium	Accuracy long
RCNN	89%	96%	95%	90%	97%	95%
CNN	90%	97%	96%	91%	97%	95%
Logistic Reg.	87%	96%	96%	89%	95%	94%
Nearest Neigh.	60%	87%	88%	76%	86%	83%
SVM	90%	96%	96%	88%	96%	96%
Decision Tree	79%	90%	93%	80%	93%	90%
Random For.	85%	95%	96%	88%	94%	94%
AdaBoost	79%	94%	95%	78%	92%	90%
SGD	86%	94%	95%	83%	94%	94%

Table 8 shows such a comparison between the average of the accuracy for the medium and long email subsets and the average accuracy of the entire testing set (short, long, medium). In both cases and in each dataset, considering any classifier, the accuracy excluding the short subset is greater respect to the accuracy of the entire testing set. Such consideration proved as the short subset influences negatively the training and the testing phase.

Table 8. Individual writing style verification results comparison.

Classifier	Public dataset				Private dataset			
	Length independent		Length dependent		Length independent		Length dependent	
	Accuracy Med/Long	Accuracy Short/Med/Long	Accuracy Med/Long	Accuracy Short/Med/Long	Accuracy Med/Long	Accuracy Short/Med/Long	Accuracy Med/Long	Accuracy Short/Med/Long
RCNN	94%	92.3%	95.5%	93.3%	94.5%	93.3%	96%	94%
CNN	95%	93.3%	96.5%	94.3%	95.5%	94%	96%	94.3%
Logistic Reg.	95.5%	94.3%	96%	93%	94%	92.3%	94.5%	92.7%
Nearest Neigh.	65.5%	68%	87.5%	78.3%	83.5%	83%	84.5%	81.6%
SVM	95.5%	94.3%	96%	94%	94%	92.6%	96%	93.3%
Decision Tree	90%	85.6%	91.5%	87.3%	89.5%	87.3%	91.5%	87.7%
Random For.	95%	93.3%	95.5%	92%	93%	92%	94%	92%
AdaBoost	93.5%	90%	94%	89.3%	85.5%	85.3%	91%	86.7%
SGD	94%	92%	94.5%	91.6%	92%	90.7%	94%	90.3%

7.2 End to End Writing Style Verification Results

As in the individual writing style verification scenario, we reported the results obtained for the end to end verification learning. Table 9, where the part related to the public dataset is detailed in [9], shows the mean accuracy of each machine learning models computed from the evaluation of every single end to end classifier trained on the sender-receiver communication independently from the email length. The table, as well as, showing the total average accuracy obtained training the overall sender-receiver communications, shows the average accuracy obtained in every subset of the testing set (short, medium, and long). The results are reported both for the public and for the private dataset. From the analysis of the results, it is possible to affirm that the models based on word embeddings outperform the feature engineering-based models. Considering the total accuracy, CNN and RCNN provide higher accuracy respect to the features engineering-based models achieving as best result 95.3% of accuracy in the public dataset and 94.9% reached by the CNN in the private dataset. Analyzing the accuracy computed for each subset, the short email set shows low accuracy in every model. As in the individual verification scenario, the accuracy increase by increasing the email length until a certain threshold, and the better accuracy is achieved with the email having length comprised between 20 and 50 words. It is possible to associate the accuracy trend obtained to the fact that short emails do not contain personal writing style features needed to the classifier to discriminate from one communication to another.

Table 9. End to end verification results length independent.

Classifier	Public dataset				Private dataset			
	Total accuracy	Short accuracy	Medium accuracy	Long accuracy	Total accuracy	Short accuracy	Medium accuracy	Long accuracy
RCNN	95.3%	91.2%	96.3%	97.1%	94.5%	89.3%	88.1%	98.3%
CNN	94.8%	92.6%	97.2%	97.4%	94.9%	89.1%	96.26%	98.4%
Logistic Reg.	94.2%	84.3%	96.5%	96.3%	94.0%	92.8%	97.07%	94.2%
Nearest Neigh.	81.4%	79.1%	85.4%	83.1%	85.5%	79.3%	86.8%	89.2%
SVM	94.2%	74.8%	98%	95.6%	94.4%	90.3%	96.2%	97.3%
Decision Tree	92.1%	76.3%	93.1%	93.9%	81.9%	83.4%	85.1%	87.3%
Random For.	93.6%	77.1%	94.6%	95.6%	92.6%	88.4%	96.2%	97.3%
AdaBoost	92.7%	80.2%	96.7%	94.3%	92.3%	87.0%	95.7%	96.8%
SGD	94.5%	80.4%	95.4%	96.0%	93.9%	91.7%	95.7%	96.8%

Table 10, where the part related to the public dataset is already presented in [9], shows the results obtained performing the training each subset defined (short, medium and long). As in the individual writing style verification test, the accuracy obtained is higher respect to the training independent approach for both the dataset and it confirms the validity of the training method proposed.

8   Discussion

In this section is discussed the effectiveness of the proposed approach in order to solve the email threats considered and a comparison between the results obtained by applying different training methods. The experiments performed have been used to demonstrate the following hypothesis: (i) Effectiveness of the email authorship attribution system in verifying the target writing style, (ii) Effectiveness of the end to end communication writing style learning respect to the individual writing style, (iii) Effectiveness of the training approach based on the partition of the dataset by length, (iv) The validation of the method applying it on a real scenario that considers a private email dataset. The results obtained, in terms of accuracy, both in the individual and in the end to end communication writing style, proved how the method is effective to learn a stylistic pattern of each user or communication. In fact, the best results obtained in the public dataset is 99.2% and 96% of accuracy given by the RCNN model trained respectively on the end to end communication and on the individual writing style. Whereas in the private dataset, we obtained 98.8% and 98.4% considering the CNN model (Table 10 and Table 9).

Table 10. End to end verification results length dependent.

Classifier	Public dataset			Private dataset		
	Short accuracy	Medium accuracy	Long accuracy	Short accuracy	Medium accuracy	Long accuracy
RCNN	91.3%	99.2%	98.8%	89.4%	98.3%	97.6%
CNN	92.5%	98.9%	98.6%	87.3%	98.8%	98.6%
Logistic Reg.	85.3%	97.2%	97.7%	90.2%	98.1%	96.7%
Nearest Neigh.	79.4%	86.5%	84.5%	79.3%	88.8%	87.5%
SVM	75.5%	98.1%	97.6%	90.8%	97.7%	97.1%
Decision Tree	77.4%	95.7%	94.6%	84.1%	88.6%	87.9%
Random For.	78.5%	96.2%	97.4%	89.3	97.9%	97.6%
AdaBoost	80.9%	97.4%	96.8%	87.9%	96.7%	97.1%
SGD	81.3%	98.0%	97.1%	91.9%	96.9%	96.8%

Such reached results proved as the authorship attribution component is able to infer with a minimum margin of error if the email is sent by a legitimate or a non-legitimate user. In such a way, it is possible, as explained in the Sect. 4 section, use the authorship component as an anti-theft or anti-scam tool on the basis of the location and the information data available to train the classification model. From the results obtained, we can infer as the training based on the partition of the dataset in subsets having different email length has produced better results in terms of accuracy. Both in the individual and in the end to end communication writing style, the accuracy obtained is greater if we consider the training customized on a specific email subset of the same length. Table 1 is shows as in every dataset the accuracy considering the length-dependent training approach outperforms the approach where the partition of the dataset is not applied. Such results derive from the fact that the classification models can learn better the pattern writing style into a subset of email having approximately the same length, instead of considering a single dataset the variance of email length can influence the content and the writing style of the sender and consequently the learning process. Hence it is possible to conclude that the writing style of a person can change depending on the length of the email. The results of such experiments have also demonstrated as the length is an important feature to characterize the writing style of a person. In fact, as reported in Table 1 the models tested on the short email subset produce low accuracy due to the fact that it is not possible to characterize the writing pattern of a person with few stylistic information. The same accuracy degradation happens for the long email subset, in that case, a long email can contain writing style variation that can alter the learning and the inference of the classification model. The summary of that result is shown in Fig. 10, it shows the mean accuracy between the classifiers used at different testing sets for each approach used. From that it is possible to deduce as the best accuracy in every experiment is obtained on the medium length testing set and the end to end communication learning provides higher accuracy respect to the individual learning due to the aforementioned explanation. The experiments conducted on the private dataset, have been used to demonstrate the effectiveness of the approach used also in a real scenario. In fact, considering the results shown in Sect. 7, the accuracy in the private dataset is aligned with the accuracy obtained in the public dataset.

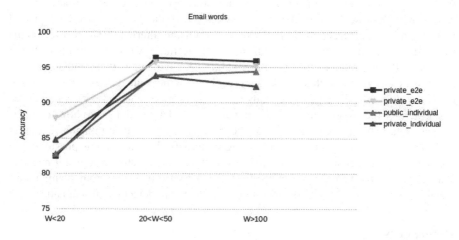

Fig. 10. Result comparison.

9   Conclusion and Future Work

We considered the problem of email attack under two different viewpoints: (i) Scam email attack where the attacker uses the email spoofing attack in order to forge the sender email address with the aim to deceive the receiver, (ii) email attack with a compromised mail account. In that case, the attacker knowing the victim's credentials tries to send an email as the legitimate sender. The countermeasures proposed is an authorship attribution system that based on the analysis of the writing style of an email, allows to infer if the email is sent or not by a legitimate user. A flexible architecture where the authorship attribution component can be placed on different locations within the mail client-server communication is presented. Different placement of the authorship attribution component can imply different learning writing style. The two approaches proposed are (i) the individual writing style and (ii) the end to end writing style learning. As a learning system, we proposed an authorship email verification based on a binary text classifier implemented considering two different classification techniques (i) features engineering and (ii) word embedding based. Two different training methods have been compared and it has been proved the effectiveness of the training mechanism based on the partition of the dataset in subsets having approximately email with the same length. The experiments are done both in a public dataset and on a private email dataset to have a better evaluation of the method on a real case. The results obtained shown (i) the effectiveness of the email authorship attribution system in verifying the target writing style and the advantage to use the end to end communication learning respect to the individual writing style learning, (ii) the effectiveness of the training approach based on the partition of the dataset by length, (iii) the higher accuracy of the word embedding based classifiers respect to the features engineering based. With the accuracy of 99% in the end to end communication writing style learning and the accuracy of 95% for the individual writing style learning reached in both the dataset, it has been proved that the authorship mechanism proposed is a promising alternative support technique to exploit as an email anti-scam or anti-theft tool. As future work, we are interested in improving the accuracy of the system including negative emails that simulate a more realistic attack. We think that the best approach to augment the dataset with a realistic email attack is to apply a generative adversarial network. Such a network is composed of a generator that given a training set (in our case sender emails) learns how to generate new data with the same statistics as the training set, and a discriminator that takes both real samples and generated data trying to classify them as well as possible. The application in our scenario would consist of applying a generator to augment negative samples in the email dataset and a discriminator to discriminate real from the malicious emails, making thus the authorship system more robust to detect email scam attacks.

References

1. Brocardo, M.L., Traore, I., Saad, S., Woungang, I.: Authorship verification for short messages using stylometry. In: 2013 International Conference on Computer, Information and Telecommunication Systems (CITS), pp. 1–6. IEEE (2013)
2. Brocardo, M.L., Traore, I., Woungang, I.: Authorship verification of e-mail and tweet messages applied for continuous authentication. J. Comput. Syst. Sci. **81**(8), 1429–1440 (2015)

3. Chen, X., Hao, P., Chandramouli, R., Subbalakshmi, K.P.: Authorship similarity detection from email messages. In: Perner, P. (ed.) MLDM 2011. LNCS (LNAI), vol. 6871, pp. 375–386. Springer, Heidelberg (2011). https://doi.org/10.1007/978-3-642-23199-5_28

4. Connor, J.T., Martin, R.D., Atlas, L.E.: Recurrent neural networks and robust time series prediction. IEEE Trans. Neural Netw. **5**(2), 240–254 (1994)

5. Dasarathy, B.V.: Nearest neighbor (NN) norms: NN pattern classification techniques. IEEE Computer Society Tutorial (1991)

6. Dewan, P., Kashyap, A., Kumaraguru, P.: Analyzing social and stylometric features to identify spear phishing emails. In: 2014 APWG Symposium on Electronic Crime Research (ecrime), pp. 1–13. IEEE (2014)

7. Donahue, J., et al.: Long-term recurrent convolutional networks for visual recognition and description. In: Proceedings of the IEEE Conference on Computer Vision and Pattern Recognition, pp. 2625–2634 (2015)

8. Freund, Y., Schapire, R., Abe, N.: A short introduction to boosting. J. Japanese Soc. Artif. Intell. **14**(771–780), 1612 (1999)

9. Giorgi, G., Saracino, A., Martinelli, F.: Email spoofing attack detection through an end to end authorship attribution system. In: Furnell, S., Mori, P., Weippl, E.R., Camp, O. (eds.) Proceedings of the 6th International Conference on Information Systems Security and Privacy, ICISSP 2020, Valletta, Malta, February 25–27, 2020. pp. 64–74. SCITEPRESS (2020). https://doi.org/10.5220/0008954600640074

10. Graves, A., Mohamed, A.r., Hinton, G.: Speech recognition with deep recurrent neural networks. In: 2013 IEEE International Conference on Acoustics, Speech and Signal Processing, pp. 6645–6649. IEEE (2013)

11. Guenther, M.: Social engineering-security awareness series. Information Warfare site UK online. http://www.iwar.org.uk/comsec/resources/sa-tools/social-engineering.pdf. Accessed 20 Dec 2006

12. Hamid, I.R.A., Abawajy, J., Kim, T.: Using feature selection and classification scheme for automating phishing email detection. Stud. Inf. Contr. **22**(1), 61–70 (2013)

13. Han, Y., Shen, Y.: Accurate spear phishing campaign attribution and early detection. In: Proceedings of the 31st Annual ACM Symposium on Applied Computing, pp. 2079–2086 (2016)

14. Ho, T.K.: Random decision forests. In: Proceedings of 3rd International Conference on Document Analysis and Recognition, vol. 1, pp. 278–282. IEEE (1995)

15. Jakobsson, M.: Modeling and preventing phishing attacks. In: Financial Cryptography, vol. 5 (2005)

16. Kiefer, J., Wolfowitz, J., et al.: Stochastic estimation of the maximum of a regression function. Ann. Math. Stat. **23**(3), 462–466 (1952)

17. Klimt, B., Yang, Y.: The enron corpus: a new dataset for email classification research. In: Boulicaut, J.-F., Esposito, F., Giannotti, F., Pedreschi, D. (eds.) ECML 2004. LNCS (LNAI), vol. 3201, pp. 217–226. Springer, Heidelberg (2004). https://doi.org/10.1007/978-3-540-30115-8_22

18. Litvak, M.: Deep dive into authorship verification of email messages with convolutional neural network. In: Lossio-Ventura, J.A., Muñante, D., Alatrista-Salas, H. (eds.) SIMBig 2018. CCIS, vol. 898, pp. 129–136. Springer, Cham (2019). https://doi.org/10.1007/978-3-030-11680-4_14

19. Mikolov, T., Chen, K., Corrado, G., Dean, J.: Efficient estimation of word representations in vector space. arXiv preprint arXiv:1301.3781 (2013)

20. Peng, C.Y.J., Lee, K.L., Ingersoll, G.M.: An introduction to logistic regression analysis and reporting. J. Educ. Res. **96**(1), 3–14 (2002)

21. Quinlan, J.R.: Induction of decision trees. Mach. Learn. **1**(1), 81–106 (1986)

22. Ruder, S., Ghaffari, P., Breslin, J.G.: Character-level and multi-channel convolutional neural networks for large-scale authorship attribution. arXiv preprint arXiv:1609.06686 (2016)
23. Sanderson, C., Guenter, S.: Short text authorship attribution via sequence kernels, markov chains and author unmasking: An investigation. In: Proceedings of the 2006 Conference on Empirical Methods in Natural Language Processing, pp. 482–491. Association for Computational Linguistics (2006)
24. Schuster, M., Paliwal, K.K.: Bidirectional recurrent neural networks. IEEE Trans. Sig. Process. 45(11), 2673–2681 (1997)
25. Shrestha, P., Sierra, S., Gonzalez, F., Montes, M., Rosso, P., Solorio, T.: Convolutional neural networks for authorship attribution of short texts. In: Proceedings of the 15th Conference of the European Chapter of the Association for Computational Linguistics, vol. 2, pp. 669–674 (2017)
26. Suykens, J.A., Vandewalle, J.: Least squares support vector machine classifiers. Neural Process. Lett. 9(3), 293–300 (1999)
27. Zhang, X., Zhao, J., LeCun, Y.: Character-level convolutional networks for text classification. In: Advances in neural information processing systems, pp. 649–657 (2015)
28. Zheng, R., Li, J., Chen, H., Huang, Z.: A framework for authorship identification of online messages: writing-style features and classification techniques. J. Amer. Soc. Inf. Sci. Technol. 57(3), 378–393 (2006)

Symmetric and Asymmetric Schemes for Lightweight Secure Communication

Simona Buchovecká[(✉)], Róbert Lórencz, Jiří Buček, and Filip Kodýtek

Department of Information Security, Faculty of Information Technology, Czech Technical University in Prague, Prague, Czech Republic
{simona.buchovecka,lorencz,jiri.bucek,kodytfil}@fit.cvut.cz

Abstract. The paper deals with the topic of lightweight authentication and secure communication for constrained hardware devices such as IoT or embedded devices. In the paper, protocols based on both symmetric and asymmetric schemes are presented, utilizing a PUF/TRNG combined module, showing it is advantageous to have single module that will allow generation of both TRNG and PUF at the same time. This approach minimizes implementation requirements and operational resource consumption. Moreover, it allows the simplification of the overall key management process as the proposed protocols do not require to store secrets on the devices themselves. This paper is the extended and revised version of the paper entitled "Lightweight Authentication and Secure Communication Suitable for IoT Devices" [1] presented at the 6th International Conference on Information Systems Security and Privacy (ICISSP) 2020.

Keywords: Authentication · Secure communication · PUF · TRNG · Key generation · Key management · IoT security

1 Introduction

With the rising usage of smart devices interconnected in Internet of Things (IoT) the importance of their security is growing. The primary security functions that needs to be established are secure authentication for ensuring only properly authenticated devices are connected to the system or network and secure communication to ensure the confidentiality of transferred data. As necessary prerequisite for both there is a need for proper use of cryptography, especially cryptographic key management, all with the constraint of limited computing resources and low power consumption.

Different communication protocols were proposed for secure authentication and communication in IoT world and are being implemented nowadays. These include machine-to-machine/Internet of Things connectivity protocol (MQTT), Constrained Application Protocol (CoAP), or Datagram Transport Layer Security (DTLS) that can be integrated with CoAP. However, there is ongoing development and lighter variants of the protocols are being continuously introduced – such as Lithe [36] or E-Lithe [20] as a lightweight variant of DTLS [46], because the originals are quite resource exhaustive for simple constrained devices.

© Springer Nature Switzerland AG 2022
S. Furnell et al. (Eds.): ICISSP 2020, CCIS 1545, pp. 97–114, 2022.
https://doi.org/10.1007/978-3-030-94900-6_5

Another problem that is often being neglected is the need for cryptographic key lifecycle and its management including the secure key generation, distribution and usage. The generation of cryptographic keys is the first and essential step in the key life cycle. The generated key needs to meet the strict requirement of its unpredictability, arising from Kerckhoffs' principle formulated by Auguste Kerckhoffs in 1883 [22]. The principle states that the cryptographic system should be secure even if everything about the system, except the key, is public knowledge. This principle is applied to all modern encryption cryptosystems and the algorithms for encryption are publicly known. Therefore, the key needs to be kept secret and unpredictable, so the attacker cannot easily guess it. In hardware, the Random Number Generators (RNGs) or Physical Unclonable Functions are used to generate unpredictable bitstream. Further, postprocessing of this bitstream allows to generate the cryptographic key.

An RNG can be defined as a device or algorithm which outputs a sequence of random (thus independent and uniformly distributed) numbers. In practical hardware implementations, the output sequence is represented as a bit stream of zeros and ones, that may be further sliced and converted to the integers, as per the need of the implemented algorithms. Nowadays, the RNGs are most often and most widely used for cryptographic key generation. The RNG can utilize non-deterministic effects in analogue or digital circuits such as noise generated in the circuit itself, including thermal noise, shot noise or avalanche noise or in case of programmable devices the advantage can be taken from the metastability of logic circuits. This is the resource and power efficient way of generating random bitstream. Once generated, keys should be stored in secure manner [19], to be protected against attacker. According to sensitivity and criticality of the information, various approaches for storage keys are used today in practical applications. For most critical applications Hardware Security Modules (HSMs) are being used, however, implementing the HSM function often required much more resources, than available on the constrained device. Therefore, the properly defined and implemented key management, consistent way of handling variety of cryptographic keys, including proper key generation, key storage, key usage for various applications (authentication, access control, encryption) and possibilities of reusing traditional security mechanisms and ensuring end-to-end integrity verification mechanisms in interconnected IoT and embedded systems, as depicted in Fig. 1 is still a challenging task [32, 37, 41]. The need for proper key management in particular applications of embedded systems and IoT started to be raised in some research papers with regards to specific areas such as automotive context [40] distributed sensor networks [8], or embedded systems in general [42].

Nowadays, PUF usage is promising to solve the issue of secure storage of cryptographic keys. The concept of PUF was originally introduced in [35] showing that instead of relying on number theory, the mesoscopic physics of coherent transport through a disordered medium can be used to allocate and authenticate unique identifiers by physically reducing the medium's microstructure to a fixed-length string of binary digits. Instead of storing the key in memory, the key is generated at the time it is needed. Moreover, PUFs are on-way, inexpensive to fabricate, prohibitively difficult to duplicate, admit no compact mathematical representation, and are intrinsically tamper-resistant, making them the ideal candidate for providing tamper resistant design for cryptographic key generation and storage.

This radically new approach to secure key storage utilizing PUF was defined in [19]. With regards to drawbacks of non-volatile storage, authors define the criteria for new approach: key should not be permanently stored in digital form on the device, key should be extracted from the device only when required, and after having been used, it should be removed from all internal registers, memories, and locations and key should be somehow uniquely linked to a given device such that it cannot be reproduced or the device with a same key manufactured.

Therefore, PUFs usage is promising to solve the issue of secure storage of cryptographic keys. Instead of storing the key in memory, the key is generated at the time it is needed. A combined PUF/TRNG circuit used in our paper is therefore a suitable alternative for the purpose of key generation and authentication in lightweight cryptographic applications, such as IoT devices and other embedded platforms.

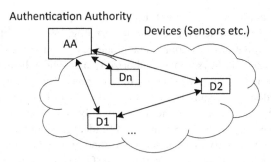

Fig. 1. Interconnected systems with an authentication authority [1].

The aim of this paper is to discuss protocols for authentication and secure communication utilizing PUF and TRNG, showing it is advantageous to have single module that will allow generation of both TRNG and PUF at the same time, since it minimizes implementation requirements and operational resource consumption. The goal we want to achieve in order to simplify the key management on the simple hardware devices and microcontrollers is to remove the requirent of storing secrets on the device itself. The paper is the extended and revised version of the paper entitled "Lightweight Authentication and Secure Communication Suitable for IoT Devices" [1] presented at the 6th International Conference on Information Systems Security and Privacy (ICISSP) 2020. This extended paper introduces the new schemes based on asymmetric cryptography (Algorithms 4 and 5). This brings the benefit that no shared keys need to be transmitted over secure channel. Further, the paper extends original Case Study, with the discussion on the length of the generated bitstream after all necessary corrections and experiment proving the quality of the generated key material.

This paper is organised as follows, related work and current State-of-the-Art is summarized in Sect. 2, providing us with the theoretical basis for our further work. In Sect. 3 our proposed approach to lightweight authentication and secure communication is presented, introducing the authentication algorithms based on symmetric and asymmetric cryptographic schemes, as well as secure communication approach. Section 4 presents a case study and feasibility review of proposed protocols with a specific PUF/TRNG circuit. Section 5 concludes this paper.

2 State-of-the-Art and Technical Background

As stated in previous paragraphs, every protocol for authentication and secure communication relies on security of used secret cryptographic keys and the security of the cryptographic system is exclusively linked to the security of the key, as discussed for instance in [14]. In critical applications, especially when used in an untrusted environment, cryptographic keys should never be generated outside the system and they should never leave the system in clear. Therefore, if the security system is implemented in a single chip (cryptographic system- on-chip), the keys should be generated inside the same chip.

The minimum common requirements for key generation and storage are summarized by Maes et al. [30]. Every system implementing a cryptographic algorithm needs a source of true randomness that ensures unpredictable and unique fresh keys and a protected memory that will shield the keys from unauthorized parties and will allow the reliable key storage and usage. This implies the need for the true randomness source that will enable generation of random bitstream. The traditional methods of generating cryptographic keys in hardware and embedded systems are mainly based on true random number generators (TRNGs). As stated by Schindler [39], ideal random number generators are characterized by the property that the generated random numbers are independent and uniformly distributed on a finite range. Various TRNG designs suitable for cryptographic key generation include purely digital designs [12, 13], Phase-Locked Loops in designs targeting FPGAs [9, 15], Random access memories [17] or multiple designs [5, 16, 27, 45] based on Ring Oscillators as a source of entropy. However, implementation of mere TRNG is not enough to resolve the problem of secure key storage.

In [30] the idea of using PUF-based key generators is presented, as using PUF it is possible to fulfill both requirements on secure key generation and storage at once. PUF is a system responding to a challenge C with a response R, referenced in general as a challenge-response pair. According to [29] PUF is best described as an expression of an inherent and unclonable instance-specific feature of a physical object and as such has a strong resemblance to biometric features of human beings, line fingerprints, and thus cloning a PUF is extremely hard if not impossible at all. Therefore, there is no need for a protected non-volatile memory since the randomness is measured only when needed. However, the PUF output may slightly vary in different measurements, and it is still challenging to get static PUF output as required by cryptographic schemes.

Existing PUF designs proposed for cryptographic applications include PUFKY based on a ring oscillator PUF [30] providing low-failure rate, generation of read-once keys [23] single-chip secure processor for embedded systems [44], arbiter PUF for device authentication and secret key generation [43] and others.

Our goal is to enable a secure communication and authentication method using a combined PUF/TRNG circuit that will allow generation of keying material using both PUF and TRNG at the same time, utilizing benefits of each one. Session keys should be periodically re-generated and are not stored in non-volatile memory in a long term, and as such the TRNG is ideal for this case. On the other hand, utilizing the PUF for asymmetric keys looks promising - as the decryption key should remain private it is ideal to utilize the PUF for key generation and storage, as the key remains private, never leaves the device and cannot be copied nor cloned to another device.

There have been several similar works published recently. The very first attempts in using PUF for the device authentication were rather simple. In [43] simple authentication against authentication authority was discussed, using pre-generated challenge-response pairs stored centrally. At the authentication time, the challenge is sent to the device and response then compared with the output. Same challenge cannot be reused again due to possible replay attacks, limiting the number of possible authentications of the device. More sophisticated PUF-based authentication protocols were reviewed in [10]. The work of [34] using reprogrammable non-volatile memory; Hammouri et al. [18] using two arbiter PUFs; protocol based on logically reconfigurable PUFs [21] which allows to recycle the challenge tokens; Reverse Fuzzy Extractor [47] allowing mutual authentication; Slender PUF protocol [31] that does not expose the full PUF responses, only the random subset instead; and Converse authentication Protocol [24] which provides one-way authentication of the server.

The protocols discussed above do not consider the need of key establishment, which is prerequisite in all the cases. Neither, the secure communication protecting the confidentiality of transmitted data is taking into the consideration. The [10], further discuss other caveats of the PUFs - responses being not perfectly reproducible, small output space of strong PUFs or need of secure TRNG, that is substantial for most of the protocols. Another issue is the privacy preservation of the devices being authenticated [2, 4] – as the PUF responses are unique per device and cannot be deliberately altered once device is manufactured, it is necessary to design the protocol in the way it preserves the privacy of the device.

3   Proposed TRNG/PUF Module for Secure Authentication and Communication

Our design aims to simplify the key management on the endpoint embedded device, allowing the efficient and secure authentication and communication, both against the Authentication Authority, as well as mutually across the interconnected devices. As discussed in the previous sections, we aim to utilize the single circuit for key generation using PUF and TRNG as a basic building block of the module so that there is no need to store secrets on the hardware device.

The overall module as presented in [1] is depicted in Fig. 2. It provides PUF authentication and PUF/TRNG based key generation. For the authentication, the PUF is used, since it provides randomness intrinsically present in the device and utilizes the fact that the generated response is unique per device. Since there is a need for both static key, as well as ephemeral keys, combination of PUF and TRNG is used in this case – the PUF is used for generation of static (private) key that never leaves the device, thus utilizing all the advantages of PUF, while TRNG is used for generation of ephemeral, one-time keys, that are shared with other communicating parties.

Asymmetric schemes are suitable if the private key is easily generated from random sequence by a Key Derivation Function (KDF), such as PBKDF2 [38]. For example, ElGamal encryption [11] and DSA/ECDSA signature schemes can be used, if good quality public parameters are chosen (generation of the public key from a private key is denoted as GENPK in Fig. 2). On the contrary, an RSA key requires more complex processing including secure prime generation. TRNG output is also used to generate random nonce and padding data.

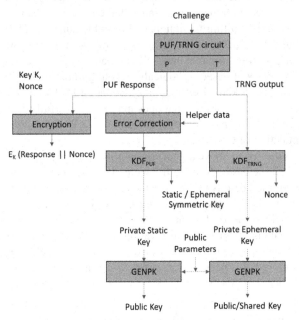

Fig. 2. Embedded module for secure authentication and communication. KDF is a Key Derivation Function, GENPK generates a public key from a private key and public parameters. Error Correction is used to obtain a stable key material from the PUF Response (see Sect. 3.1) [1].

3.1 Authentication Against Central Authentication Authority

Before the device is connected to the network and is allowed to communicate it must be properly authenticated. Since the PUF responses are unique per each device, and are intrinsically random, it makes PUF the ideal cryptographic primitive for device authentication. The authentication protocol against Authentication Authority using pre-generated challenge-response pairs that can be easily implemented in hardware devices is quite straightforward. This protocol does not require the PUF to have a large space of challenge-response pairs (even one challenge-response pair is enough). The authentication protocol consists of two phases – secure enrollment phase and authentication phase itself and is depicted in Algorithm 1 [1].

The Enrollment phase is critical for the security of all protocols based on PUFs, and (analogous to biometric authentication methods) must be performed in a secure environment. We assume that a suitable environment can be for example during the manufacturing process, but specific means are not elaborated in this paper.

During the Enrollment phase of Algorithm 1, the challenge/response pair(s) (C, R) are measured from the targeted device and securely stored at the central authenticating authority (AA), that can be either integrated into the gateway or be represented by separate device that the gateway is querying during authentication process. A database DB_{Di} of the pairs (C, R) is created for each device D_i. Furthermore, the public key (PK_{AA}) of the authenticating authority is pre-set on the device, so as the authentication data can be securely transferred. For this purpose, an asymmetric scheme (ElGamal) can be used, as proposed in the section above. We assume that PK_{AA} is protected against unauthorized changes (by the tamper-evidence property of the PUF).

The first 4 steps of the Enrollment phase are common for all 3 algorithms presented in this paper. The database DB_{Di} is used also in the Authentication phases of Algorithms 2–3.

Algorithm 1: Authentication against central Authentication Authority [1].

Enrollment phase (*Secure environment*)
Common for Algorithms 1 – 3:
1. **AA** → **D1**: Challenges $(C_1, C_2, ...)$
2. **D1**: $R_1 = PUF(C_1)$, $R_2 = PUF(C_2)$ ...
3. **D1** → **AA**: Responses $(R_1, R_2, ...)$
4. **AA**:   Store (C_i, R_i) to DB_{D1}

Specific only for Algorithm 1:
5. **AA** → **D1**: Public key PK_{AA}
6. **D1**:   Store(PK_{AA})

Authentication phase for D1
1. **AA**:   Choose (C, R) from DB_{D1}
2. **AA** → **D1**: Challenge C, Nonce N
3. **D1**: $R' = PUF(C)$
4. **D1** → **AA**: $CR = E_{PK_{AA}}(R' \; || \; N)$
5. **AA**: $(R', N') = D_{SK_{AA}}(CR)$
6.   Compare($R \approx R'$), Compare($N = N'$)

Every time device is connected to the network and needs to communicate the Authentication phase of Algorithm 1 is executed. AA randomly chooses one of the challenges C and sends it together with the nonce value N to the device to be authenticated. The nonce value is used to prevent simple replay attacks and allows each challenge-response pair to be used repeatedly. On the device that is being authenticated the appropriate PUF response is generated, concatenated with nonce value and encrypted with public key of the Authenticating Authority. Authenticating Authority then compares (strictly) if the decrypted nonce value N' = N. Since the PUF response may slightly vary across various measurements, a predetermined number of faulty bits in R' is tolerated. If both matches, the device is successfully authenticated. The disadvantage of Algorithm 1 is that it only performs authentication and does not provide a cryptographic context for future communication.

Authentication of a single device (D1) to the AA without asymmetric cryptography is depicted in Algorithm 2 [1]. (The Enrollment phase is the same as in Algorithm 1, steps 1–4) This method includes generating a shared symmetric key K, which requires a stable error-free PUF output. This is achieved by using an error-correcting code (ECC), denoted in the algorithm by its functions Encode and Decode. This code must have enough redundancy and structure to correct the maximum amount of errors assumed in the PUF when operated under various conditions (voltage, temperature etc.).

Choosing a suitable ECC depends on the bit error rate and length of PUF response while meeting the required corrected output length. The computational power of the device is also a limiting factor. In the case of "lightweight" devices, simple codes (such as a repetition code) are preferable.

The helper string H is a distance from the raw PUF response R to the random codeword Encode(r). It is computed by the AA (step 4 of Algorithm 2). The device then uses it to recover the key material (step 8), and subsequently derive the key K.

Algorithm 2: Authentication of a device D1 to the AA. [1].

Authentication phase – using symmetric cipher
1. **D1 → AA**: Call(D1)

2. **AA**: $r = TRNG()$
3.   Choose (C, R) from DB_{D1}
4. $H = R \oplus Encode(r)$
5. $K = KDF(r)$

6. **AA → D1**: Challenge C, Helper string H

7. **D1**: $R' = PUF(C)$
8. $r = Decode(R' \oplus H)$
9. $K = KDF(r)$

10. **D1 ↔ AA**: Authentication + Encryption with K

The shared key K can be used for authentication and encrypted communication, as opposed to Algorithm 1, which covers only authentication, limiting its usefulness. On the other hand, Algorithm 1 does not require the generation of a helper string, nor does it need any error correction codes.

3.2 Mutual Device Authentication

Not only the device needs to be authenticated to central authority when connected to the network, the devices must be mutually authenticated before they start to communicate, as well. Similarly, as in the previous case, central authenticating authority stores the pre-generated challenge-response pair(s), and acts as trusted 3rd party. This time though, a shared symmetric key is established between the two devices, and a conventional symmetric authenticated and encrypted session can follow afterwards. The goal is to use the PUFs in both devices D1 and D2, but not transmit any PUF response over the network. Due to the one-wayness of the hash functions used, no device gets to know other device's PUF response, even if it monitors all communication. An error correcting code is used to ensure stable PUF outputs. The codewords are selected randomly from the code space by the AA. The overall process is described in Algorithm 3 [1].

Algorithm 3: Mutual authentication of D1 and D2 using AA. [1].

Authentication phase – using symmetric cipher

1. **D1 → AA:** Call(D1, D2)

2. **AA:** r_{D1} = TRNG()
3. r_{D2} = TRNG()
4.   Choose (C_{D1}, R_{D1}) from DB_{D1}
5.   Choose (C_{D2}, R_{D2}) from DB_{D2}
6. H_{D1} = $R_{D1} \oplus$ Encode(r_{D1})
7. H_{D2} = $R_{D2} \oplus$ Encode(r_{D2})
8.   r = Hash(r_{D1}) $\oplus$ Hash(r_{D2})

9. **AA → D1:** (C_{D1}, H_{D1}, r)
10. **AA → D2:** Call(D1, D2) , (C_{D2}, H_{D2}, r)

11. **D1:** R'_{D1} = PUF(C_{D1})
12. r_{D1} = Decode($R'_{D1} \oplus H_{D1}$)
13.   Hash(r_{D2}) = Hash(r_{D1}) $\oplus$ r
14.   K = KDF(Hash(r_{D1}) || Hash(r_{D2}))

15. **D2:** R'_{D2} = PUF(C_{D2})
16. r_{D2} = Decode($R'_{D2} \oplus H_{D2}$)
17.   Hash(r_{D1}) = Hash(r_{D2}) $\oplus$ r
18.   K = KDF(Hash(r_{D1}) || Hash(r_{D2}))

19. **D1 ↔ D2:** Authentication + Encryption with K

Let us assume that D1 wants to authenticate with D2 and set up a secure communication channel. D1 initiates the process by calling the AA with the identification of D1 and D2 (Call(D1, D2)). AA contains the complete table of challenges and responses (C_{D1}, R_{D1} etc.). An error correcting code is chosen that can correct enough errors to make the PUF response stable, with the corresponding functions Encode and Decode. AA generates two random components r_{D1}, r_{D2} from the set of preimages, and encodes them, thereby forming randomly chosen codewords. The code length should correspond to the PUF response length. Helper strings H_{D1} and H_{D2} are created by XORing the expected PUF response (R_{D1}, R_{D2}) to the corresponding codeword. The two random components are hashed and the hashes XORed to form r.

To each of the devices, a triplet (C_{Di}, H_{Di}, r) with the challenge, helper string, and r is sent. Also, in step 10, AA relays the request for communication from D1 to D2. Each of the devices challenges its own PUF to get the response (R'_{D1}, R'_{D2}). By XORing the response with the corresponding helper string (H_{D1}, H_{D2}), resulting with a codeword with errors, which is then corrected by the Decode function. This way, each device recovers its component (r_{D1}, r_{D2}). D1 recovers the value Hash(r_{D2}) by XORing r with the hash of its r_{D1}, and vice versa. Moreover, both devices know the hashes of r_{D1} and r_{D2}, and can derive the shared key K by applying a key derivation function KDF on the concatenation of the hashes.

The hashing of r_{D1}, r_{D2} is done to hide the PUF responses from the other device. If D1 monitors the communication, it will know (C_{D1}, C_{D2}, H_{D1}, H_{D2}, r). It can recover r_{D1}, and if the hashing were not done, and r would be equal to $r_{D1} \oplus r_{D2}$ directly, D1 would compute r_{D2}, and using the helper string H_{D2}, it could discover the PUF response R_{D2}. We would have to either trust all devices in the network or use all challenges only once and discard them. In our case, because we do use hashing of r_{D1}, r_{D2}, D1 only gets Hash(r_{D2}), and the one-wayness of the hash function prevents it from discovering R_{D2}. Thus, we can reuse the challenges for future authentications.

PUF response correction code choice depends on the number of bitflips inherent in the PUF operation. The code length and codeword distance determine the number of information bits, thus the length of r_{D1}, r_{D2}, and limit the entropy contained in r. By using the same challenge with multiple random r_{Di}, we can extract more bits of entropy from the PUF. The entropy of the resulting shared key K is determined by the properties of used hash functions and KDF, and the inputs. If chosen correctly, it is as high as the entropies of r_{D1}, r_{D2}. The key K is always derived from randomly chosen codewords, and therefore for the same PUF challenges (C_{D1}, C_{D2}), a different K is obtained.

3.3 Secure Communication Using Asymmetric Encryption Scheme

An asymmetric scheme provides us with benefit that there are no shared keys and the keys do not need to be transferred over secure channel. Moreover, using PUF we do not need to store the secret key on the device, instead, the key is generated during initialization phase (e.g. on boot of the device or after longer period of inactivity), when needed. We propose to use the asymmetric ElGamal encryption scheme, since there are no specific requirements on private keys (such as requirement of private numbers in RSA), apart from the requirement that the private key is from an appropriate range. For digital signatures, either ElGamal or DSA, or even ECDSA can be used. In subsequent text, we assume appropriate keys are generated depending on chosen algorithms. A private-public key pair of each device must be generated and the public key stored in the Authentication Authority. In contrary to Algorithms 1–3, no challenge-response pairs are necessary to store in the authority. The private key is not stored but deleted immediately after using for generating the public key. This process is described by Algorithm 4.

Algorithm 4: Enrollment of asymmetric key of device D1 with the AA.

Enrollment phase (*Secure environment*)
1. **AA → D1**: Public parameters PP, Public key PK_{AA}

2. **D1**: Store PP, PK_{AA}
3.   Choose challenge C_{D1}
4. $R_{D1} = PUF(C_{D1})$
5. $r_{D1} = TRNG()$ so that $Encode(r_{D1})$ is a random codeword
6. $H_{D1} = Encode(r_{D1}) \oplus R_{D1}$
7.   Store (C_{D1}, H_{D1})
8.   Private key $SK_{D1} = KDF(r_{D1}, PP)$
9.   Public key $PK_{D1} = GENPK(SK_{D1}, PP)$

10. **D1 → AA**: Public key PK_{D1}

11. **AA**: Store $(D1, PK_{D1})$

After the keys are enrolled in the Authentication Authority, any device D1 can use it to establish a secure channel by requesting a fresh and authentic public key of its peer D2 from the AA. The public key query Q1 is created by encrypting the identity of D2 and a random nonce N1 with the AA's public key. The answer A1 contains a signed triplet with the identification of D2, its public key PK_{D2}, and the nonce N1. The device D1 verifies this signature using the AA's public key PK_{AA}.

The device's own private key SK_{D1} is generated using its PUF and the previously stored challenge C_{D1} and helper string H_{D1} (steps 8 and 9 of Algorithm 5). This private key is generated only for the subsequent signing operation and then deleted. It is not stored in the device. A new symmetric key K is generated randomly using the device's TRNG and sent encrypted with the peer's public key PK_{D2} and signed with SK_{D1}. Device D2 then verifies and decrypts this message to get the symmetric key K, as described in Algorithm 5.

Algorithm 5: Mutual authentication of D1 and D2 using AA.

Authentication phase – using asymmetric cipher

1. **D1:** $N1 = TRNG()$ *Generate a random challenge to ensure freshness*
2. $Q1 = E_{PK_{AA}}(D2, N1)$

3. **D1 → AA:** Call(D2, Q1)

4. **AA:** $A1 = S_{SK_{AA}}(D2, PK_{D2}, N1)$

5. **AA → D1:** A1

6. **D1:** $(D2', PK_{D2}, N1') = V_{PK_{AA}}(A1)$
7. $Compare(N1' = N1), Compare(D2' = D2)$
8. $R_{D1} = PUF(C_{D1})$ *Use PUF to recall D1's private key*
9. $SK_{D1} = KDF(Decode(R_{D1} \oplus H_{D1}), PP)$
10. $K = TRNG()$
11. $CK = S_{SK_{D1}}(E_{PK_{D2}}(K))$

12. **D1 → D2:** Call(D1, D2, CK)

13. **D2:** $N2 = TRNG()$
14. $Q2 = E_{PK_{AA}}(D1, N2)$

15. **D2 → AA:** Call(D1, Q2)

16. **AA:** $A2 = S_{SK_{AA}}(D1, PK_{D1}, N2)$

17. **AA → D2:** A2

18. **D2:** $(D1', PK_{D1}, N2') = V_{PK_{AA}}(A2)$
19. $Compare(N2' = N2), Compare(D1' = D1)$
20. $R_{D2} = PUF(C_{D2})$ *Use PUF to recall D2's private key*
21. $SK_{D2} = KDF(Decode(R_{D2} \oplus H_{D2}), PP)$
22. $K = D_{SK_{D2}}(V_{PK_{D1}}(CK))$

23. **D1 ↔ D2:** Authentication + Encryption with K

3.4   Secure Communication

After the authentication process described in the previous section, a shared key is established. At this point, a conventional symmetric authentication and session key derivation process can be performed using block ciphers such as AES. Several lightweight block ciphers suitable for embedded systems or sensor networks has been proposed, such as PRESENT [3, 28] with an 80-bit key. This allows generating the key in a single run of PUF circuit for most of the PUF designs and implementations, with no further stretching needed.

All presented algorithms in this Section utilized only PUF on the side of the devices and TRNG was used on AA. TRNG functionality on the devices is used after the secure channel establishment (steps 10 and 19) in dependence on the communication protocols. Random numbers are needed in many classical authentication protocols [33] as well as modern internet standards such as DTLS [46].

4 Feasibility Review and Testing

As results from the previous paragraphs, a combined PUF/TRNG circuit seems to be a suitable alternative for the purpose of key generation and authentication in lightweight cryptographic applications, such as IoT devices and other embedded platforms. Such PUF/TRNG based on Ring Oscillators – ROPUF circuit was presented in our previous work [6, 7, 25, 26], so the idea of the single RO circuit can be used both for PUF and TRNG generation was validated. This circuit is depicted in Fig. 3. As the design of the protocols we present relies on the module that allows secure and efficient generation of both TRNG and PUF. We used the module to test the implementation feasibility of proposed protocols.

In order to validate the proposed authentication process outlined in Sect. 3, we performed an experiment on one device containing the ROPUF design [6, 7, 25, 26]. For this purpose, we used a ROPUF design that consisted of 2 groups of ring oscillators (ROs), each group contained 150 ROs. Only ROs from different groups were selected to form a pair, which was then used to generate part of the PUF response. We extracted 3 bits from each RO pair and enhanced the stability of the PUF output by applying Gray code on these bits [26]. The selected bits from all of the RO pairs are concatenated to create the PUF response.

In the first case, we generated the PUF responses from 150 pairs of ROs (each RO from each group was used only once), in the other, each RO was used five times (one RO from the first group is paired with 5 ROs from the other group) resulting in 750 RO pairs. These two setups achieved 450 and 2250 bits of PUF response respectively. In both cases, we performed 1000 measurements, from which we obtained a majority PUF response - R_{Di} (we determined the majority for each position of the PUF output).

In our experiment, the block length of 9 bits proved to be sufficient for the repetition code. In order to create the helper string H_{Di}, we need to generate 50 or 250 random bits (r_{Di}) that are then encoded by the repetition code and XORed with the major PUF output, forming the helper string H_{Di}. This process is related to steps 2 and 4 in Algorithm 2.

The example using a simple repetition code with 5-bit block length is depicted in Fig. 4. On the device, the PUF generates a response R'_{Di} that is corrected by the helper string H_{Di}, corresponding to steps 7 and 8 in Algorithm 2. After correction, we obtained 50 and 250 bits respectively. These bits can be used to create a cryptographic key. For Algorithm 2, we can simply represent KDF as the selection of the first 128 bits (from r_{Di}) for symmetric cipher AES.

The same can be applied for Algorithm 3, where two devices are authenticating each other. However, this algorithm is more complex, since it requires implementation of suitable hash function. In case of Algorithm 1, no KDF is needed, since the AA's public key is stored on the device and PUF is not used to derive any cryptographic key.

Implementation of more efficient error would allow to increase the number of bits in generated bitstream after correction even more.

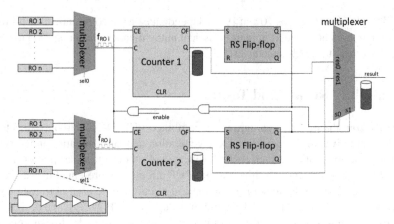

Fig. 3. PUF/TRNG circuit based on Ring Oscillators, serving as basic building block for proposed authentication and secure communication scheme [7, 25].

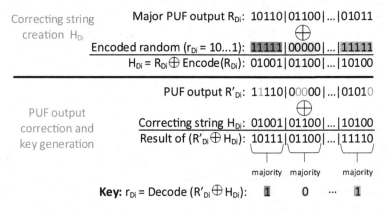

Fig. 4. Example of a simple repetition code with 5-bit groups [1].

In Fig. 5, a case study of the enrollment phase for the asymmetric key derivation according to Algorithm 4 is presented. In this case, we consider 750 ring oscillator pairs, using 3 bits from each pair [26]. This yields 2250 bits of raw PUF response, of which we use 2200 bits for key generation, using a 11 times repetition code. For this purpose, a 2200-bit helper string was derived from a 2200-bit random codeword. For this example, we consider a 200-bit private key SK of ElGamal asymmetric scheme (which corresponds to approx. 100-bit equivalent symmetric key size). The challenge C and helper string H are subsequently used to regenerate the same SK in Algorithm 5, lines 8, 9, 20, 21. The attained key lengths and the fact that the asymmetric scheme is used only once for the authentication correspond with the intended use for authentication and secure communication of IoT devices.

The experiment showed and confirmed that it is possible to generate key material for the proposed protocols, using the state of the art PUF/TRNG designs, in sufficient length and quality.

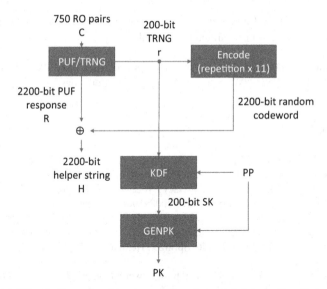

Fig. 5. Example of asymmetric key derivation for enrollment.

5 Conclusions

For the security of embedded systems, IoT and constrained devices, it is inevitable to implement the algorithms that will enable the secure authentication before the device is allowed to access the network; and secure communication to protect the confidentiality of transmitted data afterwards. In this paper we presented a set of lightweight algorithms that enable these goals even with constrained hardware, while avoiding the need to store secrets on the devices.

Several variants of authentication and secure communication protocols are presented in the paper – authentication against central authority, mutual device authentication using symmetric scheme and asymmetric encryption scheme suitable for key exchange. The combination of the protocols allows establishment of a secure communication channel – first, the devices are authenticated, then the shared session key is established, and finally, the communication may take place securely. The proposed protocols are built on PUF and TRNG as basic cryptographic primitives, as they can be efficiently implemented even in constrained devices.

Finally, a practical experiment was performed. By implementing the proposed design, following up with measurement of generated PUF responses and TRNG bistream, the feasibility of the proposed ideas was validated and confirmed. Our feasibility study and testing is utilizing the implementation a circuit combining TRNG and PUF into a unified module based on ring oscillators as it was presented in our previous work [6, 7, 25, 26] that was proved to be implementation and resource consumption efficient.

The implementation of the security measures in simple IoT devices or embedded devices is often neglected, as it is generally perceived as implementationally complex and resource exhaustive. In this paper we presented the approach and the methods that may be used to enhance the security posture of such simple devices with constrained hardware resources, without significant overhead.

Acknowledgements. The authors acknowledge the support of the OP VVV MEYS funded project CZ.02.1.01/0.0/0.0/16_019/ 0000765 "Research Center for Informatics".

References

1. Buchovecká, S., Lórencz, R., Buček, J., Kodýtek, F.: Lightweight authentication and secure communication suitable for IoT devices. In: Proceedings of the 6th International Conference on Information Systems Security and Privacy - Volume 1: ICISSP, pp. 75–83. ISBN 978-989-758-399-5 (2020). https://doi.org/10.5220/0008959600750083
2. Aysu, A., Gulcan, E., Moriyama, D., Schaumont, P., Yung, M.: End-to-end design of a PUF-based privacy preserving authentication protocol. In: Güneysu, T., Handschuh, H. (eds.) CHES 2015. LNCS, vol. 9293, pp. 556–576. Springer, Heidelberg (2015). https://doi.org/10.1007/978-3-662-48324-4_28
3. Bogdanov, A., et al.: PRESENT: an ultra-lightweight block cipher. In: Paillier, P., Verbauwhede, I. (eds.) CHES 2007. LNCS, vol. 4727, pp. 450–466. Springer, Heidelberg (2007). https://doi.org/10.1007/978-3-540-74735-2_31
4. Bolotnyy, L., Robins, G.: Physically unclonable function-based security and privacy in RFID systems. In: Fifth Annual IEEE International Conference on Pervasive Computing and Communications. PerCom 2007. IEEE (2007)
5. Bucci, M., Germani, L., Luzzi, R., Trifiletti, A., Varanonuovo, M.: A high-speed oscillator-based truly random number source for cryptographic applications on a smart card IC. IEEE Trans. Comput. **52**(4), 403–409 (2003)
6. Buchovecká, S., Kodýtek, F., Lórencz, R., Buček, J.: True random number generator based on ROPUF circuit. In: 2016 Euromicro Conference on Digital System Design (DSD). IEEE (2016)
7. Buchovecká, S., Kodýtek, F., Lórencz, R., Buček, J.: True random number generator based on ring oscillator PUF circuit. Microprocess. Microsyst. **53**(2017), 33–41 (2017)
8. Chan, H., Gligor, V.D., Perrig, A., Muralidharan, G.: On the distribution and revocation of cryptographic keys in sensor networks. IEEE Trans. Dependable Secure Comput. **2**(3), 233–247 (2005)
9. Deak N., Gyorfi T., Marton K., Vacariu L., Cret, O.: Highly efficient true random number generator in FPGA devices using phase-locked loops. In: 20th International Conference on Control Systems and Computer Science, pp. 453–458. IEEE (2015)
10. Delvaux, J., Gu, D., Schellekens, D., Verbauwhede, I.: Secure lightweight entity authentication with strong PUFs: mission impossible? In: Batina, L., Robshaw, M. (eds.) CHES 2014. LNCS, vol. 8731, pp. 451–475. Springer, Heidelberg (2014). https://doi.org/10.1007/978-3-662-44709-3_25
11. ElGamal, T.: A public-key cryptosystem and a signature scheme based on discrete logarithms. IEEE Trans. Inf. Theor. **IT-31**(4), 469–472 (1985)
12. Epstein, M., Hars, L., Krasinski, R., Rosner, M., Zheng, H.: Design and implementation of a true random number generator based on digital circuit artifacts. In: Walter, C.D., Koç, Ç.K., Paar, C. (eds.) CHES 2003. LNCS, vol. 2779, pp. 152–165. Springer, Heidelberg (2003). https://doi.org/10.1007/978-3-540-45238-6_13
13. Fairfield, R.C., Mortenson, R.L., Coulthart, K.B.: An LSI random number generator (RNG). In: Blakley, G.R., Chaum, D. (eds.) CRYPTO 1984. LNCS, vol. 196, pp. 203–230. Springer, Heidelberg (1985). https://doi.org/10.1007/3-540-39568-7_18

14. Fischer, V.: A closer look at security in random number generators design. In: Schindler, W., Huss, S.A. (eds.) COSADE 2012. LNCS, vol. 7275, pp. 167–182. Springer, Heidelberg (2012). https://doi.org/10.1007/978-3-642-29912-4_13

15. Fischer, V., Drutarovský, M.: True random number generator embedded in reconfigurable hardware. In: Kaliski, B.S., Koç, çK., Paar, C. (eds.) CHES 2002. LNCS, vol. 2523, pp. 415–430. Springer, Heidelberg (2003). https://doi.org/10.1007/3-540-36400-5_30

16. Golic, J.D.J.: New methods for digital generation and postprocessing of random data. IEEE Trans. Comput. **55**(10), 1217–1229 (2006)

17. Gyorfi, T., Cret, O., Suciu, A.: High performance true random number generator based on FPGA block rams. In: International Symposium on Parallel and Distributed Processing. IPDPS 2009, pp. 1–8. IEEE (2009)

18. Hammouri, G., Öztürk, E., Sunar, B.: A tamper-proof and lightweight authentication scheme. J. Pervasive Mob. Comput. **6**(4), 807–818 (2008)

19. Handschuh, H., Schrijen, G.J., Tuyls, P.: Hardware intrinsic security from physically unclonable functions. In: Sadeghi, A.R., Naccache, D. (eds.) Towards Hardware-Intrinsic Security. ISC. Springer, Heidelberg. https://doi.org/10.1007/978-3-642-14452-3_2

20. Haroon, A., Akram, S., Shah, M.A., Wahid, A.: E-lithe: a lightweight secure DTLS for IoT. In: 2017 IEEE 86th Vehicular Technology Conference (VTC-Fall), pp. 1–5. IEEE (2017)

21. Katzenbeisser, S., Kocabaş, Ü., Van Der Leest, V., Sadeghi, A.R., Schrijen, G.J., Wachsmann, C.: Recyclable PUFs: logically reconfigurable PUFs. J. Cryptogr. Eng. **1**(3), 177–186 (2011)

22. Kerckhoffs, A.: La cryptographie militaire. J. des sciences militaires **9**, 538 (1883)

23. Kirkpatrick, M.S., Bertino, E., Kerr, S.: PUF ROKs: generating read-once keys from physically unclonable functions. In: Proceedings of the Sixth Annual Workshop on Cyber Security and Information Intelligence Research. ACM (2010)

24. Kocabaş, Ü., Peter, A., Katzenbeisser, S., Sadeghi, A.-R.: Converse PUF-Based authentication. In: Katzenbeisser, S., Weippl, E., Camp, L.J., Volkamer, M., Reiter, M., Zhang, X. (eds.) Trust 2012. LNCS, vol. 7344, pp. 142–158. Springer, Heidelberg (2012). https://doi.org/10.1007/978-3-642-30921-2_9

25. Kodýtek, F., Lórencz, R.: A design of ring oscillator based PUF on FPGA. In: 2015 IEEE 18th International Symposium on Design and Diagnostics of Electronic Circuits and Systems (DDECS). IEEE (2015)

26. Kodýtek, F., Lórencz, R., Buček, J.: Improved ring oscillator PUF on FPGA and its properties. Microprocess. Microsyst. **47**, 55–63 (2016)

27. Kohlbrenner, P., Gaj, K.: An embedded true random number generator for FPGAs. In: Proceedings of the 2004 ACM/SIGDA 12th International Symposium on Field Programmable Gate Arrays. ACM (2004)

28. McKay, K.A.: Report on Lightweight Cryptography – NIST publication (2017). https://doi.org/10.6028/NIST.IR.8114

29. Maes, R.: Physically Unclonable Functions. Springer, Heidelberg (2016). https://doi.org/10.1007/978-3-642-41395-7

30. Maes, R., Van Herrewege, A., Verbauwhede, I.: PUFKY: a fully functional PUF-Based cryptographic key generator. In: Prouff, E., Schaumont, P. (eds.) CHES 2012. LNCS, vol. 7428, pp. 302–319. Springer, Heidelberg (2012). https://doi.org/10.1007/978-3-642-33027-8_18

31. Majzoobi, M., Rostami, M., Koushanfar, F., Wallach, D.S., Devadas, S.: Slender PUF protocol: a lightweight, robust, and secure authentication by substring matching. In: IEEE Symposium on Security and Privacy (SP), pp. 33–44 (2012)

32. Malina, L., Hajny, J., Fujdiak, R., Hosek, J.: On perspective of security and privacy-preserving solutions in the Internet of Things. Comput. Netw. **102**, 83–95 (2016)

33. Menezes, A.J., Van Oorschot, P.C., Vanstone, S.A.: Handbook of Applied Cryptography. CRC Press, Boca Raton (1996)

34. Öztürk, E., Hammouri, G., Sunar, B.: Towards robust low-cost authentication for pervasive devices. In: IEEE Conference on Pervasive Computing and Communications, PerCom (2008)

35. Pappu, R., Recht, B., Taylor, J., Gershenfeld, N.: Physical one-way functions. Science **297**(5589), 2026–2030 (2002)

36. Raza, S., Shafagh, H., Hewage, K., Hummen, R., Voigt, T.: Lithe: Lightweight secure CoAP for the Internet of Things. IEEE Sens. J. **13**(10), 3711–3720 (2013)

37. Roman, R., Zhou, J., Lopez, J.: On the features and challenges of security and privacy in distributed internet of things. Comput. Netw. **57**(10), 2266–2279 (2013)

38. RSA Laboratories: PKCS #5 V2.1: Password Based Cryptography Standard (2012)

39. Schindler, W.: Random number generators for cryptographic applications. In: Koç, Ç.K. (ed.) Cryptographic Engineering. Springer, Boston (2009). https://doi.org/10.1007/978-0-387-718 17-0_2

40. Schleiffer, C., Wolf, M., Weimerskirch, A., Wolleschensky, L.: Secure key management-a key feature for modern vehicle electronics. Technical Report, SAE Technical Paper (2013)

41. Sicari, S., Rizzardi, A., Grieco, L.A., Coen-Porisini, A.: Security, privacy and trust in Internet of Things: the road ahead. Comput. Netw. **76**, 146–164 (2015)

42. Sklavos, N., Zaharakis, I.D.: Cryptography and security in Internet of Things (IoTs): models, schemes, and implementations. In: IEEE Proceedings of the 8th IFIP International Conference on New Technologies, Mobility and Security (NTMS 2016), Larnaca, Cyprus (2016)

43. Suh, E.G., Devadas, S.: Physical unclonable functions for device authentication and secret key generation. In: Proceedings of the 44th annual Design Automation Conference, pp. 9–14. ACM (2007)

44. Suh, E.G., O'Donnell, C., Devadas, S.: AEGIS: a single-chip secure processor. IEEE Des. Test Comput. **24**, 6 (2007)

45. Tkacik, T.E.: A hardware random number generator. In: Kaliski, B.S., Koç, çK., Paar, C. (eds.) CHES 2002. LNCS, vol. 2523, pp. 450–453. Springer, Heidelberg (2003). https://doi. org/10.1007/3-540-36400-5_32

46. Tschofenig, H., Fossati, T.: Transport Layer Security (TLS)/Datagram Transport Layer Security (DTLS) Profiles for the Internet of Things. RFC 7925, July 2016

47. Van Herrewege, A., et al.: Reverse fuzzy extractors: enabling lightweight mutual authentication for PUF-Enabled RFIDs. In: Keromytis, A.D. (ed.) FC 2012. LNCS, vol. 7397, pp. 374–389. Springer, Heidelberg (2012). https://doi.org/10.1007/978-3-642-32946-3_27

Credential Intelligence Agency: A Threat Intelligence Approach to Mitigate Identity Theft

Timo Malderle[1]([⊠]), Felix Boes[1], Gina Muuss[1], Matthias Wübbeling[1,2], and Michael Meier[1,2]

[1] University of Bonn, Bonn, Germany
{malderle,boes,matthias.wuebbeling,mm}@cs.uni-bonn.de,
muuss@uni-bonn.de
[2] Fraunhofer FKIE, Bonn, Germany

Abstract. With the ongoing digitalization, identity data leakage and identity theft are a growing threat to individuals, companies and public security in general. For most existing classes of cyber threats, there exists established techniques and even services that generate valuable threat intelligence feeds, however, generating feeds about identity breaches is not deeply researched yet. Even if there are first services for preventing or mitigating identity thefts, most of these services heavily rely on the assumption that the latest leak data is discovered, however, not a single comprehensive study is known which examines how this precondition is fulfilled. In this paper, we introduce a new method for generating a threat intelligence feed about identity breaches so that all the existing preventive and mitigating services can react in a timely manner. Therefore, we develop a system that automatically classifies and extracts threat intelligence information out of an extensive amount of security related news articles. We show that this approach vastly reduces the manual effort for the identity security services, hence, increasing their efficiency.

Keywords: Identity leakage · Treat intelligence · Automated leak detection · Identity protection · Document classification

1 Introduction

Nowadays, most Internet users hold more than one email address and most of these email addresses are used for registrations at many different web services. Because of the vast amount of (more or less) useful web services, each Internet user possesses a growing number of user accounts. The increasing number of user accounts results in an ever-growing mass of passwords that each user must handle. For most users, this number of passwords leads to a confusing password management because it is too hard to memorize a unique and secure password for each user account. Unfortunately, this results in using insecure passwords or in reusing the same passwords for multiple accounts in countless cases. In addition to that security problem, a growing number of web services are affected by data breaches. Meaning, that occasionally millions of user data are stolen, which are published in identity data leaks by criminals.

To protect the users against the general problem of identity theft, various approaches and services are developed by different research groups and companies. Most of these

© Springer Nature Switzerland AG 2022
S. Furnell et al. (Eds.): ICISSP 2020, CCIS 1545, pp. 115–138, 2022.
https://doi.org/10.1007/978-3-030-94900-6_6

approaches are based on a concept in which new leak data is analyzed as soon as possible to initiate suitable countermeasures. Some of these approaches simply warn the users about their consternation, others aim to protect the infrastructure of companies or web services. All these approaches have in common that they react to security threats introduced by identity breaches. It is conceptualized how to counteract as soon as the services gets aware of a new identity breach. But a concept to get aware of it is missing in most published studies. All these services need a threat intelligence system that informs about the most recent breaching news.

To fill in the messing yet crucial foundation of said services, in this paper, we conceptualize and develop a threat intelligence system that is particularly designed for the use of alarming about the potential risk of identity theft. In order to realize that, the system analyzes automatically the latest news articles from security related news article websites. Therefore, information retrieval techniques are used to classify the articles if they are reporting about a relevant issue. If this is the case, relevant attributes are extracted from the articles, which assists an automatic processing of the data. This paper is based on the publication "Track Down Identity Leaks using Threat Intelligence" [18]. The previous work is extend by a very detailed discussion of the techniques employed in the preprocessing and classification of the news articles as well as a large scale study including more than 432 experiments, analyzing different preprocessing methods and their interplay to find out the best performing composition of preprocessing techniques. We emphasize that the system designed in this work is discussed with a strong focus on identity theft, however, it is clearly applicable to scenarios where the detection of yet unknown threats is crucial.

The remainder of this paper is organized as follows. Initially, in Sect. 2 related work is presented, covering the topics of the user perspective of passwords, identity leakage and threat intelligence. Hereafter, the full context for this work is described and the key idea for the proposed system is explained, see Sect. 3. After the key idea made clear, the concept of the automated system with its four units is introduced, see Sect. 4. In the next four sections, each unit of our system is presented in an own section in detail. The gathering of news articles (unit 1) is presented in Sect. 5. The classification of the gathered articles (unit 2) is described in Sect. 6. The subsequent attribution (unit 3) is outlined in Sect. 7, and the final presentation of the results (unit 4) is pictured in Sect. 8. In the evaluation, Sect. 9, the results of our 432 experiments are examined and the practical and scientific relevance is discussed. In the last section, the main outcome is concluded.

2   Related Work

Identity leakage is an increasingly critical problem in times of globalization and digitalization. A growing number of individuals and companies are affected by cyber-criminal activities. To mitigate the impact of this trend, manifold approaches and methods to protect victims are researched. The exact research field of identity leakage is not examined extensively. Certainly, there are other research areas which are inspecting the problem of identity leakage from different perspectives. The most influential areas focus on technical and usability aspects. The latter examines the handling of passwords from the user perspective. The former analyses the reason for identity leakage and develops methods to protect users against security problems resulting from identity theft.

2.1 The User Perspective on Passwords

From the recent perspective of security experts, the typical password handling by users is very alarming. At least 51–59% of all Internet users are reusing passwords identically or in a slightly modified form [25,43,45]. The average user reuses about 79% of its passwords [25]. In addition, the average length of passwords is only about 8.98 characters [44]. Probably, these facts are partly responsible for the growing publications of new identity leaks, because it is easier for criminals to steal identity data by making use of the insecure handling of passwords.

It is investigated how many users are affected by identity leakage. In recent literature, it is shown that 30% [28,35,37] to 83% [34] of Internet users login credentials are included in at least one data breach. Clearly, identity leakage is both a critical and a growing problem.

2.2 Identity Leakage

In the research field of identity leakage, various topics are under examination. The source and circulation of published identity leaks are analyzed [11,26].

Users affected by an identity leak stay unaware about that threat for a certain period, sometimes for more than one year [43]. At the moment, the only possibility for users to protect themselves against this threat is using *leak information services*. A *leak information service* is a web service where users proactively check whether they are affected by leaked identity data. To do so, users provide their email address as an identifier to the services website. The service searches through their leak database for the entered email address and presents the results to the user. Known *leak information services* are *Have I Been Pwned* [13], *HPI-Leakchecker* [10], *Uni-Bonn Leakchecker* [40] or the *avast heck-check* [1]. The two common problems with these services are that the users need to know such a service and that users must use it frequently to protect themselves.

In addition, methods and protocols are designed to inform users about their involvement in an identity leakage. There are different protocols for checking compromised credentials [17]. A well-known web service that provides such a protocol is *Have I Been Pwned* [13]. This service is integrated in Firefox as a plugin called *Firefox Monitor* [23]. Google develops another protocol that is deployed as a Chrome plugin [38,39].

Furthermore, there are activities for developing an automatic warning service that contacts the users by informing them about their breached identity data [19,20]. This research focuses on the development of a centralized warning service. Such a warning service offers an interface to web services to feed them with the most recent identity leak data via a protocol. This protocol transfers the data in a pseudonymized form. Then, each connected service checks whether these data contain user credentials allowing for a successful login. In the case of compromised user credentials, the service can contact the affected user to provide information on how to react. An alternative option to secure the companies infrastructure and the user can be done by disabling the potentially compromised user account.

2.3 Threat Intelligence and Information Retrieval

Threat Intelligence (TI), in contrast to legacy enterprise security, is based on the knowledge of risk, threats and vulnerabilities. Common network and host security solutions are based on rules, signatures and variants of heuristics. In contrast, the focus of TI is to minimize the attack surface as soon as possible after a vulnerability has been detected and knowledge about it becomes available. Regarding an administrators or CERTs perspective on threats like identity theft, risk assessment must be adapted to TI and means to encounter those threats must be developed [6].

One of most common buzzwords in modern cyber security research related to TI is Advanced Persistent Threats (APTs). Historically, APTs really changed the view on attacks and the intrusion kill chain [14] as a concept increases the value of TI. Kill chains model the actions taken by an attacker to successfully gain access to computers and information of a victim and to persist this access. *Reconnaissance* is the very first action of the kill chain. There, the attacker gathers as much information as possible about its victim [46]. With respect to identity theft, access to valid account credentials of employees of a targeted organization is a golden nugget of reconnaissance. An attacker that can impersonate employees is nearly incontrollable by any of the common means of cyber defense.

With APTs, TI, as a procedure to gather information from different sources, emerged. The understanding of cyberattacks, especially those that are targeted to a specific organization or a specific industry, improved the cyber defense operations. Sources of TI can be arbitrarily chosen and range from inhouse open source intelligence up to paid services providing professional TI feeds. Collaboration between peers using TI sharing platforms like MISP [21] or protocols such as STIX/TAXII [22] allows the distribution of information about indicators of compromise (IOCs) as well as vulnerability or general information about ongoing attacks [3].

Unfortunately, there is not so much about reputation of sources and, most likely, the validation of received information from a feed is not possible [15]. Acting upon TI is often limited to the generation of rules or signatures for legacy security gateways. As an example, (commercial) feeds exist that provide Snort rules for direct application to the packet filter of a firewall. Other information contained in TI is not actionable, as it is not specific enough. Assuming the TCP source port of an attack as an IOC, it is very unlikely that blocking just this port protects against this kind of attack.

Threat Intelligence, as a crucial part of cyber security, may provide valuable information about user accounts that has been leaked in the past. Already mentioned leak information services enable TI to collect information about account credentials that are available from leak data. Sharing TI between organizations allow the exchange of knowledge about account credential attacks based on leak data. An organization suffering from brute force attacks may record usernames and passwords and share this knowledge with others. This shared knowledge enables proactively limiting account capabilities or disable an account entirely, i.e., before an attack can impersonate it. This allows to increase account security and to decrease the attack surface based on impersonation [42].

Opposing other kind of TI information, leaked account credentials can be immediately checked upon receiving and validated against an organization's account database.

Although leak information services exist, there is no leak information service available that provides actionable leak data to be checked directly against an organization's authorization backend.

3   Context and Idea of the Threat Intelligence System

In this section, the context and idea of the developed system will be outlined. This is done for clarifying the basic problem and how the problem can be solved.

Generally, a threat intelligence system needs to be filled with recent information about relevant threats. In the application scenario of this research, a *warning service* for identity leaks should be operated. Such a leak warning service gathers identity leaks from the Internet, processes them and contacts the affected users and companies, who are affected by the leak. To operate such a warning service, information about recently published identity leaks, which are circulating though parts of the Internet, are needed. These information are needed to reduce the manual effort for the analysts. Analysts are staff members of this warning service and their tasks are to browse the Internet for new leak data. The analysts have a list of suitable forums, boards, download portals and searching tricks for locating new leaks. Certainly, to sweep these sources on a daily basis without any hint, which service was breached lately, is like seeking a needle in a haystack. However, when the analysts know about the latest breached web services, then they can search for the leaked data quite specifically.

An approach for gathering identity leak data is described in previous work [20]. In this work, it is outlined that it is possible to gather more than 20 billion identity data records by means of the presented method. In later examinations, some limitations for quickly finding latest articles were found. For that reason, the approach, presented in [20], are enhanced by the results of this paper. This paper presents a system for extracting threat intelligence information out of a data feed consisting of human readable news texts. In the presented individual application scenario, the threat intelligence information is about the latest identity leaks and breaches. But the general approach of the system presented here is not limited to this scenario.

Factoring in the experience of an analyst, it is helpful to read security related newspaper websites. Regularly, appropriate information was helpful to identify the most recent leaks. However, it is a time-consuming activity to read many news article websites every day. The primary idea for the designed and implemented system in this paper results out of the described problem. There is a need for an instrument that scrapes articles from feeding sources and classifies them whether they are reporting about the wanted threat intelligence topic. In the context of this research, news articles need to be classified into *leak related* and *leak unrelated* articles. *Leak related articles* are those that report about topics around identity leaks, identity theft and service breaches. Therefore, a method is in demand that realizes the classification automatically.

When skimming a few of the mentioned articles, a human can easily classify articles in the categories *leak related* and *leak unrelated* only by reading the title and looking at some paragraphs of the content part. A possibility check of an automated classification of this news articles is a part of this paper. Therefore, we present a tool that automatically classifies news articles in the categories leak-related and leak-unrelated.

In the context of the underlying research project, during the last three years over 20 billion leaked identities were gathered from relevant sources. These identities are distributed over 84 802 files and 3 752 folders. 76.18% off all files have a filename that only consists of numbers like 81537.txt. These numerical named files a belonging to so-called *Collections*. *Collections* are compilations of multiple identity leaks, which are accumulated into one newer and bigger leak. Such *Collections* are often published under a new name and its content cannot be assigned to belonging online web services because all helpful metadata is removed. However, most *Collections* are spreading older leaks under a new name and face.

Certainly, the remaining 20 199 files, which are 23.82% of all files, contain more information than only numbers. Here the question is, what information can be found in the remaining filenames. When examining these data, the file paths including the filenames are analyzed whether they contain helpful metadata that enables a mapping to a breached web service. Therefore, the file paths are handled like a string on which a domain search is performed. If a syntactically correct domain is found, then the top-level domain is checked for existence. At least, a DNS request is sent to Googles DNS server 8.8.8.8 to validate if an A or *MX* record exists for this domain. If such records exist, then the probability is high that a web service is provided under this domain to which the leak corresponds to. The result of this analysis is that 50.32% of the 20 199 files can be mapped to corresponding web services.

Coming back to the tasks of an analyst with these results, if an analyst knows the name of a breached service, it is much easier to find the related leak data because the analysts can identify the searched leak data by comparing the web service name with the filename of the leak. This is possible at a minimum of 50% by the occurrence of a valid domain in the filename or file path. The real success rate is possibly higher because the filename can include the single web service name. This name helps equally to identify the breached service, but it is not a valid domain, which is identified through the previous analyses.

4   A System for Generating Threat Intelligence Feeds

The need for an automated system that generates a threat intelligence feed for a security analyst is made clear in Sect. 3. In this paper, modern techniques from *Information Retrieval*, *Natural Language Processing* and *Machine Learning* are combined to design the system *SLAP*. In general, *SLAP* can generate threat intelligence feeds for various topics. However, in order to demonstrate its effectiveness and to ease the discussion, we present *SLAP* in the context of detecting identity leakage.

In this section, an overview of *SLAP*s core units *Scrape*, *Learn*, *Attribute* and *Present* is provided. Their interplay, culminating in the detection of recent identity leaks is shown in Fig. 1. A detailed discussion of the units is found in the following sections. *SLAP*s performance is evaluated in Sect. 9.

The unit *Scrape* monitors a set of carefully selected public sources that report on cyber security, see Sect. 5. More precisely, the unit *Scrape* is managing a swarm of scrapers. Hereby, each scraper is frequently scanning its assigned source for the most recent news articles. Those news articles are then tagged with meta information and provided to the unit *Learn*.

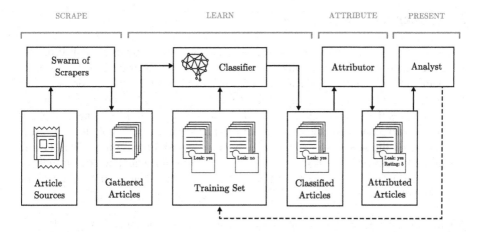

Fig. 1. *SLAP* is a system for generating a threat intelligence feed.

The unit *Learn* trains a model to classify the stream of news articles provided by *Scrape*. Hereby, *Learn* is adapting over time. More precisely, the labeled training sets, and the labeled test data, as well as the hyperparameters of the model are continuously improving.

To initialize the unit *Learn*, a proper set of labeled training and test data is provided to *SLAP*, see Subsect. 6.1. Then, these data are embedded into a high dimensional feature space, see Subsect. 6.3, and *SLAP* learns a model, see Subsect. 6.2. Both, the embedding and the model use a set of hyperparameters that are optimized automatically with respect to a given metric, see Subsect. 6.4. Tweaking the optimized hyperparameters further, using the expert's knowledge, is optional. These steps result in the initial model of the unit *Learn*. The evolution of a given generation of the unit *Learn* is sketched in the paragraphs below.

The stream of news articles collected by the unit *Scrape* are classified using the most recent generation of the unit *Learn*. Note that it is reasonable to expect that only a small portion of articles on cyber security point to identity leaks. Those articles classified as leak related are further processed by the unit *Attribute*. There, information (like the name of the service that was breached) are extracted from the article and the relevance and actuality of the leak is rated, see Sect. 7.

The unit *Present* presents articles with the highest threat rating to the security analysts for further evaluation, investigation and, in case of a yet unknown data breach, reaction, see Sect. 8. In order to obtain the next generation of the unit *Learn*, the analysts label their articles after evaluation. Once enough articles are processed, the newly labeled articles and the current generation of training and test data are used to train the next iteration of the unit *Learn*, see Subsect. 6.1 and Subsect. 6.4. The resulting model is picked by the security experts if it outperforms the current generation.

5 Gathering News Articles

The system *SLAP* collects human readable texts from news articles published online, which are then classified, attributed and presented to the security analysts. In order to obtain and prepare these articles, *SLAP* provides the unit *Scrape*. It consists of an automated scraper that gathers news articles from news article websites. A crawler, which browses the whole Internet, is for this task not as useful as it seems in the first moment. The human readable text must be extracted out of the whole html website. Depending on the source, this turns out to be a tricky task because it is a hard task to detect the human readable text and distinguish it from, for example, advertisements. To avoid an inaccurate gathering of human readable text, suitable article sources are selected. Following constraints are made to select appropriate sources [18]:

Media. In order to enable automated collection and evaluation of the articles, the sources are limited to digital media.

Language. Regarding the current preference of English in the field of Natural Language Processing as well as security research and computer science in general. We focus on this language, based on the assumption that a relevant article about a new leak is published in English, at least as translation.

Accessibility. The source must be freely accessible and not hindered by limitations like pay walls, captcha-queries or censorship. While this form of technical hurdles could be overcome, it bears additional cost, not benefiting this proof of concept.

Significance. This quality can be acquired by having a significant scope or having specialized in IT security, ensuring a good coverage or high specificity.

These constraints lead in the following news articles websites [18]: *Comodo*[1], *GBHackers*[2], *HackRead*[3], *Help Net Security*[4], *Infosecurity-Magazine*[5], *Security Gladiators*[6], *Security Week*[7], *Techworm*[8], *The Hacker News*[9], *Threat Post*[10], *The Guardian*[11], *Information Week*[12], *Naked Security* [13], *Trendmicro*[14], *Cyberdefense Magazine*[15].

Since each listed website is structured differently, there is a need to implement a specialized article extracting module for each website. The scraper modules, which are

---

[1] Comodo:https://blog.comodo.com.

[2] GBHackers: https://gbhackers.com/category/data-breach/.

[3] HackRead: https://www.hackread.com/hacking-news.

[4] Help Net Security: https://www.helpnetsecurity.com/view/news/.

[5] Infosecurity-Magazine: https://www.infosecurity-magazine.com/news/.

[6] Security Gladiators: https://securitygladiators.com/internet-security-news/.

[7] Security Week: https://www.securityweek.com.

[8] Techworm: https://www.techworm.net.

[9] The Hacker News: https://thehackernews.com.

[10] Threat Post: https://threatpost.com/blog/.

[11] The Guardian: https://www.theguardian.com/international/.

[12] Information Week: https://www.informationweek.com/.

[13] Naked Security: https://nakedsecurity.sophos.com/.

[14] Trendmicro: https://www.trendmicro.com/vinfo/us/security/news/.

[15] Cyberdefense Magazine: http://www.cyberdefensemagazine.com/category/news/.

implemented to extract the article content, are based on the framework *scrapy* [32]. The first challenge is to navigate automated through each website. Some websites use a common pagination in their article's overviews. It is a simple task to scrape these sites with *scrapy*. Other websites are adding new articles to their article overview by an AJAX request when users reach the last articles at the bottom of the website. For scraping these article websites, the provided API is used. After downloading the html of each article, the human readable text must be extracted. Therefore, two different approaches are used. The first one is to use the framework *newspaper3k*, which extracts article elements like title, author, publication date and human readable text automatically [24]. The second approach is to define an XPath expression to extract each needed article element separately. The XPath approach is used when *newspaper3k* delivers insufficient results. All gathered and parsed news articles are stored in a mongoDB.

Crawling of these news articles via the aforementioned spiders yields a total of 55 742 articles, which were saved in a mongoDB resulting in a size of 170 MiB. The number of articles from different sources varied greatly, ranging from 67 articles from thehackernews.com to 29 052 articles from helpnetsecurity.com. The average length of the articles is 2 886 characters.

In Fig. 2, the gathered articles are shown spread by the publication dates of the articles. The notable spikes at the beginning and at the end of the timeframe are due to publishers changing the dates on their articles. This appears to have two causes. The spike at the beginning seems to be caused by the fact that these articles are the initial ones, which the publisher moved to a new system, and setting all their dates to the same one in the process. The spike at the end is caused by a publisher updating a substantial number of articles. This results in the fact that our scrapers detect them as new articles and add them to the dataset. The oldest crawled articles date back to April 2002, resulting in an average of 9 articles per day for a time span of 18 years.

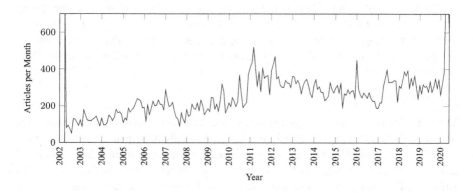

Fig. 2. Gathered news articles spread by publication date.

6   Classifying News Articles

The unit *Learn*s purpose is the binary classification of the articles provided by the unit *Scrape*. *Learn* is designed to use recent techniques from Natural Language Processing including Machine Learning. Hereby, the articles are converted into sparse vectors living in a features space of dimension 10 000. A linear SVM is used to train the classifier. Moreover, the labeled dataset and the model improve over time. The detailed choices discussed later lead to a valuable classifier that can be trained on consumer hardware in under an hour.

The quality of the classifier heavily depends on a proper representation of the features of the articles and the labeled data. The construction of the initial labeled dataset and the most important characteristics of the latest set of labeled articles is sketched in Subsect. 6.1. In order to make our design choices transparent, the details of the classifier are discussed in Subsect. 6.2 and then, in Subsect. 6.3, the representation of texts by feature vectors is outlined. The model is evaluated in Sect. 9 with a suitable quality measure that is introduced in Subsect. 6.4. How the best hyperparameter are determined is outlined in Subsect. 6.4. Lastly, the evolution of the model and the labeled data is explained in Subsect. 6.5.

6.1   Building and Evolving Test and Training Set

In order to train the classifier, a carefully assembled test set is inevitable. As pointed out before, the labeled data and the model evolve over time.

In the very first step, the security experts filter the articles provided by date, source or keywords for manual classification. This leads to a first proper labeled dataset of less than a hundred articles. The evolvement of the labeled dataset is described in Subsect. 6.5.

The latest evolution of the labeled dataset consists of 15 217 articles with a total of 1 997 classified leaks. Note that, because of the design of *SLAP*, the percentage of leak related articles in the labeled data set is considerably higher than in the complete dataset. There, the number of articles relating to identity leaks is estimated to be 3.8%.

6.2   The Classifier

A classifier that produces valuable predictions and consumes not more than a reasonable amount of time and memory in its training phase is highly anticipated. Such a classifier depends directly on the representation of significant features of the data and on the choice of a model. In the field of Natural Language Processing, an established strategy is the choice of an embedding of texts into a high-dimensional features space on which an SVM is trained [33,36]. We follow this strategy and explain our design choices.

Given feature vectors $v_1, \ldots, v_l \in \mathbb{R}^N$, the training of an SVM usually translates into a quadratic optimization problem of the following form:

$$\min_{\omega} \frac{1}{2}\omega^t Q \omega - \beta^t \omega \tag{1}$$

The non-diagonal entries of the quadratic matrix Q are $Q_{ij} = \pm v_i^t v_j$ or, if a Kernel K is used, $Q_{ij} = \pm K(v_i, v_j)$. Note that Q is dense if a common Kernel is applied (because $K \neq 0$). Note further, that two feature vectors v_i, v_j not sharing a common non-vanishing feature contribute with a zero, i.e., $Q_{ij} = 0$. In practice, SVMs benefit from the sparsity of the matrix Q with respect to time and memory complexity. In order to make use of this fact, we employ a linear SVM without Kernel and compose a text embedding that disregards features occurring too frequently.

The implementation of *SLAP* allows to choose between the SVM libraries *libsvm* [4] or *liblinear* [9]. The former applies kernels and makes use of a deterministic method to train the model [5]. The latter omits the use of kernels and employs an approximation algorithm that converges to an ε-accurate solution in $O(\log(1/\varepsilon))$ steps [12]. In our setting, *liblinear* performs two magnitudes faster and consumes less memory while producing an equally valuable model.

6.3   Preprocessing

In order to make full use of the SVM, the texts are embedded into a high dimensional feature space such that their features are sparsely scattered in the sense of Subsect. 6.2. This process is usually referred to as *preprocessing*. To this end, each text is converted to a set of features in the feature extraction phase. Next, features that occur too frequently are removed in the feature selection phase. Finally, the features are weighted and thus every text is represented by a sparse, high dimensional feature vector. In each of the three phases, *Learn* offers a variety of modular methods, which are described below. In Subsect. 6.4, it is discussed how the most suitable composition of these methods is obtained.

Let us remark, that dimension reduction techniques, for example principal component analysis, are not incorporated into *Learn*. In our setting, neither do time or memory complexity benefit from well-established techniques nor does the quality of the model.

Feature Extraction. The feature extraction stage is used to convert each document from its text representation to a set of features and it is common to refer to these features as *terms*. To this end, the unit *Learn* offers a variety of wellknown procedures that are composed consecutively, see Fig. 3. The first, the last and the *bag of words* procedure is mandatory, whilst all other procedures are optional. Which of these optional steps improve the classification process, highly depends on the use case, see also Subsect. 6.4.

To improve the quality of all procedures, all non-ASCII characters are removed, and the text is split into *tokens* in the first step. These *tokens* are typically single words obtained by splitting the text at space characters. At the end of the preprocessing phase, each word is either discarded or converted into a *term*.

The second step is optional and removes conjunctions like "and", "but" and "yet". Conjunction removal is a common step in text preprocessing [7]. The third step is also optional and performs a complexity reduction of all grammatically cases. Both *lemmatization* and *stemming* aim to achieve a linguistic aggregation of the inflected word forms to a root of the words (*tokens*). They differ in their strategies to reach said goal. On the one hand, *stemming* relies on simple rules to remove suffixes of words and trim them to their stems [27]. *Lemmatization* on the other hand, reduces the words to their lemma using more advanced rules (as well as exceptions from said rules) [29]. *Stemming* and *lemmatization* highly interfere with the effectiveness of one another and are therefore never used together. The fourth step is the removal of a given list of *stopwords* from the set of features and it is also optional. Roughly speaking, *stopwords* are the most common words in a language. There is a zoo of lists of stopwords. Here, the stopword list of the NLTK framework is used [2]. The last optional procedure is the removal of punctuation marks and replacement of numbers with the string "NUMBER" because both of these types of tokens are not expected to be useful for the classification process. This results in 24 possible preprocessing procedures in total.

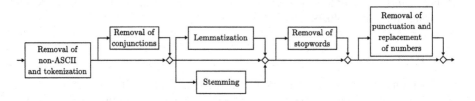

Fig. 3. The composable procedures of the preprocessing feature extraction phase.

Feature Selection. The feature extraction phase converts documents to a set of features, and it is common to refer to these features as *terms*. As the very first step of the feature selection phase, the *bag of words* corresponding to the document and the feature extraction is created. Then, most importantly, each term is ranked, and the top 10 000 terms are selected. Most modern methods rate the importance of terms according to the following criteria established in [41].

1. A term is important, if it occurs frequently in one class and is absent in the other class(es).
2. A term is relatively important, if it occurs only in some of the classes.
3. A term is unimportant, if it occurs rarely in one class and is absent in the other class(es).
4. A term is unimportant, if it occurs frequently in all classes.

Choosing the most suitable rating methods depends on the use case and is highly non-trivial.

   In our setting, we have exactly two classes (articles reporting on identity leaks or not) and the two classes are heavily unbalanced, see Subsect. 6.1. The *relative discrimination criterion, RDC* (short form), [30] and its variations [16] are filter methods, designed for unbalanced classes. They produce the most promising results in our preliminary tests. In the following paragraphs, the *relative discrimination criterion* and its variations are described.

   In order to rank a term t with the *relative discrimination criterion*, the following notations are introduced. For simplicity, a document is called positive if it reports

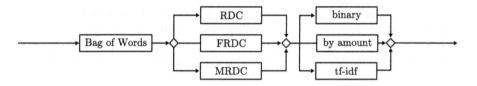

Fig. 4. The composable procedures of the feature selection and feature weighting phase.

on an identity leak and it is called negative otherwise. The number of positive documents is *Pos* and the number of negative documents is *Neg*. Given a term count c, the number of positive (resp. negative) documents containing t exactly c times is $tp(t, c)$ (resp. $fp(t, c)$). Normalizing the unbalanced classes yields $tpr(t, c) = tp(t, c)/Pos$ and $fpr(t, c) = fp(t, c)/Neg$. The *relative discrimination criterion* of t with respect to the term count c is:

$$RDC(t, c) = \frac{|tpr(t, c) - fpr(t, c)|}{c \cdot \min(tpr(t, c), fpr(t, c))} \tag{2}$$

In case a term does occur exactly in one class, $RDC(t, c)$ is not infinite but the denominator is replaced by $c \cdot \varepsilon$ for a suitably small value ε. The *RDC-rank* of a term t is the discrete integral:

$$RDC(t) = \int RDC(t, x) dx \tag{3}$$

For further details and comparisons with other, well known ranking methods, the reader is referred to [30].

The purpose of the *multivariate relative discrimination criterion* (MRDC) is the selection of terms with the highest RDC-ranking while avoiding redundancies [16]. To this end, terms are selected iteratively using the MRDC-ranking. Denoting the set of already selected features by S and the correlation of two terms t and s by $\sigma(t, s)$, the *MRDC-rank* of t with respect to S is the following [16].

$$MRDC_S(t) = RDC(t) - \sum_{t \neq s \in S} |\sigma(t, s)| \tag{4}$$

Removing correlating features is clearly desirable. However, in our setting, the MRDC-ranking performed almost always worse compared to the RDC-ranking, see Sect. 9. This is potentially caused by the fact, that the RDC-ranking and the correlation coefficient are not on the same scale. Hence, the above formula does not allow for a direct interpretation to us.

To overcome the shortcomings of the *MRDC-rank*, we introduce the *fitted relative discrimination criterion*. The *FRDC-rank* of t with respect to a set of already chosen terms S is:

$$FRDC_S(t) = RDC(t) \cdot \prod_{t \neq s \in S} (1 - |\sigma(t, s)|) \tag{5}$$

In order to iteratively construct the set of selected features S, the term with the highest FRDC-ranking is selected in each step until 10 000 features are selected.

Observe that $FRDC_S(t) = 0$ if t correlates perfectly with at least one term in S. On the other hand, $FRDC_S(t) = RDC(t)$ if t does not correlate at all with any term in S.

Observe further, that an implementation of $FRDC_S$ will most probably lead to $FRDC_S(t) = 0$ if S is large because large products of factors $0 \leq 1 - |\sigma(t, s)| < 1$ vanish numerically. One way out is taking only a small amount of the terms with the highest correlation into account. In our experiments, up to ten features that minimized $1 - |\sigma(t, s)|$ are used. This leads to promising results, see Sect. 9. A further evaluation of the FRDC-ranking is in the scope of future work.

Feature Weighting. In the final step of the preprocessing, the selected features are weighted in order to convert a given document into a high dimensional feature vector. To this end, the unit *Learn* offers three methods. Utilizing *binary weights*, a selected feature is represented by 1 if is present in the document and by 0 otherwise. Therefore, the feature vector of the document consists only of zeros and ones. Similarly, *counting features*, the entries of the feature vector equals the number of occurrences of a given feature in the given document. Lastly, the well-known *Term-Frequency-Inverse-Document-Frequency* weights the feature frequency (in the given document) by its inverse document frequency in a logarithmic scale, see [31].

Finally, the imbalance in the volume of the two classes is handled to improve the quality of the SVM. Each feature vector is normalized (to have Euclidean distance one) and is then weighted with $|Samples|/|Leaks|$ or $|Samples|/|NoLeaks|$ respectively.

6.4 Choosing Suitable Quality Measures and Hyperparameter

A reasonable quality measure is fundamental to properly evaluate a given classifier. However, finding a suitable quality measure depends heavily on the use case. In our setting, news articles are classified, rated and, if their respective threat rating is high enough, presented to the security analysts. Hereby, a single security expert must process only a hand full of articles on average per day. Note that false positives are quickly handled and therefore, minimizing the number of false positives is desired but not crucial. However, being informed on recent data breaches as soon as possible is highly anticipated, i.e., the number of false negatives must be small. Moreover, the dataset is unbalanced because the vast number of articles on cyber security do not report on identity theft, see Subsect. 6.1. Therefore, the well-known F_1-score (being the harmonic mean of recall and precision) is not suitable. To evaluate *SLAP*, we choose the weighted harmonic mean of recall and precision with recall amounting for 95% of the total weight, i.e., our performance metric is

$$F_\beta = (1 + \beta^2) \cdot \frac{\text{prec} \cdot \text{rec}}{(\beta^2 \cdot \text{prec}) + \text{rec}} \quad \text{with } \beta = \frac{0.95}{1 - 0.95} = 19. \tag{6}$$

Similarly, to finding a suitable quality measure, it is highly non-trivial to determine the best parameters for the model consisting of the text embedding composition in combination with the hyperparameters of the SVM. Besides using *expert knowledge*, the unit *Learn* offers an automated search for optimal parameters. More precisely, for each composition of the preprocessing methods, the best hyperparameter for the SVM are determined via grid search with tenfold cross-validation.

6.5   Evolving the Model and the Labeled Dataset

The unit *Learn* evolves over time by improving both the model and the labeled data. Given the latest labeled data set T_i, the best performing model $\mathfrak{M}_i$ is determined as described in Subsect. 6.4. If $\mathfrak{M}_i$ outperforms its predecessor $\mathfrak{M}_{i-1}$ it is picked by the security expert.

With the latest model, the articles provided by the unit *Scrape* are classified by the unit *Learn* (see below), attributed by the unit *Attribute* (see Sect. 7) and presented to the security experts by the unit *Present* (see Sect. 8). The manual classification of the presented articles yields the next preliminary labeled data set $T_i \subset \tilde{T}_{i+1}$. Using the expert's knowledge, $\tilde{T}_{i+1}$ is further refined, e.g., by removing all articles from $\tilde{T}_{i+1}$ exceeding a certain age. This results in the latest set of labeled articles T_i.

7   Attributing Articles

Valuable threat intelligence feeds contain clear structured threat information. The classification of news articles in the categories *leak related* and *leak unrelated* is the first task of *SLAP*. For a threat intelligence feed only the *leak related* articles are needed because they are reporting about a security incident in the category of identity leaks. However, whole news articles are unsuitable to fit in serialized thread intelligence feed formats like *STIX* [8]. Therefore, *SLAP* extracts specified attributes from the news articles utilizing its unit *Attribute* (see Fig. 1).

The attribution of the articles is done using multiple modules. Each module has a specified kind of information that is to be extracted from the news articles. These modules are presented in greater detail in the previous work [18].

The first module is the *Service Detection Module*, which extracts the name of the affected web service or company. The second modules purpose is the detection of identity data types that are mentioned to be included in the appropriate leak file. The third module is for searching for the number of affected user accounts that are included in the leak. *SLAP* scrapes news articles from multiple news article websites. For that reason, it is possible that also multiple news article agencies are reporting about the same security incident. To avoid multiple warnings about the same event the *Clustering Module* aggregates articles that are reporting about the same incident.

The last module, which is presented in [18], is the *Threat Level Calculation*. This module determines a threat level of the incident with the help of the results of the previous modules. Hereby, each article is tagged with a value from 1 (*smallest potential risk*) to 9 (*biggest potential risk*) [18]. The complete model for the risk calculation is presented in [18][Fig.1].

8   Presenting the Threat Intelligence Feed

The classified and attributed articles need to be presented to the analyst. For a usable and rapid user interaction, in the previous work, a user interface is designed to present an analyst the latest classified articles. In [18][Fig. 3], the graphical user interface, consisting of a dashboard, allows the analyst to read the classified articles and to label them, if an article is about a leak or not. If an article is classified into a wrong category the analyst corrects that by clicking the appropriate button. Based on these labels, a retraining of the classifier is performed for an improvement of the classified results, see Subsect. 6.5.

9   Evaluation of the Unit Learn

The quality of *SLAP* is evaluated in this section. More precisely, the evaluation concentrates on the quality of the unit *Learn* introduced in Sect. 6. For an evaluation of the other units, the reader is referred to [18].

The specification of the datasets and the hardware is given in Subsect. 9.1. Then, in Subsect. 9.2, the quality of *Learn* is evaluated on the large scale with the quality measures Recall and Precision. The best performing models are described and evaluated in Subsect. 9.3 using the F_1-score and the quality measure F_β introduced in Subsect. 6.4. Lastly, the evolution of *Learn* is briefly evaluated in Subsect. 9.4.

9.1   Specification of Datasets and Hardware

The labeled dataset consists of 15 211 articles with a minimum length of the content of 200 characters. Shorter articles are discarded. The average length of the articles is 2 966 characters. A total of 1 997 articles are classified to report on identity leakage by a human.

From the labeled dataset, three labeled datasets are derived and used in the evaluation. The dataset *Titles* disregards the text of the article, only the title is kept. The dataset *Article* disregards the title of the article, only the article body is incorporated. Lastly, the dataset *Both* integrate both, the title and the articles text.

For each of the three categories *Titles*, *Articles* and *Both* a total of 432 experiments are performed. To obtain a reliable performance estimation, each experiment is carried out with a tenfold cross-validation.

For each configuration of preprocessing methods, the model can be trained on consumer hardware equipped with an Intel Core i7 8700k and 16 GiB of RAM. There, the training phase of the model consumes 8:25 min of Wall-Time and 20:30 min of CPU time on average. During said training phase the maximum memory usage is 2.6 GiB, the average CPU usage is 260% and the maximum CPU usage is 710%.

The actual evaluation runs on a Kubernetes cluster with up to 80 instances being executed in parallel. There, the average Wall-Time of one cross-validation step including training and validation is estimated to be 14 min with a variance of 3 min and 30 s.

9.2   Large Scale Analysis

In this section, the most significant impacts on the quality are discussed in the large scale. Picking the right number of features influences the quality the most. Then, having the number of features fixed to be 10 000, choosing the best feature selection methods improves the precision further. Fixing the best feature selection methods also, the effect of feature extraction and feature weighting methods are discussed.

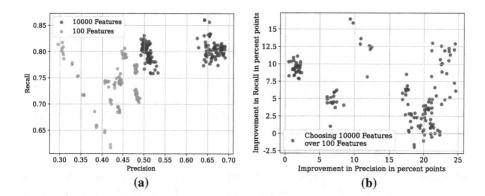

Fig. 5. a Each of the 288 experiments in the category *Article* is represented by a dot. The model benefits from choosing 10 000 features. **b** Each dot represents the improvement in percent points of an experiment in the category *Article* by choosing 10 000 over 100 features.

Number of Features. In the category *Article*, choosing 10 000 or 100 features to train the model affects its quality the most. From Fig. 5a it is evident, that the model benefits from choosing 10 000 features instead of 100. Figure 5b depicts the improvement in percent point of each experiment in the category *Article* by choosing 10 000 over 100 features. The improvement in recall ranges from −1.95 percent points (pp) to 16.44 pp with a median of 5.49 pp and a variance of 16.91 pp. The improvement in precision ranges from 0.49 pp to 24.64 pp with a median of 17.91 pp and a variance of 68.93 pp. The same effects are observed in the classes *Title* and *Both*. We conclude, that choosing more features leads to a significant increase in quality in almost all cases.

Feature Selection Methods. Continuing the large-scale analysis, we concentrate on the category *Both* while fixing the number of features to be 10 000. After removing two outlines, we are left with a total of 210 experiments. For the category *Both*, it is evident from Fig. 6a that MRDC leads to a worse precision. Figure 6b depicts the improvement in percent point of each experiment in the category *Both* by disregarding MRDC. Choosing RDC over MRDC leads to an improvement in recall that ranges from −4.33 pp to 5.07 pp with a median of 0.97 pp and a variance of 6.12 pp. The improvement in precision ranges from −4.33 pp to 5.07 pp with a median of 0.97 pp and a variance of 6.12 pp. Choosing FRDC over MRDC leads to an improvement in

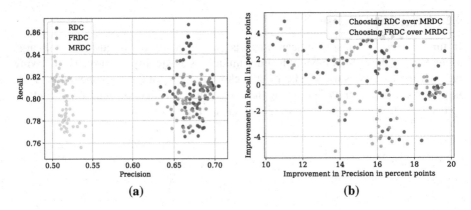

Fig. 6. a Each of the 210 experiments in the category *Both* is represented by a dot. The number of features is 10 000. The model benefits from not choosing MRDC. **b** Each dot represents the improvement in percent points of an experiment in the category *Both* by choosing RDC respectively FRDC over MRDC.

recall that ranges from –5.14 pp to 4.97 pp with a median of –0.05 pp and a variance of 6.90 pp. The improvement in precision ranges from 10.41 pp to 19.68 pp with a median of 16.01 pp and a variance of 5.62 pp. Choosing RDC over FRDC leads to a neglectable improvement in recall and precision with medians around 0.15 pp. The same tendencies are observed in the categories *Article* and *Title*. We conclude that choosing RDC or FRDC over MRDC leads to a vast increase in precision. Moreover, a deeper evaluation of the FRDC-ranking is in the scope of future work.

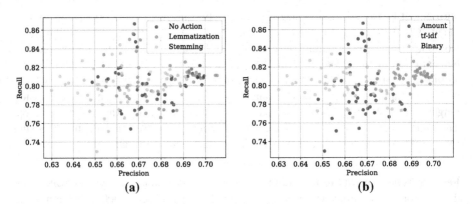

Fig. 7. a Each of the 142 experiments in the category *Both* is represented by a dot. The number of features is 10 000, the feature selection method is RDC or FRDC. **b** Each of the 142 experiments in the category *Both* is represented by a dot. The number of features is 10 000, the feature selection method is RDC or FRDC.

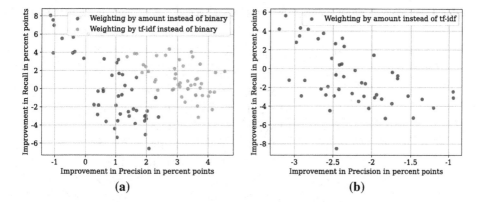

Fig. 8. a Each dot represents the improvement in percent points of an experiment by choosing a feature weighting method over binary. **b** Each dot represents the improvement in percent points of an experiment by weighting the features by amount instead of binary.

Feature Weighting and Feature Extraction. At the end of the large-scale analysis, we concentrate on the categories *Both* while fixing the number of features to be 10 000 and the feature selection method to be RDC or FRDC. Therefore, a total of 142 experiments per category is considered. Aside from feature weighting, the remaining steps did not significantly correlate with an improvement of the quality of the model, see Fig. 7a for an example. Most interestingly, Fig. 7b shows that weighting the features by the amount of words leads to the best results with respect to recall while tf-idf leads to the best results with respect to precision. Analyzing further, Fig. 8a depicts the improvement of precision and recall if the features are weighted by amount or tf-idf instead of the binary weighting. From Fig. 8b it is clear that weighting features by amount instead of tf-idf leads to a significant increase in recall while reducing the precision. Overall, this leads to a significant improvement of the model with respect to our quality measure F_β.

The same tendencies are observed for the category *Article*. We conclude that weighting the features by amount for the categories *Both* and *Article* improves the quality with respect to F_β most likely if 10 000 features are selected with RDC. However, if only 100 features are selected or if RDC is not used, the analogous prediction cannot be drawn.

9.3   Analyzing the Best Performing Models

In this section, the ten best performing models are discussed. The top-three of each of the categories *Title*, *Article* and *Both* are seen in Table 1. Hereby, the first column states the respective F_β-rating.

The configuration of the model achieving the best result is presented in Table 2. The best model achieves an F_β-score of 0.866 for *Both* respectively 0.855 for *Title* and *Article*. This is a decent quality for the heavily unbalanced dataset, see Subsect. 6.1 and compare [36].

The top ten models use RDC to select 10 000 features. For the categories *Both* and *Article*, these features are weighted by amount. The steps in the preprocessing phase

Table 1. For each category, the three best performing models, according to the F_β-rating, are shown.

F_β-rating	Category	Recall	Precision	F_1	F_β
1	Both	0.866565	0.668323	0.754465	0.865852
6	Both	0.855905	0.667691	0.749856	0.855234
7	Both	0.855290	0.668046	0.749442	0.854617
2	Title	0.861454	0.617852	0.719428	0.860513
8	Title	0.854399	0.607984	0.710120	0.853438
10	Title	0.851844	0.608536	0.709763	0.850901
3	Article	0.860404	0.641942	0.735011	0.859591
4	Article	0.860404	0.641942	0.735011	0.859591
5	Article	0.856412	0.653497	0.741152	0.855676

do not correlate with improving the quality with statistical significance. For the category *Title* the best weighting method varies but the removal of punctuation and the replacement of numbers improves the quality significantly.

Let us discuss the performance of *SLAP* in the perspective of a real-world scenario. Using the public resources suggested in Sect. 5, an analyst must read about 100 articles every week on average since the beginning of 2019. In our dataset, the number of articles reporting about identity leaks is estimated to be about 4%, see Subsect. 6.1. Using *SLAP*, an analyst needs to read, on average, about 5 to 6 articles every week, with approximately 3 to 4 of which are about an identity leak and 1 to 2, which are not. It is reasonable to assume that every leak is covered in at least two public resources. Even with these conservative assumptions, at most 2% of not covered are filtered out

Table 2. For each category, the selected procedures of the best performing models, according to the F_β-rating, are shown. The procedures are removal of conjunctions (Conj), Lemmatization, stemming, or none (L/S/N), Removal of stopwords (Stopwords), Removal of punctuations and replacement of numbers (P+N), Feature selection (Select) and Feature weighting (Weighting).

F_β-rating	Category	Conj	L/S/N	Stopwords	P+N	Select	Weighting
1	Both	No	No	No	Yes	RDC	Amount
6	Both	No	Lem	No	Yes	RDC	Amount
7	Both	Yes	No	No	Yes	RDC	Amount
2	Title	Yes	Lem	Yes	Yes	RDC	tf-idf
8	Title	No	No	Yes	Yes	RDC	Binary
10	Title	Yes	No	Yes	Yes	RDC	Amount
3	Article	No	Stem	No	Yes	RDC	Amount
4	Article	Yes	Stem	No	Yes	RDC	Amount
5	Article	No	Stem	No	Yes	RDC	Amount

by *SLAP*. We conclude that *SLAP* is a highly valuable system for generating an automated threat intelligence feed for a security analyst.

9.4   A Brief Evaluation of the Evolution Step

As mentioned in Sect. 4 and explained in Subsect. 6.5, *SLAP* uses the articles classified by an analyst to train the next iteration of the unit *Learn*. To briefly evaluate the evolution step, the full labeled dataset is divided into the chronologically first 80% and the latest 20%. Then, the first iteration of the model is generated using the first 80% of the labeled data, see Subsect. 6.5. The performance metrics of this first iteration are recorded. After that, the remaining 20% are classified with the previously trained iteration. Using this model, all articles classified as leak are added to the test set, because these are the ones an analyst would have classified, see Subsect. 6.5. The performance measurements are then recalculated by training the second iteration of the process chosen before on said test set. Again, cross-validation is used. Overall, the models recall improves by 1% and its precision increases non-significantly by 0.01%. Therefore, evolving both the model and the dataset yields promising results. The evolution is studied more extensively in future work.

10   Conclusion

Organizations use threat intelligence for a better understanding and prediction of behaviors of attackers. Armed with this knowledge, defences against threats, we face, can be realized. There are many sources of threat intelligence feeds, most of which require a significant amount of manual analysis and investigation by analysts to create useful knowledge.

In this paper, we propose an automatic system that supports analysis of open sources for security news information as well as the selection, enrichment, and refinement of relevant information for specific threats. This idea of a system supporting threat intelligence analysts is discussed and demonstrated for the specific use case in the field of identity theft.

We present and evaluate a system that combines several natural language processing and machine learning techniques to analyze, classify and attribute news articles. Our evaluation shows that using the system the weekly number of articles to be analyzed manually can be reduced from about 100 to 6. Thus, the system provides significant support for threat intelligence analysts.

Acknowledgements. We thank Christian Bungartz for helpful discussions on the implementation. We thank Faye Jennifer Lee for designing the pretty pictures in Sect. 4.

References

1. Avast Software s.r.o.: Avast Hack Check (2020). https://www.avast.com/hackcheck. Accessed 24 June 2020

2. Bird, S., Loper, E., Klein, E., Nltk, T.: Natural language toolkit (2020). https://www.nltk. org/. Accessed 23 June 2020

3. Brown, S., Gommers, J., Serrano, O.: From cyber security information sharing to threat management. In: Proceedings of the 2nd ACM Workshop on Information Sharing and Collaborative Security, pp. 43–49 (2015)

4. Chang, C.C., Lin, C.J.: LIBSVM: a library for support vector machines. ACM Trans. Intell. Syst. Technol. **2**, 27:1–27:27 (2011). http://www.csie.ntu.edu.tw/~cjlin/libsvm

5. Chang, C.C., Lin, C.J.: Libsvm: a library for support vector machines. ACM Trans. Intell. Syst. Technol. (TIST) **2**(3), 1–27 (2011)

6. Chismon, D., Ruks, M.: Threat Intelligence: Collecting, Analysing, Evaluating. MWR InfoSecurity Ltd., Basingstoke (2015)

7. Cios, K.: Data Mining?: A Knowledge Discovery Approach. Springer, New York (2007)

8. Committee C.T.I.T.: Introduction to STIX. https://oasis-open.github.io/cti-documentation/ stix/intro. Accessed 24 June 2020

9. Fan, R.E., Chang, K.W., Hsieh, C.J., Wang, X.R., Lin, C.J.: LIBLINEAR: a library for large linear classification. J. Mach. Learn. Res. **9**, 1871–1874 (2008)

10. Hasso-Plattner-Institut: Wurden Ihre Identitätsdaten ausspioniert? (2020), https://sec.hpi.de/ ilc. Accessed 24 June 2020

11. Holz, T., Engelberth, M., Freiling, F.: Learning more about the underground economy: a case-study of keyloggers and Dropzones. In: Backes, M., Ning, P. (eds.) ESORICS 2009. LNCS, vol. 5789, pp. 1–18. Springer, Heidelberg (2009). https://doi.org/10.1007/978-3-642-04444-1_1

12. Hsieh, C.J., Chang, K.W., Lin, C.J., Keerthi, S.S., Sundararajan, S.: A dual coordinate descent method for large-scale linear SVM. In: Proceedings of the 25th International Conference on Machine Learning, pp. 408–415 (2008)

13. Hunt, T.: Have I been pwned? (2020). https://haveibeenpwned.com/. Accessed 24 June 2020

14. Hutchins, E.M., Cloppert, M.J., Amin, R.M., et al.: Intelligence-driven computer network defense informed by analysis of adversary campaigns and intrusion kill chains. Lead. Issu. Inf. Warf. Secur. Res. **1**(1), 80 (2011)

15. Kilinc, H.H., Cagal, U.: A reputation based trust center model for cyber security. In: 2016 4th International Symposium on Digital Forensic and Security (ISDFS), pp. 1–6. IEEE (2016)

16. Labani, M., Moradi, P., Ahmadizar, F., Jalili, M.: A novel multivariate filter method for feature selection in text classification problems. Eng. Appl. Artif. Intell. **70**, 25–37 (2018)

17. Li, L., Sullivan, N., Pal, B., Chatterjee, R., Ali, J., Ristenpart, T.: Protocols for checking compromised credentials. In: Proceedings of the ACM Conference on Computer and Communications Security, pp. 1387–1403 (2019)

18. Malderle, T., Knauer, S., Lang, M., Wübbeling, M., Meier, M.: Track down identity leaks using threat intelligence. In: Furnell, S., Mori, P., Weippl, E., Champ, O. (eds.) ICISSP 2020 - Proceedings of the 6th International Conference on Information Systems Security and Privacy. SCITEPRESS - Science and Technology Publications, Valetta (2020)

19. Malderle, T., Wübbeling, M., Knauer, S., Meier, M.: Warning of affected users about an identity leak. In: Madureira, A.M., Abraham, A., Gandhi, N., Silva, C., Antunes, M. (eds.) SoCPaR 2018. AISC, vol. 942, pp. 278–287. Springer, Cham (2020). https://doi.org/10.1007/978-3-030-17065-3_28

20. Malderle, T., Wübbeling, M., Knauer, S., Sykosch, A., Meier, M.: Gathering and analyzing identity leaks for a proactive warning of affected users. In: Proceedings of the 15th ACM International Conference on Computing Frontiers, CF 2018, pp. 208–211. ACM, New York (2018). https://doi.org/10.1145/3203217.3203269

21. MISP: Misp - open source threat intelligence platform & open standards for threat information sharing, https://www.misp-project.org/. Accessed 24 June 2020

22. MITRE: Cyber threat intelligence. https://www.mitre.org/capabilities/cybersecurity/cyber-threat-intelligence. Accessed 24 June 2020
23. Mozilla Foundation: Firefox Monitor - Frequently asked questions (2020). https://support.mozilla.org/en-US/kb/firefox-monitor-faq. Accessed 24 June 2020
24. Ou-Yang, L.: Newspaper3k: Article scraping & curation (2019). https://github.com/codelucas/newspaper. Accessed 17 Dec 2019
25. Pearman, S., et al.: Let's go in for a closer look: observing passwords in their natural habitat. In: Proceedings of the ACM Conference on Computer and Communications Security, pp. 295–310 (2017)
26. Peng, P., Xu, C., Quinn, L., Hu, H., Viswanath, B., Wang, G.: What Happens After You Leak Your Password: Understanding Credential Sharing on Phishing Sites. In: Asia CCS 2019: Proceedings of the 2019 ACM Asia Conference on Computer and Communications SecurityJuly 2019, pp. 181–192 (2019)
27. Porter, M.F.: An algorithm for suffix stripping. Program **14**(3), 130–137 (1980)
28. PricewaterhouseCoopers GmbH: Identitätsklau - die Gefahr aus dem Netz (2016). https://www.pwc.de/de/handel-und-konsumguter/assets/cyber-security-identitaetsdiebstahl-2016.pdf. Accessed 24 June 2020
29. Princeton University: About wordnet. (2010), https://wordnet.princeton.edu. Accessed 24 June 2021
30. Rehman, A., Javed, K., Babri, H.A., Saeed, M.: Relative discrimination criterion-a novel feature ranking method for text data. Exp. Syst. Appl. **42**(7), 3670–3681 (2015)
31. Salton, G., Buckley, C.: Term-weighting approaches in automatic text retrieval. Inf. Process. Manag. **24**(5), 513–523 (1988)
32. Scrapinghub: Scrapy (2019). https://scrapy.org/. Accessed 17 Dec 2019
33. Silva, C., Ribeiro, B.: On text-based mining with active learning and background knowledge using SVM. Soft Comput. **11**(6), 519–530 (2007)
34. Sood, G., Cor, K.: Pwned: The risk of exposure from data breaches. In: WebSci 2019 - Proceedings of the 11th ACM Conference on Web Science, pp. 289–292 (2019)
35. Statista GmbH: Waren Sie schon einmal von Identitätsdiebstahl betroffen, hat also schon einmal jemand Ihre persönlichen Daten missbräuchlich genutzt und Ihnen Schaden zugefügt? (2019). https://de.statista.com/prognosen/953397/. Accessed 24 June 2020
36. Sun, A., Lim, E.P., Liu, Y.: On strategies for imbalanced text classification using SVM: a comparative study. Decis. Supp. Syst. **48**(1), 191–201 (2009)
37. Symantec Corporation: 2017 - Norton Cyber Security Insights Report - Global Results (2017). https://www.nortonlifelock.com/content/dam/nortonlifelock/docs/about/2017-ncsir-global-results-en.pdf. Accessed 24 June 2020
38. Thomas, K., et al.: Data breaches, phishing, or malware? In: Proceedings of the 2017 ACM SIGSAC Conference on Computer and Communications Security - CCS 2017, pp. 1421–1434 (2017)
39. Thomas, K., et al.: Protecting accounts from credential stuffing with password breach alerting. 28th USENIX Security Symposium, USENIX Security 2019, Santa Clara, CA, USA, August 14–16, 2019, pp. 1556–1571 (2019)
40. Universität Bonn: identity leak checker (2020). https://leakchecker.uni-bonn.de/. Accessed 24 June 2020
41. Uysal, A.K., Gunal, S.: A novel probabilistic feature selection method for text classification. Knowl.-Based Syst. **36**, 226–235 (2012)
42. Vakilinia, I., Cheung, S., Sengupta, S.: Sharing susceptible passwords as cyber threat intelligence feed. In: MILCOM 2018–2018 IEEE Military Communications Conference (MILCOM), pp. 1–6. IEEE (2018)

43. Wang, C., Jan, S.T., Hu, H., Bossart, D., Wang, G.: The next domino to fall: empirical analysis of user passwords across online services. In:CODASPY 2018 - Proceedings of the 8th ACM Conference on Data and Application Security and Privacy, pp. 196–203 (2018)
44. Wash, R., Rader, E., Berman, R., Wellmer, Z.: Understanding password choices: how frequently entered passwords are re-used across websites. In: Twelfth Symposium on Usable Privacy and Security (Soups), p. 175 (2016)
45. Web.de: Was ist Ihre bevorzugte Methode, die notwendige Menge an Passwörtern zu verwalten? (2019). https://www.slideshare.net/WEBDE_DEUTSCHLAND/passwortstudie-59-der-deutschen-internetnutzer-verwenden-passwrter-mehrfach. Accessed 24 June 2020
46. Yadav, T., Rao, A.M.: Technical aspects of cyber kill chain. In: Abawajy, J.H., Mukherjea, S., Thampi, S.M., Ruiz-Martínez, A. (eds.) SSCC 2015. CCIS, vol. 536, pp. 438–452. Springer, Cham (2015). https://doi.org/10.1007/978-3-319-22915-7_40

Key Agreement in the Lightning Network Protocol

Hans Hüttel$^{(\boxtimes)}$ and Vilim Staroveški

Department of Computer Science, Aalborg University, Aalborg, Denmark
hans@cs.aau.dk

Abstract. The Lightning Network is a decentralized bidirectional payment solution using the Bitcoin blockchain. In an earlier paper, we analyzed the secrecy and authenticity properties of the four subprotocols of the network and found that the key agreement protocol does not guarantee authenticity wrt. the responder. In this paper, we continue the analysis of the key agreement protocol using ProVerif and amend the protocol such that authenticity holds.

Keywords: Cryptographic protocols · Protocol verification · Blockchain

1 Introduction

The Lightning Network is a decentralized network of bidirectional payment channels that sits on top of the Bitcoin blockchain. The design of the protocol used in the network dates back to 2014 and version 1.0 was released in December 2017. At the time of writing, the Lightning Network consists of about 8000 nodes and has about 37000 payment channels that altogether contain about 1000 bitcoins.

One of the limitations of the Lightning Network is that users needs to be online when receiving a payment. This could potentially expose their private keys, which would give an attacker full access to user funds. The secrecy of the user private key is therefore the main security property of the Lightning Network. Another important security property that the Lightning Network must satisfy is user authenticity. The protocol must be able to guarantee that if user A believes that is interacting with user B, then this is the case.

At present little has been done to provide a formal analysis of the security properties of the network. There is work by Kiayias et al. [10] but the focus is on the properties of the cryptographic primitives used in the protocols.

A paper by Seres et al. [14] carries out an analysis of the topology of the Lightning Network and finds that high-level depictions of the network topology give "...a false image of security and robustness" and that the network is "structurally weak against rational adversaries". This, too, calls for a further security analysis.

The Lightning Network consists of four cryptographic protocols that must be analyzed separately.

The Key Agreement Protocol: establishes a secure and authenticated connection to another user

The Channel Opening Protocol: opens a payment channel to another user

S. Furnell et al. (Eds.): ICISSP 2020, CCIS 1545, pp. 139–155, 2022.
https://doi.org/10.1007/978-3-030-94900-6_7

The Onion Routing Protocol: carries out a payment to a user and the
The Channel Closing Protocol: closes an existing payment channel.

In an earlier paper [9] we used the automatic protocol verifier ProVerif [4] to give a fully automated analysis of the security properties of the Lightning Network by analyzing these subprotocols. The channel opening protocol and the onion routing protocol were found to satisfy the expected properties of secrecy and authenticity. However, this was not the case for the key agreement protocol; the analysis reveals that the authenticity does not hold for the responder. This implies that in the key agreement protocol, that should provide mutual authentication, the initiator of the protocol cannot be sure that it is actually running the protocol with the responder it has in mind.

In this paper we therefore continue our analysis with the focus on the key agreement protocol and show that the problem does not lie with the assignment of asymmetric keys. Based on this observation, we propose an amendment of the key agreement protocol that ensures authenticity in both directions.

The rest of our paper is organized as follows. In Sect. 2 we describe the analysis methodology that we follow, and in particular the Dolev-Yao attacker model and the applied π-calculus that form the basis of ProVerif. Section 3 describes our model of the key agreement protocol. Section 4 gives an overview of the results of our analysis as well as our proposed amendment to the protocol.

Since we use ProVerif code from our earlier paper [9] and the same version of in the applied π-calculus in order to make the paper self-contained, these references to existing work are reproduced with citations to [9] in order to make the paper self-contained.

2   The Symbolic Approach to Security Analysis

As in [9] we use the symbolic approach to protocol analysis based on the Dolev-Yao assumptions [7].

2.1   The Dolev-Yao Model

In the symbolic approach we assume that all messages exchanged in the protocol will be sent through public channels. We assume that every public channel is controlled by an attacker that can

- obtain any message passing through the network
- is a legitimate user of the network and can interact with other users
- has the opportunity to be a receiver to any user.

Furthermore, the attacker can modify, delete and inject messages as well as apply the user-defined cryptographic functions to manipulate the data obtained (for instance by accessing a given element of a tuple, by constructing a tuple or decrypting a message). On the other hand, the attacker cannot perform any sort of cryptoanalysis or any operation that would break the cryptography properties of the defined cryptographic functions (e.g. finding an inverse of an one-way hash function used in the protocol).

2.2 ProVerif

For the analyses that follow, we use the ProVerif tool, which is a tool for automatically analyzing the security of cryptographic protocols [3] based on the Dolev-Yao assumptions. ProVerif is able to prove secrecy, authenticity and observational equivalence properties of cryptographic protocols. Its analysis considers a unbounded number of sessions and unbounded message space and performed on a symbolic model of a protocol [3].

ProVerif works by translating a protocol described in the applied π-calculus into a collection of Horn clauses. Security properties can then be checked by performing queries for this system of Horn clauses using the usual notion of resolution.

2.3 The Applied π-Calculus

ProVerif uses a version of the applied π-calculus for modelling cryptographic protocols. This lends itself well to a protocol analysis that uses the Dolev-Yao-assumptions; as pointed out by Abadi and Gordon [1], we can then view any attacker as a process that interacts with the protocol that is the protocol itself. Our version of the applied π-calculus is that of [2], which is used in the ProVerif protocol analyzer described in Sect. 2.2.

We consider an infinite set of *names* (channels) $\mathcal{N}$ and an infinitive set of *variables* $\mathcal{X}$. We let a, b and c range over $\mathcal{N}$ and x, y and z range over $\mathcal{X}$. We will use the letters M and N for *terms* and the letters P, Q and R for *processes*.

The syntax of processes is presented in Table 1. Here, the process **0** is the inactive process. The output process $\overline{a}\langle N \rangle.P$ outputs the term N on the channel a and continues as P. The input process $a(x).P$ inputs a term on the channel a and then binds the term to x within the continuation P. The process $P \mid Q$ denotes the parallel execution of processes P and Q. In order to allow for infinite behaviour we introduce *replication*. The process $!P$ denotes an infinite supply of copies of process P. Finally, and importantly, we must be able to compare terms. The *match* process **if** $M = N$ **then** P compares the terms M and N; if M and N are the same term, we continue with the process P, otherwise, nothing happens.

If a name n is not bound by a restriction or an input in P we say that n is *free* in P. The set of free names in P is denoted by $fn(P)$. In the following, we assume that all bound names are pairwise distinct and distinct from any free name. If P contains no free names, we say that P is *closed*.

Table 1. Formation rules for terms and processes in the applied π-calculus [9].

$$M, N ::= x, y, z \mid a, b, c \mid f(M_1, ..., M_n)$$
$$P, Q ::= \mathbf{0} \mid \overline{a}\langle N \rangle.P \mid a(x).P \mid P \mid Q \mid !P \mid (\nu a)P$$
$$\mid \textbf{if } M = N \textbf{ then } P \mid \textbf{let } x = g(M_1, ..., M_n) \textbf{ in } P$$

In the original π-calculus, the only terms that can be transmitted along channels are names. However, we now allow a richer set of data terms that let us describe the messages that can be communicated in cryptographic protocols. Table 1, f describes the formation rules for terms.

Message terms $M, N \ldots$ are built from a *signature*, a finite set of function symbols Σ representing the cryptographic primitives. We distinguish between *constructors*, denoted by f, that are used for building terms (e.g. in encryption), while others are *destructors*, denoted by g, used for taking terms apart (e.g. in decryption).

For every destructor in our signature there are zero or more reduction rules that define how message terms are to be evaluated. We write $M \rightarrow M'$ if the term M evaluates to M' and $M \nrightarrow$ if the term M cannot be evaluated.

The semantics of the π-calculus is given by a *reduction* relation. We write $P \rightarrow P'$ if P by performing a computation step evolves to P'.

In the reduction semantics, we use the notion of *structural congruence* to identify processes that are identical up to structure. For instance, we would like to identify the processes $P \mid Q$ and $Q \mid P$ and they should have the same behaviour. The rules defining the relation are presented in Table 2.

The reduction relation $\rightarrow$ is defined inductively by a collection of reduction rules on closed processes, shown in Table 3. We write $P \rightarrow^* P'$ if either $P = P'$ or P reduces to P' in 1 or more reduction steps.

Table 2. The rules and axioms defining structural congruence [9].

$$P \equiv P \qquad\qquad P \mid \mathbf{0} \equiv P$$

$$P \mid Q \equiv Q \mid P \qquad P \mid (Q \mid R) \equiv (P \mid Q) \mid R$$

$$(\nu a)(\nu b)P \equiv (\nu b)(\nu a)P \qquad (\nu a)\mathbf{0} \equiv \mathbf{0}$$

$$(\nu a)(P \mid Q) \equiv P \mid (\nu a)Q \quad \text{if } a \notin \mathrm{fn}(P)$$

$$\frac{P \rightarrow Q}{P \equiv Q} \qquad \frac{P \equiv Q}{Q \equiv P} \qquad \frac{P \equiv Q \quad Q \equiv R}{P \equiv R}$$

$$\frac{P \equiv Q}{P \mid R \equiv Q \mid R} \qquad \frac{P \equiv Q}{(\nu a)P \equiv (\nu a)Q}$$

Table 3. The rules defining the reduction relation [9].

$$\overline{a}\langle M\rangle.P \mid a(x).Q \rightarrow P \mid Q\{M/x\}$$

$$\frac{P \rightarrow Q}{P \mid R \rightarrow Q \mid R} \qquad\qquad !P \rightarrow P \mid !P$$

$$\frac{P \equiv P' \quad P' \rightarrow Q' \quad Q' \equiv Q}{P \rightarrow Q} \qquad \frac{P \rightarrow Q}{(\nu a)P \rightarrow (\nu a)Q}$$

$$\text{if } M = M \text{ then } P \rightarrow P$$

To the reduction rules for the π-calculus we add the reduction rules in Table 4; they describe how terms are evaluated by applying destructors in let-expressions. If a term $g(M_1, \ldots, M_n)$ evaluates to M', the process continues as $P\{M'/x\}$, otherwise, it terminates.

Table 4. Reduction rules for let-expressions [9].

$$\frac{g(M_1, \ldots, M_n) \to M'}{\textbf{let } x = g(M_1, \ldots, M_n) \textbf{ in } P \to P\{M'/x\}}$$

$$\frac{g(M_1, \ldots, M_n) \not\to}{\textbf{let } x = g(M_1, \ldots, M_n) \textbf{ in } P \to 0}$$

2.4 Secrecy and Authenticity

In the following, when defining security properties, we use the Dolev-Yao attacker model with the capabilities previously defined. In a process calculus setting, an adversary is any process that has a set of public names S in its initial knowledge and does not contain correspondence assertions (defined below).

Definition 1. *Let S be a finite set of names. A closed process Q is an S-adversary if and only if $fn(Q) \subseteq S$ and Q does not contain correspondence assertions or executed correspondence assertions.*

The *secrecy* of a term M is preserved in the protocol, if M will never be sent on any public channel such that it can be obtained by the attacker.

Definition 2 [2]. *Let P be a closed process and M be a message. We say that P outputs M on c if and only if $P \to^* \overline{a}\langle M \rangle.R \mid R'$ for some process R and R' and channel a. We say that P preserves the secrecy of M from S if and only if $P \mid Q$ does not output M on c for any S-adversary Q and any $c \in S$.*

In the case of *authenticity*, we say that the principal A is authentic to the principal B, if whenever B completed a protocol run believing that A was the initiator, then this was indeed the case. To capture this, following Woo and Lam [15], we use *correspondence assertions* that are labelled with terms and are of the form **begin**(M) and **end**(M). Here, the intention is that in every run of a protocol, if an end-expression **end**(M) appears, a begin-expression **begin**(M) with the same label M has to have appeared earlier in the run. We incorporate this into the syntax of the process calculus as shown in Table 5.

Table 5. Formation rules for correspondence assertions [9].

$$P ::= \textbf{begin}(M).P \mid \textbf{end}(M).P$$
$$\mid \textbf{begin\_ex}(M).P \mid \textbf{end\_ex}(M).P$$

Table 6 shows the reduction rules for correspondence assertions: **begin**$(M).P$ evolves to **begin_ex**$(M) \mid P$ and **end**$(M).P$ evolves to **end_ex**$(M) \mid P$.

Table 6. Reduction rules for correspondence assertions [9].

$$\textbf{begin}(M).P \to \textbf{begin\_ex}(M) \mid P$$
$$\textbf{end}(M).P \to \textbf{end\_ex}(M) \mid P$$

An important distinction is that between non-injective and injective agreement.

Definition 3. *Suppose P is a closed process P. Then P satisfies non-injective agree-ment with respect to S-adversaries if and only if for any S-adversary Q, for any P′ such that P | Q →* P′, for any M, if* **end_ex**(M) *occurs in P′, then* **begin_ex**(M) *also occurs in P′ [2].*

If we want to express that an event **end**(M) has happened after the event **begin**(M) and at most as many times as event **begin**(M), the appropriate notion is that of injective agreement.

Definition 4. *Let P be a closed process. We say that P satisfies injective agreement with respect to S-adversaries if and only if for any S-adversary Q, for any P′ such that P | Q →* P′, for any M, the number of occurrences of* **end_ex**(M) *in P′ is at most the number of occurrences of* **begin_ex**(M) *in P [2].*

3   Modelling the Lightning Network Key Agreement Protocol

The Lightning Network key agreement protocol is intended to provide a mutual authen-tication between two participants (i.e. nodes) and to create secret session keys (asym-metric encryption key-pair: ek_I and dk_I for the protocol initiator and ek_R and dk_R for the protocol responder). The newly generated session keys will be used for encrypting all future messages between the participants and authenticating any information adver-tised on behalf of a participant.

We will present the security properties the protocol needs to satisfy in Sect. 3.1 followed by the protocol signature in Sect. 3.2. In Sect. 3.3 will present and describe a model of the protocol using the applied π-calculus.

3.1   Security Properties

We can summarize the security properties that the protocol must satisfy as follows:

- The initiating node must be authentic to the responding node
- The responding node must be authentic to the initiating node
- The secrecy of the generated secret session keys ek_I and dk_I must hold
- The secrecy of the generated secret session keys ek_R and dk_R must hold.

The authenticity property of the initiating node to the responding node means that, if the responding node reaches the end of the protocol with a belief that it has done so with a initiating node, then the initiating node has actually engaged a session with the responding node. The same must hold for the authentication of the responding node to the initiating node.

The secrecy of a secret session key ek_I and dk_I implies that if the initiating node has reached the end of the protocol with the responding node, then the keys ek_I and dk_I, generated at the initiating node side as a result of the protocol, are secret and can be used for encrypting and decrypting future communication with the responding node. For the secrecy of the secret session keys ek_R and dk_R generated at the responding node side, the same must be the case.

3.2 Principals and Signature

The protocol will have the following *signature* $(\mathcal{S}, \Sigma)$, where $\mathcal{S}$ is a set of sorts and Σ is a set of function symbols. $\mathcal{S}$ contains two sorts: $\mathcal{S} = \{term, key\}$. The sort $term$ will be used for all hashes, encrypted data and messages exchanged between the nodes, while the sort key will be used for all types of keys used (e.g. ephemeral and static keys, encryption key, etc.).

In the signature $(\mathcal{S}, \Sigma)$, the function symbols are: $\Sigma = \{\bot, pk, hash, ECDH, HKDF, senc, sdec, [\,], ith_i\}$ and their definitions are given in the Table 7.

Table 7. Cryptographic primitives.

$$\bot \; : \; \to term \qquad\qquad HKDF \; : \; key \times term \to term$$
$$ECDH \; : \; key \times key \to key \qquad hash \; : \; term \to term$$
$$senc \; : \; term \times key \to term \qquad [\,] \; : \; term \times term \to term$$
$$sdec \; : \; term \times key \to term \qquad ith_i \; : \; term \to term$$
$$pk \; : \; key \to key$$

Where:

- $\bot$ represents a null or empty data
- $ECDH(k_1, k_2)$ is an abstraction of the Elliptic Curve Diffie-Hellman [6] operation which combines two keys k_1 and k_2 and produces a new key
- $senc(d, k)$ encrypts data d with a symmetric key k and produces a ciphertext
- $sdec(d, k)$ decrypts data d with a symmetric key k and produces its plaintext version
- $pk(k)$ is a public key generation function that takes a private key k and returns its public key pair
- $HKDF(k, x)$ represents a Hashed Message Authentication Code (HMAC)-based key derivation function [11], where a key k and data x are combined to create a new term; newly created term is actually a key which is used to derive more additional keys
- $hash(d)$ is a representation of a standard hash function that takes a data d and returns its hash value
- $[x, y]$ is a tuple creation function in which we also consider the short form $[x_1, x_2, ..., x_{n-1}, x_n]$ for the expression $[x_1, [x_2, [..., [x_{n-1}, x_n]]]]$
- $ith_i(M)$ function that returns i-th element of a tuple M.

We will also extend the applied π-calculus reduction system with additional reduction rules for the destructors we will use:

$$\text{(Red Decrypt)} \quad sdec(senc(M, N), N) \to M$$
$$\text{(Red Ith}_i) \quad ith_i([M_1, ..., M_n]) \to M_i$$

3.3 The Behaviour of the Protocol

The handshake chosen for the authenticated key exchange in the Lightning Network is Noise_XK [12]. Noise_XK is one of twelve fundamental interactive handshake patterns of the Noise Protocol Framework [13]. Here, the letter 'X' in the name of the protocol refers to the fact that the static key of the initiator will be transmitted to the responder. The letter 'K' refers to the fact that the key of the static responder is known to the initiator. Throughout the handshake process, each side will maintain the following variables.

- e: a freshly generated ephemeral key-pair; e_priv is the private and e_pub is the public component
- s: a static key-pair; s_priv is the private and s_pub is the public component
- ck: the chaining key which is an accumulated hash of all previous ECDH outputs and is used to derive the encryption keys at the end of the protocol
- h: the handshake hash which is an accumulated hash of all handshake data sent and received; it is never transmitted, but used as the Associated Data in the AEAD messages
- $temp\_k_1$, $temp\_k_2$, $temp\_k_3$: the intermediate keys which are used for encrypting messages during the handshake [12].

Table 8 shows the message exchanges of the protocol. The messages will be exchanged through a public channel c.

Table 8. The key agreement protocol message sequence [9].

Message 0	$node_R$	$\rightarrow$	$node_I$	: s_pub_R
Message 1	$node_I$	$\rightarrow$	$node_R$	: $[e\_pub_I, senc(\bot, [temp\_k_1, 0, h_1])]$
Message 2	$node_R$	$\rightarrow$	$node_I$	: $[e\_pub_R, senc(\bot, [temp\_k_2, 0, h_2])]$
Message 3	$node_I$	$\rightarrow$	$node_R$	: $[senc(s\_pub_I, [temp\_k_2, 1, h_3]), senc(\bot, [temp\_k_3, 0, h_4])]$

The protocol has three phases but before the phase one, both parties initialize their handshake state (i.e. ck and h) to the same values on each side.

We first describe the actions of the protocol initiator using the applied π-calculus model from Table 9.

The initiating node carries out the following actions.

- Generate a new ephemeral key pair e (line 2)
- Compute the first intermediary key. Update the chaining key ck_I using the outputs from HKDF function (lines 3, 4)

$$k_1 = ith_0(HKDF(ck_I, ECDH(e\_priv_I, s\_pub_R)))$$

$$ck_I = ith_1(HKDF(ck_I, ECDH(e\_priv_I, s\_pub_R)))$$

- Encrypt an empty text ($\bot$) with k_1. Send it together with the ephemeral public key (e_pub_I) to the responding node (line 5)
- Receive a response from the responding node. Extract e_pub_R and the encrypted data from it (line 6)

Table 9. The initiating node process [9].

$$node_I(s\_priv_I, s\_pub_R, h_0, ck_0) = \tag{1}$$

$$(\nu e\_priv_I)c(s\_pub_X).\textbf{begin}(s\_pub_X). \tag{2}$$

$$\textbf{let } k_1 = ith_0(HKDF(ck_0, es)) \textbf{ in} \tag{3}$$

$$\textbf{let } ck_1 = ith_1(HKDF(ck_0, es)) \textbf{ in} \tag{4}$$

$$\overline{c}\langle[pk(e\_priv_I), d_1]\rangle.c(m_2). \tag{5}$$

$$\textbf{let } e\_pub_R = ith_0(m_2) \textbf{ in} \tag{6}$$

$$\textbf{let } k_2 = ith_0(HKDF(ck_1, ee)) \textbf{ in} \tag{7}$$

$$\textbf{let } ck_2 = ith_1(HKDF(ck_1, ee)) \textbf{ in} \tag{8}$$

$$\textbf{let } d_2 = ith_1(m_2) \textbf{ in} \tag{9}$$

$$\textbf{let } k_3 = ith_0(HKDF(ck_2, se)) \textbf{ in} \tag{10}$$

$$\textbf{let } ck_3 = ith_1(HKDF(ck_2, se)) \textbf{ in} \tag{11}$$

$$\textbf{let } dd_2 = sdec(d_2, [k_2, 0, h_3]) \textbf{ in} \tag{12}$$

$$\textbf{if } dd_2 = \bot \textbf{ then } \overline{c}\langle m_3\rangle. \tag{13}$$

$$\textbf{if } s\_pub_X = s\_pub_R \textbf{ then end}(pk(s\_priv_I)) \tag{14}$$

$$\text{where} \begin{cases} h_1 = hash([h_0, pk(e\_priv_I)]) \\ es = ECDH(e\_priv_I, s\_pub_X) \\ d_1 = senc(\bot, [k_1, 0, h_1]) \\ h_2 = hash([h_1, d_1]) \\ h_3 = hash([h_2, e\_pub_R]) \\ ee = ECDH(e\_priv_I, e\_pub_R) \\ h_4 = hash([h_3, d_2]) \\ d_3 = senc(pk(s\_priv_I), [k_2, 1, h_4]) \\ h_5 = hash([h_4, d_3]) \\ se = ECDH(s\_priv_I, e\_pub_R) \\ ek_I = ith_0(HKDF(ck_3, \bot)) \\ dk_I = ith_1(HKDF(ck_3, \bot)) \\ m_3 = [d_3, d_4] \end{cases}$$

- Compute a new intermediary key and update the chaining key ck_I using the outputs from HKDF function (line 7):

$$k_2 = ith_0(HKDF(ck_I, ECDH(e\_pub_R, e\_priv_I)))$$

$$ck_I = ith_1(HKDF(ck_I, ECDH(e\_pub_R, e\_priv_I)))$$

- Validate the encrypted data. If validation fails, stop (line 8)

- Encrypt the static public key with k_2 (line 9)
- Compute a new intermediary key and update the chaining key ck using the outputs from HKDF function (lines 10, 11)

$$k_3 = ith_0(HKDF(ck_I, ECDH(s\_priv_I, e\_pub_R)))$$

$$ck_I = ith_1(HKDF(ck_I, ECDH(s\_priv_I, e\_pub_R)))$$

- Encrypt an empty text ($\perp$) with k_3 and send it together with encrypted static public key to the responding node (line 12)
- Derive the session keys from the chaining key using the HKDF function.

Table 10 shows the responding node process as described in the applied π-calculus. The actions of the responding node are

- Receive a message from the initiating node and extract e_pub_I (line 16) and encrypted data from it
- Compute the first intermediary key (line 17) and update the chaining key ck_R using the outputs from the HKDF function (lines 18, 19)

$$k_1 = ith_0(HKDF(ck_R, ECDH(e\_pub_I, s\_priv_R)))$$

$$ck_R = ith_1(HKDF(ck_R, ECDH(e\_pub_I, s\_priv_R)))$$

- Validate the encrypted data (line 20). If validation fails, stop
- Generate a new ephemeral key pair e
- Compute a new intermediary key. Update the chaining key ck_R using the outputs from HKDF function (lines 21, 22)

$$k_2 = ith_0(HKDF(ck_R, ECDH(e\_priv_R, e\_pub_I)))$$

$$ck_R = ith_1(HKDF(ck_R, ECDH(e\_priv_R, e\_pub_I)))$$

- Encrypt an empty text ($\perp$) with k_2 and send it together with the ephemeral public key (e_pub_R) to the initiating node (line 23)
- Receive a message from the initiating node. Decrypt s_pub_I from and save the additional encrypted data (line 24)
- Compute a new intermediary key. Update the chaining key ck_R using the outputs from HKDF function (lines 23, 24)

$$k_3 = ith_0(HKDF(ck_R, ECDH(e\_priv_R, s\_pub_I)))$$

$$ck_R = ith_1(HKDF(ck_R, ECDH(e\_priv_R, s\_pub_I)))$$

- Validate the encrypted data from the previous message; if it fails, stop (line 30)
- Derive the session keys from the chaining key using the HKDF function (line 31).

In both of these descriptions we have omitted some details (such as the update of the handshake hash h). However, these can easily be found read from the process calculus descriptions given in Tables 9 and 10.

Table 11 shows the main process that start the processes of the initiating and responding nodes. Moreover, the static public keys of the participants are output to the public channel to make sure that the attacker receives them.

4   Representing and Analysing the Protocol Using ProVerif

The representation of the protocol in ProVerif is a straightforward translation of the specifications in Tables 9, 10 and 11.

Table 10. Responding node process [9].

$$node_R(s\_priv_R, s\_pub_I, h_0, ck_0) = \tag{15}$$

$$(\nu e\_priv_R)c(m_1). \tag{16}$$

$$\textbf{let } e\_pub_X = ith_0(m_1) \textbf{ in} \tag{17}$$

$$\textbf{let } d_1 = ith_1(m_2) \textbf{ in} \tag{18}$$

$$\textbf{let } k_1 = ith_0(HKDF(ck_0, se)) \textbf{ in} \tag{19}$$

$$\textbf{let } ck_1 = ith_1(HKDF(ck_0, se)) \textbf{ in} \tag{20}$$

$$\textbf{let } dd_1 = sdec(d_1, [k_1, 0, h_1]) \textbf{ in} \tag{21}$$

$$\textbf{if } dd_1 = \perp \textbf{ then} \tag{22}$$

$$\textbf{let } k_2 = ith_0(HKDF(ck_1, ee)) \textbf{ in} \tag{23}$$

$$\textbf{let } ck_2 = ith_1(HKDF(ck_1, ee)) \textbf{ in} \tag{24}$$

$$\bar{c}\langle[pk(e\_priv_R), d_2]\rangle.c(m_3). \tag{25}$$

$$\textbf{let } d_3 = ith_0(m_3) \textbf{ in} \tag{26}$$

$$\textbf{let } d_4 = ith_1(m_3) \textbf{ in} \tag{27}$$

$$\textbf{let } s_p ub_X = sdec(d_3, [k_2, 1, h_4]) \textbf{ in begin}(s\_pub_X). \tag{28}$$

$$\textbf{let } k_3 = ith_0(HKDF(ck_2, es)) \textbf{ in} \tag{29}$$

$$\textbf{let } ck_3 = ith_1(HKDF(ck_2, es)) \textbf{ in} \tag{30}$$

$$\textbf{let } dd_4 = sdec(d_4, [k_3, 0, h_5]) \textbf{ in} \tag{31}$$

$$\textbf{if } dd_4 = \perp \textbf{ then} \tag{32}$$

$$\textbf{if } s\_pub_X = s\_pub_I \textbf{ then end}(pk(s\_priv_R)) \tag{33}$$

$$\text{where} \begin{cases} h_1 = hash([h_0, e\_pub_X]) \\ se = ECDH(s\_priv_R, e\_pub_X) \\ h_2 = hash([h_1, d_1]) \\ h_3 = hash([h_2, pk(e\_priv_R)]) \\ ee = ECDH(e\_priv_R, e\_pub_X) \\ d_2 = senc(\perp, [k_2, 0, h_3]) \\ h_4 = hash([h_3, d_2]) \\ h_5 = hash([h_4, d_3]) \\ es = ECDH(e\_priv_R, s\_pub_X) \\ dk_R = ith_0(HKDF(ck_3, \perp)) \\ ek_R = ith_1(HKDF(ck_3, \perp)) \end{cases}$$

4.1 Two Models of Key Assignment

In our analysis we have to decide whether we will test with the attacker (who already has the abilities of a Dolev-Yao attacker explained in Sect. 2.1) is able to assign static public keys to the protocol participants – this is the *generalized model* – or they will be hardcoded in the protocol – this is the *pre-assigned key* model. We have carried out both of these, as it turns out that the preassigned keys model can be used as a sanity check for the generalized model but also gives an extra scenario that gets tested. The specifications for protocol participants in Table 9 and 10 represent the pre-assigned key model while the generalized model has a difference in the first lines of the model (i.e. it expects as an input the static key it will use and the static key the other party is using).

Table 11. The main process [9].

$$P = (\nu s\_priv_I, s\_priv_R, h_0, ck_0) \tag{34}$$

$$\textbf{let } s\_pub_I = pk(s\_priv_I) \textbf{ in } \overline{c}\langle s\_pub_I \rangle. \tag{35}$$

$$\textbf{let } s\_pub_R = pk(s\_priv_R) \textbf{ in } \overline{c}\langle s\_pub_R \rangle. \tag{36}$$

$$((!node_I(s\_priv_I, s\_pub_R, h_0, ck_0))| \tag{37}$$

$$(!node_R(s\_priv_R, s\_pub_I, h_0, ck_0))) \tag{38}$$

The following part of the code is shared between both of the models and it tests whether the aforementioned security properties hold.

```
query attacker(secret_ek_I);
        attacker(secret_dk_I);
        attacker(secret_ek_R);
        attacker(secret_dk_R).
```

```
query x:public_key, y:public_key; inj−event(end_I(x,y)) ==> inj−event(begin_I(x,y)).
query x:public_key, y:public_key; inj−event(end_R(x,y)) ==> inj−event(begin_R(x,y)).
```

The keys $secret\_ek\_I$, $secret\_dk\_I$, $secret\_ek\_R$ and $secret\_dk\_R$ are free names, not available to the attacker which will be encrypted using session keys: ek_I, dk_I, ek_R and dk_R respectively and output to the public channel. If the attacker is able to obtain (decrypt) the encrypted form of these names, then we know that it has obtained some of the session keys. The queries for testing whether the injective agreement holds in both way, work as described in Sect. 2.4 where the first one is testing is the responding node authentic to the initiating node, while the second one is testing whether the initiating node is authentic to the responding node.

4.2 The Analysis of the Generalized Model

The results that ProVerif outputs for the generalized model are the following.

RESULT not attacker(secret_ek_I[]) is true.
RESULT not attacker(secret_dk_I[]) is true.
RESULT not attacker(secret_ek_R[]) is true.
RESULT not attacker(secret_dk_R[]) is true.
RESULT inj−**event**(end_I(x_229,y_230)) ==> inj−**event**(begin_I(x_229,y_230)) is false.
RESULT inj−**event**(end_R(x_231,y_232)) ==> inj−**event**(begin_R(x_231,y_232)) is true.

The results show that the secrecy of the session keys holds for the protocol. Neither the keys owned by the initiating node and the ones owned by the responding node were leaked to the attacker. However, we see that the responding node is not authentic to the initiating node. This means that the initiating node can be tricked into thinking that it is running a protocol with the responding node, when in fact it is running it with the attacker. The second result proves that the initiating node is authentic to the responding node.

In addition to the results, ProVerif provided us with the detailed analysis of a potential attack in which responder authentification fails. Since the complete ProVerif output is quite large in size, we will give a short description of the attack, while referencing the lines of the protocol model in Table 9, 10 and 11.

1. the attacker obtains $pk(s\_priv_I)$ and $pk(s\_priv_R)$ from the public channel (lines 35, 36) and creates a tuple out of them
2. the attacker sends the tuple from step 1 to the initiating node (which assigns its static key and tells the initiating node about the responder static public key)
3. the initiating node is sending back a message containing its ephemeral public key together with the message MAC (Message Authentication Code), denoted as $[pk(e\_priv_I), d_1]$ (line 5)
4. the attacker receives the message from step 3 and extracts its elements to obtain $pk(e\_priv_I)$ and d_1
5. the attacker now sends to the responding node, the static public key that belongs to the initiating node which was obtained in step 1, which the responding node will use as its own (this means that both of the participants are using the same static public key)
6. the attacker now sends the ephemeral public key that the initiating node uses which was obtained in step 4, to the responding node (line 16)
7. the responding node sends the message m_2 to the attacker containing $pk(e\_priv_R)$ and d_2 (where d_2 is the MAC of the message) (line 25)
8. the attacker receives the message m_2 and extracts $pk(e\_priv_R)$ and d_2 from it
9. the attacker sends a message to the initiating node containing a tuple: $[pk(e\_priv_R), d_2]$
10. the initiating node receives the message (line 5), finishes the rest of the protocol and finally sends a message m_3 which contains its static public key and emits the event $end\_I(s\_pub_I, s\_pub_Y)$ where s_pub_Y is the responder static public key (this line is not present in the pre-assigned model, but corresponds to line 14)
11. the attacker can intercept the message $m3$ and the responding node would never finish the protocol run (while on the other side, the initiating node has finished a protocol run); this would also mean that due to the fact that the responding node has never received the static public key that the initiating node is using, it would

never emit $begin\_I(s\_pub_X, s\_pub_R)$ where s_pub_X is the other party static public key (this line is not present in the pre-assigned model, but corresponds to line 28).

After the potential attack analysis, a new question emerges: Is this attack only possible due to the generalization of our code and the fact that the attacker is assigning the static keys to the protocol participants? We have decided to provide the answer empirically.

4.3   The Analysis of Pre-assigned Key Model

To answer the question that was produced by the generalized model we have modified out ProVerif code to remove the generalization. This analysis also serves as a sanity check of the previous, more complicated model.

In the pre-assigned key model of the protocol, the attacker is not able to assign the static public keys to the protocol participants. The static public keys are predetermined for each participant. This means that the model perfectly matches the one described in Table 9, 10 and 11.

The results that ProVerif outputs for the pre-assigned key model are

RESULT not attacker(secret_ek_I[]) is true.
RESULT not attacker(secret_dk_I[]) is true.
RESULT not attacker(secret_ek_R[]) is true.
RESULT not attacker(secret_dk_R[]) is true.
RESULT inj$-$**event**(end_I(x_229,y_230)) ==> inj$-$**event**(begin_I(x_229,y_230)) is false.
RESULT inj$-$**event**(end_R(x_231,y_232)) ==> inj$-$**event**(begin_R(x_231,y_232)) is true.

Again, along with the results, ProVerif provided us with the steps the attacker needs to take for the responder authetication to fail, which we have briefly described as follows:

1. attacker obtains the responders static public key $pk(s\_priv_R[])$ (line 36)
2. attacker sends $pk(s\_priv_R[])$ to the initiator (line 2) who responds with its ephemeral public key and message MAC $[pk(e\_priv_I), d_1]$ (line 5)
3. attacker then sends $[pk(e\_priv_I), d_1]$ to the responder who responds with its ephemeral public key and a message MAC $[pk(e\_priv_R), d_2]$ (line 25)
4. attacker then sends $[pk(e\_priv_R), d_2]$ to the initiator who ends the protocol by emitting $end_I(pk(s\_priv_I[]), pk(s\_priv_R[]))$ (line 14)
5. the responder never receives the message (m_3 containing the encrypted initiator static public key) the initiator tries to send to it (line 13).

This means that the analysis of the pre-assigned key model produces the same results as that of the analysis of the general model and it indicates that the problem does not lie with the assignment of asymmetric keys.

4.4   A Solution to the Responder Authentication Failure

It seems that the root cause for the responder authentication failure is the fact that the attacker intercepts the last message the initiator send to the responder. A potential solution to the problem is to introduce an additional (encrypted) message exchange.

Our hypothesis is that when the initiator finishes the protocol, it could send a message to the responder with a text that would say: "I am ready to communicate with a node that owns s_pub_R", encrypted with the encryption key that was established in the protocol (i.e. ek_I). The responder would send a similar message back. The encryption keys were proven to remain secret in the protocol, so the attacker can not read or change these messages in a meaningful way. By doing this, both initiator and responder would know that the other party has finished the protocol, as well as that it knows with who they have finished the protocol with. Then the authenticity would hold for both parties.

In order to determine if this actually is the case, we changed the models for initiator and responder by adding an additional message exchange. The changes made to the initiator model, included only the last line (14) and it was replaced by the code in Table 12. Similarly, the last line (33) in the responder model was changed with the code in Table 13.

Table 12. Changes to the initiating node model (replacing line 14 in Table 9)

if $s\_pub_Y = s\_pub_R$ **then**	(39)
let $m\_end_I = senc(s\_pub_I, ek_I)$ **in**	(40)
$\overline{c}\langle m\_end_I \rangle c(m\_end_R)$	(41)
let $s\_pub_Z = sdec(m\_end_R, dk_I)$ **in**	(42)
if $s\_pub_Z = s\_pub_R$ **then** $\mathbf{end}(pk(s\_priv_I))$	(43)

Table 13. Changes to the responding node model (replacing line 33 in Table 10).

if $s\_pub_X = s\_pub_I$ **then**	(44)
let $m\_end_R = senc(s\_pub_R, ek_R)$ **in**	(45)
$\overline{c}\langle m\_end_R \rangle c(m\_end_I)$	(46)
let $s\_pub_W = sdec(m\_end_I, dk_R)$ **in**	(47)
if $s\_pub_W = s\_pub_I$ **then** $\mathbf{end}(pk(s\_priv_R))$	(48)

We used the same ProVerif query for testing the authenticity property as before:

query x:public_key, y:public_key; inj−**event**(end_I(x,y)) ==> inj−**event**(begin_I(x,y)).
query x:public_key, y:public_key; inj−**event**(end_R(x,y)) ==> inj−**event**(begin_R(x,y)).

The output provided by ProVerif is

RESULT inj−**event**(end_I(x_91,y_92)) ==>
inj−**event**(begin_I(x_91,y_92)) is true.
RESULT inj−**event**(end_R(x_93,y_94)) ==>
inj−**event**(begin_R(x_93,y_94)) is true.

The results show that for the model with proposed changes, both initiator and responder authenticity property hold and we have proven the hypotesis made earlier.

5   Conclusions and Ideas for Further Work

This paper continues the analysis of the key agreement protocol of the Lightning network using ProVerif that was begun in [9]. The key agreement protocol does not satisfy the authenticity property in one direction, namely that of the authenticity of the protocol responder to the initiator. This implies that in the key agreement protocol, that should provide mutual authentication, the protocol initiator cannot be sure that it is running the protocol with the responder it has in mind. On the other hand, it turns out to be easy to amend the protocol such that the authenticity problem goes away.

Other information leaks appear to be possible for the Lightning Network. Herrera-Joancomartí et al. [8] present an attack that is can disclose the balance of a channel in the Lightning Network. The attack is based on carrying out multiple payments while ensuring that none of them will be finalized. It would be interesting to model this attack using the symbolic approach but this calls for a more refined model.

An analysis of the anonymity properties of the Lightning Network protocols is another topic for further work. An attacker must be prevented from learning anything about the secrets (in this case the sum of the secrets), and the support given by ProVerif for proving indistinguishability is likely to be useful in for analyzing both anonymity and the balance confidentiality property mentioned above.

Moreover, one should carry out further analyses of the other sub-protocols. In particular, it would be important to carry out a further analysis of the onion routing protocol using ProVerif. Our analysis in [9] was only concerned with authenticity and secrecy but for routing protocols, route establishment is itself highly important. Cortier et al. have shown [5] that one can use ProVerif to analyze the routing properties of protocols by means of a reduction that allows one to consider topologies with only four nodes – meaning that only five distinct topologies need to be considered.

References

1. Abadi, M., Gordon, A.D.: A calculus for cryptographic protocols: the spi calculus. Inf. Comput. **148**(1), 1–70 (1999)
2. Blanchet, B.: From secrecy to authenticity in security protocols. In: Hermenegildo, M.V., Puebla, G. (eds.) SAS 2002. LNCS, vol. 2477, pp. 342–359. Springer, Heidelberg (2002). https://doi.org/10.1007/3-540-45789-5_25
3. Blanchet, B.: Automatic verification of security protocols in the symbolic model: the verifier ProVerif. In: Aldini, A., Lopez, J., Martinelli, F. (eds.) FOSAD 2012-2013. LNCS, vol. 8604, pp. 54–87. Springer, Cham (2014). https://doi.org/10.1007/978-3-319-10082-1_3
4. Blanchet, B., Smyth, B., Cheval, V., Sylvestre, M.: ProVerif 2.00: automatic cryptographic protocol verifier, user manual and tutorial (2018)
5. Cortier, V., Degrieck, J., Delaune, S.: Analysing routing protocols: four nodes topologies are sufficient. In: Degano, P., Guttman, J.D. (eds.) POST 2012. LNCS, vol. 7215, pp. 30–50. Springer, Heidelberg (2012). https://doi.org/10.1007/978-3-642-28641-4_3
6. Diffie, W., Hellman, M.: New directions in cryptography. IEEE Trans. Inf. Theory **22**(6), 644–654 (1976)
7. Dolev, D., Yao, A.C.: On the security of public key protocols (extended abstract). In: 22nd Annual Symposium on Foundations of Computer Science, Nashville, Tennessee, USA, 28–30 October 1981, pp. 350–357 (1981). https://doi.org/10.1109/SFCS.1981.32

8. Herrera-Joancomartí, J., Navarro-Arribas, G., Ranchal-Pedrosa, A., Pérez-Solà, C., Garcia-Alfaro, J.: On the difficulty of hiding the balance of lightning network channels. In: Proceedings of the 2019 ACM Asia Conference on Computer and Communications Security, Asia CCS 2019, pp. 602–612. ACM, New York (2019). https://doi.org/10.1145/3321705.3329812. http://doi.acm.org/10.1145/3321705.3329812
9. Hüttel, H., Staroveski, V.: Secrecy and authenticity properties of the lightning network protocol. In: Proceedings of the 6th International Conference on Information Systems Security and Privacy, ICISSP 2020, Valletta, Malta, 25–27 February 2020, pp. 119–130 (2020). https://doi.org/10.5220/0008974801190130
10. Kiayias, A., Litos, O.S.T.: A composable security treatment of the lightning network. IACR Cryptol. ePrint Arch. **2019**, 778 (2019)
11. Krawczyk, H., Eronen, P.: HMAC-based extract-and-expand key derivation function (HKDF) (2010)
12. lightningnetwork: Github - lightningnetwork-rfc/08-transport.md (2017). https://github.com/lightningnetwork/lightning-rfc/blob/master/08-transport.md
13. Perrin, T.: The noise protocol framework. PowerPoint Presentation (2016)
14. Seres, I.A., Gulyás, L., Nagy, D.A., Burcsi, P.: Topological analysis of Bitcoin's lightning network. In: Pardalos, P., Kotsireas, I., Guo, Y., Knottenbelt, W. (eds.) Mathematical Research for Blockchain Economy. SPBE, pp. 1–12. Springer, Cham (2020). https://doi.org/10.1007/978-3-030-37110-4_1
15. Woo, T.Y.C., Lam, S.S.: A semantic model for authentication protocols. In: Proceedings of the 1993 IEEE Symposium on Security and Privacy, SP 1993, pp. 178–194. IEEE Computer Society, Washington, DC (1993). http://dl.acm.org/citation.cfm?id=882489.884188

Effects of Explanatory Information on Privacy Policy Summarization Tool Perception

Vanessa Bracamonte[1(✉)], Seira Hidano[1], Welderufael B. Tesfay[2], and Shinsaku Kiyomoto[1]

[1] KDDI Research, Inc., Saitama, Japan
va-bracamonte@kddi-research.jp
[2] Goethe University Frankfurt, Frankfurt, Germany

Abstract. Privacy policies summarization tools can provide information about the contents of a privacy policy in a short and usable format. Although these automated tools can support users in understanding the information in privacy policies, they rely on machine learning techniques for the analysis of textual data to generate these summaries and can therefore contain errors which may affect the reliability of their results. A few of the existing privacy policy summarization tools provide some explanatory information about their performance, but the effects of this information on the user have not been validated. In this paper, an experimental study was conducted to evaluate whether explanatory information, in the form of justification and confidence measures, has an effect on understanding of the privacy policy content and on perception of the tool. The results indicate that participants have a more positive perception of the tool in terms of behavioral intention, perceived trustworthiness and usefulness when the summary includes a fragment of the policy as justification for the outcome. However, including a confidence measure in the summary did not have a significant effect on perception of the tool, and did not appear to communicate the possibility of incorrect results. This study contributes findings regarding user perception of automated privacy policy summarization that takes into consideration how explanatory information affects this perception. The implications of the findings for the design of privacy policy summarization tools are discussed.

Keywords: Privacy policy summarization tools · Explanatory information · Trust · User study

1 Introduction

Regulation such as the GDPR [7] has encouraged recent efforts to make privacy policies more understandable to users. Research has proposed the use of shorter notices in graphical and standardized formats [8,13] as alternatives to these lengthy pieces of text, and these have been proved to succeed in communicating

© Springer Nature Switzerland AG 2022
S. Furnell et al. (Eds.): ICISSP 2020, CCIS 1545, pp. 156–177, 2022.
https://doi.org/10.1007/978-3-030-94900-6_8

information about the privacy policy to users. In practice, however, the privacy policies of many companies and service providers remain too long and difficult for users to read and comprehend.

In order to provide more user-friendly privacy policy information, there are projects such as ToS; DR [24] which relies on a community of volunteers to manually analyze and categorize the content of existing privacy policies and generate a readable summary. However, reliance on human analysis makes it very difficult to scale the work to cover every existing privacy policy. In order to address this problem, there are projects that propose to automatize the analysis of privacy policies using machine learning techniques. Examples of these projects are Privee [28], PrivacyCheck [27], Polisis [10] and PrivacyGuide [23]. Privacy policy summarization tools are automated applications, implemented using different machine learning and natural language processing techniques, that analyze the content of a privacy policy text and provide a summary of the results of that analysis. These tools can be a solution to the problem of scale in the analysis of privacy policies, but they introduce a different challenge: users express concern regarding the trustworthiness and accuracy of a privacy policy summarization tool when they know that the process is automated [4]. Explanations can help to improve trust perception in automated tools [25], but there are no studies that evaluate how explanatory information affects user perception of automated privacy policy summarization. Although research has evaluated perception and understanding of usable privacy policy formats produced by humans, aspects related to the reliability of the privacy policy information have not been previously considered.

The purpose of this study is to address this gap. To achieve this, an experiment was conducted to evaluate understanding and perception of the results of an automated privacy policy summarization tool. Different conditions were created based on whether the results of the tool showed information about justification and confidence of the results, and asked participants about the content of the privacy policy and their perception of the tool in each of these conditions. The results show that justification information increased behavioral intention and trustworthiness and usefulness perception. Justification information also helped users qualify the answers provided by the tool, although the effect was not present for every aspect of the policy. Confidence information, on the other hand, did not have a positive effect on perception of the tool or on understanding of the results of the tool. These findings are discussed in the context of providing usable automated tools for privacy policy summarization and the challenges for the design of these tools.

This paper is an extended version of the paper "Evaluating the Effect of Justification and Confidence Information on User Perception of a Privacy Policy Summarization Tool" presented at the 6th International Conference on Information Systems Security and Privacy (ICISSP 2020) [3]. It includes additional details on the user study conducted, and new data analysis (quantitative and qualitative) and discussion of the findings.

2   Related Work

2.1   Automated Privacy Policy Summaries

The design of the result summary of automated privacy policy summarization tools often follows guidelines for usable formats aimed at presenting privacy policy information. Research on alternative ways of presenting privacy policies indicates that shortened versions of these texts, supplemented with icons, can provide users with the necessary information for them to understand their content [8]. Not only the length of the privacy policy is important, but also how the information is presented: standardized graphical formats can better provide information than text [12,13]. Automated privacy policy summarization tools follow these guidelines and use a similar approach in their summary result format, in the sense that they provide a standardized category-based summary of the privacy policy. Privee [28], PrivacyCheck [27] and PrivacyGuide [22], for example, show a policy summary based on pre-established categories and risk levels. The visual design of their summary result includes icons and standard descriptions, although the details are different and they use a different criteria for their policy categorization and for assigning risk levels. Polisis [10] takes a different and more complex approach for the privacy policy analysis and classification, but also provides standard categories and fragments of the original privacy policy text. PriBot, a chatbot tool related to Polisis, shows privacy policy fragments in answer to freely composed questions from users.

In addition to the summary result, some privacy policy summarization tools also provide information related to the reliability and performance of the machine learning techniques used. Two of the tools mentioned in the previous section, PrivacyGuide and PriBot, include information that may be considered as explanation of performance of the tool. PrivacyGuide shows a fragment of the original privacy policy that the tool identifies as related to a privacy aspect and uses to assign a risk level. PriBot, on the other hand, shows a confidence percentage that works as a proxy for how accurately the fragment it returns answers a user's question [10].

2.2   Explanatory Information in Automated Systems

When results are provided by automated tools, users have questions about the reliability of those results. One way of influencing this perception is through providing some explanation about the system. For example, offering some justification for outcomes can positively influence perception of accuracy [2] and information about accuracy can improve trust [16]. Although there is no predefined way of communicating to the user about the performance of automated privacy policy summarizing tools, existing tools provide some information. PrivacyGuide shows a fragment of the privacy policy, which can be classified as a justification or support explanation [9]. Similarly, information about the confidence of results such as the one shown by PriBot can also be considered a dimension of explanation [25]. This serves as a measure of uncertainty [5] of the results and therefore as an indication of performance.

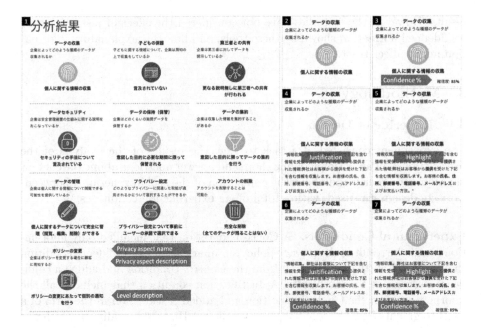

Fig. 1. Privacy policy summary result interface for the experiment. 1: Full summary in the *Control* condition. 2: *Control*, 3: *Confidence*, 4: *Justification*, 5: *Highlight*, 6: *Justification + Confidence* and 7: *Highlight + Confidence* conditions fragments. The full content of the interface (English translation) is detailed in the Appendix.

Although explanatory information, including confidence, has been found to increase trust when users interact with automation [25], its effect is not always positive. Research indicates that certain types of explanatory information about the performance of a system, for example an F-score accuracy measure, may not be useful in applications intended for a general audience [11]. In addition, it has also been found that too much explanatory information could have a negative effect on aspects such as trust [14]. These studies show that simply providing more information may not result in a positive effect; therefore, it is important to evaluate the effect of explanatory information, such as justification and confidence, provided by privacy policy summarization tools.

One limitation in this area is that there are few user evaluations of automated privacy policy summarization tools. For Polisis, a user study was conducted that evaluated only the perception of the accuracy of results, independent from the interface of the tool [10]. The study found that users considered the results of the tool were relevant, although users' perception of the quality of the answers was different from the accuracy of the predictive model. A user study was also conducted to evaluate whether PrivacyGuide results, which found that the tool partially achieved the goal of informing users about the risk of a privacy policy and increasing interest in its content [4]. The study also found that users indicated concern about the trustworthiness of the tool and the accuracy of its results. However, these studies have not considered the effect of justification or confidence information shown by these tools, and how this explanatory information might affect trust.

3   Methodology

3.1   Experiment Design

The experiment consisted of a task to view the results of the analysis of the privacy policy of an fictional online shop, and answer questions about the content of the privacy policy and about the perception of the tool in general. A between-subjects design was used, with a total of six experimental conditions.

Experimental Conditions. A Control condition that included only information about the result of the privacy policy summarization. A Confidence condition that included all the information from the Control condition and added a confidence percentage for the results. A Justification condition that included all the information from the Control condition and added justification in the form of a short fragments from the original privacy policy. A Highlight condition, which was a second form of justification where relevant words were emphasized in the privacy policy fragments. Finally, two conditions that showed both confidence percentage and justification (Justification + Confidence and Highlight + Confidence).

The Control condition result included the basic information about the each privacy aspect, including icons and descriptions of the risk levels. The Justification condition result interface was based on the Control condition, and also included a text fragment for each privacy aspect. The Highlight condition result interface was based on the Justification result, with emphasis on the justification by highlighting words relevant to the corresponding privacy aspect. The Confidence condition was also based on the Control condition, and added a confidence percentage for each privacy aspect result. The Justification + Confidence and Highlight + Confidence conditions result interfaces showed both justification/highlight information (respectively) and confidence percentages.

Regarding the values of the confidence percentages, since confidence and justification information would be shown together for these last two conditions, the confidence values were set by manually evaluating how accurately the fragments represented the privacy aspect risk level. The confidences assigned to each privacy aspect are shown in Table 1. Confidence percentages for the privacy aspect results ranged from 70% to 95%, with the exception of Privacy Settings. For Privacy Settings, the confidence percentage was set to 45% and a fragment that did not accurately represent the corresponding privacy aspect was chosen. This was done to evaluate the influence of incorrect information and low confidence on users' response to questions about the content of the privacy policy.

Privacy Policy Content. Text fragments selected from real privacy policies were used in the experiment. PrivacyGuide was used to generate the summaries of English language privacy policies of well known international websites that also provided an equivalent Japanese language privacy policy. Results that matched the privacy aspect risk level defined were chosen, but the fragment from the matching Japanese language privacy policy was selected. This procedure resulted in fragments that were obtained from different privacy policies; therefore, the texts were reviewed and modified so that they would be congruent with each other in style and content. In addition, any reference to the original company were anonymized.

Interface. The design of the privacy policy summary result interface was based on PrivacyGuide and defined that the result would correspond to a low risk privacy policy, as defined by [4]. In PrivacyGuide, an icon in a color representing one of three levels of risk (Green, Yellow and Red) is assigned to each result category (privacy aspect) depending on the content of the privacy policy corresponding to that aspect [23].

The interfaces also included a help section at the top of the result interface screen, which described every element of the results from the privacy aspect name to the confidence percentage (where applicable). Because users need time to familiarize themselves with elements in a privacy notice [19], the help section was included to compensate for the lack of time, although such a section would not normally be prominently displayed. Figure 1 shows the details of the interface used in the experiment. The details of the content of the interface translated to English language are shown in Appendix A.2.

3.2 Questionnaire

Questions about the privacy policy were included, to evaluate participants' understanding of the privacy practices of the fictional company based on what was presented on the result interface. The questions were adapted from [13] and addressed each of the privacy aspects.

Table 1 shows the content questions and the expected answers for conditions that showed the confidence measure. It was established that the correct option for all questions would be a positive answers (Definitely yes or Possibly yes), with two exceptions: the questions corresponding to the Protection of Children and Privacy Settings aspects. For these questions, the correct option was different depending on the experimental condition, because the Protection of Children aspect was not included in the policy and the Privacy Settings aspect was assigned a low confidence percentage and an incorrect justification fragment (as defined in the previous section). Therefore, in the experimental conditions that included these pieces of information, the correct answer was expected to *not* be a positive answer.

Items for measuring behavioral intention and perception of usefulness, understandability and trustworthiness of the tool were included, as well as questions addressing the perceived appropriateness of using AI for this use case and questions to measure privacy attitude using Westin's Privacy Index [15]. The items were rated on a six-point Likert scale, ranging from Completely disagree to

Completely agree. In addition, an open-ended question on the opinion of participants regarding the privacy policy summarization ("Please tell us what you think about (the tool)") was included.

The detail of the measurement items are shown in Appendix A.1.

Translation. The questionnaire was developed in English; since the survey was conducted in Japan with Japanese participants, the questionnaire was translated with the following procedure. First, two native Japanese speakers independently translated the whole questionnaire, including the statements explaining the survey and privacy policy summarization tool. The translators and a person fluent in Japanese and English reviewed the translated statements one by one, verifying that both translations were equivalent to each other and had the same meaning as the original English statement.

The reviewers found no contradictions in meaning in this first step. The reviewers then chose the translated statements that more clearly communicated the meaning of the questions, instructions or explanations. Finally, the translators reviewed the whole questionnaire to standardize the language, since they had originally used different levels of formality.

Table 1. Questions regarding the content of the result interface. Response options: definitely yes, possibly yes, possibly no, definitely no, it doesn't say in the result, it's unclear from the result.

Privacy aspect	Confidence	Content question	Expected answer
Data collection	85%	Does the online store (company) collect your personal information?	Positive
Privacy settings	45%	Does the online store give you options to manage your privacy preferences?	Positive (for Control condition)/Not positive (for the rest)
Account deletion	75%	Does the online store allow you to delete your account?	Positive
Protection of children	95%	Does the online store knowingly collect information from children?	Does not say
Data security	90%	Does the online store have security measures to protect your personal information?	Positive
Third-party sharing	90%	Does the online store share your personal information with third parties?	Positive
Data retention	85%	Does the online store indicate how long they retain your data?	Positive
Data aggregation	70%	Does the online store aggregate your personal information?	Positive
Control of data	70%	Does the online store allow you to edit your information?	Positive
Policy changes	95%	Does the online store inform you if they change their privacy policy?	Positive

3.3 Data Collection

The survey was conducted using an online survey company, which distributed an invitation to participate in the survey to their registered users. The recruitment process was targeted to obtain a sample with sex and age demographics similar to those of the Japanese population according to the 2101 census [20], but limited participation to users who were 18 years-old or older. Participants were compensated by the online survey company.

Participants were randomly assigned to one of the six experimental conditions and filled the survey online. Pseudonymized data from participants was received from the online survey company, which also included demographic data. In addition, the survey also registered the total time taken for the survey.

The survey was conducted from December 12–14, 2018.

4 Results

4.1 Sample Characteristics

The online survey returned a total of 1054 responses. Suspicious responses were first identified, with the following criteria: (1) cases where all questions were answered with the same extreme points of the response scale, and (2) cases where the total survey answer time was lower than 125 s. The minimum response time of 125 s was calculated as the time it would take to read the full survey at a high reading speed, considering the length (number of Japanese characters) of the online survey and the result screen for the Control condition. With these criteria, 110 cases were identified which were manually reviewed and removed from further analysis.

The sample after removing these data consisted of 944 cases (Table 2). 51% of the participants were female, and the age range was 19–69 years. The distribution these demographic characteristics is similar to that of the Japanese population [20], as established in the data collection process.

Table 2. Sample characteristics. Table from Bracamonte et al. [3].

		n	%	Job		n	%
Total		944	100%	Job	Government employee	35	4%
Gender	Male	458	49%		Company Employee	373	40%
	Female	486	51%		Own business	59	6%
Age	19–20s	168	18%		Freelance	17	2%
	30s	175	19%		Full-time homemaker	174	18%
	40s	200	21%		Part time	112	12%
	50s	185	20%		Student	42	4%
	60s	216	23%		Other	27	3%
					Unemployed	105	11%

The number of cases in each conditions were: 161 cases in the *Control* condition, 160 cases in the *Confidence* condition, 153 cases in the *Justification* condition, 158 cases in the *Highlight*, 153 in the *Justification + Confidence* condition and 150 in the *Highlight + Confidence* condition.

Appropriateness of AI. With regards to the appropriateness of using AI for summarizing privacy policies, the results of a Kruskal-Wallis test showed that there were no significant differences between groups. The median value was 4 ("Somewhat agree") for all conditions except the Control condition, which had a median value of 3 ("Somewhat disagree").

4.2   Westin Privacy Segmentation Index

Answers to the Westin Privacy Segmentation Index questions were analyzed to classify respondents into Privacy Pragmatists, Fundamentalists and Unconcerned. For the classification, the rules described in Woodruff et al. [26] (adjusted for a 6-point Likert scale) were followed: respondents that gave privacy concerned answers to every question were classified as Fundamentalists, respondents that gave privacy unconcerned answers to every question were classified as Unconcerned, and the remaining respondents were classified as Pragmatists. Table 3 shows the results of the classification, and the percentages from existing surveys conducted online in the USA [21,26] for reference.

The results show that the majority of our sample of respondents fall under the category of Privacy Pragmatists, followed by Fundamentalists. Comparatively very few respondents fall under the category of Unconcerned. Although direct comparisons are difficult due to differences in methodology and analysis, previous studies have found a similar proportion of Westin privacy categories in respondents [15,26].

Table 3. Westin's Privacy Segmentation Index classification results for this study and for previous studies, for reference.

	Current study 2018 (n = 944)	Woodruff et al. 2014 [26] (n = 1500)	Harris 2003 [21] (n = 1529)
Pragmatist	60%	58%	64%
Fundamentalist	36%	37%	26%
Unconcerned	4%	5%	10%

4.3   Understanding of the Privacy Policy Content

Fig. 2. Association plot of the relationship between privacy policy questions and their responses for each experimental condition. Blue and red areas indicate significantly higher and lower response proportion than expected (i.e. if all questions had the same response proportion), respectively. Figure from Bracamonte et al. [3]. (Color figure online)

The categorical responses to the questions about the privacy policy were analyzed using chi-square tests. The differences between the responses to each privacy aspect question were of interest, so contingency tables were used to represent the relationship between questions and answers in each experimental condition. As indicated previously, whether participants had understood the results of the tool was of interest, and whether differences in the information shown in each condition were reflected in their answers. The results of the chi-square test of independence are shown in Fig. 2. Association plots [18] were used to visualize areas with significantly higher or lower response proportion, compared between privacy aspect questions.

Responses corresponding to the Control condition provide a base for how participants understand the content of the privacy policy from the results of the tool. The majority of participants chose a positive answer for all of the questions except the one corresponding to Protection of Children, indicating that the result of the tool communicated the expected information in the Control condition. However, the results show that there were no differences in the proportion of responses corresponding to the question regarding Privacy Settings compared to other aspects in any of the experimental conditions. As can be observed in Fig. 2, there are no significant differences in the proportions of responses to the Privacy Settings question compared to the responses to the Control of Data or Data Aggregation questions, for example. This lack of significant differences indicates that participants' responses were not influenced by either the low confidence percentage nor the incorrect justification in the result for the Privacy Settings aspect. However there is some evidence that at least some participants considered the justification information in their response. For the conditions that include justification, the proportion of *Does not say* responses in the Data Retention question is higher. A review of the fragment corresponding to this privacy aspect indicates that there is no mention of a specific time for the retention of the data. This lack of detail may have resulted in at least some participants considering that the question was not answered in the privacy policy. This difference was not seen in the Control condition nor in the Confidence condition, which do not include the justification fragment.

Differences in the time taken to answer the full survey between conditions were also tested. The distribution of time was similar for all conditions and highly skewed, so non-parametric Kruskal-Wallis tests were used for the difference in median. No significant differences were found, indicating that the additional information of justification and confidence conditions did not have an influence on the time taken to finish the survey.

In addition, Kruskal-Wallis tests for the difference in how confident respondents were in their answers and how easy it was to answer the questions indicated that there were no significant differences between conditions for both variables.

4.4   Perception of the Tool

Composite variables were created by summing the items corresponding to attitudes and perception of usefulness, understandability and trustworthiness. A Cronbach's alpha measure for the items corresponding to each composite variable was calculated. In the case of usefulness, the recoded reverse-worded item was negatively correlated and removed from the analysis. After removal, Cronbach's alpha values indicated good internal consistency (all values above 0.9.). Figure 3 shows the median in each experimental condition for all variables.

All composite variables had a similar non-normal distribution shape; therefore, non-parametric Kruskal Wallis tests for the difference between their medians were used, and Dunn's test for multiple comparisons. To control for false positives, p-values were adjusted using the Benjamini-Hochberg procedure [1]. Significant differences between groups for all variables were found, according to the results of Kruskal-Wallis tests. Chi-square values (df $= 5$) for the variables were: (a) Behavioral Intention: 11.694 (p $= 0.33$); (b) Usefulness: 17.217 (p $= 0.004$); (c) Trustworthiness: 17.028 (p $= 0.004$) and (d) Understandability: 11.715 (p $= 0.039$).

Post-hoc comparisons using Dunn's tests were conducted to evaluate which of the groups were significantly different. The results are shown in Fig. 3. Only p-values for comparisons that were significant (p < 0.5) are shown. No significant

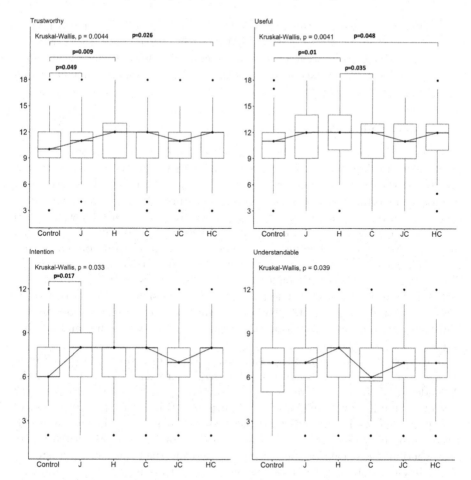

Fig. 3. Boxplots indicating differences in median between the experimental conditions: Control, Justification (J), Highlight (H), Confidence (C), Justification + Confidence (JC), Highlight + Confidence (HC). The p-values of the Kruskal-Wallis test and Dunn's test (in bold) are included for comparisons where there was a significant difference.

differences were found for perceived understandability. The Highlight and Highlight + Confidence conditions were more positively perceived in terms of usefulness and trustworthiness than the Control condition. For behavioral intention, a significant difference was found only between the Control and Justification conditions. No differences in the perception of any of the variables of interest were found between the Control and Confidence conditions, nor between the between the Justification and Highlight conditions; in the latter case, this may be due to the relatively subtle effect of bolding the words. Nor were there significant differences between similar experimental conditions with or without confidence information. In addition, although the Kruskal-Wallis test indicated significant difference for understandability, the post hoc Dunn test did not find significant differences between any condition, based on the adjusted p-value (Fig. 3)

Finally, with regard to the appropriateness of using AI for summarizing privacy policies, the results of a Kruskal-Wallis test showed that there were no significant differences between conditions. The median value was 4 ("Somewhat agree") for all conditions except the Control condition, which had a median value of 3 ("Somewhat disagree").

4.5   Open-Ended Comments

The content of the answers to the open-ended question was analyzed. All comments were in Japanese language, and the thematic analysis was conducted directly on the Japanese comments, without a translation step. There were 656 comments in total; from these, an initial read-through of the data identified non-relevant comments: comments that indicated an "I don't know" or "No comment" response, and blank responses. These responses were not included in subsequent analyses. The data after eliminating non-relevant comments consisted 400 valid responses, corresponding to 42% of participants of the study. There was a similar rate of female and male respondents, and a similar rate of respondents in terms of age. The responses were classified based on their content and themes were identified based on technology acceptance factors and on dimensions of trust in automation [17]. Figure 4 shows the themes and number of comments per theme.

Participants mentioned concerns regarding the performance ("If there's even a 1% probability of error it should not be used."), process ("How much does the AI understand the damage regarding privacy policy, how does it calculate risk? The algorithm is a bit suspicious.") and purpose ("How is the trustworthiness of the application itself assessed? (Because there is a possibility that it's an application favorable to the creator)") of the tool. General concerns about trust were also mentioned ("It can be one guide, but I'm concerned if it can be trusted"). When intention of using the tool was mentioned, it often included certain conditions to be fulfilled ("If it's easy to use and accurate I want to use it.", "If it can judge accurately I think it is ok to use it."). Performance in particular was mentioned by several participants as a reason for concern ("I don't know about its accuracy, so I cannot say I want to proceed to use it."), even when these participants had been assigned to experimental conditions where the tool included explanatory information.

Other comments by participants referred to understandability of the tool, both positively ("I felt it was more understandable than I expected") and negatively ("In any case I want it to be understandable to laymen"). Similarly, the design of the tool was mentioned in both positive and negative terms ("It makes a long, complicated text into (something) visually concise and easy to understand so I thought it was useful", "There are too many sections, I did not understand very well"). These types of comments occurred regardless of whether the experimental condition contained more or less information. Finally, positive and negative attitudes towards the use of AI for this type of applications were mentioned in the comments ("This is what AI-based analysis is appropriate for.", "It is the result of an analysis done by AI, so it's difficult to trust it").

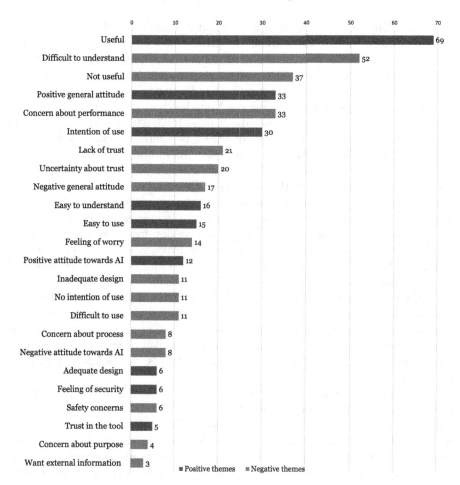

Fig. 4. Themes identified in participants' open-ended comments about their opinion on the privacy policy summarization tool, ordered by number of comments per theme.

5   Discussion

The results show that providing privacy policy information fragments as justification, with and without highlighted words, improved perception of the tool compared to not showing that information, albeit on different dimensions. On the other hand, the results show that confidence information did not have any influence. Based on previous research on the confidence explanations [25], showing a confidence percentage was expected to improve perception of trustworthiness in particular, but there was no effect on any of the measured perception variables. The results show that the short summary format (Control condition) can inform users of the overall privacy policy contents as categorized by the tool. This result is in line with research on shorter privacy policy formats [8]. On the other hand, the additional explanatory information of justification and result confidence included in other experimental conditions did not greatly alter the responses to the questions about the privacy policy content, even when the fragment did not accurately justify the result or the confidence percentage was low. One possibility is that participants may have relied mainly on the privacy aspect's icons and descriptions to answer the questions about the privacy policy, even when there was additional information that was in contradiction of the overall result. This may have been due to the fact that no explicit attention was brought to the justification and confidence percentage, beyond including its description in the help section of the interface. In addition, the questions asked to participants were straightforward and for the most part targeted information that was already available in the elements of the Control condition interface.

However, the results indicate that participants did consider justification information, at least to some extent, as evidenced by the answers to the Data Retention question in conditions where the privacy policy fragment was shown. As for the incorrect fragment corresponding to the Privacy Settings aspect, it may be that participants were not sufficiently familiar with this type of settings, and therefore could not judge whether the fragment was incorrect or not. In the case of confidence information, another possibility is that the users did not think to question the results of the tool and therefore ignored the contradictory information of low confidence. This can happen when the user considers that the system is reliable [25]. Figure 3 shows that the median of trustworthiness perception is higher than the midpoint for all conditions, which lends support to this hypothesis.

In general, the results of this study suggest that adding explanatory information in the form of justification can be beneficial to automated privacy policy summarization tools. However, post-hoc power analysis indicates that the sample is large enough to detect small differences, meaning that it is possible that statistically significant improvements in perception of usefulness and trustworthiness may not be relevant in practice. Conversely, the findings that not all explanatory information had a significant positive effect suggest that it is important to evaluate whether this additional information can truly benefit users, before considering adding it to the result interface of an automated privacy policy summarization tool. Although our results do not indicate that there would be negative effects if explanatory information is shown, future research should consider evaluating any possible tradeoffs in terms of usability.

The content of participants' comments suggest that concerns the about performance of the tool were not addressed by the information presented. This points to the difficulty of providing information that can target concerns related to trust in automation, in a way that users can understand and use. From participant's comments it can be gathered that accuracy of the tool is an important piece of information for users, but this information is particularly difficult to show. Information about the performance of AI or machine learning-based systems (e.g. accuracy) are highly dependent on the training and validation data. Automated privacy policy summary tools could show accuracy metrics obtained during the initial development of the tool, but not for the current privacy policy that is being summarized. In addition, information about process, which describes the operation of the automated tool, can also be difficult to show when the AI or machine learning models used are black boxes. The challenge is how to communicate the information about trustworthiness dimensions (performance, process and purpose) in order to lessen users' concerns. Due to the characteristics of machine learning, users are interested in how these type of automated systems generate their results but are unclear on how they may verify this information even if it is shown:

"Even if a percentage is shown, there is not enough basis to know whether that number itself can be trusted; in this situation it is difficult to trust to that extent"

In the particular case of automated summarization of privacy policies, performance is not easy to verify as it would require either reading the privacy policy or encountering an error. In the first case, even if a user were to read a privacy policy they may not have the specialist knowledge to determine whether a risk assessment is correct or incorrect, even with the assumption that there is such a clearly established baseline. In the case of errors, privacy policy violations may not be easily detectable even if they occur. Although improving trust by addressing these factors is possible, designing automated systems that provide performance, process and purpose information is not trivial. In particular, if the goal is appropriate trust then simply providing information is not considered sufficient [17]. More research is needed to identify what information to present to users in order to improve efficacy as well as perception of these automated privacy tools.

5.1 Limitations

The study conducted had the following limitations. In the study, the risk level of the privacy policy was not manipulated, and only a privacy policy defined as low risk was considered. The number of privacy aspects and corresponding risk levels result in a large number of possible combinations, making it impractical to test them all. Consequently, it may be that the results of the study are not generalizable to other risk levels besides the one chosen for the study.

In addition, a process to validate that the participants had indeed comprehended every aspect of the result interface was not included, beyond the straightforward questions about the content of the privacy policy. The consideration was that if more detailed questions were included, the behavior of the participant would deviate further from a normal interaction with these type of tools. Nevertheless, this means that the results of this study reflect an evaluation of perception rather than objective measures of comprehension.

Lastly, in the study PrivacyGuide's privacy aspect categorization was used, which is based on the European Union's GDPR, and showed it to Japanese participants. However, the GDPR-based categories are considered relevant for our Japanese participants. For one, there is a degree of compatibility between the GDPR and Japanese privacy regulation [6]. And the Japanese language privacy policies used in the experiment come from international websites aimed at Japanese audiences, and are direct translations of English privacy policies created to comply with the GDRP.

6   Conclusions

In this paper, an experimental evaluation of the effects of explanatory information on the perception of the results of an automated privacy policy tool was
conducted. In particular, it was evaluated whether justification and confidence
of the results can help users correctly interpret the summarization results and
whether showing this information has influence in user perception. The results
showed that perception of usefulness, trustworthiness and behavioral intention
are positively influenced by including a privacy policy fragment as result justification, but that a result confidence percentage did not have such an effect, even
when it indicated a low reliability in the results.

In general, the findings suggest that explanatory information of the results
of an automated privacy policy summarization tool can improve perception of
the tool, but that not all explanatory information is the same. What type of
explanatory information should be included, and how to show this information
need to be evaluated before inclusion. Future research should investigate how to
best provide the type of explanatory information that will help users understand
the limitations of the results of these tools.

A   Appendix

A.1   Questionnaire Items

The response scale is Completely agree, Agree, Somewhat agree, Somewhat disagree, Disagree, Completely disagree.

1. *Usefulness*
   (a) The application answers my questions about the privacy policy of the
       online store
   (b) The application addresses my concerns about the privacy policy of the
       online store
   (c) The application is useful to understand the privacy policy of the online
       store
   (d) The application does not answer what I want to know about the privacy
       policy of the online store (Reverse worded).
2. *Trustworthiness*
   (a) The results of the application are trustworthy
   (b) The results of the application are reliable
   (c) The results of the application are accurate.
3. *Understandability*
   (a) The results of the application are understandable
   (b) The reason for the results is understandable.
4. *Behavioral Intention*
   (a) I would use this application to analyze the privacy policy of various online
       stores
   (b) I would use this application to decide whether or not to use various online
       stores.

5. *Appropriate AI Use*
   (a) The use of AI is appropriate for this kind of application.
6. *Westin's Privacy Index*
   (a) Consumers have lost all control over how personal information is collected and used by companies.
   (b) Most businesses handle the personal information they collect about consumers in a proper and confidential way.
   (c) Existing laws and organizational practices provide a reasonable level of protection for consumer privacy today.
7. *About Content Questions*
   (a) I'm confident in my answers to the above questions.
   (b) It was easy to answer the above questions.

A.2 Interface Information

Information presented in the result interface for each privacy aspect, in English language.

1. *Data Collection*
   - Description: What type of data is collected by the company?
   - Risk level description: Collection of personal information
   - Privacy policy fragment: "collection of information we receive and store information about you such as: information you provide to us: we collect information you provide to us which includes: your name, email address, address or postal code, payment method(s), and telephone number".
2. *Protection of Children*
   - Description: Does the company knowingly collect data of children?
   - Risk level description: Not mentioned
   - Privacy policy fragment: n/a.
3. *Third-party Sharing*
   - Description: Does the company disclose the data to third parties?
   - Risk level description: Third party sharing with no further explanation
   - Privacy policy fragment: "There are also other parties which can receive some of your data, which are parties we involve to provide you with our services. This includes for example - financial institutions, advertisers, subsidiaries of our company's corporate family and other affiliates of our company's corporate family or in some cases, if we are required by applicable law, governmental or other authorities."
4. *Data Security*
   - Description: Does the company mention any kind of safeguarding mechanisms?
   - Risk level description: Security measures mentioned
   - Privacy policy fragment: "security we use reasonable administrative, logical, physical and managerial measures to safeguard your personal information against loss, theft and unauthorized access, use and modification".

5. *Data Retention*
   - Description: How long does the company store the collected data?
   - Risk level description: Data is kept as long as it is necessary for the intended purpose
   - Privacy policy fragment: "we may retain information as required or permitted by applicable laws and regulations, including to honor your choices, for our billing or records purposes and to fulfill the purposes described in this privacy statement".

6. *Data Aggregation*
   - Description: Does the company aggregate the collected information?
   - Risk level description: Data aggregation only for the intended purpose
   - Privacy policy fragment: "Our partners and advertisers share information with us we also get information about you and your activity outside our website from our affiliates, advertisers, partners and other third parties we work with, or other publicly available sources".

7. *Control of Data*
   - Description: Does the company offer the possibility to review personal information?
   - Risk level description: Full control of personal data (review, edit and deletion)
   - Privacy policy fragment: "choices relating to your registration and account information if you have an account, you generally may review and edit personal data by logging in and updating the information directly or by contacting us".

8. *Privacy Settings*
   - Description: Is it possible to choose which privacy related practices will be applied?
   - Risk level description: User has the option to opt-in for privacy related practices
   - Privacy policy fragment: "if you no longer want to receive certain communications from us via email or text message, simply access the communications settings option in the account section of our website and uncheck those items to unsubscribe".

9. *Account Deletion*
   - Description: Is it possible to delete an account?
   - Risk level description: Full deletion (no remaining data) possible
   - Privacy policy fragment: "Please note that after you close an account, you will not be able to sign in or access any of your personal information. [However, you can open a new account at any time.]. Please also note that we may retain certain information associated with your account in our archives, including for analytical purposes as well as for recordkeeping integrity."

10. *Policy Changes*
    - Description: Does the company inform their customers in case of a policy change?
    - Risk level description: Individual notification in case of policy changes

- Privacy policy fragment: "the most current version of the policy will govern our processing of your personal data and will always be at our website. If we make a change to this policy that, in our sole discretion, is material, we will notify you via an email to the email address associated with your account".

References

1. Benjamini, Y., Hochberg, Y.: Controlling the false discovery rate: a practical and powerful approach to multiple testing. J. Royal Stat. Soc. Ser. B (Methodological) **57**(1), 289–300 (1995)
2. Biran, O., McKeown, K.: Human-centric justification of machine learning predictions. In: Proceedings of the 26th International Joint Conference on Artificial Intelligence, IJCAI 2017, pp. 1461–1467. AAAI Press (2017)
3. Bracamonte, V., Hidano, S., Tesfay, W., Kiyomoto, S.: Evaluating the effect of justification and confidence information on user perception of a privacy policy summarization tool. In: 6th International Conference on Information Systems Security and Privacy, pp. 142–151. SciTePress (2020)
4. Bracamonte, V., Hidano, S., Tesfay, W.B., Kiyomoto, S.: Evaluating privacy policy summarization: an experimental study among Japanese users. In: Proceedings of the 5th International Conference on Information Systems Security and Privacy - Volume 1: ICISSP, pp. 370–377. INSTICC, SciTePress (2019). https://doi.org/10.5220/0007378403700377
5. Diakopoulos, N.: Accountability in algorithmic decision making. Commun. ACM **59**(2), 56–62 (2016). https://doi.org/10.1145/2844110
6. European Commission: European Commission - PRESS RELEASES - Press release - European Commission adopts adequacy decision on Japan, creating the world's largest area of safe data flows (2019). http://europa.eu/rapid/press-release_IP-19-421_en.htm
7. European Parliament: Regulation (EU) 2016/679 of the European Parliament and of the Council of 27 April 2016 on the protection of natural persons with regard to the processing of personal data and on the free movement of such data, and repealing Directive 95/46 (2016)
8. Gluck, J., et al.: How short is too short? Implications of length and framing on the effectiveness of privacy notices. In: Twelfth Symposium on Usable Privacy and Security (SOUPS 2016), pp. 321–340. USENIX Association (2016)
9. Gregor, S., Benbasat, I.: Explanations from intelligent systems: theoretical foundations and implications for practice. MIS Q. **23**(4), 497–530 (1999). https://doi.org/10.2307/249487
10. Harkous, H., Fawaz, K., Lebret, R., Schaub, F., Shin, K.G., Aberer, K.: Polisis: automated analysis and presentation of privacy policies using deep learning. In: 27th USENIX Security Symposium (USENIX Security 2018), pp. 531–548. USENIX Association (2018)
11. Kay, M., Patel, S.N., Kientz, J.A.: How good is 85%?: A survey tool to connect classifier evaluation to acceptability of accuracy. In: Proceedings of the 33rd Annual ACM Conference on Human Factors in Computing Systems, CHI 2015, pp. 347–356. ACM (2015). https://doi.org/10.1145/2702123.2702603

12. Kelley, P.G., Bresee, J., Cranor, L.F., Reeder, R.W.: A "nutrition label" for privacy. In: Proceedings of the 5th Symposium on Usable Privacy and Security, SOUPS 2009, pp. 4:1–4:12. ACM (2009). https://doi.org/10.1145/1572532.1572538

13. Kelley, P.G., Cesca, L., Bresee, J., Cranor, L.F.: Standardizing privacy notices: an online study of the nutrition label approach. In: Proceedings of the SIGCHI Conference on Human Factors in Computing Systems, CHI 2010, pp. 1573–1582. ACM (2010). https://doi.org/10.1145/1753326.1753561

14. Kizilcec, R.F.: How much information?: Effects of transparency on trust in an algorithmic interface. In: Proceedings of the 2016 CHI Conference on Human Factors in Computing Systems, CHI 2016, pp. 2390–2395. ACM (2016). https://doi.org/10.1145/2858036.2858402

15. Kumaraguru, P., Cranor, L.F.: Privacy indexes: a survey of Westin's studies. Carnegie Mellon University, Technical report (2005)

16. Lai, V., Tan, C.: On human predictions with explanations and predictions of machine learning models: a case study on deception detection. In: Proceedings of the Conference on Fairness, Accountability, and Transparency, FAT 2019, pp. 29–38. ACM (2019). https://doi.org/10.1145/3287560.3287590

17. Lee, J.D., See, K.A.: Trust in automation: designing for appropriate reliance. Hum. Factors **46**(1), 50–80 (2004). https://doi.org/10.1518/hfes.46.1.50.30392

18. Meyer, D., Zeileis, A., Hornik, K.: The strucplot framework: visualizing multi-way contingency tables with VCD. J. Stat. Softw. **17**(3) (2006). https://doi.org/10.18637/jss.v017.i03

19. Schaub, F., Balebako, R., Durity, A.L., Cranor, L.F.: A design space for effective privacy notices. In: Eleventh Symposium On Usable Privacy and Security (SOUPS 2015), pp. 1–17 (2015)

20. Statistics Bureau, Ministry of Internal Affairs and Communications: Population and Households of Japan 2010 (2010)

21. Taylor, H.: Most people are "privacy pragmatists" who, while concerned about privacy, will sometimes trade it off for other benefits. Harris Poll **17**(19), 44 (2003)

22. Tesfay, W.B., Hofmann, P., Nakamura, T., Kiyomoto, S., Serna, J.: I read but don't agree: privacy policy benchmarking using machine learning and the EU GDPR. In: Companion Proceedings of the The Web Conference 2018, WWW 2018, pp. 163–166. International World Wide Web Conferences Steering Committee (2018). https://doi.org/10.1145/3184558.3186969

23. Tesfay, W.B., Hofmann, P., Nakamura, T., Kiyomoto, S., Serna, J.: PrivacyGuide: towards an implementation of the EU GDPR on internet privacy policy evaluation. In: Proceedings of the Fourth ACM International Workshop on Security and Privacy Analytics, IWSPA 2018, pp. 15–21. ACM (2018). https://doi.org/10.1145/3180445.3180447

24. ToSDR: Terms of Service; Didn't Read (2019). https://tosdr.org/

25. Wang, N., Pynadath, D.V., Hill, S.G.: Trust calibration within a human-robot team: comparing automatically generated explanations. In: The Eleventh ACM/IEEE International Conference on Human Robot Interaction, HRI 2016, pp. 109–116. IEEE Press (2016)

26. Woodruff, A., Pihur, V., Consolvo, S., Schmidt, L., Brandimarte, L., Acquisti, A.: Would a privacy fundamentalist sell their DNA for 1000...if nothing bad happened as a result? The Westin categories, behavioral intentions, and consequences. In: Proceedings of the Symposium On Usable Privacy and Security: SOUPS 2014 (2014)

27. Zaeem, R.N., German, R.L., Barber, K.S.: PrivacyCheck: automatic summarization of privacy policies using data mining. ACM Trans. Internet Technol. **18**(4), 53:1–53:18 (2018). https://doi.org/10.1145/3127519
28. Zimmeck, S., Bellovin, S.M.: Privee: an architecture for automatically analyzing web privacy policies. In: 23rd USENIX Security Symposium (USENIX Security 2014), pp. 1–16. USENIX Association, August 2014

Harmonic Group Mix: A Framework for Anonymous and Authenticated Broadcast Messages in Vehicle-to-Vehicle Environments

Mirja Nitschke$^{(\boxtimes)}$ (ID), Christian Roth (ID), Christian Hoyer, and Doğan Kesdoğan

University of Regensburg, Regensburg, Germany
{mirja.nitschke,christian.roth,christian.hoyer,
dogan.kesdogan}@ur.de

Abstract. Nowadays Vehicle-to-Vehicle communication (V2V) plays an increasingly important role, not only in terms of safety, but also in other areas of Intelligent Transport Systems (ITS). However, privacy is often underestimated in this context. In this paper we describe an extended version of our Harmonized Group Mix (HGM). HGM has the objective of enabling the privacy-friendly data exchange between vehicles in an ITS without neglecting other requirements such as integrity. In contrast to other approaches a complex organizational structure is not required and HGM is thus easily applicable. Rather, the idea of a Mix system is transferred to ITS communication, but the ITS-specific real-time requirements can still be met. The simultaneous use of group signatures can ensure a high degree of k-anonymity and prevent the tracking of participants. A distributed knowledge approach provides trust but at the same times allows revealing fraudsters. In addition to a detailed security analysis, this paper evaluates the approach using the simulation framework Veins and focuses on the exact vehicle movements and the groups formation respectively changes over time and their influence on each other.

Keywords: V2V communication · Mix · Privacy · k-Anonymity · ITS

1 Introduction

In the course of the last century, vehicle development has undergone a major evolution in terms of safety. While in the last decades the safety of vehicles has been increased mainly by the fact that more and more safety systems, such as seat belts or airbags, have been built directly into the vehicles, car manufacturers today try to increase safety by allowing vehicles to communicate with each other. Especially in the EU and the USA the potential of Vehicle-to-Vehicle (V2V) communication was identified years ago. So that the vehicles can also understand each other, efforts are being made to standardize communication in this field. This has been promoted through the establishment of the CAR 2 CAR Communication Consortium[1] and the Transportation Systems Committee[2]. However, new ITS-based applications also require very high standards for the

---

[1] https://www.car-2-car.org.
[2] https://sites.ieee.org/ias-tcs.

© Springer Nature Switzerland AG 2022
S. Furnell et al. (Eds.): ICISSP 2020, CCIS 1545, pp. 178–200, 2022.
https://doi.org/10.1007/978-3-030-94900-6_9

processed data. The data has to be precise, up-to-date, and most importantly integer. The exact location of every user must be known local at all times in order to provide a safe and secure environment, although, this may conflict with interests of the privacy of the participants. For example, location traces are sensitive because they give insight into a user's behavior and daily routine. Although, current standards are usually little oriented towards privacy, it has become a topic of interest for science and industry.

Our contribution is an architecture extension for V2V communication that provides anonymous and yet authenticated broadcast messages by incorporating the idea of mix technology to harmonize the appearance of different messages of miscellaneous users. Our *Harmonized Group Mix (HGM)* is designed to be compatible to current standards, like the IEEE Standard for Wireless Access in Vehicular Environments (WAVE). Our architecture has several advantages, e.g.

1. the organizational structure is simple, beside the users we only need one other, merely semi-trusted, entity,
2. we limit cryptographic overhead by only using group signatures, and
3. a sender cannot easily be identified because the collaboration of several tracing authorities is needed to decrypt the group signature, providing maximum privacy.

We follow the classical approach of the triple bottom line of security "algorithm, adversary and evaluation". In addition to our original paper [32], we contribute in this extended version with i.a.

– a detailed description of the blame process by explaining the use of a cuckoo filter,
– an enlarged security analysis, and
– an extended evaluation with a focus on the exact vehicle movements and the groups formation respectively changes over time and their influence on each other.

The remainder of this paper is organized as follows. After a review of related work in Sect. 2, we discuss the system model in Sect. 3. We present our approach *Harmonized Group Mix (HGM)* to provide anonymous and yet authenticated broadcast messages in the context of the ITS in Sect. 4. In Sect. 5 we evaluate the proposed approach and discuss the results. Section 6 concludes the paper and names possible extensions of our approach. A list of notation can be found in Appendix A.

2   Related Work

The issue of privacy in vehicular ad-hoc networks (VANETs) has been investigated in various papers, e.g. [33] focus on management of identities and cryptographic keys, [39] focus on the possibility of tracking broadcast communications. [6] investigate pseudonym-based authentication in their architecture, while [24] investigate a Vehicular Public Key Infrastructure. Further interesting approaches are [1, 26, 35]. [5] propose a security credential system that uses certificates to balance privacy and anonymity. In contrast to our work, however, this approach is based on a complex structure of several organizations. [20] propose a superficial security framework based on group signature in which a person's identity can be revealed by a single other entity. [44] use short time certificates where multiple deactivated certificates are issued to a vehicle during a setup phase. Activation can be then be performed once a central authority sends activation keys for a particular certificate, but the vehicle must be connected to the network to receive the codes. The certificate holder can modify the certificate so that messages are signed at a specific time to protect himself against location based attacks.

There is also a significant amount of literature on architectures that enable anonymous V2V communication [21,22,39,41,48,50]. However, most of these papers rely on Road-Side-Units (RSU), which are either autonomous or controlled by a single trusted third party. Upon reviewing other architecture proposals, we identified several roles that RSUs can assume, of which they can hold one or more roles at once. In most papers we found RSUs act as communication relays, which handle information dissemination between network entities [17,34,37,49], computational devices, which handle calculations for vehicles, monitor the flow of traffic and control traffic lights [31,36,38], or take up tasks in the areas of group management, which mean they handle the setup and administration of groups [46,50]. They can also act in the areas of key management, in a role where they are in control of handing out asymmetrical and symmetrical keys to secure communication [6,18,21,28,31], or resource management and provision, which means they provide vehicles with internet access or access to specific services proposed by the architecture [12,25,27,34]. Another disadvantage is the price of RSUs. We identified three documents [42,47,49] where the authors calculate the cost of installing RSUs in an urban scenario. The following example calculation is based on the area of Munich (310.71 Km^2)^3 and an average range per RSU of 400 m. Using the numbers for calculation, we estimated installation costs of 8.0 million euros and operating and maintenance costs of 1.6 million euros per year. Cutting these costs would be a huge advantage over other architectures. Therefore, the goal of our approach is to reduce costs by eliminating RSUs and to provide a privacy enhanced service.

As already mentioned, we focus our work on the unlinkability of messages. We try to propagate the idea of linking individual messages not to a specific (pseudonymized) entity, but to a group of people. Thus we combine the idea of a Mix network with group signatures to deliver a location aware message without revealing a specific identity.

3   System Model

Our system model is compatible with the typical Intelligent Transportation System (ITS) scenario. Vehicles (i.e. users $u \in \mathcal{U}$) drive along a road network in different trajectories and eventually pass other vehicles, usually quite fast. Each vehicle is inseparably equipped with communication devices, so-called On-Board-Units (OBUs; see [33]), which enable an authenticated and unforgeable exchange of information. It can be preloaded with cryptographic material.

In typical ITS scenarios, vehicles have to exchange information, so silent periods are not acceptable and the ability to send messages must be available at all times. Messages are broadcasted within the network and can be relayed by all participants $\mathcal{U}$ and/or external (static) entities such as Road-Side-Units. The set $\mathcal{M}$ describes all sent messages $m \in \mathcal{M}$.

---

^{3} https://www.muenchen.de/sehenswuerdigkeiten/muenchen-in-zahlen.html.

Each user u is uniquely identifiable via his vehicle ID $id(obu)$ which is inseparably linked to its OBU. The OBU is responsible for signing messages so that each m can be traced back to u via $id(obu)$. The information is generally arbitrary, but due to the nature of ITS is always enriched with a timestamp and a GPS location. Since each message can be traced to a specific location, it is obvious that such messages pose a threat to a participant's privacy. A trajectory of multiple messages that can be traced to a single user provides information about a user's behavior and is therefore a sensitive asset that must to be protected. Therefore, every participant has an interest in hiding his or her true identity in combination with the originating messages.

3.1 Group Signatures

A useful approach to ensure anonymity is the use of group signatures, first introduced in [8] and extended by [4, 7, 10, 29]. Group signatures allow members of a group to sign messages on behalf of the entire group. They are verifiable with a single public verification key associated to the whole group. As a result, no one can identify the originator of this signature or link signed messages from the same originator, except for a tracer authority that has a special opening key. A second role, called group leader, distributes the signing keys to all members. In addition, group signatures provide anonymity and traceability as well as non-frameability and unforgeability, essential building blocks for a vehicle communication protocol. In particular, we select a group signature scheme that offers the following functionality:

- Users may join a group after it is created (dynamic groups).
- A group leader may not be the only tracer (two authorities).
- The ability to identify the originator of a message must be divided among several entities (distributed tracers).
- No central key distributing agency or other similarly trusted third party.
- CCA-full-anonymous [16] properties against insider attacks, as any vehicle can be a potential attacker.
- Very short signatures due to limited packet size (around 1024 byte) while providing enough space for the payload.

Such a protocol can be realized with the help of the group signature scheme of [3], which is based on the work [4] and extends it with distributed traceability. Furthermore, we adapt [14] to allow dynamic groups.

3.2 Mix Network

A viable approach to anonymise communication between two users is the Mix network presented in [9]. In simple terms, a Mix network is a chain of nodes that a message from a user must pass through to reach its destination. A Mix node collects multiple messages from different people, which the originator have to encrypt in multiple layers using known asymmetric keys of all Mix nodes in the chain. Then each Mix node decrypts the respective layer of the message using its private key, thus changing the appearance of the message. It now outputs all messages in a changed order, and the next Mix node performs the same operation until the message reaches its destination. As a result, an eavesdropper cannot establish a connection between incoming and outgoing messages in the system due to changes in shape and order. We take up this idea by harmonizing the appearance of multiple messages from different users through group signature encryption. Since the users themselves act as mix, see Fig. 1, no one sees the incoming messages and the mix does not need to collect multiple messages. Instead, an attacker can only associate a message with a group of users, and not with a single user.

3.3 WAVE

This section gives a brief derivation of the requirements for our approach based on the IEEE 802.11p standard and the IEEE 1609 extension. Together they are collectively referred to as WAVE (Wireless Access for Vehicular Environments) [23]. To exchange information, participants form a WAVE Basic Service Set (WBSS, c.f. IEEE 1609.3) for the organization of our anonymity groups (see [43]).

The IEEE 1609.4 standard offers multi-channel operation over WAVE PHY and MAC layers. It provides one control channel (CCH) and 6 service channels (SCH) that can be used by different applications. Each channel has different characteristics in terms of maximum transmit power or frequency depending on the application requirements. Depending on the speed of a vehicle, packet loss and bandwidth may vary [2]. Due to its safety-critical nature, the control channel is best suited for stable and long-range communication in an urban context [19]. From this we derive the following requirements: Communication exchange on SCHs should be minimal and must be completed during the close range of the vehicles. The protocol should be as efficient and robust as possible.

WAVE Short Messages, as defined in the IEEE 1609.3 standard, are the actual data packets and are permitted on any type of channel. To exchange information, the participants use a specific SCH. Together they form a group, a so-called WAVE Basic Service Set (WBSS), which synchronizes certain parameters, such as the time of switching to the SCH [43]. We use WBSS to organize our anonymity groups.

3.4 Attacker

All participants are considered to be honest-but-curious, i.e. they respect every step of the protocol, but want to gain more knowledge about others. Given this, the attacker in our system is in general anyone who can actively interact with the system, such as replaying messages. Therefore we need CCA full-anonymity. As a result, every user is able to collect messages distributed in the system and store them in a message log $\hat{\mathcal{M}}$. The attacker's primary goal is to link multiple messages m to a single user u, however, a user may use different pseudonyms π at the same time to create messages m. In the end, the attacker can then use the log of collected messages $\hat{\mathcal{M}}$ and his knowledge about his own behavior together with π to create a complete location trajectory of a user u.

In our setup we assume that the attacker knows all system parameters. This leads to an even more severe threat to stress our algorithm. He starts his attack to link messages to the user and derive information about the path driven by this user. However, as mentioned above, it is very resource-intensive for an attacker to gain access to multiple

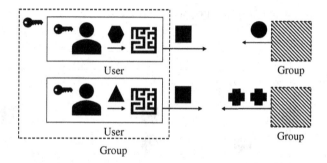

Fig. 1. White- and Blackbox view on the Mix groups each producing harmonized messages unlinkable to the originator. Because every user operates his own Mix node the group does not need to communicate after exchanging the group keys (taken from [32]).

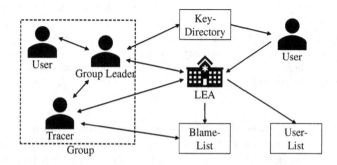

Fig. 2. A organizational overview of *HGM*'s entities and roles including their relationship (taken from [32]).

OBUs, so we assume that he is not able to control a large part of the network. We do not focus in this paper on approaches to validate the content (i.e. the substance) of a message. For example, [11] can be relied upon this. However, we do provide a method to reveal the originator of a message.

4   Harmonized Group Mix

We now present *Harmonized Group Mix* (HGM) for ITS. Our approach combines ideas from Mixes to change the shape of a message, i.e. harmonize it, with group signatures to dynamically create new Mix groups.

4.1   High Level Overview

HGM relies only on two basic entities to balance anonymity and integrity. It is therefore noticeably less complex than other approaches. In addition to all users, there is a semi trusted third party called *Law Enforcement Agency (LEA)* that maintains a user list containing $\mathcal{U}$. Figure 2 illustrates all entities and relationships. Each user can have multiple roles in the system.

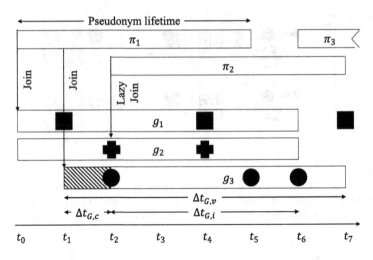

Fig. 3. Process flow of *HGM*. A user holds multiple pseudonyms π which he uses to participate in different groups g. Each message (rectangle, circle, plus) is only linkable to a group but not the pseudonym. A user can select a pseudonym to join multiple groups at once even his own enhancing anonymity (taken from [32]).

In general, there is no need to attach personally identifiable information to a message, or even to restrict access to it. In the real world, however, it is likely that dishonest users will try to attack the system, for example by flooding it with fake information. This is especially true in the open nature of V2V architectures, where dishonest users are eventually present. Therefore, countermeasures are required to exclude such users from the system; possible threats are discussed later in Sect. 4.4.

HGM uses separation of duties to isolate the activity of a user from his identity. Messages are not directly linkable to a user u or his respective pseudonym π_i, but with arbitrary groups $g_i \in \mathcal{G}$. A group is managed by another user (called group leader $l(g_i) = \pi_x$, where π_x is the pseudonym of the group leader) who is responsible for creating groups or adding new members, avoiding the need for a trusted third party. All messages from a group are *harmonized*, i.e. identifiable information of a user is obfuscated. Therefore, any member of a group can be the sender of a message, making it difficult for an adversary to obtain additional information about a user. To spread the power further, this obfuscation can only be removed if the majority of a user group (called tracers) agrees. After a message is sent, it is impossible for a recipient to identify the sender of a message because all messages within the group have been *mixed*. Messages are created locally in a user's domain using their private group key (see Fig. 1), as only the local vehicle is assumed to be fully trusted.

Unlike existing approaches, no silent periods are required when switching from one π to another, because a user holds multiple π and is always a member of multiple groups. Figure 3 shows an except of the lifetime of a single user u. He can use any $\pi \in \Pi$ during its pseudonym lifetime to join groups at any time as long as they accept new users (up to $\Delta t_{G,i}$ after creation). He can then randomly use each joined group to create messages breaking up a potential location trajectory. Groups also have a certain lifetime of $\Delta t_{G,v}$ to ensure that expired or blocked pseudonyms can no longer send messages. As a result, messages from such groups are discarded on reception. A new group can be created at any time, but must be completed within $\Delta t_{G,c}$.

4.2 Roles

Our approach uses different entities to distribute knowledge and control. Communication between these different entities should be minimized, not only because of the performance aspect, but also because of anonymity.

Law Enforcement Agency (LEA): The LEA, for example administrated by the government, keeps track of all $\mathcal{U}$ and acts as a doorkeeper. It is a semi-trusted party, since all users trust authenticated entities from it. The LEA is not considered and needed to be fully trusted, since it can only recognize that users want to participate, but cannot obtain any knowledge about their activities. This is important because this entity is a global attacker in the honest-but-curious attacker model. For example, the LEA is interested in the GPS trajectory of a specific OBU – something that *HGM* is supposed to protect itself against.

Participant: A user becomes a participant if he has an authorized OBU that allows him to interact with the system. This is the most basic role in our system. Participants can use multiple signed pseudonyms π to enroll in dynamically created anonymity groups. Only participants in a group can create messages. The permission of a user to be a participate in the ITS network is controlled by the LEA.

Group Leader: Since anonymity in our system is achieved by organizing multiple and unique participants into groups, there must to be a managing entity called group leader. A group leader is responsible for the management of groups, including the distribution of keys, although he is not needed during crunch time. Furthermore, he does not gain any additional knowledge about his group participants, except that he knows which pseudonym has joined with what role. He is not able to tell whether different signed pseudonyms refer to the same $id(obu)$.

Tracer: Since any group member can create valid messages on behalf of their anonymity group, the entire group is to blame if, for example, the messages are forged. Therefore, the system allows to reveal the true identity of the originator. We split the ability to map $m \rightarrow \pi$ between multiple, randomly chosen group members, so-called tracers. A certain percentage of these tracers must work together to reveal the originator of the message. In this way, they are accountable for the integrity of the entire group, including their own messages.

4.3 Protocol

We now present a detailed examination of the protocol. Users communicate via V2V communication channels (e.g. WAVE), while information exchange between users and LEA, and directory lookups are performed out-of-band, e.g. via LTE, which supports higher ranges and bandwidth. In Figs. 4, 5 and 6 we refer to out-of-band communication using - before the entity.

Notation. c, d denote a public private key pair that is used for encryption and decryption as well as for signing and verifying. A group g with n members is denoted as $u_1, \ldots, u_n \in g$, where g contains a subgroup $\mathcal{U}_g$ of all users $\mathcal{U}$ and all groups $\mathcal{G}$. $|\mathcal{U}_g|$ defines the number of members in this group. As mentioned in Sect. 3.1, we use group signatures by [3] with the specified extension. For simplicity, we do not list all parameters of this group signature scheme, but only name extensions needed for *HGM*. If stated, $\mathcal{X}$ and $\mathcal{Y}$ always denote parameters for the group signature scheme. All symbols used in this paper can found in Appendix A.

Initialization of the System. *HGM* offers anonymity by using pseudonyms among other things. These pseudonyms are derived from a users $id(obu)$ in a reversible manner to protect integrity. However, the disclosure of these pseudonyms is only possible through the LEA. Requesting pseudonyms can be upstreamed so that problems with unreliable long-range communication can be mitigated.

To request an authenticated pseudonym, a user sends a PSEUDOSIGNREQUEST($\triangle$) to the LEA using a user-generated signing payload $\triangle = \{id(obu) \parallel \{0,1\}^k\}^{c_{LEA}}, zk$ with k random bits. The LEA is then responsible for signing the $\triangle$ to confirm the legitimate participation of the user. LEA responds with a PSEUDOSIGNSUCCESS($\{\triangle, ts\}^{d_{LEA}}$) using the input from the PSEUDOSIGNREQUEST. The payload of this response is called π, which is created at timestamp ts. However, the LEA can also deny a signing request if the user's vehicle ID is not in the user list or blacklisted for to various reasons. In that case, a PSEUDOSIGNDENIAL is sent and the user cannot participate.

Since our system uses the WAVE protocol, every message is broadcasted, therefore such π are easy to intercept. Thus a user must prove his rightful possession of this pseudonym. This is done by a zero knowledge proof of knowledge when showing π to other users. Public parameters zk are therefore included.

Managing Groups. Each participant can become a group leader if necessary. There are two different strategies when a member decides to offer a new group to other participants:

- A user can enter an area where he can admittedly connect to others, but none of these users in range intend to be a group leader. As a result, the new user decides to open his own group according to our protocol.
- To avoid situations where not enough groups are available, a user decides with a probability ζ to open a new group.

HGM requires a setup phase for new groups according to the step *Setup* [3] of the group signature scheme, however, no central key creating instance is used, but certain steps are distributed. We separate the sign ability from the trace capability according to our restrictions. Since this process requires that all participants must be able to communicate and exchange information, data size and number of communications are minimized. The setup phase consists of two steps (see Fig. 4), but must be completed within $\Delta t_{G,c}$ seconds.

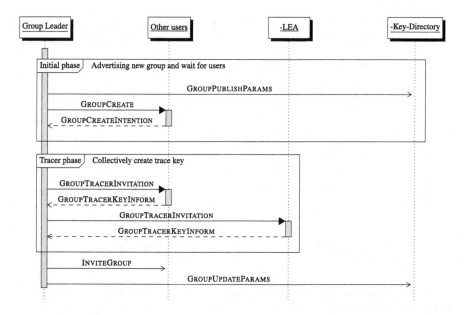

Fig. 4. Sequence of GROUPCREATE (taken from [32]).

First, in the initial phase, the group leader signals to create a new group g_k by updating the central key directory with the required information of his group $((id(g_k), ts, \mathcal{X})$, where ts is the creation timestamp) using GROUPPUBLISHPARAMS message, followed by a GROUPCREATE broadcast inviting other users to join his group. So a GROUPCREATE$(\pi, id(g_k), SCH\_RC, ts_{exp})$ message is broadcasted on the WAVE Control Channel (using an unused $\pi \in \Pi$ and a group ID $id(g_k) \equiv \mathcal{H}\left(\pi \parallel \{0.1\}^k\right)$. In our scheme, each group is organized in a WBSS (WAVE Basic Service Set) using one of the several channels (the selected one is SCH_RC) to minimize packet collisions between different groups. At least θ^P users must indicate their intention to join (GROUPCREATEINTENTION). Otherwise, the group creation phase may fail due to a timeout. This is a precautionary measure because during the setup phase, no user will be able to send payload messages (using this specific group) and will only passively wait for a response from $l(g_k)$.

Assuming that θ^P members are found, the group leader starts the tracer phase by selecting $\theta^T - 1 < \theta^P$ users using a direct message GROUPTRACERINVITATION. Hopefully, $\theta^T - 1$ members will respond with GROUPTRACERKEYINFORM providing each information about their secret key part $sk_{0,...,\theta^T-1}$, the group leader will request the remaining tracer part sk_l from the LEA as well. The LEA always responds. Eventually the group leader can generate the verification key VK and the public key PK (see [3]).

The setup is now complete and the group is ready to accept members ($\mathcal{U}_{g_k} = \emptyset$), by having the group leader broadcast INVITEGROUP$(\pi, id(g_k))$ for $\Delta t_{G,i}$ seconds. At the same time, he stores the member list, the public group key and the verification key in

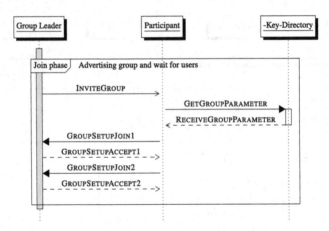

Fig. 5. Sequence of GROUPJOIN (taken from [32]).

an online directory for others can download as soon as they want to verify a signature (GROUPUPDATEPARAMS).

Joining an Existing Group. A participant u_i uses a $\pi_j \in \Pi_{u_i}$ to join the group g_k (equivalent to *Join* from [3] with the extension of [14]). To find a group, the participant observes the Control Channel for INVITEGROUP messages sent by $l(g_k)$ and then checks the key directory, which he can cache locally, for all necessary information (cf. Fig. 5). Once a user finds such a message indicating that a group leader accepts new members, he will ask to join the group in a two-step process using GROUPSE-TUPJOIN1,2$(\pi_j, \mathcal{X}, id(g_k))$. A successful join is completed when the group leader replies with GROUPSETUPACCEPT1,2$(id(g_k), \mathcal{Y})$ and executes $\mathcal{U}_{g_k} \leftarrow u_i$.

A group leader is not able to recognize if two distinct pseudonyms refer to the same user. Therefore a group leader only checks the received pseudonym π_j for a correct signature from the LEA. He also uses the timestamp ts in π to enforce certain joining constrains.

Sending Messages. A user u_i can send messages at any time, but normally every $\Delta t_{M,b}$ seconds, as long as $u_i \in \mathcal{U}_{g_k}$ (equivalent to *Sign* of [3]). They then send messages on behalf of this group. So if a user wants to send some payload $\square$, he uses his private part of the group key to create a message $m = (\square, ts, id(g_k), \sigma)$. σ is the signature of the message m. To save space, $\mathcal{H}(\sigma)$ is the ID of the message. Also $id(g_k)$ is included in the message. This serves two purposes. First, a user who receives a message can validate the signature by simply obtaining the group's public key from the online directory and then using that key to verify the signature. Second, $id(g_k)$ is used for the blame process explained in the next section.

By design, a user should be a member of different groups at the same time. Therefore he can send messages with any of his private group keys. In this way, he can

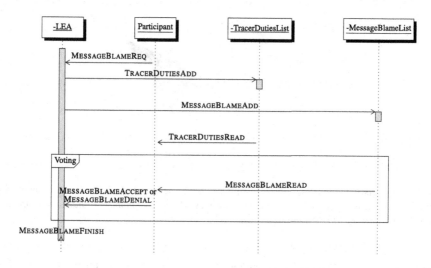

Fig. 6. Sequence of MESSAGEBLAME.

become untraceable by interrupting any message flow. As a note, all other identifying information (e.g. MAC address) must also be changed.

Messages are relayed by other members who receive them. However, they always check the signature of the message first[4] (using *SignatureVerify* from [3]) before resending the message without changing it. Also, users do not relay messages if the geographic location of the payload is too far from the user's current location. This is done to reduce the load on the network. Also, messages are discarded if they are too old.

Blaming a Message. Our system allows users to send any payload (including sensitive GPS-coordinates) without revealing their identity, yet all messages are authenticated, making *HGM* an integer system. Maintaining this state is achieved by an intentional backdoor. A user who suspects a message m from group g_k can start a blame process (cf. Fig. 6) which may reveal the originator of m (i.e. find $m \rightarrow \pi$). This can only be done with the support of the tracers of the message's group. The LEA itself is not able to obtain more information about the message conforming our requirements. We recall that the message $m = (\square, ts, id(g_k), \sigma)$ contains all the necessary information, especially the group ID $id(g_k)$.

The blaming of a m requires a valid π. Every user who owns π_b sends a MESSAGE-BLAMEREQ(m, π_b) to the LEA. The LEA validates the blame request by extracting the $id(obu)_b$ from the pseudonym π_b using their private key d_{LEA}. The LEA keeps records of all blame request for each $id(obu)_b$ to prevent abusive use of the blame. An unsuccessful blame request (i.e. a blame request rejected by tracers) increases the penalty score of $id(obu)_b$ on the userlist.

Since *HGM* is a distributed system with volatile participants, the blame process is implemented as a pull process. This means that tracers, who are needed to reveal the

---

[4] Required information can be looked up in the key directory and cached locally.

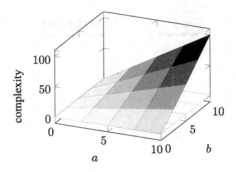

Fig. 7. Comparison of the complexity of using a cuckoo filter (white plane) and searching in a list structure (grayscaled plane) for new blame messages while a = *number of total groups* and b = *number of groups in which the user is a tracer.*

originator of a message, actively pursue their role by analyzing an online list called TRACERDUTIESLIST which is provided by LEA. Recall that the participants know in which groups they had a tracer role, so they only need to search the online list for these group IDs. To make the lookup space efficient, we use a cuckoo filter [15]. A cuckoo filter is a space-efficient data structure that can be used to check whether a value is an element of a set. The cuckoo filter is the TRACERDUTIESLIST list and can be downloaded via TRACERDUTIESREAD. Tracers search for each group ID if it is part of the filter. If it is included the set, the tracer knows that he is needed to reveal the sender of a message. This is a very efficient way without the need to read full messages. Only then he request, in a more expensive process, a full list MESSAGEBLAMELIST with assignments of $id(g_k) \rightarrow [m_i, m_{i+1}, ...]$ is requested from LEA to lookup the actual message (MESSAGEBLAMEREAD). However, since a cuckoo filter is a compressed data structure, false positives may occur in some cases. In this case a tracer tries to execute MESSAGEBLAMEREAD even though the result is an empty set. Figure 7 shows that the complexity for this whole process using a cuckoo filter is always $\mathcal{O}(1)$, while the use of a plain list structure is $\mathcal{O}(ab)$ with a = *number of total groups* and b = *number of groups in which the user is a tracer.*

To make the process work, the LEA therefore adds an $id(g_k)$ to TRACER-DUTIESLIST (TRACERDUTIESADD) and also sets m_k to MESSAGEBLAMELIST (MESSAGEBLAMEADD).

When a tracer reads a message, he decides whether to use its part of the tracer key to reveal its part of the user's real identity (*ShareOpen* from [3]). The process must be completed within $\Delta t_{G,b}$ or it will fail. Depending on his decision, he then sends his reply to LEA:

- MESSAGEBLAMEACCEPT: A tracer also doubts that the payload of the message is true, e.g. because he has seen otherwise or he tries to compromise a user.
- MESSAGEBLAMEDENIAL: A confirmation of the payload ultimately leads to this behavior of a tracer, but it is also possible that an unfavourable tracer shields the causer.

Since we are in a highly dynamic network, it may happen that a proportion of the former tracers leave the network or do not answer the blame request. Therefore *HGM* does not require all θ^T tracers to accept an blame request. Instead, only $\lambda * \theta^T < \theta^P$ tracers must accept a blame request. This is sufficient to reveal the real identity (i.e. the π used in this group) of the message originator. Once λ percent of $\mathcal{T}(g_k)$ have worked together to reveal the π, LEA can perform *ShareVerify* in combination with *ShareCombine* from [3] and then extract the $id(obu)$ and add a penalty point, which may lead to putting it on the blacklist if a penalty point threshold is exceeded (MESSAGEBLAMEFINISH).

4.4 Security and Anonymity

The LEA is responsible for authenticating the pseudonyms of the individual users. Only she can match different pseudonyms to a single user. Thus, she is able to limit the amount of pseudonyms a user can have at the same time and is essential for the protection against Sybil attacks. She sends a PSEUDOSIGNDENIAL once a user already exceeds the limit of valid pseudonyms allowed at a particular time. A pseudonym is considered valid as long it is not expired. The LEA is unable to tell if a pseudonym is in active use, so every π given to a user counts towards the limit θ^π.

HGM is build on the idea that people hold multiple pseudonyms at once which sounds counterintuitive at first. However, there are multiple features build-in which prevent abusive behavior. We now discuss four possible attacks, namely *Altering*, *Suppressing*, *Replaying*, and *Injecting*. Depending on the attacking instance (*Participant*, *Group Leader*, *Tracer*), each attack targets different attributes.

Alter. Most attributes in the system are read-only, thus there is no need to modify them afterwards. As a consequence, altering is unintended and has to be prevented.

- *Participants* might want to change the payload or timestamp of a message for various reasons. However, σ prevents to change $\square$ or ts. Pointing to another group by changing $id(g)$ to blame it also does not work since other users then use the other group's public key to verify σ which eventually fails.
- Let's discuss the *group leader*'s ability to change key parameters. One reason to do so might be to illegally track a single user by offering unique parameter settings to each interested user. However, forging any key parameters is easily detectable by a user via the public group key directory which has to show the same attributes for each group.
- The ability of *tracers* to alter artifacts is limited. Tracers are only used to reveal a user identity once a valid MESSAGEBLAMEREQ is placed by LEA. Hence, they cannot alter this request at all.

Suppress. Suppressing any information sent in the system might lead to service unavailability and thus has to be handled by *HGM*.

- *Participants* can suppress individual messages, but since they are forwarded by all other participants similar to a mesh network, this only has an effect in very limited cases (e.g. sparse areas).

- *Group Leaders* have two possibilities in this scenario. First, they can not broadcast GROUPPUBLISHPARAMS or INVITEGROUP messages. Participants will then ignore the group leader and choose other groups instead. Furthermore, a group leader can decide to not answer messages, although, this is handled by a timeout on the user side.
- Similar to altering messages, *tracers* are unable to manipulate the system in an unintended way. Ignoring a MESSAGEBLAMEREQ message, i.e. not answering, is similar to sending a MESSAGEBLAMEDENIAL message and thus is a legitimate behavior in *HGM*.

Replay. The ITS scenario places special demands on the authenticity and integrity of the messages in the system, otherwise correct and error-free operation cannot be guaranteed. Replay attacks must therefore be prevented.

- *Participants* may send a single message multiple times, however, message are uniquely identified via $\mathcal{H}(\sigma)$. Hence, replayed messages can be always matched to the same message. In fact, *HGM* relies on replaying messages for distribution. Using another user's π to join another group is not possible because of a zero knowledge proof.
- A *group leader* is solely responsible for the group creation process. Therefore, only related parameters are subject to this attack. Resending key parameters during create or join to trap other participants is impossible since a fake group leader may not know the respective secrets to these parameters.
- Each *tracer* only has one vote (either MESSAGEBLAMEACCEPT or MESSAGE-BLAMEDENIAL) and successive responses may be discarded by LEA.

Inject. Similar to replay attacks, injecting artificial or wrong information in the system may lead to service disruption. *HGM* is designed to ensure service quality.

- In principle, *participants* share information by sending messages, i.e. they inject new messages in the system to be distributed by others. However, participants control which information they want to send. According to our attacker model, a user might craft bogus messages to e.g. gain a benefit. *HGM* offers methods to take that into account. Recipients decide if they trust a message. If not, they further have the option to start a blame process.
- A *group leader* can violate θ^P and/or θ^T. He can either track a user by performing an $n-1$ attack or create a group without LEA as a tracer or any other independent tracers. As a consequence each blame request will eventually fail. Such a rogue group can be easily identified by LEA with the group leader being ultimately responsible for it.
- A *tracer* can only inject two messages, either MESSAGEBLAMEACCEPT or MES-SAGEBLAMEDENIAL. However, without a proper MESSAGEBLAMEREQ, these messages have no effect.

Furthermore, for integrity, it is also important to consider the ratio of θ^T and θ^P, i.e. the minimum number of tracers and users during group setup phase (and in particular

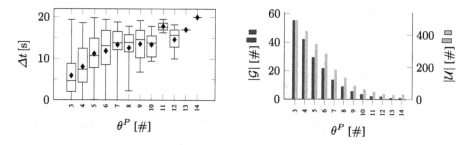

Fig. 8. Impact of θ^P on group creation time Δt and the number of groups $|\mathcal{G}|$ and number of participants $|\mathcal{U}|$ for $\Delta t_{G,c} = 20$ s, $\Delta t_{G,v} = 80$ s, $\Delta t_{G,i} = 60$ s.

GROUPTRACERKEYNEGOTIATION). If $\theta^T = \theta^P$ then the group leader is forced to select every member of the group as a tracer resulting in predictability to become a tracer. An adversary user may circle the group leader with all of his θ^π pseudonyms knowing that he will later hold θ^π parts of the tracer key. Therefore, it is recommended to set $\theta^T \ll \theta^P$.

5   Evaluation

We now evaluate *HGM* using the state-of-the-art vehicular network simulation framework Veins [40]. Veins combines SUMO [30], a microscopic simulator for urban mobility, and OMNeT++[5], an event-based network simulation framework. Veins is particularly well suited for our purposes as it supports the IEEE 802.11p standard and WAVE. In the following we will outline the setup and the parametrization of our simulation model. Next we give an overview of our results and show the impact of *HGM* on users' privacy and performance in terms of the group formation.

An urban area around the city of Regensburg, Germany (about $5\,km^2$ in size), see Fig. 10, was extracted from OpenStreetMap[6] and prepared using `netconvert`, `randomTrips`, and `polyconvert` for Veins. The chosen area includes different aspects of an urban area. Besides residential areas with side streets and main roads, motorways are also included. To present realistic results, we use `SimpleObstacleShadowing` included in Veins to simulate radio interference due to obstacles, e.g. buildings. For the sake of simplicity, we disabled WAVE channel switching in our simulation, although, *HGM* is designed to work with different channels.

Our model depends on several parameters that we have changed during the simulation process to determine their impact on the privacy and performance of the system. The parameters are the following, each of which is listed with its default values: $\theta^\pi = 3$, $\theta^P = 5$, $\theta^T = 3$, $\rho_{U,b} = 0$, $\rho_{G,o} = 0$, $\rho_{G,j} = 1$, and $\Delta t_{M,b} = 1$ s. Every second a new vehicle is randomly generated, which then drives along a random path. To ensure that there are enough vehicles in the system, at the beginning of the simulation, a warm-up

---

[5] https://omnetpp.org/.

[6] https://www.openstreetmap.de/.

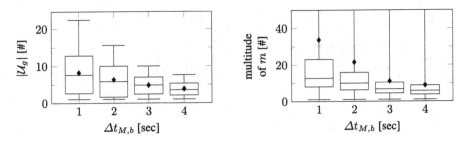

Fig. 9. Anonymity set size defined by the user who send a safety beacon message under the same group ID for $\Delta t_{G,c} = 20$ s, $\Delta t_{G,v} = 80$ s, $\Delta t_{G,i} = 60$ s (taken from [32]).

period of 10 min is performed. Only then does the actual simulation begin, which in turn takes another 10 min. Since the simulation is based on many random events, each parameter configuration is simulated at least five times. Then the mean of the results is calculated.

In our previous work [32], we already discussed the privacy of our system using the two metrics *anonymity set size*, which describes "the set of users that the adversary cannot distinguish from u" [45], and *size of uncertainty region*, which illustrates "the minimal size of the region R_U to which an adversary can narrow down the position of a target user u" [45]. Here we want to present a summary of these results and go more deeply into the exact vehicle movements and the groups formation respectively changes over time and their influence on each other.

In theory, the *anonymity set size* is at least θ^P. Therefore, it would be wise to choose θ^P as big as possible. However, from a performance perspective, the upper bound of θ^P is limited since larger groups are more unlikely to be successfully created (c.f. Fig. 8). Thus, our algorithm allows subsequent group joins, subsequently increasing the anonymity set size. To extract feasible values, we track the position of the sender of a payload message and his group affiliation. On that, we derive the ratio of messages sent by a user in comparison to all messages sent by the affiliated group called multitude of messages. Also, we count the average number of users within each group ($|\mathcal{U}_g|$). As Fig. 9 illustrates, there is a direct correlation between $\Delta t_{M,b}$ and these parameters indicating that low values for $\Delta t_{M,b}$ are to prefer.

Figure 10 illustrates movements of the vehicles of four different groups at four different simulation times t where every group is represented by another color. Only those vehicles are shown that are sending a message using the corresponding group ID (although, it is possible that a vehicle sends a message using another group key). In reality, more vehicles than shown can be part of the respective group. This is obvious as at $t = 680$ s five vehicles are displayed in the green group, however, at $t = 700$ s only four vehicles are shown. Furthermore, the figure shows that the individual vehicles within the group are distributed over a larger area over the course of time, i.e. the size of the uncertainty region increases. It also shows that the groups overlap more and more over time. This fact enhances the privacy of the users, because a user can be a member of several groups at the same time and could send a message via one group one second and a message via another group the next second.

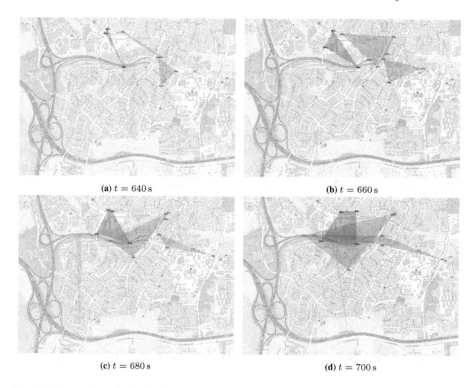

(a) $t = 640\,\text{s}$ **(b)** $t = 660\,\text{s}$

(c) $t = 680\,\text{s}$ **(d)** $t = 700\,\text{s}$

Fig. 10. Extract from the Vehicle movements and group formations for different simulation times t and $\Delta t_{G,c} = 20$ s, $\Delta t_{G,v} = 60$ s, $\Delta t_{G,i} = 80$ s, and $\Delta t_{M,b} = 1$ s.

To gain insight into the *size of uncertainty region*, we collect payload messages sent by users $\mathcal{U}_{g_i}$ of a group g_i. With the help of the Gauss's area formula, we calculate the region span of $\mathcal{U}_{g_i}$ that sent a safety beacon message at the same time. However, this yields just the minimum size of the uncertainty region because not all $u \in \mathcal{U}_{g_i}$ may have send a safety beacon message using that specific group g_i. Figure 11 shows the uncertainty region size in comparison to the number of messages send in one simulation time step for one group. It demonstrates that the uncertainty region increases strongly over time and only slowly decreases again towards the end of the group's existence. At the last possible time still more people send a message via the group than θ^P specifies. Furthermore, one can see that at most times more than the minimum number of participants send a message through the group which ensures a high value of k-anonymity. In addition, Fig. 12 shows that θ^P can be chosen small because the uncertainty region stays more or less constant with a decrease of θ^P.

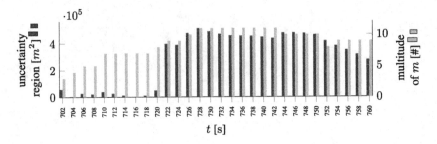

Fig. 11. Uncertainty region size and number of messages at different simulation times t for one group and $\Delta t_{G,c} = 20$ s, $\Delta t_{G,v} = 80$ s, $\Delta t_{G,i} = 60$ s, and $\Delta t_{M,b} = 1$ s.

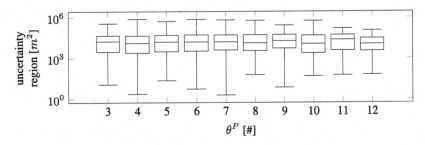

Fig. 12. Boxplot of the uncertainty region (taken from [32]).

6   Conclusion

In this paper, we presented a privacy-friendly approach for anonymous and yet authenticated broadcast messages in Vehicle-to-Vehicle environments called *Harmonized Group Mix (HGM)*. Our proposal can be used with current communication standards such as WAVE. *HGM* uses a state-of-the-art group signature scheme that meets the high requirements of ITSs. It relies only on a merely semi-trusted instance called LEA and is otherwise fully decentralized. We strive to reconcile both requirements, data privacy and integrity. The integrity of the system is protected by the fact that in case of misuse the identity of a participant can be uncovered. However, this cannot be done by one instance alone, but requires the participation of several participants, namely tracers of a group and LEA. To optimize the tracing process, a cuckoo filter is used to enable an efficient way to identify bogus message originators.

Our evaluation was conducted using the vehicular network simulation framework Veins and real world road network. It showed that *HGM* improves the privacy of users by allowing them to group with other participants and thus become k-anonymous. Among other things, we were able to show that even a small minimal group size results in good anonymity, since over time more participants can join the group. We also showed that group boundaries mix over time, which further increases the level of anonymity, as one participant in our protocol can be a member of several groups at the same time. Thus, it is not possible to uniquely identify a single user on the basis of a message since messages from a group are successfully harmonized, i.e. user-identifying information is stripped from each message.

In future work, we would like to extend our analysis to a more realistic scenario like [13] with users having specific daily routines. This information can lead to a stronger attacker who can then incorporate external knowledge such as derived user behavior to track users. Furthermore, we want to analyze the robustness of *HGM* more thoroughly. Eventually, we want to remove the semi-trusted LEA as it is the only centralized entity in the system. Also we want to first analyze the throughput of the system in terms of performance and then optimize it using e.g. channel switching of WAVE.

Appendix

A   Notation

See Table 1.

Table 1. Notation used throughout the paper.

Symbol	Description	Symbol	Description
u	Known user in the system	$\mathcal{U}$	Set of all users
g	Existing group in the system	$\mathcal{G}$	Set of all groups with $id(g)$
$\mathcal{U}_g$	Users in group g	l	Group leader
t	Tracer	$\mathcal{T}$	Set of tracers
π	Pseudonym signed by LEA	Π	Set of all signed pseudonyms
$\mathcal{H}$	Hash function	m	Message
$\mathcal{M}$	Set of all messages	σ	Signature of a message m
zk	Public parameters of a zero knowledge proof	θ^T	Minimum number of tracers
θ^P	Minimum number of group users	θ^π	Maximum number of concurrent pseudonyms of a user
λ	Proportion of tracers needed to reveal	k	Length of randomness
α	Percentage of dishonest users in the system	$\Delta t_{G,c}$	Group creation time
$\Delta t_{G,v}$	Group valid time	$\Delta t_{G,i}$	Group invition time
$\Delta t_{G,b}$	Blame duration time	$\Delta t_{M,b}$	Message safety beacon time interval
$\rho_{G,o}$	Probability of opening a group	$\rho_{G,j}$	Probability of joining a group
$\rho_{U,b}$	Probability of being blocked		

References

1. Alexiou, N., Laganà, M., Gisdakis, S., Khodaei, M., Papadimitratos, P.: VeSPA. In: Proceedings of the 2nd ACM Workshop on Hot Topics on Wireless Network Security and Privacy - HotWiSec 2013, p. 19. ACM Press, New York (2013)
2. Bilgin, B.E., Gungor, V.C.: Performance comparison of IEEE 802.11p and IEEE 802.11b for vehicle-to-vehicle communications in highway, rural, and urban areas. Int. J. Veh. Technol. **2013**, 1–10 (2013)
3. Blömer, J., Juhnke, J., Löken, N.: Short group signatures with distributed traceability. In: Kotsireas, I.S., Rump, S.M., Yap, C.K. (eds.) MACIS 2015. LNCS, vol. 9582, pp. 166–180. Springer, Cham (2016). https://doi.org/10.1007/978-3-319-32859-1_14
4. Boneh, D., Boyen, X., Shacham, H.: Short group signatures. In: Franklin, M. (ed.) CRYPTO 2004. LNCS, vol. 3152, pp. 41–55. Springer, Heidelberg (2004). https://doi.org/10.1007/978-3-540-28628-8_3
5. Brecht, B., et al.: A security credential management system for V2X communications. CoRR abs/1802.05323 (2018)
6. Calandriello, G., Papadimitratos, P., Hubaux, J.P., Lioy, A.: Efficient and robust pseudonymous authentication in VANET. In: Proceedings of the Fourth ACM International Workshop on Vehicular Ad Hoc Networks, VANET 2007, pp. 19–28. ACM, New York (2007)
7. Camenisch, J.: Efficient and generalized group signatures. In: Fumy, W. (ed.) EUROCRYPT 1997. LNCS, vol. 1233, pp. 465–479. Springer, Heidelberg (1997). https://doi.org/10.1007/3-540-69053-0_32
8. Chaum, D., van Heyst, E.: Group signatures. In: Davies, D.W. (ed.) EUROCRYPT 1991. LNCS, vol. 547, pp. 257–265. Springer, Heidelberg (1991). https://doi.org/10.1007/3-540-46416-6_22
9. Chaum, D.L.: Untraceable electronic mail, return addresses, and digital pseudonyms. Commun. ACM **24**(2), 84–90 (1981)
10. Chen, L., Pedersen, T.P.: New group signature schemes. In: De Santis, A. (ed.) EUROCRYPT 1994. LNCS, vol. 950, pp. 171–181. Springer, Heidelberg (1995). https://doi.org/10.1007/BFb0053433
11. Chen, L., Ng, S.L., Wang, G.: Threshold anonymous announcement in VANETs. IEEE J. Sel. Areas Commun. **29**, 605–615 (2011)
12. Chinnasamy, A., Sivakumar, B., Selvakumari, P., Suresh, A.: Minimum connected dominating set based RSU allocation for smartCloud vehicles in VANET (2018)
13. Codeca, L., Frank, R., Engel, T.: Luxembourg SUMO traffic (LuST) scenario: 24 hours of mobility for vehicular networking research. In: IEEE Vehicular Networking Conference, VNC, January 2016, pp. 1–8. IEEE Computer Society (2016)
14. Delerablée, C., Pointcheval, D.: Dynamic fully anonymous short group signatures. In: Nguyen, P.Q. (ed.) VIETCRYPT 2006. LNCS, vol. 4341, pp. 193–210. Springer, Heidelberg (2006). https://doi.org/10.1007/11958239_13
15. Fan, B., Andersen, D.G., Kaminsky, M., Mitzenmacher, M.: Cuckoo filter: practically better than bloom. In: Seneviratne, A., Diot, C., Kurose, J., Chaintreau, A., Rizzo, L. (eds.) Proceedings of the 10th ACM International on Conference on Emerging Networking Experiments and Technologies, CoNEXT 2014, Sydney, Australia, 2–5 December 2014, pp. 75–88. ACM (2014)
16. Fischlin, M.: Communication-efficient non-interactive proofs of knowledge with online extractors. In: Shoup, V. (ed.) CRYPTO 2005. LNCS, vol. 3621, pp. 152–168. Springer, Heidelberg (2005). https://doi.org/10.1007/11535218_10
17. Fogue, M., Sanguesa, J., Martinez, F., Marquez-Barja, J.: Improving roadside unit deployment in vehicular networks by exploiting genetic algorithms. Appl. Sci. **8**(1), 86 (2018)

18. Freudiger, J., Raya, M., Félegyházi, M., Papadimitratos, P., Hubaux, J.P.: Mix-zones for location privacy in vehicular networks. In: ACM Workshop on Wireless Networking for Intelligent Transportation Systems (WiN-ITS) (2007)
19. Gräfling, S., Mähönen, P., Riihijärvi, J.: Performance evaluation of IEEE 1609 WAVE and IEEE 802.11p for vehicular communications. In: ICUFN 2010–2nd International Conference on Ubiquitous and Future Networks, pp. 344–348 (2010)
20. Guo, J., Baugh, J.P., Wang, S.: A group signature based secure and privacy-preserving vehicular communication framework. In: 2007 Mobile Networking for Vehicular Environments, pp. 103–108. IEEE (2007)
21. Hao, Y., Cheng, Y., Ren, K.: Distributed key management with protection against RSU compromise in group signature based VANETs. In: GLOBECOM - IEEE Global Telecommunications Conference, pp. 4951–4955. IEEE (2008)
22. Hu, W., Xue, K., Hong, P., Wu, C.: ATCS: a novel anonymous and traceable communication scheme for vehicular Ad hoc networks. Int. J. Netw. Secur. 13(2), 71–78 (2011)
23. IEEE 1609 Working Group: IEEE Guide for Wireless Access in Vehicular Environments (WAVE) - Architecture. IEEE Std 1609.0-2013, pp. 1–78 (2017)
24. Khodaei, M., Papadimitratos, P.: The key to intelligent transportation: identity and credential management in vehicular communication systems. IEEE Veh. Technol. Mag. 10(4), 63–69 (2015)
25. Kim, S.: Effective crowdsensing and routing algorithms for next generation vehicular networks (2017)
26. Laurendeau, C., Barbeau, M.: Secure anonymous broadcasting in vehicular networks. In: 32nd IEEE Conference on Local Computer Networks (LCN 2007), pp. 661–668. IEEE (2007)
27. Ligo, A.K., Peha, J.M.: Cost-effectiveness of sharing roadside infrastructure for internet of vehicles. IEEE Trans. Intell. Transp. Syst. 19(7), 2362–2372 (2018)
28. Lin, X., Lu, R., Zhang, C., Zhu, H., Ho, P.H., Shen, X.: Security in vehicular ad hoc networks [security in mobile ad hoc] (2008)
29. Lin, X., Sun, X., Ho, P.H., Shen, X.: GSIS: a secure and privacy-preserving protocol for vehicular communications. IEEE Trans. Veh. Technol. 56(6 I), 3442–3456 (2007)
30. Lopez, P.A., et al.: Microscopic traffic simulation using sumo. In: The 21st IEEE International Conference on Intelligent Transportation Systems. IEEE (2018)
31. Lu, R., Lin, X., Zhu, H., Ho, P.H., Shen, X.: ECPP: efficient conditional privacy preservation protocol for secure vehicular communications. In: Proceedings - IEEE INFOCOM, pp. 1903–1911. IEEE (2008)
32. Nitschke, M., Roth, C., Hoyer, C., Kesdoğan, D.: Harmonized group mix for ITS. In: Proceedings of the 6th International Conference on Information Systems Security and Privacy - Volume 1: ICISSP, pp. 152–163. INSTICC, SciTePress (2020)
33. Papadimitratos, P., Buttyan, L., Hubaux, J.P., Kargl, F., Kung, A., Raya, M.: Architecture for secure and private vehicular communications. In: 2007 7th International Conference on ITS Telecommunications, pp. 1–6. IEEE (2007)
34. Patil, P., Gokhale, A.: Voronoi-based placement of road-side units to improve dynamic resource management in Vehicular Ad Hoc Networks. In: Proceedings of the 2013 International Conference on Collaboration Technologies and Systems, CTS 2013, pp. 389–396 (2013)
35. Plossl, K., Nowey, T., Mletzko, C.: Towards a security architecture for vehicular ad hoc networks. In: First International Conference on Availability, Reliability and Security (ARES 2006), pp. 8 pp.-381. IEEE (2006)

36. Pradweap, R.V., Hansdah, R.C.: A novel RSU-aided hybrid architecture for anonymous authentication (RAHAA) in VANET. In: Bagchi, A., Ray, I. (eds.) ICISS 2013. LNCS, vol. 8303, pp. 314–328. Springer, Heidelberg (2013). https://doi.org/10.1007/978-3-642-45204-8_24

37. Reis, A.B., Sargento, S., Tonguz, O.K.: On the performance of sparse vehicular networks with road side units. In: IEEE Vehicular Technology Conference (2011)

38. Reis, A.B., Sargento, S., Tonguz, O.K.: Smarter cities with parked cars as roadside units. IEEE Trans. Intell. Transp. Syst. 19(7), 2338–2352 (2018)

39. Sampigethaya, K., Huang, L., Li, M., Poovendran, R., Matsuura, K., Sezaki, K.: CARAVAN: providing location privacy for VANET. Embedded Security in Cars, pp. 1–15 (2005)

40. Sommer, C., German, R., Dressler, F.: Bidirectionally coupled network and road traffic simulation for improved IVC analysis. IEEE Trans. Mob. Comput. 10(1), 3–15 (2011)

41. Sun, J., Zhang, C., Fang, Y.: An ID-based framework achieving privacy and non-repudiation in vehicular ad hoc networks. In: Proceedings - IEEE Military Communications Conference MILCOM, pp. 1–7. IEEE (2007)

42. US Department of Transportation: Unit Cost Element - Communications Equipment - Wireless Unit Cost Component - DSRC Roadside Unit (2017). https://www.itsknowle dgeresources.its.dot.gov/ITS/benecost.nsf/0/D34CF040283762B2852581F700556636?Ope nDocument&Query=Hometechcrunch.com/2017/11/13/tampa-offers-first-demo-of-its-con nected-vehicle-technology-project-launching-with-1600-cars-in-2018

43. Uzcategui, R.A., De Sucre, A.J., Acosta-Marum, G.: Wave: a tutorial. IEEE Commun. Mag. 47(5), 126–133 (2009)

44. Verheul, E.R.: Activate later certificates for v2x - combining its efficiency with privacy. IACR Cryptol. ePrint Arch. 2016, 1158 (2016)

45. Wagner, I., Eckhoff, D.: Technical privacy metrics. ACM Comput. Surv. 51(3), 1–38 (2018)

46. Wasef, A., Lu, R., Lin, X., Shen, X.: Complementing public key infrastructure to secure vehicular ad hoc networks. IEEE Wirel. Commun. 17(5), 22–28 (2010)

47. Wright, J., et al., Transportation: National Connected Vehicle Field Infrastructure Footprint Analysis (2014)

48. Xiaonan, L., Zhiyi, F., Lijun, S.: Securing vehicular ad hoc networks. In: Ning, P., Du, W. (eds.) 2007 2nd International Conference on Pervasive Computing and Applications, ICPCA 2007, vol. 15, pp. 424–429. IOS Press (2007)

49. Xue, L., Yang, Y., Dong, D.: Roadside infrastructure planning scheme for the urban vehicular networks. In: Transportation Research Procedia, vol. 25, pp. 1380–1396. Elsevier (2017)

50. Zhang, L., Wu, Q., Solanas, A., Domingo-Ferrer, J.: A scalable robust authentication protocol for secure vehicular communications. IEEE Trans. Veh. Technol. 59(4), 1606–1617 (2010)

Contextual Factors in Information Security Group Behaviour: A Comparison of Two Studies

Dirk Snyman[(✉)] [iD] and Hennie Kruger [iD]

School of Computer Science and Information Systems, North-West University,
11 Hoffman Street, Potchefstroom 2531, South Africa
{dirk.snyman,hennie.kruger}@nwu.ac.za

Abstract. Group behaviour is a relatively under researched field in research pertaining to information security. Most behavioural studies in information security focus on the individual and how he/she reasons and eventually behaves. Recent investigations into security group behaviour have revealed that the context within which the members of a group function plays an important role. Behavioural threshold analysis has been identified as a possible tool to evaluate security group behaviour and provide insights into the possible influence of the group's contextual milieu. Based on earlier research on contextual factors in information security, this paper embodies an elaboration on the theoretical and practical implications of the previous work by comparing two distinct information security group behaviour experiments. The contextual environments for the two experiments include a group of employees in an industry setting, as well as a group of students that reside together in a university residence. These experiments are discussed, firstly by looking at the information security behavioural threshold analysis results for the two groups, and secondly, by expounding on the external contextual factors that play a part in the formation and eventual practice of information security behaviour in a group setting. The paper concludes by reflecting on the research aims and possible future work. This research has shown that external contextual factors play an important role in information security group behaviour and its effect should be taken into account in the strategies of managing information security.

Keywords: Information security behaviour · Contextual factors · Human factor in information security

1 Introduction

Human behaviour remains one of the more challenging information security aspects to understand and, by extension, to manage [1]. Issues that complicate the understanding thereof, include phenomena such as the privacy paradox, i.e. willingly providing your own sensitive information in the full knowledge that it is unwise to do so [2]. Differences between the behaviour of individuals in seclusion, in contrast to group behaviour, is another contributing factor that hampers the effective management of the human factor, which is further exacerbated by the influence of external contextual factors. The circumstances and setting in which attitude and intention towards human behaviour is

© Springer Nature Switzerland AG 2022
S. Furnell et al. (Eds.): ICISSP 2020, CCIS 1545, pp. 201–221, 2022.
https://doi.org/10.1007/978-3-030-94900-6_10

formed has a marked effect on the behaviour that is eventually acted upon. The way in which one behaves in a social setting among friends surely differs from the sort of behaviour one exhibits in a corporate environment. This difference in behaviour is due to the contextual factors that are different between the two settings.

In terms of the information security behaviour of individuals, many attempts to understand its nuances exist. Often, psychological models are used to examine how intention, and eventually behaviour, is formed as part of an individual's cognition. This theoretical foundation sees many recurring models that guide information security behaviour research, notably knowledge, attitude, behaviour (KAB), the theory of reasoned action (TRA), protection motivation theory (PMT), and the theory of planned behaviour (TPB) [1, 3]. Once a model is selected, it is used to try to explain both cases of straightforward security behaviour where the motivations for behaviour are uncomplicated, but it is also used to understand paradoxical behaviour where the reasoning behind the behaviour and the behaviour itself, seem contradictory. For the evaluation of group behaviour, models like that of [4] and recently [5], that contemplate the use of threshold analysis to explain the intricacies of group behaviour in information security exists. Similarly, there is also research such as that of Willison and Warkentin [6], supported by more recent research [7–9] that indicate the need to understand the context and contextual factors to be able to better evaluate and comprehend information security (group) behaviour.

In an attempt to contribute to the abovementioned body of knowledge, this paper constitutes an extension of previously published work by Snyman and Kruger [10]. This extension draws on the theoretical foundations as described in [10] but augments the understanding of the practical implications by providing more in-depth results and discussions on the contextual factors that influence information security behaviour. Furthermore, the results from the previous work are expanded here to include more examples of information security group behaviour focus areas and are compared to that of another practical application by providing a two-fold comparison by 1) comparing the results of the two studies in terms of the predicted information security behaviour of the two groups, and 2) discussing the similarities and differences in the contextual factors of the two studies as described in the previous research.

The aim of this study is therefore to firstly, theorise on the external contextual factors that will influence information security behaviour, and secondly, to present the application of a model that considers external contextual factors in the prediction of group behaviour in information security. Thirdly, and finally, to compare the group behaviour of two distinct groups, based on the aforementioned model and discuss the influence that the identified contextual factors might have on the security behaviour of said groups.

The remainder of the paper is structured as follows: Sect. 2 gives an introductory overview of contextual factors that typically influence human behaviour and indicates its relevance in information security behaviour., In Sect. 3 a short overview of the experimental background for evaluating group behaviour, the contextual environments, and behavioural threshold analysis is given, while Sect. 4 provides a comparison of the experimental results from Sect. 3. Section 5 reflects on the underlying contextual factors that influence information security group behaviour and a final reflection on the contributions made in this research conclude the study in Sect. 6.

2 Information Security Behaviour: A Product of Circumstance?

Exploiting the preceding, related work [10], the concept of contextual factors in information security behaviour is revisited in this section. The contextual factors that were identified in [10], were based on the initial influential work of Belk [11], which were also used in a more recent study by Kirova and Thanh [12] to investigate the influence of contextual factors on smartphone use.

The five contextual factors which they identified were:

- *Physical milieu;*
- *Social milieu;*
- *Perspective of elapsed (or remaining) time;*
- *Individual predisposition; and*
- *Individual intention.*

Following a critical reflection on these identified contextual factors, with due consideration of the predominant psychological theories and approaches to evaluating information security behaviour, an emergent taxonomy became apparent. This allows for the classification of the five contextual factors as being either intrinsic or extrinsic to an individual and were grouped as follows in Table 1:

Table 1. Categorisation of contextual factors in behaviour [10].

Contextual factors in behaviour	
Extrinsic factors	Intrinsic factors
Physical milieu	Perspective of elapsed (or remaining) time
Social milieu	Individual predisposition
	Individual intention

Many of the aforementioned psychological models and theories already address the intrinsic factors when used to evaluate information security behaviour, e.g. individual predisposition (which relates to intention). Intention is one of the core indicators which guides behaviour in the TPB. In contrast thereto, the extrinsic factors are not explicitly provided for in these frameworks.

Due to the fact that intrinsic factors are commonly considered in these theories, the focus of this research revolves around the extrinsic factors and how they influence behaviour with specific reference to information security behaviour. A short description is provided below for each of the extrinsic factors from Table 1:

The material environment in which an individual functions, comprises their *physical milieu.* The corporeal experiences of the individual, based on their sensory perception, are relevant here. These experiences include, what a person, feels (both in terms of touch and emotion), hears, tastes, and smells.

Social milieu refers to the effect of other people in the environment of an individual. Others may be present in the physical milieu, thereby directly influencing the behaviour of an individual by his/her exposure to their example. The social milieu can also extend beyond the physical proximity of an individual to include, for example, interactions across digital communication channels. The other people that influence the individual's behaviour may either be formal acquaintances including their close social network or may be strangers with whom the individual has (coincidental) contact.

In terms of information security behaviour, it is imperative to understand how these external factors manifest in the environments where security behaviour is performed. For instance, the physical milieu also includes aspects that may be considered intangible in terms of a person's senses, e.g. ease of access to systems and information can be thought of as part of the physical milieu as it relates to processes in the physical world. Similarly, interactions that relate to the social milieu of information security behaviour do not only refer to the overtly observable actions of others, but also incorporate aspects of an interpretive nature, e.g. social cues such as body language, and (implied) peer pressure.

Table 2 shows some examples of what these factors might look like in terms of information security behaviour as conceptualised by the authors. The conceptualisation is based on the extrinsic contextual factors as identified from the work of Kirova and Thanh [12]. The extrinsic factors that are shown here do not comprise an exhaustive list. Depending on the specifics of different scenarios, many other examples may exist.

Table 2. Extrinsic contextual factors in information security behaviour (adapted from [10]).

Extrinsic contextual factors in information security behaviour	
Physical milieu	Social milieu
– Ease of access to systems, processes and people – Level of convenience associated with certain tasks – Availability of technical expertise – Presence of security controls	– Peer pressure – Presence of co-workers/family/friends – Organisational structure – Required to work together with others – Collective purpose – Exposed to the actions/behaviours of others

In a related study, Snyman and Kruger [13] investigate information security behaviour in terms of the TPB model. In contrast to other studies that use TPB as the underlying theoretical framework, their study theorises that TPB on its own is not sufficient for evaluating behaviour. They argue that (external) contextual influences should be taken into account in conjunction with the intrinsic motivations that form the basis of the model. The effect that contextual factors might exert on the eventual behaviour is only discussed on a theoretical level and was not specifically applied in practice. Expanding upon their theoretical work and incorporating the two external contextual factors that are identified in this research, it will inform the practical part of this study.

To contextualise the TPB (as applied in [13]) with the current research presented in this paper, a graphical depiction is provided in Fig. 1.

Figure 1 shows a conceptual diagram in which the external contextual factors in this research, relates to the TPB and the intrinsic contextual factors that are implicitly

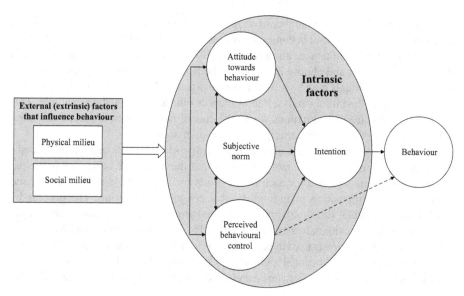

Fig. 1. Conceptual model of the influence of contextual factors in relation to the TPB [10].

included therein. The intrinsic factors form the basis for the establishment of intention (informed by attitude, norms, and perceived behavioural control) and ultimately the resulting behaviour. All the while, the intrinsic factors being affected by the external factors. An approach for evaluating group behaviour, identified in [13] as being able to implicitly encapsulate the influence of external factors, was first proposed by Granovetter [4]. The model is known as Threshold models of collective behaviour.

Granovetter [4] contends that behaviour and the underlying motivation for behaviour is rarely self-informed. Behaviour is said to be the product of circumstance, where circumstance (an extrinsic factor) refers to the observed, or perceived, behaviour of others. Given a situation with only two possible avenues of behaviour (i.e. acting or choosing not to act), an individual is thought to always try to enhance their efficacy in the given situation by electing how to behave, based on the perceived risk versus reward in choosing one alternative over the other.

Arguably, one would always choose the behaviour with the highest associated benefit, relative to the associated cost. However, as the number of individuals that perform one of the behaviours increases, the perceived benefit of also participating in the behaviour increases along with it. Even if the cost was initially, and in reality, probably still is higher than the benefit. The decision-making process is often taking place sub-consciously and is said to be based on the concept of behavioural thresholds.

Granovetter [4] hypothesises that each individual has an intrinsic threshold for participation in behaviour. In a group setting, the aforementioned mechanism of determining behaviour changes due to the influence of external contextual factors as the behaviour of other people become part of the equation. Choosing which behaviour to act on becomes a function of one's intrinsic threshold, expressed as the number of other people that should first be engaging in a behaviour before the associated benefit will outweigh the cost in one's mind. Once the number of actors in a behaviour outweighs one's threshold, participation in the behaviour becomes almost inevitable. When left to their own devices, without any external influence, an individual will mostly follow their own perception of cost versus benefit and choose in favour of the behaviour with the highest perceived benefit. Such individuals may be referred to as instigators. In a group setting, instigators are required to be the initial catalyst that influences others to follow their example. This specifically holds true for situations where the cost of participation is particularly high and very few individuals will participate of their own accord.

In order to apply this theoretical model in a real-world situation, behavioural threshold analysis is employed. This analysis entails that the threshold values for participation in a behaviour is known for each of the group members and is dependent on, and specific to, the composition of individuals that constitute the group. The process by which these individual thresholds may be elicited from the group members by means of self-reporting questionnaires is presented in [5]. Given the individual thresholds, mathematical aggregation is used to provide an outlook for the eventual group behaviour.

To relate the threshold model and analysis of Granovetter [4] back to information security, two practical exercises were conducted which are described in the following section.

3 Experimentation

This section describes two information security group behaviour experiments with reference to the experimental setup, contextual factors, and behavioural threshold analysis.

3.1 Experimental Setup

To practically evaluate the idea of external contextual factors and to see the influence of these factors on the information security behaviour of people in groups, behavioural threshold analysis exercises were conducted in two discrete organisational settings i.e. an academic setting, specifically where students live together in a university residence, and an industry setting where people work together.

The first experiment [10] was conducted to examine the information security behaviour of students at a predominantly residential university in South Africa. The threshold questionnaires were digitally distributed to residents at a single-sex (male) university residence. A group of students were asked to distribute the questionnaire in the residence and ask willing participants to forward the questionnaire to other possible candidates in the residence. Participation was voluntary and all responses were anonymous. Due to the relatively sensitive nature of questions that relate to personal information security behaviour, along with participation not being compulsory, suitable responses were obtained from 52 respondents This resulted in a notional response rate of around 30%, based on the total number of residents as it is unknown how many students were eventually targeted by the word of mouth type distribution of the questionnaires. Of these 52 respondents, 17 were self-identified as first-years (typically 19 years old), 15 as second years (20 years old), 13 as third years (21 years old), and 7 as being fourth-year and above (22 years old and over). The respondents represented students studying in seven different academic faculties.

The relatively low response rate and the possible influence of phenomena such as selection bias notwithstanding, the distribution between four year-groups and seven faculties were considered to be representative enough to allow for the useful application of information security behavioural threshold analysis [5].

The second experiment was conducted in an industry setting (first reported in [14]). The experiment was specifically chosen for comparison due to the difference in the sets of contextual influences in mind when compared to that of [10].

The experiment was performed with working adults within a utility company. A behavioural threshold analysis questionnaire was distributed within a risk assurance department. Supervisors were asked to distribute the questionnaire which was completed by 63 employees. Once again, the nature of the online, self-reporting approach does not provide an indication of the number of respondents who were targeted but based on the number of employees in the department, a notional response rate of 50% is plausible. Three categories of the type of employment were identified as management (14%), contractors (53%), and permanent staff (33%).Given the compulsory nature of the information security assessment in the second experiment, a 100% response rate was achieved. This is in contrast to the 28% response rate reported on in [10] which can be ascribed to the voluntary nature of completing the questionnaire for the first experiment. The response rate was dependent on students dedicating time and effort into completing the survey. They were not compensated for their participation and therefore seemed reluctant to do so if there was no direct gain to be had.

The questionnaires which were distributed to both groups of respondents in experiments one and two, consisted of six questions relating to information security behaviours. To cover a range of common information security themes, selected focus areas of the Human Aspects of Information Security Questionnaire (HAISQ) were employed as the topics for the questions [3]. The six questions related to *information security training, password management, incident reporting, social media use, internet use,* and *email use.*

A four-point Likert scale was used for the question responses. The respondents rate their predisposition for participating in the security behaviour, relative to the percentage of other group members that perform the behaviour [5]. This predisposition for participation is used as the behavioural threshold for the respondent. Responses from all the respondents were mathematically aggregated and analysed.

In the next section, a high-level overview of the contextual environments is presented.

3.2 Contextual Environment

Given the distinctly different natures of the two environments in which the abovementioned experiments were performed, this section provides a summary of the two contexts in terms of the physical milieu and the social milieu as identified in Table 1. The summary is provided in the form of Table 3, based on the general contextual factors from Table 2.

Information security behavioural threshold analysis from [5] was subsequently implemented in the specific contexts as described above in Table 3. In the following section, a cursory reflection is provided on the process of behavioural threshold analysis.

Table 3. External factors that influence information security behaviour.

External factors in information security behaviour		
Extrinsic factor	Factors in student information security behaviour	Factors in industry information security behaviour
Physical milieu	**– Ease of access to systems, processes and people** Common areas (lounges, television rooms, kitchens, laundry rooms, public computer rooms, reception), as well as private sleeping quarters which houses one or two students per room. The close proximity of this kind of living arrangement provides the members of the residence with unprecedented access to the behaviour of others. Both in practical terms that allow the observation of the behaviour of others, and physical terms in which access is afforded to personal and university computers and networks	**– Ease of access to systems, processes and people** In contrast to people that live together, co-workers rarely have unrestricted access to each other's private spaces like workstations, cubicles, or offices. A level of professional distance is expected that limits the observation of the behaviour of others. Access to systems and processes are strictly controlled and enforced to prevent unauthorised access and behaviour
	– Level of convenience associated with tasks A certain level of convenience is conveyed by living in close quarters. For instance, if network access is required after business hours and a person's credentials have expired, it is easy to simply ask any other inhabitant of the residence to supply their details. It is convenient for the borrower as their ability to access the network is instantly restored without the need to contact the helpdesk which will not respond in real-time	**– Level of convenience associated with tasks** Within larger organisations, convenience of performing everyday tasks is diminished by the associated red tape and governing policies. In terms of the levels of information security within the organisation, this can be seen as both a hindrance and a help. Tighter control and oversight might help prevent human error but might also lead to security fatigue [15] which can lead to employees trying to find workarounds for frustrating security controls
	– Availability of technical expertise Given the combination of different academic levels, fields of study, and technical proficiencies that cohabit, it is probable that someone with a high level of know-how or expertise can readily be found to help circumvent security controls that stand in the way of quickly or conveniently completing a task An example of such a circumvention is accessing dubious websites that are restricted on the university network by means of masking their network traffic by employing virtual private networks to third party providers	**– Availability of technical expertise** Industries tend to group different functions that logically belong together within departments or sections. With reference to the availability of technical expertise, this might lead to a scenario where expertise is concentrated (e.g. within the IT department) and not readily accessible to many of the members of other groupings. Dedicated persons are appointed to fulfil technical roles and are typically well versed in good security hygiene. Such employees would ideally not assist others in performing unwanted security behaviour and will preferably report any security circumventions
	– Presence of security controls In the specific university and residence environment, no formal information security training is provided. The only mechanism that is used to raise awareness is notifications when accessing the university network and posters stating relevant rules for the use of university computer labs	**– Presence of security controls** In the industry setting, formal information security training is provided to the employees which should ensure an enhanced level of awareness and compliance

(*continued*)

Table 3. (*continued*)

External factors in information security behaviour		
Extrinsic factor	Factors in student information security behaviour	Factors in industry information security behaviour
Social milieu	**– Organisational structure and peer pressure** A strict hierarchy prevails where a pecking order distinction is made based on the number of years someone has been residing in the specific residence. There is also a specific distinction between junior (usually first-year students or first-time entrants) and senior students. In this hierarchy, juniors have very little autonomy and, especially during an initial orientation, are forced to obey senior residents [17]. The peer pressure and hierarchy that is present in residences are usually seen as factors in hazing [17] and alcohol consumption in literature [15, 16] but is also applicable to security behaviour. A resident may easily be coerced, through this hierarchical structure and peer pressure, into divulging credentials, downloading illicit content, etc	**– Organisational structure and peer pressure** Organisations, specifically larger organisations, typically have fixed organisational structures with clearly defined levels and roles. In such a hierarchy there is a noticeable unidirectional balance of authority, e.g. a manager has influence over an employee, but the reverse is rarely true. When viewed in terms of information security, this control of the upper echelons over the lower can have either a positive or a negative effect. An authority figure can serve as the embodiment of policy and procedure and can be a strong deterrent for unsafe security behaviour. Contrariwise, such a figure can, for example, strong-arm a subordinate into not reporting security incidents or performing other negative security behaviours
	– Presence of co-workers, family, or friends and being exposed to the actions/behaviours of others In a residence, there is a constant presence of other people. Even in a private space like sleeping quarters, there might be another resident present. This implies that some actions of an individual, that would normally go unnoticed, are being observed. If they visit a dubious website, someone may be there to observe it. When password sharing occurs between two parties it may be witnessed by any or all of the others present. Therefore, this constant presence may convey an unprecedented sense of awareness of the information security habits of the resident corps. The awareness may set the precedent for future behaviour	**– Presence of co-workers, family, or friends and being exposed to the actions/behaviours of others** Arguably the most important, distinction between the physical environment in industry and that of the university residence is the amount of time that the members of the two groups spend together. Assuming a typical eight-hour workday, this is the only exposure that the members of the industry group will have to the behaviour (including information security behaviour) of others on a regular day. This is in contrast to the residence where the exposure is constant except for the interruptions of attending classes. This reduced contact time leads to a different dynamic in the *social milieu*
	– Collective purpose and working with others Even though the abovementioned hierarchy may be seen in a negative light as illustrated above, it may also contribute to a sense of belonging and camaraderie [17]. There is an implied level of trust associated with shared experiences. This is compounded by the compulsory attendance of events [15, 17] that are meant to reaffirm the bond between the residents. This trust allows for a false sense of safety where security is concerned. For instance, one might not appropriately scrutinise an email that was (presumably) sent by a confidant and assume it to be safe. The assumption will leave one open to malware and phishing attacks	**– Collective purpose and working with others** It stands to reason that the ultimate purpose of an organisation is to be successful and sustainable. The specific measure of what successfulness entails notwithstanding, it should be the clear collective vision of the members of the organisation to contribute to reaching this goal. This vision serves as a moral compass that guides their behaviour and by extension should influence information security behaviour. Especially when confronted with security behaviour is known to be imprudent, the collective purpose of the group should guide the individual to behave in a positive way

3.3 Behavioural Threshold Analysis

For a detailed description on behavioural threshold analysis in general terms, the reader is referred to [4] as only a brief overview is presented here, followed by the specific descriptions of the behavioural threshold analysis results in the following section.

To interpret the behavioural thresholds that were reported by the respondents, the thresholds are aggregated by calculating the cumulative frequencies for each threshold interval. In order to simplify the analysis, behavioural thresholds are grouped into intervals of 10%. These frequencies are then graphed as a line of participation level (y) versus cumulative behavioural thresholds (x). Furthermore, Granovetter [4] stipulates that the cumulative frequencies of the respondents' behavioural thresholds should be graphed in relation to a uniform distribution of thresholds. This uniform distribution is referred to as the equilibrium line and is represented by the $y = x$ line. The intersection (if present) of the two lines may indicate that the group behaviour has reached an equilibrium point, i.e. the number of participants in the behaviour has stabilised. Behaviour that has reached equilibrium will not gain any new participants, but neither will any participants desist from their current behaviour.

Granovetter [4] states that the requirement for equilibrium is that the two line segments to the left and right of the intersection have gradients ($m = \Delta y/\Delta x$) of less than one. This implies that an equilibrium state requires the threshold line to intersect the equilibrium line from above. An intersection from below does not constitute an equilibrium state, i.e. the gradient is greater than one. When $m < 1$ to the left of the intersection, the number of participants will not decrease in and of itself. An external influence or stimulus (e.g. information security training or awareness campaigns) is required to reduce the participation rate. In the same manner, to the right of the intersection, the number of participants will not increase.

In the following section, a comparison of the results for experiments one and two (explained in Sect. 3.1) in the application of behavioural threshold analysis are presented.

4 A Comparison of Two Studies Through Behavioural Threshold Analysis

As per its definition, contextual factors in information security behaviour is dependent upon the environment in which such behaviours are to be performed. The influence of such factors may be assessed by means of behavioural threshold analysis. Therefore, in this section, a pairwise comparison of two behavioural threshold analysis experiments are presented.

As mentioned before in Sect. 2, two main classes for external contextual factors were identified, i.e. physical milieu, and social milieu. For the purposes of the comparison between the two experiments (experiments one and two from Sect. 3.1), only three information security focus areas are presented here namely, information security training, social media use, and internet use. The cumulative threshold graphs for the remaining three focus areas (password management, incident reporting, and email use) are included in the Appendix for reference. This is due to page restriction considerations and it was reasoned that the similarity in the behavioural threshold analysis results of the graphs in the Appendix, compared to those that already form part of the discussion, are such that including them do not contribute significantly to the arguments presented here.

A concern that often comes with employing measuring instruments (questionnaires) for evaluating behaviour, is social desirability [16], i.e. respondents report on what they suppose the "correct" response is rather than responding candidly. This problem can also occur in behavioural threshold analysis experiments and in previous studies it has been provided for in the form of adapted responses [5]. For the purpose of this study, it was decided to use the original data that was not adjusted for social desirability, specifically to show the effect of the original data. Because these are two such divergent examples, using the unaltered data should provide a more accurate picture of the effect of the contextual factors on the behaviour of the two groups.

In Sect. 3.3, the process of behavioural threshold analysis was described. The principles that were discussed are now applied to evaluate the behaviours that relate to the focus areas from Sect. 3.1.

Information security training – The behaviour of voluntarily completing information security training is considered a positive behaviour. One would therefore expect that others should ideally copy this behaviour from the example that is set by the group. The cumulative threshold graph for information security training behaviour is presented in Fig. 2.

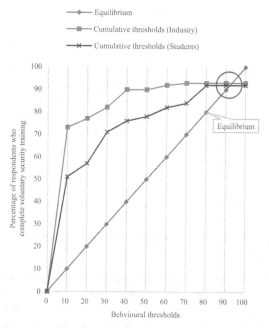

Fig. 2. Behavioural threshold analysis graph – Information security training (Industry vs. Students).

From Fig. 2 it can be observed that respondents that work together in an industry setting are more willing to initially follow the behaviour of their peers in attending voluntary information security training than students that live together in a university residence. However, as participation in this behaviour gains traction, the difference in the eventual predicted participation is very low, i.e. 92% for students, and 93% for industry workers. These percentages are derived from where the two cumulative frequency lines for the industry and student respondents intersect the equilibrium line (highlighted in Fig. 2). Both groups exhibit low thresholds for participation which means that they will easily follow the group example. Seeing as security training contributes positively to the levels of information security in the organisations, this behaviour should be encouraged and reinforced.

Social media use – In the context of this research, social media use refers to the use of company or university resources and time to access social media websites. The intersections of the cumulative thresholds for the two groups for this behaviour are once again highlighted in Fig. 3.

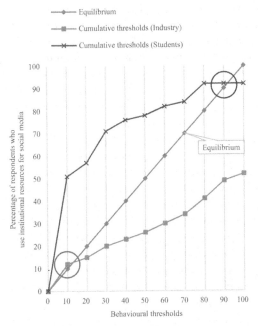

Fig. 3. Behavioural threshold analysis graph – social media use (industry vs. students).

Contrary to the information security training example, the predicted behaviour for the two groups for social media use, shows a stark contrast. An early equilibrium is reached for the industry group. The green highlighted area at the bottom left of the graph (Fig. 3) shows that only between 12% and 13% of industry workers will eventually follow the social media behaviour of others. This low level of behavioural compliance indicates that the industry group members retain high threshold values against participation. The behaviour cannot propagate to other group members beyond this point.

Students, on the other hand, will follow the social media behaviour of their cohorts until it reaches a 92% participation rate (red highlighted area, Fig. 3) They show low behavioural thresholds for this behaviour. Furthermore, as many as 51% of the student respondents will start to participate if they think that as little as 10% of their group are already taking part. This pattern foretells a rapid preliminary uptake in the behaviour and thereafter a steady increase until the equilibrium is reached. A participation level of 92% in any improper information security behaviour should be considered problematic. The group behaviour will remain unchanged unless specific action is taken to rectify it. With reference to the human aspect of information security, awareness campaigns are thought to be one of the more effective interventions whereby to ensure good information security practices within an organisation and effect change in behaviour [7]. Such awareness campaigns can be tailored to fit the focus areas that need to be addressed to raise awareness, i.e. social media use in this particular case.

Internet use – This focus area refers to risky behaviour when using the Internet, e.g. visiting dubious websites which exposes one to possible malware attacks and the interception of sensitive information. The cumulative behavioural threshold graph for Internet use behaviour presents an interesting case that differs from the preceding three focus areas. The participation rate of 69% for the student group (see the red highlighted area in Fig. 4), indicates that the respondents, are quite willing to follow the example of their fellow residents. However, the aggregated reported thresholds for the industry respondents do not intersect the equilibrium line when plotted.

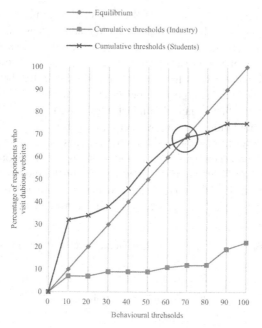

Fig. 4. Behavioural threshold analysis graph – Internet use (Industry vs. Students).

This occurrence is an example of what Growney [17] refers to as a dying problem. In a dying problem scenario, there is not enough initial stimulus to get the underlying individual behaviour to grow into an accepted group behaviour. In the example of internet use behaviour, an instigator (or several instigators) might initially perform the behaviour of visiting dubious websites. They do not require anyone else to exhibit the behaviour and they will perform it out of their own intrinsic motivations. This number of initial actors does not, however, satisfy the chief requirement of the threshold models of collective behaviour, stating that the number of people that perform a certain behaviour must exceed an individual's internal threshold before the individual will join in the behaviour. At all the threshold levels, the plotted cumulative thresholds for the industry respondents remain below the equilibrium line. This contrasts with the threshold graph for the students, which remains above the equilibrium line for the most part. With the current composition of the industry group, there is no individual that will be convinced to join in the behaviour because their own threshold for participation has not been exceeded. Given the nature of the behavioural thresholds model, the dying problem might even cause the process to work in reverse. If an instigator notices that very few others, if any, take part in the behaviour that they themselves perform, they might reconsider their own behaviour and desist from any future action.

The commonalities and differences in their contextual environments and the influence that context has on behaviour is now discussed in Sect. 5.

5   Discussion

In the previous section, a comparison of the predicted information security behaviour for the two groups, based on behavioural threshold analysis, was presented. It is notable that for each of the information security focus areas, the industry respondents fare better than their opposite number in the academic setting. The results are summarised in Table 4 which shows the mean values for the reported thresholds for the two groups. Note that the training behaviour is a positive behaviour (indicated with*). This is opposed to the other behaviours that negatively impact information security. Therefore, in these instances, the threshold model should be interpreted in reverse, i.e. it can be considered a good thing if positive information security behaviour spreads through a group.

The mean behavioural thresholds (μ) for all of the listed behaviours are higher (save for * where lower thresholds are considered better) for the industry respondents (μ_2) than for the student respondents (μ_1), i.e. the chances that unwanted security behaviour will propagate within the industry group, based on the principles of threshold models of

Table 4. Mean reported behavioural thresholds per group.

	Security behaviour	Students (μ_1)	Industry (μ_2)
Mean behavioural threshold (μ)	Information security training*	23.65	21.27
	Social media use	31.15	74.44
	Incident reporting	51.15	70.79
	Email use	51.92	86.51
	Internet use	50.96	90.00
	Password management	68.27	90.95

collective behaviour, are lower than for the student group by a margin as big as 43.29 percentage points for the social media use behaviour.

The two experiments that were described in Sect. 3.1, were conducted in exactly the same manner, i.e. the same methodology [5] was used in both cases. This means that the data collection methods, information security focus areas, the way the questions were worded, and the question layouts were kept constant in both settings. The main differences between the experiments, were differences in the contexts in which they were performed (issues such as age and gender notwithstanding). Hence, one possible conclusion is that the differences in predicted behaviour for the groups, can be attributed to the considerable influence that the different external contextual factors have on the two groups.

The remainder of this section is dedicated to a discussion of how the two external contextual factors that were identified, i.e. physical milieu and social milieu, may have influenced the way in which the two groups go about information security behaviour for the different focus areas.

Information Security Training. Formal information security training is not provided in the specific university context for this research, apart from inconsequential notices in the university computer labs and login screens. In industry however, there is a marked tendency to provide training to employees in an attempt to protect the digital and financial assets of the organisation. It stands to reason then, that the motivations of the groups to perform the behaviour differ. Their heightened knowledge of the importance of security training, in comparison to that of the students, influence employees to choose voluntary training. Receiving security training can be seen as part of their physical milieu that provide the availability of and access to expertise. Students, on the other hand, having not received any previous formal security training, may opt to choose voluntary training due to their social milieu. Taking part in activities as a group is a common occurrence in the residence setting and gives a sense of collective purpose.

Social Media Use – In the two contexts under review, the security implications of the use of social media are quite different in terms of their physical aspects. In an industry context, social media use might expose the organisation to phishing attacks, or accidental dissemination of proprietary information, and the like. The risk for the student is, however of a personal nature, e.g. identity theft, even if the student does use the university infrastructure for their social media interactions. Undergraduate students rarely (if ever) have access to information of a sensitive nature relating to the university itself. Based on the differences in security implications, the motivations for exercising caution with social media behaviour is also different. Students also experience the influence of the social milieu as many of their events and activities use social media platforms for interaction and organisation. This further contributes to their willingness of using social media, even when information security circumstances dictate that it should best not be done.

Internet Use. Student behavioural thresholds are low, i.e. it takes little motivation or the perception that only a few others already perform the behaviour for them to also perform the behaviour. On the physical level, this may be attributed to the access that the student respondents have to technologically knowledgeable peers. An example scenario can include that academic institutions often employ firewalls and other network infrastructure to prohibit access to websites and other network protocols they deem to be dubious in terms of security or questionable in terms of the content they provide [18]. Residences provide the ideal environment where these restrictions may be circumvented by a knowledgeable person and the method of access disseminated to others. The social factor determines how dissemination might take place: The required awareness that such circumventions are possible is created through constant presence and observation within the residence. The student that originally exploited the circumvention is then either coerced to help others bypass the existing security (through peer pressure or levels of hierarchy) or might provide other students with the solution willingly because of a sense of solidarity and collective purpose.

Stricter policies and deterrence measures, as an example of the physical milieu, might be the reason why their industry counterparts are less willing to follow bad examples of internet use. Similar to the physical aspect, the social aspect in the workplace can be interpreted as the reason for the high thresholds for the industry respondents. Being aware of the security and disciplinary risks associated with disregarding policies and accessing dubious websites and possibly having to circumvent technical security measures to achieve this, should cause a certain reluctance to follow the example of others. Also, if an individual is performing such actions, it will be done in secret and kept hidden from the observation of his/her co-workers.

The following three focus areas did not form part of the comparison between the predicted information security behaviour of the two groups in Sect. 4. The resulting behavioural threshold graphs are available in the Appendix. However, a cursory overview of the possible underlying contextual factors is presented here.

Incident Reporting. Although incident reporting is often touted as being important in the management of information security, it is rarely being practised. One of the main impeding problems is that without a clearly defined process of reporting, responsibility and accountability guided by policy [19], reporting will not take place as it should without the proper commitment of the members of the organisation. Conceivably, it is often easier to just ignore incidents, due to security fatigue [15], than to navigate the process of reporting them, if such a process exists. The actual and perceived ease associated with reporting an incident, is one of the barriers that translate to how an employee or student will behave when an incident occurs. Convenience and access are considered factors that inform behaviour and therefore these reporting mechanisms can be considered part of the physical milieu of an organisation. Existing hierarchies and mutual experiences (social milieu) can be considered as another stumbling block for reporting security incidents. An individual might be reluctant to be an informant on the security transgressions of others for fear of retribution or for simply being ostracised from the group.

Password Management. The sharing and mismanagement of passwords is said to be one of the main security threats that relates to the human aspect of information security [20], and as such it is one of the most common topics in information security awareness programs. Both formally (through such programs) and informally (through media and many websites) people are warned to take the security of their passwords seriously. Often, the social milieu is an external contextual stimulus for password sharing. This is both relevant for the industry and residence settings as one of the main reasons for sharing passwords is to simply "get the job done". As mentioned before, expired or forgotten credentials stand in the way of completing tasks and are therefore circumvented by using another's credentials to avoid the inconvenience of retrieving them.

Email Use. The use of email for communication is common in both the academic and industry settings. Phishing attacks, social engineering, and the distribution of malware are prevalent in the email ecosystem [21]. Email servers and their technical configuration, including spam filtering functionality, and antimalware and antivirus capabilities all comprise the physical milieu in relation to email use behaviour. Reliance on the protection afforded by these functionalities may lead to complacency and an unwarranted sense of security. However, if these technical measures fail, the success of these attacks draws on the interactions between people on a social level. The social milieu will therefore influence the related behaviours. In the context of the university students, the reasons for unwanted behaviour in terms of email security can once again be linked to the common practice of digital piracy that is rife in university settings [22, 23]. Many different file formats are used to encode, compress, or hide illicit content. Email attachments may therefore not be scrutinised thoroughly if a file with a strange or unknown file extension is accompanied by a convincing message. The implied sense of trust and camaraderie that forms part of the social milieu further exacerbates the problem by strengthening the associated credibility of an email and its attachments if the source appears to be from within one's social milieu. Similarly, in industry the social milieu may influence even well-trained employees with the necessary awareness to lower their guard with respect to email security.

In the final section, the study is summarised. The aims of the study are revisited, and a reflection is provided on the contributions and limitations of this research. A look ahead to possible future work concludes the article.

6   Conclusion

This paper presented an extension of previously published work [10] in which external contextual factors and their possible influence on information security behaviour were studied.

The aims of this research were to firstly provide a theoretical discourse about the applicability of external contextual factors to information security behaviour and then to apply a model to evaluate information security group behaviour. Secondly, this model should be able to observe the influence of contextual factors on the way in which a group behaves. Finally, the evaluations of the security behaviour of two different groups through the identified model, including the underlying contextual factors, were to be compared. The contributions to the field of information security behaviour, by virtue of addressing these three aims, are shortly discussed here.

Aim 1 – A literature review on how context influences human behaviour in general revealed five distinct factors that play a role in how humans behave. Two distinct classifications of contextual factors were identified and conceptualised in terms of the theory of planned behaviour (TPB). TPB was consequently used as the theoretical foundation for connecting the extrinsic contextual factors to information security behaviour. Even though TPB is often used in information security behaviour studies, TPB on its own only considers individual cognition and does not provide insights into behaviour in groups. This limitation was addressed in the second aim.

Aim 2 – Behavioural threshold analysis was recognised as a suitable approach to evaluate information security group behaviour and is conceptually compatible with TPB. Furthermore, this approach implicitly takes the influences of external contextual factors on information security group behaviour into account.

Aim 3 – Two group behaviour experiments were conducted in which behavioural threshold analysis was applied and the different behaviours of the two experiment groups were compared. The information security group behaviour was found to be consistently better for the industry stetting in comparison to that of the university residence setting. The behavioural threshold analysis comparison for the two groups was further augmented by a discussion that highlighted the differences in the external contextual factors that ultimately affected the information security behaviours of these two groups. This discussion demonstrates the importance of taking into account the contextual environment when seeking to address information security behaviour in an organisation.

Lastly, this paper only reflects on the influence of the extrinsic contextual factors on information security behaviour. This is due to the intrinsic factors already being implicitly addressed in other security studies that are based solely on TPB. However, future studies may seek to investigate the applicability of these factors to group behaviour, especially how these contextual factors influence the individual's thresholds and related susceptibility to follow the behaviour of others.

Acknowledgements. The authors would like to thank Johan Allers and Wayne Kearney for their assistance with the experiments.

Appendix

As mentioned in Sect. 4, this Appendix shows the cumulative behavioural threshold graphs for the information security focus areas for *Email use, Password management* and *Incident reporting* in Figs. 5, 6, and 7 respectively. The external contextual factors that contribute to the predicted eventual group behaviours for these three focus areas were discussed in Sect. 5.

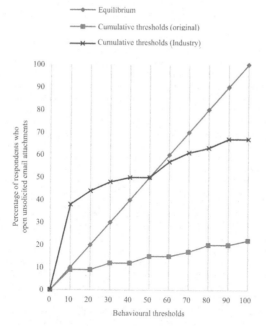

Fig. 5. Behavioural threshold analysis graph – Email use (Industry vs. Students)

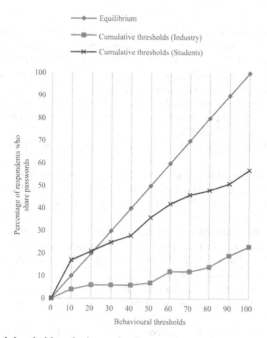

Fig. 6. Behavioural threshold analysis graph – Password management (Industry vs. Students)

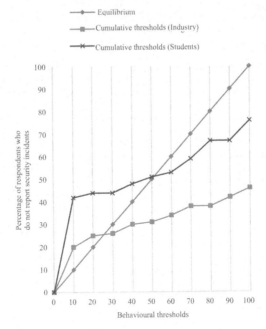

Fig. 7. Behavioural threshold analysis graph – Incident reporting (Industry vs. Students)

References

1. Shropshire, J., Warkentin, M., Sharma, S.: Personality, attitudes, and intentions: predicting initial adoption of information security behavior. Comput. Secur. **49**, 177–191 (2015)
2. Barth, S., De Jong, M.D., Junger, M., Hartel, P.H., Roppelt, J.C.: Putting the privacy paradox to the test: online privacy and security behaviors among users with technical knowledge, privacy awareness, and financial resources. Telemat. Inform. **41**, 55–69 (2019)
3. Parsons, K., Calic, D., Pattinson, M., Butavicius, M., McCormac, A., Zwaans, T.: The human aspects of information security questionnaire (HAIS-Q): two further validation studies. Comput. Secur. **66**, 40–51 (2017)
4. Granovetter, M.: Threshold models of collective behavior. Am. J. Sociol. **83**, 1420–1443 (1978)
5. Snyman, D.P., Kruger, H.A.: Behavioural threshold analysis: methodological and practical considerations for applications in information security. Behav. Inf. Technol. **38**, 1–19 (2019)
6. Willison, R., Warkentin, M.: Beyond deterrence: an expanded view of employee computer abuse. MIS Q. **37**, 1–20 (2013)
7. Johnston, A.C., Di Gangi, P.M., Howard, J., Worrell, J.: It takes a village: understanding the collective security efficacy of employee groups. J. Assoc. Inf. Syst. **20**, 186–212 (2019)
8. Wu, P.F., Vitak, J., Zimmer, M.T.: A contextual approach to information privacy research. J. Am. Soc. Inf. Sci. **7**, 485–490 (2019)
9. Kroenung, J., Eckhardt, A.: The attitude cube—A three-dimensional model of situational factors in IS adoption and their impact on the attitude–behavior relationship. Inf. Manag. **52**, 611–627 (2015)
10. Snyman, D.P., Kruger, H.A.: External contextual factors in information security behaviour. In: 6th International Conference on Information Systems Security and Privacy (ICISSP 2020), pp. 185–194. SCITEPRESS – Science and Technology Publications, Lda (2020)

11. Belk, R.W.: Situational variables and consumer behavior. J. Consum. Res. **2**, 157–164 (1975)
12. Kirova, V., Thanh, T.V.: Smartphone use during the leisure theme park visit experience: the role of contextual factors. Inf. Manag. **56**, 742–753 (2019)
13. Snyman, D.P., Kruger, H.A.: The application of behavioural thresholds to analyse collective behaviour in information security. Inf. Comput. Secur. **25**, 152–164 (2017)
14. Snyman, D.P., Kruger, H.A., Kearney, W.D.: I shall, we shall, and all others will: paradoxical information security behaviour. Inf. Comput. Secur. **26**, 290–305 (2018)
15. Furnell, S., Thomson, K.-L.: Recognising and addressing 'security fatigue.' Comput. Fraud Secur. **2009**, 7–11 (2009)
16. Fisher, R.J.: Social desirability bias and the validity of indirect questioning. J. Consum. Res. **20**, 303–315 (1993)
17. Growney, J.S.: I will If You Will: Individual Thresholds and Group Behavior - Applications of Algebra to Group Behavior. COMAP Inc., Bedford (1983)
18. Miller, C., Stuart Wells, F.: Balancing security and privacy in the digital workplace. J. Chang. Manag. **7**, 315–328 (2007)
19. Wiant, T.L.: Information security policy's impact on reporting security incidents. Comput. Secur. **24**, 448–459 (2005)
20. Furnell, S., Esmael, R.: Evaluating the effect of guidance and feedback upon password compliance. Comput. Fraud Secur. **2017**, 5–10 (2017)
21. Security, I.B.M.: IBM X-Force Threat Intelligence Index 2018: Notable Security Events of 2017, and a Look Ahead. IBM Corporation, New York (2018)
22. Lee, B., Fenoff, R., Paek, S.Y.: Correlates of participation in e-book piracy on campus. J. Acad. Librariansh. **45**, 299–304 (2019)
23. Gan, L.L., Koh, H.C.: An empirical study of software piracy among tertiary institutions in Singapore. Inf. Manag. **43**, 640–649 (2006)

Using MedBIoT Dataset to Build Effective Machine Learning-Based IoT Botnet Detection Systems

Alejandro Guerra-Manzanares(✉) , Jorge Medina-Galindo, Hayretdin Bahsi ,
and Sven Nõmm

Department of Software Science, Tallinn University of Technology, Tallinn, Estonia
{alejandro.guerra,hayretdin.bahsi,sven.nomm}@taltech.ee

Abstract. The exponential increase in the adoption of the Internet of Things (IoT) technology combined with the usual lack of security measures carried by such devices have brought up new risks and security challenges to networks. IoT devices are prone to be easily compromised and used as magnification platforms for record-breaking cyber-attacks (i.e., Distributed Denial-of-Service attacks). Intrusion detection systems based on machine learning aim to detect such threats effectively, overcoming the security limitations on networks. In this regard, data quantity and quality is key to build effective detection models. These data are scarce and limited to small-sized networks for IoT environments. This research addresses this gap generating a labelled behavioral IoT data set, composed of normal and actual botnet network traffic in a medium-sized IoT network (up to 83 devices). Mirai, BashLite and Torii real botnet malware are deployed and data from early stages of botnet deployment is acquired (i.e., infection, propagation and communication with C&C stages). Supervised (i.e. classification) and unsupervised (i.e., anomaly detection) machine learning models are built with the data acquired as a demonstration of the suitability and reliability of the collected data set for effective machine learning-based botnet detection intrusion detection systems (i.e., testing, design and deployment). The IoT behavioral data set is released, being publicly available as MedBIoT data set.

Keywords: Botnet · Internet of Things · Dataset · Intrusion detection · Anomaly detection · IoT · Machine learning

1 Introduction

The inter-connectivity of nowadays world's elements is a fact. Internet has extended the connectivity and communication capabilities like never before, not only to humans but also for everyday objects. Now it is possible to interact and control via Internet objects such as TV's, refrigerators, light bulbs or thermostats. The so-called Internet of Things (shortened as IoT) has just started its expansion, expecting a major growth in the near future. It was estimated that there were around 22 billion connected IoT devices by 2018, a figure expected to reach 50 billion by 2030 [52]. Globally, 127 new IoT devices are connected to the Internet every second [34] encompassing a wide range of

© Springer Nature Switzerland AG 2022
S. Furnell et al. (Eds.): ICISSP 2020, CCIS 1545, pp. 222–243, 2022.
https://doi.org/10.1007/978-3-030-94900-6_11

applications from healthcare and manufacturing to automotive and agriculture. A typical consumer owns an average of four IoT devices that communicate directly with the cloud [34]. The global IoT market size is estimated to grow over $248 billion by 2020 and reach the $1.6 trillion figure by 2025 [51]. In spite of its wide spread and significant growth, the IoT technology still poses concerns even to the early adopters and eager customers, mostly related to security and data privacy [10,34,50]. IoT devices have been identified as potential entry points and enticing targets for cyberattacks, exposing their vulnerabilities and facing challenges for their massive adoption [34]. Thus, despite its vast growth, the Internet of Things market blast is still constrained by its main barrier: security [5,10,42].

The ubiquity of IoT devices might pose a major challenge to security as IoT devices have traditionally lacked of proper control measures, maintenance and proactive security management (e.g., usage of default passwords, no firmware updates, no access control policy), featuring them as highly vulnerable and easy to be compromised devices [5,34]. These weaknesses have been exploited by attackers, being able to compromise the defenseless devices by exploiting its vulnerabilities, thus gaining remote control and using them as amplification platforms for their massive disruptive attacks [25].

Effective IoT botnet attack anomaly detection methods rely on the usage of appropriate data. These data sets are characterized by the collection of normal (legitimate) and malicious (botnet) behavioral data from IoT networks. Anomaly detection models are built on the basis of legitimate data, establishing a normality pattern. The induced models are assessed using normal and malicious data. Performance metrics are computed and used to evaluate the model's detection capabilities. Therefore, accurate and complete data are key elements to build highly effective intrusion detection systems (IDS).

In this regard, as can be observed in Table 1, all the available data sets focus on small-sized IoT networks and on a specific and small variety of devices, mostly cameras. As a result, the behavior of a small set of devices is acquired, considerably limiting the scope of the IoT devices analyzed from the vast and varied domain of the existing IoT devices. Furthermore, none of the data sets use a combination of real and emulated IoT devices, which impacts and limits the scope of their results to either real or emulated devices.

This research aims to fill this substantial gap by providing a novel IoT data set acquired from a medium size IoT network architecture (i.e., 83 devices), including normal and malicious behavioral traffic from both real and emulated devices and the deployment of three prominent IoT botnets (i.e., Mirai, BashLite and Torii). The size extension allows to capture malware spreading patterns and interactions that cannot be observed in small-sized networks, providing a more realistic environment. Furthermore, no data set uses the combination of emulated and real devices within the same network. Additionally, this data set includes the behavior of Torii botnet malware, being the first publicly available data set to deploy it. Lastly, this data set provides and focuses on malware infection, propagation and communication with C&C server phases, the first stages of actual botnet deployment, while the other data sets focus on the last stages of the botnet life cycle, the attack phase [29]. In this relation, this data set can be seen as a complement of the already available data sets, which mainly focus on attack detection, the main outcome and part of the later stages of the botnet life cycle [22,29].

This paper is an extension of the original paper [21] which presented the novel Med-BIoT data set. This paper builds up on the original paper by adding more detailed analysis and comparison of publicly released data sets for IoT botnet detection (Sect. 2.4), recently published research literature on the field (Sect. 2.3) and, more significantly, extends the experimentation performed with MedBIoT data set to anomaly-based detection models (Sect. 4.2, anomaly detection). In this regard, while the original paper focused on supervised machine learning (i.e., classification) this paper provides tests and experimentation using unsupervised machine learning models (i.e., anomaly detection) which show and emphasize the goodness of the data to build any kind of effective machine learning-based intrusion detection system. The data set is available at https://cs.taltech.ee/research/data/medbiot/.

The paper structure is as follows: background information and literature review are provided in Sect. 2, while Sect. 3 explains the methodology implemented in the experimental setup. Section 4 shows a comprehensive overview of the main outcome of this research, a novel IoT botnet data set, and its verification. Lastly, Sect. 5 wraps up the study and highlights its major contributions.

2 Background Information

2.1 Botnets and DDoS Attacks

An IoT botnet is a specific type of computer botnet in which the compromised devices are IoT devices, thus presenting analogous schemes and dynamics as computer botnets. In this regard, when a device has its vulnerabilities exploited, thus being compromised, it becomes a *bot*. Bots are grouped on a large community of compromised devices, called *botnet*. A botnet is typically under the control of a malicious actor, the *botmaster*. The botmaster controls remotely the bot over the Internet, using Command & Control (C&C) servers [49]. This privileged access is unauthorized, there is no consent or awareness from the real owner of the compromised device.

IoT Botnets are used to perpetrate a wide scope of attacks, from massive SPAM and phishing campaigns to distributed denial-of-service (DDoS), the most common attack performed using botnets. A DDoS attack aims to compromise the availability of online resources, such as websites or services. This goal is achieved overloading the targeted server or network with more traffic than it can handle (e.g., sending an overwhelming amount of messages, connection requests or forged packets) and provoking the service or website to get saturated and crashing. As a result, the crashed machine becomes unavailable and unresponsive to the legitimate users requests [56]. In this regard, KrebsOnSecurity.com, the blog of the journalist Brian Krebs, was the target of a record-breaking attack (i.e., 620 Gpbs) in 2016. The attack, performed using Mirai botnet, was specifically tailored to tackle the site down [27]. Just a month later, the company OVH, a well-known hosting provider, was attacked by BashLite botnet hitting 1 Tbps and involving over 140.000 compromised cameras/dvr [43]. The same year, Dyn, a domain name system provider of well-known websites and services such as Netflix, PayPal, Visa, CNN and Amazon was attacked by 100.000 IoT devices belonging to Mirai botnet. The attack reached up to 1.2 Tbps, disrupting the services and causing the servers to be inoperative and the websites unavailable for several hours [23,56].

As a collateral damage from the attack and the loss of trust, it is estimated that Dyn lost around 8% of its customers (i.e., 14000 domains) [55]. And these attacks were just the beginning. Since then, IoT botnet-based attacks have not stopped. On the contrary, they have evolved in sophistication and capabilities, influenced by the public release of the source code behind some prominent botnet malware [2]. According to F-secure, in 2019, cyber attacks on IoT devices rouse 300%, reaching the unprecedented figure of 3 billion attacks [14]. Therefore, the threat is still alive and growing, mainly caused by the conjunction of factors such as the increase of the number of devices deployed worldwide and the inherent vulnerabilities that characterise them, which also poses at risk the data they carry and store, usually in an unencrypted manner [40], which might be deemed as confidential and related to medical or control issues in many applications. Nevertheless, one of the major threats is the leveraging of IoT endpoints, such as printers or fridges, as highly vulnerable entry points to wider and otherwise considered to be secure networks [14].

Consequently, cyber security for the IoT domain, in the form of early detection of such a threats becomes a key issue to detect and mitigate such attacks. For that purpose, intrusion detection systems are widely deployed network security tools aiming to detect security threats and attacks where preventive security measures are infeasible to implement [4,53].

2.2 Intrusion Detection Systems

The concept of intrusion can be defined as the set of actions or activities that compromise either one or more components of the CIA triad, the IT security model that refers to the confidentiality, integrity and availability elements of a specific system or entity. Whereas system refers not only to computers, firewall, network equipment, routers or networks but to any information technology system under the scope of the monitoring capabilities of an intrusion detection system [53]. Within this context, an intrusion detection system is a security tool which aims to detect and identify unauthorized accesses that target to misuse the system but also authorized accesses which abuse of their privileges within the system [53]. Four main approaches are used to build intrusion detection systems: misuse, anomaly, specification and hybrid [4,11,53,58]. They are outlined as follows:

- Misuse detection systems use known fingerprints or signatures of attacks stored in a database. The IDS tries to find a match between the known signatures and the current activities within the system. If a match is found, the alarm is raised about the detected suspicious behavior. Also known as signature-based systems, they are prone to be easily bypassed by unknown and novel attacks, where the signature is not yet available.
- Anomaly-based detection systems are dependant on the creation of a typical or normal activity profile or pattern. Current actions within the system are compared against the normality pattern. If the IDS finds a significant deviation or discrepancy from the normality model, the alarm is raised about the suspicious behavior. These systems are capable of detect novel attacks but they are prone to false alarms or false

positives (i.e., normal behavior is detected as malicious behavior) as the normality pattern might be difficult to model accurately. Thus, these systems are sensitive to the correctness of the normality model created.

- Specification-based detection systems use a combination of features of misuse and anomaly approaches. More concretely, anomaly-based principles are applied on a set of human-generated specifications or constraints about the normal or legitimate behavior. These systems aim to detect novel attacks using the anomaly principles and improve the limitations of anomaly-based models by reducing the amount of false positives.
- Hybrid detection systems combine any of the previous approaches, with the purpose of overcoming the weaknesses of a particular approach with the strengths of another.

The anomaly-based approach is one of the most used and effective detection methods, enabling to detect novel attacks with the inevitable trade-off of being sensitive to the correctness of the generated normality model. In this regard, statistical methods and machine learning algorithms are usually used to build the normality profile [58]. Therefore, valid behavioral models must be used to optimize the benefits obtained when using this approach, which is directly dependant on the training data used [8]. In the specific case of an IoT network, where a wide variety of devices may coexist, it is highly likely to have different normality profiles. This fact evidences the actual need of accurate IoT behavioral data which enable the implementation of effective anomaly-based intrusion detection systems. However, there is a significant lack of available data addressing the different network architectures, devices and behaviors that can be found in IoT networks and its major threats. As a result, in order to build intrusion detection systems for effective intrusion detection in IoT networks the use of proper IoT behavioral data is key.

2.3 Literature Review on Machine Learning-Based IDS

The application of machine learning to computer botnet detection first and lately to the specific case of IoT botnet detection has demonstrated encouraging results [31,58]. The noteworthy increase in IoT-related security incidents has provoked the reorientation of researchers' focus to the IoT field, thus promoting the investigation of effective and feasible IoT botnet detection methods involving anomaly-based machine learning approaches. The main aim of these approaches is to overcome the intrinsic hardware and software constraints and limited capabilities of these devices related to security [58].

In [36], Deep Autoencoders, Local Outlier Factor, One-Class Support Vector Machines and Isolation Forest models were built and tested using the N-baiot dataset. All models, except Isolation Forest, effectively detected all the simulated attacks using Mirai and BashLite malware. Deep Autoencoders provided the lowest ratio of false positives and provided the fastest attack detection times. Logistic Regression algorithm was used in [44] to estimate the likelihood for a device to be part of an IoT botnet by analyzing the connection initiation at the propagation stage. [30] developed an IoT botnet detection method combining Artificial Fish Swarm and Support Vector Machines algorithms. A different method was proposed in [48] using Convolutional Neural Networks and binary visualization technique feed with network traffic. The novel detection approach provided fast detection times for zero-day malware. A novel application for a text recognition deep learning algorithm (Bidirectional Long Short Term Memory based Recurrent Neural Network) was developed in [33]. The suggested approach demonstrated remarkable success on Mirai botnet attack detection. In [15], different network features were used to build and assess the accuracy of traditional machine learning algorithms such as k-Nearest Neighbors, Support Vector Machines, Decision Tree, Random Forest and Artificial Neural Networks to test their detection capabilities on Mirai DDoS attacks. Traditional unsupervised anomaly-based learning algorithms were used on [39] to perform botnet detection using reduced feature sets by applying different feature selection techniques. Dimensionality reduction and discriminatory feature analysis was performed in [3] to build fast, efficient and interpretable models. Hybrid feature selection methods were evaluated in [19] to induce faster and more efficient IoT botnet detection methods.

As can be noted, the implementation of anomaly detection requires the acquisition of malicious data that is tested against the normality patterns in order to assess the goodness of the proposed detection model. Therefore, the used data sets must provide both kinds of network traffic data in order to assess effectively the detection of the threats. In this regard, we provide demonstrability of the generated data set both on classification issues (i.e., supervised learning), for the easiness of interpretation of the results and comparison and also on anomaly-based scenarios (i.e., unsupervised learning). This facts evidences the suitability of this data set to build effective anomaly detection models.

2.4 IoT Botnet Attack Anomaly Detection Datasets

As already mentioned, an vast amount of scientific literature deals with the botnet detection phenomenon in computer networks [16,17], with many publicly available data sets for experimentation [47]. On the contrary, the more recent IoT botnet phenomenon has not attracted the required attention yet, evidenced by a notable scarcity on available data sources. Table 1 provides and overview of the publicly released IoT botnet data sets which are used to build and test IoT anomaly-based intrusion detection systems. As can be observed, a small amount of data sets are available, showing common and similar characteristics in their scenarios.

Mirai, the most prominent IoT botnet and perpetrator of record-breaking attacks [9], is deployed in the vast majority of the data sets (all except Bot-IoT). Mirai, "the future" in japanese, discovered in 2016, was designed to exploit vulnerabilities on low-secured Linux-based IoT devices (i.e., consumer devices such as cameras, printers and routers) to perform massive DDoS attacks [1,9,57]. Mirai is capable to perform 10 different DDoS attacks, which can be customized using several parameters [57]. Since the release of the source code, it has been used as a basis to create other IoT botnet malware [13], but also facilitated its deployment it in a contained manner in lab environments, improving knowledge and data set creation. BashLite, also known as Lizkebab, Qbot, Torlus, Gafgyt and LizardStresser, is a notorius botnet in the IoT botnet landscape and the second most deployed in the data sets. Discovered in 2014 and made public in 2015, it is the antecessor of Mirai [45]. As one of the oldest IoT malware, there are many variants of this malware in the wild. Since its inception, BashLite was designed to exploit devices running BusyBox (e.g., routers) evolving later to exploit any IoT device, thus enhancing its possibilities to be perform large-scale DDoS attacks [54].

Half of the data sets use emulated IoT devices, usually running on a *Raspberry Pi*. Emulators are a cheap and more scalable alternative to the usage of real IoT devices in lab environments, thus preferred in some cases. The IoT landscape embraces a wide variety of different devices used for different applications, so that is also the case for the type of devices used on the data sets, showing a great variability among data sets. Camera is the only IoT device type that can be found in more than 2 data sets. Regarding the data format, all the studies except one provide the raw *pcap* file while some also provide an structured feature data set. N-Baiot data set provides only structured data thus restricting the possibilities of perform further experimentation using this data set.

When analyzing the data sets based on the botnet lifetime cycle they encompass [22], it is shown that none of the data sets encompass all the botnet life-cycle steps, thus focusing the majority of them on the attack and post-attack phases. The data sets simulate different attacks that botnets can perform and also the scanning attack for the recruitment of new members, part of the post-attack stage. MedBIoT data set is the only data set that deals with the early stages of botnet deployment, focusing on formation and C&C stages, two of the core components of botnet deployment [29]. In this sense, this data set provides the opportunity to perform early detection of the threat, previous to the perpetration of an attack, key to prevent attacks and botnet growth.

3   Method

The main contribution of this study is the generation of a fully-labelled behavioral IoT data set and the demonstration of its suitability to induce effective machine learning-based detection systems. The data set is composed of normal and actual botnet malicious network data acquired in a medium-sized IoT network infrastructure (i.e., 83 IoT devices). The focus was placed on the acquisition of network traffic from all the end-points and servers during the initial propagation steps performed by Mirai, BashLite and Torii botnet malware.

3.1   IoT Network Topology

The network infrastructure topology built for the purpose of this research is provided in Fig. 1. As can be observed, it is composed of three connected networks: internet network, monitoring network and IoT LAN network. Their roles, tasks and components are described as follows:

- The internet network is directly connected to the Internet and provides internet connectivity to the whole setup, for the initial configuration of different devices. A different sub-network mask is on place to restrict the connectivity between networks.
- The monitoring network provides the storage and processing capabilities for the data set creation. It receives the network data from the switch. It is composed of:

Table 1. Data sets for IoT anomaly-based IDS.

Name	Botnet	Number of devices	Device type	Real or Emulated	Net. Size	Data format	Date	References
N-Baiot	Mirai BashLite	9	Doorbell Webcam Thermostat Baby monitor Security Camera	R	Small	structured	2018	[35,36]
IoT host-based datasets for ID research	Hajime Aidra BashLite Mirai Doflo Tsunami Wroba	2	Multimedia Center Security Camera	E	Small	pcap structured	2018	[6,7]
IoT Network Intrusion Dataset	Mirai	2	Speaker Wi-Fi Camera	R	Small	pcap	2019	[24]
Bot-IoT	No actual malware - simulated	5	Refrigerator Smart Garage door Weather Monitoring Smart Lights Smart thermostat	E	Small	pcap structured	2019	[26,38]
Aposemat IoT-23	Mirai Torii Trojan BashLite Kenjiro Okiru Hakai IRCBot Muhstik Hide&Seek	4	Raspberry Pi Lamp Amazon Echo Lock	R	Small	pcap	2020	[41]
MedBIoT	Mirai BashLite Torii	83	Switch Fan Light bulb Lock	E+R	Medium	pcap structured	2020	[20,21]

- Capture server: responsible for the collection and storage of all the network packets captured within the whole network infrastructure. In our setup, *Tcpdump* was used to monitor and log the network traffic. Data was stored as *pcap* file format, which was later further processed by the SIEM server.
- Security Information and Event Management (SIEM) server: responsible for data indexing, filtering, analysis and data set generation (i.e., data processing and labelling). In our setup, the SIEM server was a *Splunk* software instance.
- The IoT LAN network is a local area network (LAN) which allows malware spreading in a contained manner. It is composed of both real and virtual IoT devices. These devices generate all the behavioral traffic (i.e., benign and malicious) that is collected by the monitoring network. Containerization software (i.e., *Docker*) was used to

deploy the virtual devices. The composition and capabilities of the network devices are outlined as follows:

- Router: this networking device is responsible for the creation of an isolated network segment thus allowing only communication internally between devices. This is achieved using firewall rules. It also assigns IP addresses to the internal devices using Dynamic Host Configuration Protocol (DHCP).
- Switch: this networking device is responsible for the acquisition and transfer of the network packets. This is achieved using *port mirroring* technique. *Port mirroring* is used to clone and transfer network packets flowing through a port to another port. It can be made in real time and without any affectation on the network's performance. In this setup, all the data generated by all devices was captured and transferred to the monitoring network by this mean.
- IoT Management System: this software allows the management of all the IoT devices within the network in a single and centralized point. In our setup, it was deployed using *Hassio* software on a *Raspberry Pi*, allowing to simulate the same network behavior of the real implementations. Four types of IoT devices were emulated: switch, light bulb, lock and fan. Each type allows the remote management of different features. For instance, the emulated fan allows to turn on/off, speed selection, oscillation state and get current fan state.
- Virtual IoT devices: these IoT devices were virtualized using *Docker* containers. They are deployed using a *Raspberry Pi* thus emulating the behavior of an IoT device.
- Wireless Access Point: this networking device provided network connection to the non-ethernet compatible devices. To avoid the existence of duplicated IP addresses, it is configured to delegate on the router the capabilities of assigning IP addresses (via DHCP).
- BashLite C&C server: this server acts as the command and control unit for the BashLite malware botnet. In order to allow the spreading of the malware within the network, web and FTP services are installed. It also performs the compilation of the malware binaries used to propagate the malware infection.
- Mirai C&C server: this server acts as the command and control unit for the Mirai malware botnet. Role and tasks are analogous to BashLite C&C server.
- DNS server sinkhole: this server has two main tasks. It provides domain name resolution for the Mirai botnet and it acts as a sinkhole for the connection requests to the domains that Torii malware performs. This task provides effective malware contention within the network by avoiding the actual connection between Torii and the domain of its remote C&C server.
- Physical devices: these are the real IoT devices deployed within the network. Three different devices were used: Sonoff tasmota smart switch, TpLink smart switch and TpLink smart bulb. All these devices allow external device management and control of different features. For instance, the light bulb provides control of turn on/off, light intensity and get the device status.

To create a medium-sized network, 80 virtual devices are created and 3 physical devices are deployed. As a result, the total amount of IoT devices deployed in the LAN network is 83. The virtual devices have ARM architecture, inherited from the *Raspberry*

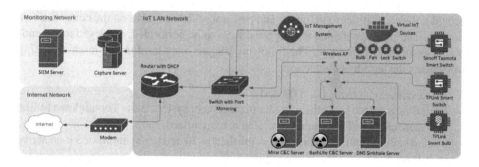

Fig. 1. Medium-sized IoT network topology. Extracted from the original paper [21].

Pi used to create them. All the real devices have MIPS architecture. The architecture of the device determines the malware binary used to infect the device. Having different types of architectures generates a wider variety of devices which enriches the spectrum of the data collected.

Regarding the virtual devices deployed, 20 instances of each type were created (i.e., fan, switch, lock and light bulb). All these devices provided different features to be controlled remotely. More specifically, all the devices allowed to active/deactivate them (on/off status). Additionally, the fan allowed to control its speed and oscillation and the light bulb its intensity.

Regarding the real devices, one instance of each type was in place (i.e., two different switches and a light bulb). All the devices allowed to active/deactivate them remotely. Additionally, the light bulb allowed control of intensity.

3.2   IoT Behavior

To simulate the behavior of IoT devices different approaches can be used, ranging from the manual usage of the devices aiming to mimic the behavior to a more automated solution using *scripts* to trigger scheduled functions/tasks. The quality and consistency of the simulated behavior is the most important element on the generation of a high quality data set that could be used as a realistic input data on effective intrusion detection systems. In such cases, the collection of relevant and real statistics of normal usage patterns offers a realistic baseline for the behavior simulation. As an example, in a average living room, a light bulb has a average usage of 1.7 h per day while in a kitchen it reaches 2.3 h [18]. These statistics provided the baseline for the simulation of normal behavior in our experimental setting. In the case of malware, the behavior was simulated by the execution of the different modules within the botnet, providing a real output of the actual botnet malware behavior.

Normal Behavior. An automated approach is selected for the simulation of the benign or normal behavior. It takes into account the architecture of the device and its performed using a Python *script* and MQ Telemetry Transport (MQTT) protocol. MQTT is a communication protocol used to manage IoT devices. The IoT management system provides the capabilities to automate and perform scheduled tasks on the controlled IoT devices. The *script* contained the trigger actions to be performed, conveyed to the end-points using MQTT protocol. The following triggers were used in this research setting to simulate the legitimate behavior:

- All devices are activated at 8.00 AM
- Each time a device state changes, the management system starts a countdown for the next state change. The countdown value is randomized.
- The maximum limit of changes is established in 20 and a maximum of 3 h on active state is set.
- All devices are deactivated at 07.00 PM
- To simulate a working environment, the execution of the triggers is limited to week-days

These triggers provoked the generation of network packets along the network, which are captured and stored. The acquired network packets provide the following communication data: time, protocol used, TCP stream, TCP stream size, source IP, destination IP, MAC addresses, TCP raw message and response code.

Malicious Behavior. Three prominent botnet malware are deployed within the controlled environment. Mirai [1], BashLite [32] and Torii [28] actual malware are used to generate the malicious behavior. Mirai and BashLite botnets have been widely researched and their source code is publicly available. For that reason, their deployment is fully controlled within the experimental setup using a Command & Control server for each botnet and modifying the source code to connect only with each specific C&C server. On the contrary, Torii source code is not available, thus actual samples were used to deploy it. The samples were obtained from Hybrid Analysis archive [12]. To safely contain Torii malware within the network and avoid the connection with its real C&C server, extra contention measures are in place. As a result, Mirai, BashLite and Torii malware propagation is performed and controlled in our restricted network setting using different strategies, they are summarized in the following paragraphs.

- **Botnet Malware Propagation Techniques.** Three botnet malware are deployed within the controlled environment. Mirai and BashLite source code was publicly released, thus facilitating their contention in a similar fashion. Torii needed special measures for its unknown spreading and behavior patterns.
  - Mirai and *Yakuza* version of BashLite are configured and executed after modifying the malware source code to connect with the corresponding C&C servers within the controlled network. Mirai and BashLite use dropper as a method to download and install the appropriate infection binaries in the targets, according to their architecture. Once the binary is executed, the bot daemon will run and the compromised device will become a bot.
  - Torii behavior has not been so deeply studied yet so its deployment involves further risks. To contain and mitigate the risk of improper use of the infected devices by the actual botmaster, firewall rules and a DNS sinkhole are used. Thus Torii connection attempts with the remote C&C server are permanently

denied and redirected to the sinkhole. As a result of the actual lack of knowledge about Torii spreading methods and information about its source code, the infection binary is manually deployed in the infected devices. The sample used is tailored to infect ARM devices. The malware is run by executing the binary as root in the target devices, allowing to spread the malware through the IoT devices.

- **Botnet Contention Methods.** One of the greatest risks of deploying actual malware is the abuse of the infected devices by the real attackers. In the case of Torii, its unknown spreading methods and lack of knowledge about this malware this implies a greater challenge. In the eventuality of an unsuccessful malware contention, real attackers might be able to control the infected devices and use them to perpetrate attacks or collect relevant data. In this regard, two major risks are identified and addressed:

  1. The possibility of hidden code in Mirai's source code to establish connection with the actual C&C server
  2. Lack of knowledge about Torii's spreading techniques and capabilities

  Although Mirai spreading method is well-known, extra security measures are taken to contain the malware effectively. Firewall rules and a DNS sinkhole are in place to avoid any effective connection to the real C&C servers. The sinkhole purpose is to redirect the connection attempts, resolving the name resolution request with a controlled IP address. The firewall rules placed on the router allow to control and block traffic based on known network masks.

In this experimental setup, the three botnet malware were deployed at different times within 6 days (i.e., each let run free for 2 consecutive days). The main aim was to obtain relevant botnet data while eliminating the risk of data overlapping between different malware. Additionally, one of the Mirai malware capabilities is to detect other malware running on devices and remove it, to take the single control of it. A limited and randomized number of devices are infected for each botnet deployment. Thus, 40 devices were infected using BashLite malware, selected in a pseudo-randomized way by constraining the scope of the reachable devices. 25 devices were infected by Mirai malware, limited by restricting the internal scanner to spread on the network IP ranges. Finally, Torii malware was manually deployed in 12 devices, all under the scope of the DNS sinkhole.

3.3 IoT Behavior Verification

The generated data set was further processed and machine learning models were induced. The purpose of this experimental implementation is to verify the suitability of the generated data set for machine learning-based intrusion detection systems. In this regard, classification and anomaly detection machine learning models were built. They are briefly described as follows:

- Classification models are a kind of supervised learning which main aim is to correctly predict the class or label of an unknown data point based on specific features, also called predictors, found on the training data provided during the model building phase. When the data points are labelled into two mutually exclusive classes or categories (e.g., legitimate and malicious traffic), binary classification is used, while when more than two categories are present in the data (e.g., legitimate, Mirai, Bash-Lite and Torii), multiclass or multinomial classification is performed. In order to validate the outcome of this research, both approaches are implemented and validated using k-fold cross validation.

- Anomaly detection models are a type of unsupervised learning that aim to detect and identify observations that do not conform with an expected pattern or feature values in a data set. Commonly, legitimate data are used to build models that aim to detect and identify observations (i.e., malware generated points) that deviate significantly from the learnt expected normality pattern. Eventually, any data point that deviates significantly, thus seemingly not belonging to the same (legitimate) data distribution, is detected and categorized them as anomalous data points or anomalies by the learning models.

Data features are extracted from the *pcap* files acquired in this experimental setup. These features are used as predictors/inputs for all the machine learning models. More specifically, the features used in this research are computed as in [37]. Thus, 100 statistical features are generated from the network traffic, encompassing different time windows. Table 2 provides an overview of the extracted features. As it is shown, statistical features are generated for 4 main categories and 5 time windows for each one.

Table 2. Feature categories.

Category	Statistic	Time window	Features
Host-MAC&IP	Packet count Mean	100 ms 500 ms	15
Network Jitter	Variance	1.5 s	15
Channel	Packet count Mean Variance Magnitude Radius Covariance	10 s 1 min	35
Socket	Correlation		35

After the extraction of the features, a random sample for each class is generated and used to train and test 10-fold cross validated machine learning models. Four traditional machine learning classification algorithms are implemented: k-Nearest Neighbors (k-NN), Support Vector Machines (SVM), Decision Tree (DT) and Random Forest (RF). The main objective of these classifier models is to demonstrate the suitability of the generated data set for machine learning-based anomaly detection and classification models. No hyper-parameter optimization was performed, leaving room for improvement on the induced models. In this regard, default *scikit_learn* library (version 0.22.2) values are used. For each model, four performance metrics are reported: accuracy, precision, recall and F_1 score. They are defined as follows:

- Accuracy: ratio of the correctly classified test instances from all test instances.
- Precision: fraction of positive instances correctly classified among all the positive classified instances.
- Recall: fraction of positive instances correctly classified among all the actual positive instances.
- F_1 score: harmonic mean of precision and recall.

All the metrics reported range from 0 to 1. In this sense, a reported value closer to 1 is generally deemed as a positive or good result for the given metric while a value close to 0 as a bad or negative performance. Thus, for classification tasks, the greater the value the better the classifier's performance on label discrimination task, thus evidencing that the data and the classifier are suitable for that purpose. In our case, obtaining values closer to 1 in all classifiers' metrics could be used to infer that the data is suitable for machine learning-based IoT botnet detection and also that the data labels (e.g., legitimate and malware) can be effectively discriminated.

4   Results

4.1   IoT Botnet Data Set

All the network packets generated within the IoT LAN network were collected and redirected using port mirroring to the monitoring network. There, a SIEM software instance was used to perform data processing and labelling, creating the final data set. The data set is generated in two formats: structured (i.e., tabular features are extracted from the raw data) and unstructured (i.e., raw *pcap* files). The number of packets captured and provided within the whole data set are provided in Table 3.

Table 3. Data set composition.

Data source	Number of devices	Number of packets	Proportion
Normal	83	12,540,478	70.27%
BashLite	40	4,143,276	23.22%
Mirai	25	842,674	4.72%
Torii	12	319,139	1.79%
All	All	17,845,567	100%

As can be observed, the majority of the traffic is deemed as normal or legitimate IoT traffic (i.e., 70.27%) while around 30% is originated and acquired from different IoT botnet malware sources. The SIEM software used (i.e., *Splunk*) allowed further analysis and acquisition of more fine-grained of the communication details. In this regard, 32% of the normal network traffic is related to system updates, 53% to device communication (i.e., MQTT protocol) and 15% to other network data (e.g., TLS errors, pings, etc.). Regarding the malicious data, 68% of the traffic is related to malware propagation actions while 32% to direct communication between bots and C&C servers. It is worth to note that Mirai and BashLite source codes were configured to perform these different types of communications using different ports, thus facilitating the posterior data analysis. Torii's data only includes traffic regarding the initial infection of the devices as the contention measures were explicitly established to avoid any remote communication with the actual C&C, thus preventing posterior botnet events such as propagation. The generated data set is made publicly available in the following url: https://cs.taltech.ee/research/data/medbiot/.

4.2 IoT Behavior Verification

Binary Classification. Four traditional and widely used machine learning classification models for binary classification (i.e., two class classification) are induced and 10-fold cross validated. To perform such a classification task, the data is split into two groups or labels: legitimate/normal and malware. Thus the malware class contains mixed data from the three malware deployed. More specifically, the legitimate class data is composed of 15000 randomly selected data points from the acquired legitimate traffic. The malware class is composed of 5000 randomly selected data points for each of the malware deployed within the network, summing up to 15000 data points for this class. As a result, a balanced data set is generated and used for the binary classification task. The results of models built are provided in Table 4. The table does not reflect the performance metrics for Support Vector Machines algorithm as it showed poor performance in all the assessed metrics.

Table 4. Binary classification.

Model	Acc.	Prec.	Rec.	F_1
k-NN	0.8871	0.9034	0.8871	0.8842
DT	0.9541	0.9582	0.9541	0.9538
RF	0.9702	0.9731	0.9702	0.9700

Table 5. RF confusion matrix.

		Predicted	
		Malware	Legitimate
Actual	Malware	1443	57
	Legitimate	19	1481

As can be observed, Random Forest model is able to discriminate effectively the vast majority of the network traffic, as over 97% of the data points are detected correctly. k-NN and Decision Tree models reported lower discriminatory capabilities but with performance metrics over 88% and 95%, respectively. The confusion matrix provided in Table 5, extracted from a Random Forest model, confirms that the mixed malware traffic is effectively discriminated from the normal traffic with a few misclassified points. As already stated, SVM results are not reported as they showed poor performance on all metrics. This fact may suggest that the data is not linearly separable, thus linear classifiers such as SVM or Logistic Regression may not be suitable for the classification task using this data set. Nevertheless, the results obtained using the other algorithms evidence the effective capabilities of machine learning approaches to detect botnet malware traffic, in the first stages (i.e., infection, propagation and communication with the C&C server stages) and disregarding the malware type. Furthermore, it is demonstrated that the data set generated in this research is suitable to be used as a medium-sized realistic IoT data set for IoT botnet detection scenarios and IDS training and testing purposes.

Multiclass Classification. For this task, the data set was divided in four classes or labels according to the data source: normal, Mirai, BashLite and Torii. Four-class or multiclass classification models were induced and 10-fold cross validated using the same algorithms as in the binary task. The data set used was generated by random selection of 10000 data points for each of the classes, summing up to 40000 data points. The data set is balanced, thus data points were evenly distributed within the four labels. The purpose of this task is not only to test discrimination capabilities of legitimate/malware labels but also the discrimination of the specific malware source. Table 6 shows the results obtained for this task. As in the binary approach, Support Vector Machines algorithm is not reported, showing a poor performance in all metrics.

Table 6. Multiclass classification.

Model	Acc.	Prec.	Rec.	F_1
k-NN	0.8990	0.9073	0.8990	0.8958
DT	0.9379	0.9478	0.9379	0.9347
RF	0.9617	0.9692	0.9617	0.9602

Table 7. RF confusion matrix.

		Predicted			
		Mirai	BashLite	Torii	Leg.
Actual	Mirai	983	3	3	11
	BashLite	14	974	2	10
	Torii	5	5	978	12
	Leg.	11	3	3	983

As can be observed, in a similar fashion as in the binary models, Random Forest model outperforms Decision Tree and k-NN algorithms in the multiclass classification task. More specifically, RF algorithm provides similar discrimination performance in the multiclass task and in the binary setting, achieving over 96% accuracy in all metrics. The Random Forest model confusion matrix provided in Table 7, emphasizes the significant accuracy of this classification model in all cases, not being significantly biased towards any of the possible classes. These results suggest that network traffic source can be effectively discriminated, even in the earliest stages of botnet infection. It also demonstrates that the learning capabilities of machine learning-based detection methods can be accurate both in the general detection task (i.e., legitimate vs. malware) and in the detection of different sources of malicious traffic in medium-sized IoT networks.

Anomaly Detection. This task involves the identification of abnormal or unusual observations within the data distribution, the so-called *anomalies*. In our case, these abnormal observations are the ones generated by the non-normal behavior of the IoT devices, mainly caused by malware activity. Depending on the purpose of anomaly detection it can be further divided into *outlier* detection and *novelty* detection. In outlier detection, the training data set contains outliers (i.e., observations that deviate significantly from the rest) and the goal of the algorithms is to identify regions where data is most concentrated thus ignoring the data that lie far from that regions, the *outliers*. The observations on concentrated areas, which belong to the same data distribution, are called *inliers*. In the case of novelty detection it is assumed that the training data set does not contain outliers and the goal is, given a new observation, detect whether it can be categorized as an outlier or an inlier. In this case, the outlier observation is called *novelty*. Both anomaly detection approaches were used and tested with the data set generated in this research. The anomaly detection algorithm used was Local Outlier Factor (LOF), which is capable to perform both novelty and outlier detection tasks. LOF's algorithm *Scikit-learn* library implementation was used to build and test all the anomaly-based models [46].

In order to build the models, the data was sampled using random sampling. Thus, for each benign data set 100.000 observations were randomly selected (i.e., 90.000 for training and 10.000 for testing) and 10.000 observations for each malware data set (i.e., BashLite, Mirai and Torii). Prior to induce the models, data was pre-processed by using standardization and Principal Component Analysis (PCA) to reduce data dimensionality, from high dimensionality data to lower dimensionality (i.e., ranging from 10 to 30 Principal Components on all induced models). Principal components are new generated features by PCA algorithm, created from the linear combination of the original features of the data set, aiming to capture the maximum variance within the data points. Based on that, the new generated features possess no real meaning or category and they are just called Principal Components or PC (i.e., 1PC is the first principal component). Two different scenarios were tested in the anomaly-based induced models. In the first scenario, legitimate data captured during the time a specific malware was running was used to build the models. The testing sets correspond to held-out legitimate data and malware data from that specific collection time-frame. For example, as can be observed in the first row in Table 8, the training data corresponds to legitimate data acquired during the deployment of BashLite malware. The testing samples correspond to legitimate data from the same period of time and BashLite malware generated data. The detection performances for this first scenario are provided in Table 8. The column *training*, specifies the normal data training source used to build the corresponding model while the *test malware* and *test normal* refer to the source of data used for testing purposes. The *mixed total* column provides the average of the previous two columns, as the same amount of legitimate and malware instances were tested against the model (i.e., 10.000 samples). The *All* value refers to a stratified mix of the legitimate data (i.e., 1/3 of each of the previous data sets). The performance metric used is accuracy, which provides the ratio of correctly classified instances among all the testing samples. Accuracy ratios closer to 1 indicate a good performance metric while closer to 0 a poor detection performance.

Table 8. Novelty detection performance - first scenario.

Training	Test normal	Test malware	Mixed total
BashLite	0.9486	0.9628	0.9557
Mirai	0.9331	0.8552	0.8942
Torii	0.9433	0.9515	0.9474
All	0.9444	0.9129	0.9286

As can be observed on Table 8, models built with BashLite, Torii and combined legitimate data provide detection performances over 91% on malware and over 93% on the held-out legitimate data. Legitimate data belonging to Mirai deployment provides less accuracy on the malware data and test data, suggesting that the malware is more similar to legitimate traffic but prone to be discriminated effectively. It is worth to note that these models are not optimized and there is room to improvement as mostly default values were used on the generation of the models. According to the results, BashLite malware provides a differentiated profile from normal traffic that make the models more effective in the detection of this specific malware. Torii and the mixed model (i.e., using stratified randomly sampled legitimate data from the three data sets) provide high accuracy ratios for malware detection based on anomaly models. In any case, these results evidence IoT malware can be discriminated from legitimate and effectively detected using anomaly-based detection models in the early stages of a botnet deployment (i.e., prior to any attack).

In the second scenario, the same models built on the first scenario were tested against other test sets belonging to different malware data. For example, the first row in Table 9, the training data corresponds to legitimate data acquired during the deployment of BashLite malware. The testing samples correspond to the same time-frame BashLite generated data, and also data belonging to the deployments of Torii and Mirai malware. This setting allows to test the goodness of the anomaly detection models to detect different types of malware. The column *training* in Table 9 specifies the normal data training source used to build the corresponding model while the rest of columns specify what malware data test was tested. The *All* value refers to a stratified mix of the legitimate data (i.e., 1/3 of each of the previous data sets). The *Test Mixed* column provides the performance when a mixed data set of the three malware data sets was combined and tested against the model. This test data set was generated using stratified random sampling (i.e., the same amount of samples extracted from each malware data set, 33%). The performance metric reported is the detection accuracy.

Table 9. Novelty detection performance - second scenario.

Training	Test Mirai	Test Torii	Test BashLite	Test mixed
BashLite	0.9066	0.9842	0.9628	0.9536
Mirai	0.8552	0.9665	0.9643	0.9262
Torii	0.8839	0.9515	0.9618	0.9120
All	0.8407	0.9594	0.9615	0.9074

The results provided in Table 9 suggest that the anomaly-based detection models built in the first scenario are capable to detect effectively not only its specific malware but also the other IoT botnet malware. With the exception of the detection of Mirai malware, which is slightly worse than the other malware, the detection ratios are over

91% in all models, whatever the data source used, except the Mirai-based model. These results emphasize the goodness of the anomaly-based models to detect malware effectively and the goodness of the generated data set to build effective anomaly-based IoT malware detection models on early stages of botnet deployment.

5 Conclusions

The Internet of Things is growing exponentially and these devices will become ubiquitous in the following years. This fact, in combination with the traditional lack of security measures associated to them, make IoT devices an appealing objective for cyber attackers. The vulnerable IoT devices are compromised and become part of a *botnet*, which is mainly used as amplification platform for cyber attacks. In this regard, botnets have been used to perpetrate massive DDoS attacks against companies and individuals, leading to nefarious consequences. As a result, the security of these devices is a critical issue to be addressed. The most recent solutions involve machine learning techniques, which are providing notable and promising results.

The performance of machine learning models is directly related with the amount of data used to build the models and its quality to capture the phenomenon. In the specific case of IoT botnet detection, there is a remarkable lack of data sets which limits the possibilities of building efficient machine learning-based models. This paper elaborates on the original research where MedBIoT data set was introduced [21] by adding more experimentation with the acquired data, demonstrating the suitability of MedBIoT data set to build effective machine learning-based IoT botnet detection models. As provided in [21], the data set focuses on the early stages of botnet deployment in a medium-sized IoT network (i.e., 83 IoT devices). Three prominent botnet malware were deployed (i.e., Torii, Mirai and BashLite) in different IoT devices within the network. The network traffic data is provided labelled according to its source: botnet malware or normal.

Supervised (i.e., classification) and unsupervised (i.e., anomaly detection) machine learning models are induced and tested. The obtained results evidence the goodness of MedBIoT data set to build effective IoT botnet detection models, using both machine learning-based approaches. In this regard, the performance metrics obtained in all the tested scenarios (i.e., over 85% in all cases) prove that IoT botnet detection can be achieved with high accuracy even in the early stages of botnet deployment, thus preventing the attack phase and avoiding its nefarious consequences. As a result, MedBIoT data set complements the existing data sets, which mainly focus on attack scenarios, by putting emphasis on the early stages of botnet deployment. Early detection may help to prevent attacks and botnet growth in a significant manner.

The extensive experimentation performed in this research proves the suitability of MedBIoT data set as a reliable data source for IoT botnet detection in general and intrusion detection systems' testing, design and deployment in particular. The data set is available at https://cs.taltech.ee/research/data/medbiot/.

References

1. Antonakakis, M., et al.: Understanding the mirai botnet. In: 26th $USENIX$ Security Symposium ($\{USENIX\}$ Security 17). pp. 1093–1110 (2017)
2. Asokan, A.: Massive botnet attack used more than 400,000 IoT devices (2019). https://www.bankinfosecurity.com/massive-botnet-attack-used-more-than-400000-iot-devices-a-12841
3. Bahşi, H., Nõmm, S., La Torre, F.B.: Dimensionality reduction for machine learning based IoT botnet detection. In: 2018 15th International Conference on Control, Automation, Robotics and Vision (ICARCV), pp. 1857–1862 (2018)
4. Benkhelifa, E., Welsh, T., Hamouda, W.: A critical review of practices and challenges in intrusion detection systems for IoT: toward universal and resilient systems. IEEE Commun. Surv. Tutor. **20**(4), 3496–3509 (2018)
5. Bertino, E., Islam, N.: Botnets and internet of things security. Computer **2**, 76–79 (2017)
6. Bezerra, V.H., da Costa, V.G.T., Martins, R.A., Junior, S.B., Miani, R.S., Zarpelao, B.B.: Data set (2018). http://www.uel.br/grupo-pesquisa/secmq/dataset-iot-security.html
7. Bezerra, V.H., da Costa, V.G.T., Martins, R.A., Junior, S.B., Miani, R.S., Zarpelao, B.B.: Providing IoT host-based datasets for intrusion detection research. In: Anais do XVIII Simpósio Brasileiro em Segurança da Informação e de Sistemas Computacionais, pp. 15–28. SBC (2018)
8. Bolzoni, D.: Revisiting Anomaly-based Network Intrusion Detection Systems. University of Twente, Enschede (2009)
9. Bonderud, D.: Leaked mirai malware boosts IoT insecurity threat level (2016). https://securityintelligence.com/news/leaked-mirai-malware-boosts-iot-insecurity-threat-level/
10. Bosche, A., Crawford, D., Jackson, D., Schallehn, M., Schorling, C.: Unlocking opportunities in the internet of things (2018). https://www.bain.com/contentassets/5aa3a678438846289af59f62e62a3456/bain_brief_unlocking_opportunities_in_the_internet_of_things.pdf
11. Butun, I., Morgera, S.D., Sankar, R.: A survey of intrusion detection systems in wireless sensor networks. IEEE Commun. Surv. Tutor. **16**(1), 266–282 (2013)
12. Crowdstrike: Hybrid analysis (2019). https://www.hybrid-analysis.com/
13. DeBeck, C., Chung, J., McMillen, D.: I can't believe mirais: tracking the infamous IoT malware (2019). https://securityintelligence.com/posts/i-cant-believe-mirais-tracking-the-infamous-iot-malware-2/
14. Doffman, Z.: Cyberattacks on IoT devices surge 300% in 2019, 'measured in billions', report claims (2019). https://www.forbes.com/sites/zakdoffman/2019/09/14/dangerous-cyberattacks-on-iot-devices-up-300-in-2019-now-rampant-report-claims/#574229995892
15. Doshi, R., Apthorpe, N., Feamster, N.: Machine learning DDoS detection for consumer internet of things devices. In: 2018 IEEE Security and Privacy Workshops (SPW), pp. 29–35. IEEE (2018)
16. Feily, M., Shahrestani, A., Ramadass, S.: A survey of botnet and botnet detection. In: 2009 Third International Conference on Emerging Security Information, Systems and Technologies, pp. 268–273. IEEE (2009)
17. Garcia, S., Grill, M., Stiborek, J., Zunino, A.: An empirical comparison of botnet detection methods. Compu. Secur. **45**, 100–123 (2014)
18. Gifford, W.R., Goldberg, M.L., Tanimoto, P.M., Celnicker, D.R., Poplawski, M.E.: Residential lighting end-use consumption study: estimation framework and initial estimates (2012). https://www1.eere.energy.gov/buildings/publications/pdfs/ssl/2012_residential-lighting-study.pdf
19. Guerra-Manzanares, A., Bahsi, H., Nõmm, S.: Hybrid feature selection models for machine learning based botnet detection in IoT networks. In: 2019 International Conference on Cyberworlds (CW), pp. 324–327 (2019)

20. Guerra-Manzanares, A., Medina-Galindo, J., Bahsi, H., Nõmm, S.: Medbiot data set archive (2020). https://cs.taltech.ee/research/data/medbiot/

21. Guerra-Manzanares, A., Medina-Galindo, J., Bahsi, H., Nõmm, S.: Medbiot: generation of an IoT botnet dataset in a medium-sized IoT network. In: Proceedings of the 6th International Conference on Information Systems Security and Privacy - Volume 1: ICISSP, pp. 207–218. INSTICC, SciTePress (2020). https://doi.org/10.5220/0009187802070218

22. Hachem, N., Mustapha, Y.B., Granadillo, G.G., Debar, H.: Botnets: lifecycle and taxonomy. In: 2011 Conference on Network and Information Systems Security, pp. 1–8. IEEE (2011)

23. Hilton, S.: DYN analysis summary of Friday October 21 attack (2016). https://dyn.com/blog/dyn-analysis-summary-of-friday-october-21-attack/

24. Kang, H., Ahn, D.H., Lee, G.M., Yoo, J.D., Park, K.H., Kim, H.K.: IoT network intrusion dataset(2019). http://dx.doi.org/10.21227/q70p-q449

25. Kolias, C., Kambourakis, G., Stavrou, A., Voas, J.: Ddos in the IoT: Mirai and other botnets. Computer 50(7), 80–84 (2017)

26. Koroniotis, N., Moustafa, N., Sitnikova, E., Turnbull, B.: Towards the development of realistic botnet dataset in the internet of things for network forensic analytics: Bot-IoT dataset. Fut. Gene. Comput. Syst. 100, 779–796 (2019)

27. Krebs, B.: Krebsonsecurity hit with record Ddos (2016). https://krebsonsecurity.com/2016/09/krebsonsecurity-hit-with-record-ddos/

28. Kroustek, J., Iliushin, V., Shirokova, A., Neduchal, J., Hron, M.: Torii botnet - not another mirai variant (2018). https://blog.avast.com/new-torii-botnet-threat-research

29. Leonard, J., Xu, S., Sandhu, R.: A framework for understanding botnets. In: 2009 International Conference on Availability, Reliability and Security, pp. 917–922. IEEE (2009)

30. Lin, K.C., Chen, S.Y., Hung, J.C.: Botnet detection using support vector machines with artificial fish swarm algorithm. J. Appl. Math. 2014 (2014)

31. Livadas, C., Walsh, R., Lapsley, D.E., Strayer, W.T.: Using machine learning techniques to identify botnet traffic. In: LCN, pp. 967–974. Citeseer (2006)

32. Marzano, A., et al.: The evolution of bashlite and mirai IoT botnets. In: 2018 IEEE Symposium on Computers and Communications (ISCC), pp. 00813–00818. IEEE (2018)

33. McDermott, C.D., Majdani, F., Petrovski, A.V.: Botnet detection in the internet of things using deep learning approaches. In: 2018 International Joint Conference on Neural Networks (IJCNN), pp. 1–8. IEEE (2018)

34. McKinsey: What's new with the internet of things? (2017). https://www.mckinsey.com/industries/semiconductors/our-insights/whats-new-with-the-internet-of-things

35. Meidan, Y., et al.: detection_of_iot_botnet_attacks_n_baiot data set (2018). http://archive.ics.uci.edu/ml/datasets/detection_of_IoT_botnet_attacks_N_BaIoT

36. Meidan, Y., et al.: N-baiot-network-based detection of IoT botnet attacks using deep autoencoders. IEEE Perva. Comput. 17(3), 12–22 (2018)

37. Mirsky, Y., Doitshman, T., Elovici, Y., Shabtai, A.: Kitsune: an ensemble of autoencoders for online network intrusion detection. arXiv preprint arXiv:1802.09089 (2018)

38. Moustafa, N.: The bot-IoT dataset. http://dx.doi.org/10.21227/r7v2-x988 (2019). 10.21227/r7v2-x988

39. Nõmm, S., Bahşi, H.: Unsupervised anomaly based botnet detection in IoT networks. In: 2018 17th IEEE International Conference on Machine Learning and Applications (ICMLA), pp. 1048–1053 (2018)

40. O'Donnell, L.: More than half of IoT devices vulnerable to severe attacks (2020). https://threatpost.com/half-iot-devices-vulnerable-severe-attacks/153609/

41. Parmisano, A., Garcia, S., Erquiaga, M.J.: Stratosphere laboratory. a labeled dataset with malicious and benign IoT network traffic (2020). https://www.stratosphereips.org/datasets-iot23

42. Pratt, M.K.: Top challenges of IoT adoption in the enterprise (2019). https://internetofthingsagenda.techtarget.com/feature/Top-challenges-of-IoT-adoption-in-the-enterprise
43. Pritchard, M.: Ddos attack timeline: time to take Ddos seriously (2018). https://activereach.net/newsroom/blog/time-to-take-ddos-seriously-a-recent-timeline-of-events/
44. Prokofiev, A.O., Smirnova, Y.S., Surov, V.A.: A method to detect internet of things botnets. In: 2018 IEEE Conference of Russian Young Researchers in Electrical and Electronic Engineering (EIConRus), pp. 105–108. IEEE (2018)
45. Radware: A quick history of IoT botnets (2018). https://blog.radware.com/uncategorized/2018/03/history-of-iot-botnets/
46. Scikit-Learn: novelty and outlier detection (2020). https://scikit-learn.org/stable/modules/outlier_detection.html
47. Shiravi, A., Shiravi, H., Tavallaee, M., Ghorbani, A.A.: Toward developing a systematic approach to generate benchmark datasets for intrusion detection. Comput. Secur. 31(3), 357–374 (2012)
48. Shire, R., Shiaeles, S., Bendiab, K., Ghita, B., Kolokotronis, N.: Malware squid: a novel iot malware traffic analysis framework using convolutional neural network and binary visualisation. In: Internet of Things, Smart Spaces, and Next Generation Networks and Systems, pp. 65–76. Springer, Cham (2019). https://doi.org/10.1007/978-3-030-01168-0
49. Silva, S.S., Silva, R.M., Pinto, R.C., Salles, R.M.: Botnets: a survey. Comput. Netw. 57(2), 378–403 (2013)
50. Sklavos, N., Zaharakis, I.D., Kameas, A., Kalapodi, A.: Security & trusted devices in the context of internet of things (IoT). In: 2017 Euromicro Conference on Digital System Design (DSD), pp. 502–509. IEEE (2017)
51. Statista: Forecast end-user spending on iot solutions worldwide from 2017 to 2025 (2019). https://www.statista.com/statistics/976313/global-iot-market-size/
52. Statista: Number of internet of things (IoT) connected devices worldwide in 2018, 2025 and 2030 (2019). https://www.statista.com/statistics/802690/worldwide-connected-devices-by-access-technology/
53. Sun, B., Osborne, L., Xiao, Y., Guizani, S.: Intrusion detection techniques in mobile ad hoc and wireless sensor networks. IEEE Wirel. Commun. 14(5), 56–63 (2007)
54. TrendMicro: Bashlite IoT malware updated with mining and backdoor commands, targets WeMo devices (2019)
55. Weagle, S.: Financial impact of mirai Ddos attack on DYN revealed in new data (2017). https://www.corero.com/blog/797-financial-impact-of-mirai-ddos-attack-on-dyn-revealed-in-new-data.html
56. Weisman, S.: Emerging threats - what is a distributed denial of service attack (Ddos) and what can you do about them? (2019). https://us.norton.com/internetsecurity-emerging-threats-what-is-a-ddos-attack-30sectech-by-norton.html
57. Winward, R.: IoT attack handbook: A field guide to understanding IoT attacks from the mirai botnet to its modern variants (2018). https://www.datacom.cz/userfiles/miraihandbookebook_final.pdf
58. Zarpelão, B.B., Miani, R.S., Kawakani, C.T., de Alvarenga, S.C.: A survey of intrusion detection in internet of things. J. Netw. Comput. Appl. 84, 25–37 (2017)

Author Index

Printed in the United States
by Baker & Taylor Publisher Services